Leaving Certificate Home Economics

Lifelines

SECOND EDITION

Carmel Enright and Maureen Flynn

FOLENS

Editor
Sinéad Keogh

Design and layout
Artwerk Ltd

Cover Design
Design Image

Illustration
David Benham/Graham Cameron Illustration
Steph Dix/Graham Cameron Illustration
Sarah Wimperis/Graham Cameron Illustration

© 2010 Carmel Enright and Maureen Flynn

ISBN: 978-1-84741-572-1

Folens Publishers,
Hibernian Industrial Estate,
Greenhills Road,
Tallaght,
Dublin 24

Preface

Lifelines Second Edition consists of the three core areas of the Leaving Certificate Home Economics Scientific and Social syllabus: Food Studies; Resource Management and Consumer Studies; and Social Studies. Two of the three electives are also included: Home Design and Management; and Social Studies.

Lifelines Second Edition has been updated and improved with a number of new features including:

► Syllabus referencing
Topics are numbered to match the Home Economics Scientific and Social syllabus document for ease of reference. (See 'Food Choices' on page 2 for an example.)

► Cross-referencing within the text
A blue bar – See Page – is used to highlight page numbers where more information on a topic may be found. This extensive cross-referencing facilitates an integrated approach to learning.

► Current information
Revised text and up-to-date statistics are given to take account of various social and economic changes.

► Study-friendly layout
Many paragraphs have been broken down into manageable bullet points to facilitate learning.

► Sample Food Studies Assignment
An A-grade sample of a 2008 Food Studies Assignment is included in full at the back of the textbook.

► Verified information
A number of topics have been written in consultation with relevant bodies to ensure accuracy of information. The Department of Agriculture, Fisheries and Food; The Food Safety Authority of Ireland; and The Osteoporosis Society of Ireland have all contributed to topics relating to their work.

► PowerPoint CD
An accompanying Teacher CD contains 27 PowerPoint presentations and other resources for use in the classroom. The topics covered are indicated with the symbol *PPP* in the table of contents.

► Revised workbook
  – The textbook is intended to be used with the accompanying workbook. The workbook has been updated to include material from all available exam questions since the introduction of the syllabus in 2004.
  – The workbook contains questions for each of the 28 chapters of the textbook, with exam questions now integrated into each chapter to facilitate revision.
  – The workbook now features a blank sample of the journal pages used to record the Food Studies Assignment.

Lifelines Second Edition also retains many of the popular features which appeared in the first edition of the textbook, including:

► Content that is closely aligned to the requirements of the syllabus and the examination.

► All five areas of study colour-coded for ease of reference.

► Up-to-date photographs, graphics and statistics to assist comprehension of the subject areas.

► The use of clear and simple language, suited to students of all levels.

► Both Higher and Ordinary Levels are covered, with the material for Higher Level only clearly indicated. (Higher Level is indicated by a line down the side.)

Carmel Enright and Maureen Flynn

Acknowledgements

The authors and Publisher would like to thank the following for permission to reproduce photographs, logos and other material: Alamy Images, ACCORD Marriage Care Service, Advertising Standards Authority for Ireland, Argos, Camera Press Ireland, Corbis, County Clare Enterprise Board, Declan Corrigan Photography, Department of Agriculture, Fisheries and Food, Department of Health and Children, Elizabeth Whiting and Associates, ENFO, Enterprise Ireland, FÁS, Food Safety Authority of Ireland, Galway Eggs Ltd, Getty Images, Institute of Leisure and Amenity Management of Ireland (ILAM), Just Eggs Ltd, Kelloggs, the National Consumer Agency (NCA), National Standards Authority of Ireland, www.plan-a-home.ie, St. Tola Organic Goat Cheese, Science Photo Library, Vocational Training Opportunities Scheme (VTOS), Youthreach.

Contents

Syllabus Reference Guide

Syllabus Headings	Lifelines Reference
1 Food Studies (45%)	**AREA ONE**
1.1 Food science and nutrition	**Chapter 1: Food Science and Nutrition, p 2**
1.1.1 Food choices	Chapter 1, p 2
1.1.2 Protein	Chapter 1, p 5
1.1.3 Carbohydrates	Chapter 1, p 13
1.1.4 Lipids	Chapter 1, p 19
1.1.5 Vitamins	Chapter 1, p 26
1.1.6 Mineral	Chapter 1, p 34
1.1.7 Water	Chapter 1, p 39
1.2 Diet and health	**Chapter 2: Diet and Health, page 40**
1.2.1 Energy	Chapter 2, p 40
1.2.2 Dietary guidelines	Chapter 2, p 42
1.2.3 Dietary and food requirements	Chapter 2, p 46
1.2.4 The Irish diet	**Chapter 5: The Irish Diet and Food Industry, p 135**
1.3 Preparation and processing of food	
1.3.1 The Irish food industry	Chapter 5, p 141
1.3.2 Food commodities	**Chapter 3: Food Commodities, p 62**
1.3.3 Meal management and planning	**Chapter 4: Meal Planning and Preparation, p 108**
1.3.4 Food preparation and cooking processes	Chapter 4, p 109
1.3.5 Food processing and packaging	**Chapter 6: Food Processing and Packaging**, p 147
1.3.6 Food additives	Chapter 6, p 155
1.3.7 Food legislation	**Chapter 9: Food Safety and Hygiene, p 186**
1.3.8 Food spoilage	**Chapter 7 Microbiology, p 160 HL only**
	Chapter 8: Food Spoilage and Food Preservation, p 170
1.3.9 Preservation	Chapter 8, p 174
1.3.10 Food safety and hygiene	Chapter 9, p 186
2 Resource Management and Consumer Studies (25%)	**AREA TWO**
2.1 Family resource management	**Chapter 11: Family Resource Management, p 218**
2.1.1 Components of management	Chapter 11, p 219
2.1.2 Attributes affecting management	Chapter 11, p 222
2.1.3 Management of household financial resources	**Chapter 12: Management of Household Finances, p 224**
	Chapter 13: Housing Finance, p 244
2.1.4 Housing	Chapter 13, p 248
2.1.5 Household technology	**Chapter 14: Household Technology, p 250**
2.1.6 Textiles	**Chapter 15: Textiles, p 260**
2.2 Consumer studies	**Chapter 16: Consumer Studies, 266**
2.2.1 Consumer choices	Chapter 16, p 266
2.2.2 Consumer responsibility	Chapter 16, p 272
2.2.3 Consumer protection	Chapter 16, p 274

Syllabus Headings (continued)	Lifelines Reference (continued)
3.1 Social Studies (10%)	AREA THREE
3.1 The family in society	Chapter 17: The Family in Society, page 284
3.1.1 Introducing sociological concepts	Chapter 17, p 284
3.1.2 Defining the family	Chapter 17, p 286
3.1.3 Family structures	Chapter 17, p 286
3.1.4 Family functions	Chapter 17, p 290
3.1.5 Marriage	Chapter 18: Marriage, p 294
3.1.6 Family as a caring unit	Chapter 19: The Family as a Caring Unit, p 302
3.1.7 Family law	Chapter 19, p 310
4. Elective 1 – Home Design and Management (20%)	ELECTIVE ONE
4.1 Housing	Chapter 20: Housing, p 314
4.1.1 Housing styles	Chapter 20, p 314
4.1.2 Housing provision	Chapter 20, p 319
4.2 House building and design	Chapter 20, p 325
4.3 Designing the house interior	Chapter 21: Designing the House Interior, p 332
4.4 The energy efficient home	Chapter 22: The Energy Efficient Home, p 358
4.5 Systems and services	Chapter 23: Systems and Services, p 366
4.5.1 Electricity	Chapter 23, p 366
4.5.2 Water	Chapter 23, p 370
4.5.3 Heating	Chapter 23, p 372
4.5.4 Insulation	Chapter 23, p 377
4.5.5 Ventilation	Chapter 23, p 379
4.5.6 Lighting	Chapter 23, p 382
6. Elective 3 – Social Studies (20%)	ELECTIVE THREE
6.1 Social change and the family	Chapter 24: Social Change and the Family, p 388
6.2 Education	Chapter 25: Education, p 394
6.3 Work	Chapter 26: Work, p 406
6.3.1 Concepts of work	Chapter 26, p 406
6.3.2 Reconciling employment with family responsibilities	Chapter 26, p 414
6.4 Leisure	Chapter 27: Leisure, p 422
6.5 Unemployment	Chapter 26, p 419
6.6 Poverty	Chapter 28: Poverty, p 428
6.6.1 Concepts of poverty	Chapter 28, p 428
6.6.2 Causes and effects of poverty	Chapter 28, p 430
6.7 Statutory and community responses to creating employment and eliminating poverty	Chapter 28, p 433

AREA ONE
FOOD STUDIES

Chapter 1 | Food Science and Nutrition (1.1)

CONTENTS INCLUDE:

► Food choices: the factors that affect decisions in relation to food
► A detailed study of nutrients: protein, carbohydrates, lipids, vitamins, minerals and water
► The inter-relationships between various nutrients in the diet

Food Choices (1.1.1)

Food is a basic human need and links between food choices and health are well recognised. The type of food people eat is influenced by a number of different factors including: culture, eating patterns, sensory aspects, nutritional awareness, health status, availability, finance, marketing and advertising.

Culture

Culture and its associated beliefs and values have an impact on food choices. Certain foods have always been associated with particular countries. For example, pasta is commonly eaten in Italy, spices are widely used in India and rice and noodles are the staple food in China. Religion also affects food choices, for example, practising Jews do not eat pig meat and practising Hindus are vegetarians. Television, travel, immigration and improved methods of food processing and transportation have brought multicultural influences to bear on the Irish diet.

A Chinese meal

Eating Patterns

The lifestyle of the family influences eating patterns, which in turn affects food choices. Busy lifestyles have increased the demand for convenience foods, which are ready-to-eat or require very little preparation. Fast foods and take-aways often take the place of more elaborate family meals, with individual family members eating irregularly and at different times.

Sensory Aspects

The senses – in particular sight, smell and taste – have a major impact on food choices. Consumers have varied expectations of food in terms of flavour, texture, temperature and appearance, many of which may have been established in childhood. Much research is carried out on a continuous basis to identify factors which make food

2

attractive to consumers. The colour and design of the packaging must have instant appeal and the food itself must look attractive, fresh and wholesome. Food samples are cooked and served at promotion stands in supermarkets, so that consumers are attracted by the sound and smell of cooking food and are encouraged to taste the cooked product. When people have choice, the influence of the sensory aspects of food cannot be underestimated.

Attractive buffet meal

Nutritional Awareness

Irish people are becoming more nutritionally aware and more health conscious in their food choices. The work of organisations such as The Health Promotion Unit and An Bord Bia ensures that the majority of people are aware of what constitutes a healthy diet. It should consist of a variety of fresh foods which are low in sugar, fat and salt, and are rich in fibre, vitamins and minerals. Informed consumers make food choices regarding such issues as genetically modified food (`See Page` 149), fat content and artificial additives. Fewer people lack the nutritional awareness necessary to make healthy food choices.

Health Status

Health status may dictate food choices. A family that is generally healthy is free to follow a varied diet while maintaining good health. An individual on a restricted diet, such as a diabetic or coeliac, must make more discerning food choices. Medical conditions, such as heart disease, will restrict food choices. Food allergies, such as a nut allergy that could be fatal, make careful food choices a necessity.

Availability

The availability, or otherwise, of particular foods influences choices. Seasonal foods, such as Irish strawberries, are only available fresh at certain times of the year. Imported equivalents can be expensive. Location can affect availability. People in rural areas often have fewer shops to choose from and less choice in food range within shops. Take-away foods and restaurants may also be less readily available.

An allergy label

Finance

More affluent people eat out more often and holiday abroad, so they are exposed to multicultural food choices. A family living on a tight budget needs to shop wisely to keep within their means, for example choosing minced beef rather than the more expensive fillet steak.

Marketing and Advertising

Marketing strategies and advertising greatly influence food choice. Their aim is to encourage consumers to choose one product over a range of others. Marketing strategies include the layout of supermarkets and the positioning of foods makes the consumer aware of new products.

A supermarket interior

Nutrition

To study nutrition it is necessary to understand the following terms:

► **Nutrition** is the study of food, its composition, structure, properties, amounts required and its effects on the body.

► **Nutrients** are the chemical components of food which can be digested and absorbed by the body to produce heat and energy, promote growth and repair or regulate biological processes. Nutrients are required by the body in varying amounts.

► **Macronutrients** are nutrients required in large amounts. They are proteins, lipids and carbohydrates. The amounts are measured in grams (g).

| 1 g = 1000 mg |

► **Micronutrients** are nutrients needed in very small amounts. They are minerals and vitamins which are usually measured in milligrams (mg) and micrograms (µg):

| 1 mg = 1000 µg |

► An **element** is the simplest form of a substance. Each nutrient is made up of molecules, which in turn are made up of elements. For example, proteins are made up of amino acid molecules. These amino acid molecules are made up of the elements carbon, hydrogen, oxygen and nitrogen.

▶ **Organic nutrients** are those that contain the element carbon. Organic nutrients include proteins, lipids, carbohydrates and vitamins.

▶ **Inorganic nutrients** do not contain carbon. The mineral elements are inorganic nutrients, e.g. iron and calcium.

▶ **Antioxidants** are substances which protect the body from damage caused by free radicals which are by-products of metabolism, helping to prevent conditions such as coronary heart disease and certain types of cancer.

▶ **Metabolism** is the total of all chemical reactions which occur in the body. Some metabolic processes use energy, e.g. growth. This is called *anabolism*. Some metabolic processes produce energy, e.g. digestion. This is called *catabolism*.

▶ **Enzymes** are organic catalysts which control all chemical reactions in the body.

A child suffering from malnutrition

▶ The **substrate** is the matter upon which the enzyme works, e.g. starch is the substrate of the enzyme amylase.

▶ The **product** is the end result of an enzymic action, e.g. maltose is the product of amylase activity.

▶ **Malnutrition** is the general term for dietary imbalance. It may occur as a result of too little of a nutrient, e.g. anaemia is due to insufficient iron; or because of the excess of a nutrient. Obesity is often due to too much fat and sugar in the diet.

▶ **Undernutrition** results from starvation. Food intake is inadequate to supply sufficient nutrients. Kwashiorkor and marasmus are diseases that occur due to undernutrition particularly in children. These diseases develop because of insufficient protein in the diet.

Proteins (1.1.2)
Composition of Proteins

▶ Proteins are composed of the elements carbon (C), hydrogen (H), oxygen (O) and nitrogen (N).

▶ Protein is the only nutrient that contains nitrogen, an element which is essential for growth.

▶ Some proteins also contain small amounts of sulphur (S), phosphorus (P) and iron (Fe).

▶ The elements are arranged into basic units called amino acids.

Basic structure of amino acid

C	= Carbon atom
H	= Hydrogen atom
NH_2	= Amino group (basic/alkaline)
COOH	= Carboxyl group (acidic)
R	= Variable – different in each amino acid

$$NH_2 \text{——} \underset{\underset{R}{\overset{H}{\mid}}}{C} \text{——} COOH$$

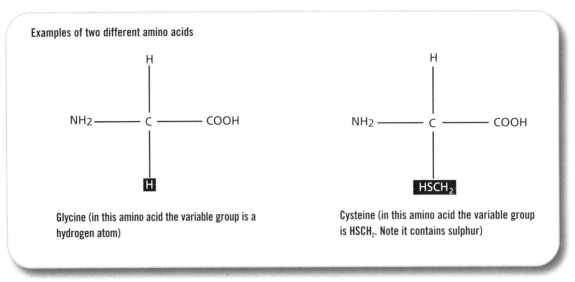

Examples of two different amino acids

Glycine (in this amino acid the variable group is a hydrogen atom)

Cysteine (in this amino acid the variable group is $HSCH_2$. Note it contains sulphur)

▶ Each protein molecule contains a number of amino acids.

▶ The amino acids are joined together by peptide links or bonds.

▶ A number of linked amino acids are referred to as a polypeptide chain.

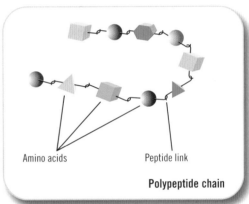

Amino acids

Peptide link

Polypeptide chain

Essential and Non-essential Amino Acids

▶ Food contains about 20 different amino acids, eight of which are essential for adults.

▶ **Essential amino acids** cannot be manufactured in the body, and therefore they must be obtained from food.

▶ The amino acids which can be manufactured by the body are known as **non-essential amino acids**.

Essential amino acids	Non-essential amino acids
Valine	Glycine
Lysine	Serine
Leucine	Proline
Isoleucine	Alanine
Tryptophan	Aspartic acid
Methionine	
Threonine	
Phenylalanine	
Children require 2 extra: **arginine** and **histidine**	

Peptide Bonds or Links

Peptide bonds form when amino acids join together. This reaction, which results in the loss of a water molecule, is called a **condensation reaction**.

▶ The NH₂ group (alkaline) of one amino acid reacts with the COOH group (acidic) of another amino acid.

$$NH_2 - C - COOH \qquad NH_2 - C - COOH$$

(with H above and R below each C)

▶ The NH₂ group loses a hydrogen atom.

▶ The COOH group loses an OH group.

▶ The hydrogen atom and the OH group join together to form a molecule of water.

$$N - C - C-OH \; + \; N - C - C-OH$$

▶ The resulting bond is CONH bond.

▶ Two amino acids join to form a dipeptide (one bond); many amino acids join to form a polypeptide (many bonds).

$$N - C - C - N - C - C-OH + H_2O$$

(Peptide link/bond)

The reverse of condensation is called **hydrolysis** and involves the addition of water and enzyme action. This occurs during digestion when proteins are broken down into individual amino acids for absorption.

Protein Structure

Primary Structure

Primary structure is the sequence/order and the number of amino acids in a chain. Insulin is made up of 51 amino acids arranged in a definite order.

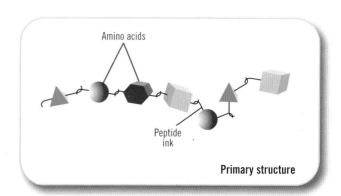

Amino acids

Peptide ink

Primary structure

Secondary Structure

In a protein molecule a polypeptide chain, or two different polypeptide chains, can be interlinked giving shape, e.g. coiled or spiral. These links are known as *cross-links* or *bridges* and give proteins their properties, e.g. the protein gluten is elastic.

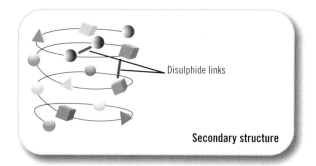

Disulphide links

Secondary structure

Examples of Cross-links

Disulphide links: This link occurs when two sulphurs join together. The amino acid cysteine contains sulphur. When two cysteine units, either in the same chain or in two different polypeptide chains, are adjacent, a disulphide link may be formed. Insulin has disulphide links.

Hydrogen bonds: Polypeptide chains can also be linked by hydrogen bonds. The hydrogen in one chain joins with the oxygen in a neighbouring chain. Collagen has hydrogen bonds.

Tertiary Structure

Tertiary structure relates to the pattern of folding of the polypeptide chains. The coiled or spiral shape of the secondary structure may be folded over to form a globule, a three-dimensional organisation of the polypeptide chain held firmly by links. Tertiary structures may be either:

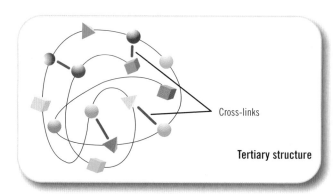

Cross-links

Tertiary structure

► **Fibrous:** The polypeptide chain is arranged in a straight, spiral or zigzag shape, e.g. gluten and collagen which are are insoluble in water.

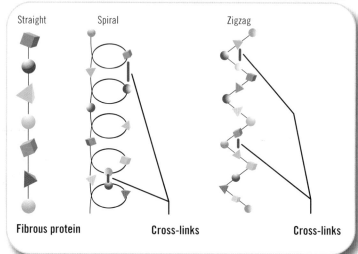

Straight   Spiral   Zigzag

Fibrous protein   **Cross-links**   **Cross-links**

► **Globular:** The polypeptide chain is arranged in a globe shape, e.g. ovalbumin and myoglobin which are soluble in water.

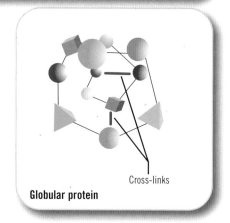

Cross-links

Globular protein

Classification of proteins

1. **Simple**	2. **Conjugated**

(a) **Animal** *shape*
  (i) Fibrous, e.g. collagen in skin, myosin in muscle.
  (ii) Globular, e.g. albumin in egg, myoglobin in meat.
	Consist of amino acids + a non-protein molecule, e.g.
	
	• Lipoproteins (lipid + protein), e.g. lecithin in egg yolk.
	
	• Phosphoprotein (phosphate + protein), e.g. caesinogen in milk. *nucleoprotein*

(b) **Plant** *solubility* *GAA*
  (i) Glutelins (insoluble in water soluble in acids and alkalis), e.g. glutenin in wheat, oryzenin in rice.
  (ii) Prolamines (insoluble in water, soluble in alcohol), e.g. gliadin in wheat, zein in maize.
  (glutenin + gliadin = gluten)
	Non-protein molecule
	
	Conjugated protein

Some important proteins are found in the following foods:

Protein	Food
Casein	Cheese
Collagen	Meat connective tissue
Myosin/albumin/actin	Meat fibres
Gelatine	Meat bones
Myosin/collagen/actin	Fish
Albumin	Eggs
Lactalbumin/caseinogen	Milk
Gluten	Wheat

Learn ∞

Sources of protein

Animal protein		Plant protein	
Cheese		Soya beans	
Chicken		TVP foods	
Meat		Nuts	
Fish		Lentils	
Eggs		Peas	
Milk		Beans	
		Cereals	

Listed in decreasing amounts of protein

Properties of Protein

1. Denaturation

Proteins can be denatured. This is an unfolding of the protein chain resulting in an irreversible change in shape. *Coagulation* of protein is an example of denaturation. Proteins may be denatured by:

Causes of denaturation
(a) **Heat**, e.g. albumin in egg hardens/coagulates. *Moist heat*, e.g. boiling, changes collagen to gelatine thereby tenderising meat. *Dry heat*, e.g. grilling causes shrinkage and toughening of meat therefore is only suitable for expensive tender cuts.
(b) **Acids** which lower the pH, e.g. milk-souring bacteria, change lactose to lactic acid which causes the caseinogen in the milk to coagulate. Vinegar (acetic acid) in a marinade denatures protein thereby tenderising meat.
(c) **Enzymes** e.g. rennin in the stomach, coagulate milk. Tenderising salts contain enzymes which tenderise meat.
(d) **Mechanical action**, e.g. whisking egg whites causes them to foam (**Foam formation** See Page 79).

2. Solubility

Most proteins are *insoluble* in water except egg white in cold water and collagen in hot water.

3. Maillard reaction

The Maillard reaction is the browning of food that is not caused by enzymes. It occurs as a result of a reaction between amino acids and carbohydrates on heating, e.g. fried potatoes, brown crusts on bread.

4. Elasticity

Elasticity is a property of some proteins, including gluten, which allows baked goods to rise.

5. Gel formation/gelling

Gelatine can absorb large amounts of water forming a gel. This property enables gelatine to be used as a setting agent, e.g. in soufflés and mousses (See Page 65).

Effects of dry and moist heat on protein	
1. Coagulation: Proteins set or harden when subjected to heat.	Egg proteins solidify on cooking.
2. Colour change. Millard Reaction	Myoglobin (red pigment) in meat turns brown (haematin).
3. Maillard reaction (dry heat).	Roast potatoes.
4. Tenderising (moist heat). Stew	Collagen in meat changes to gelatine causing the fibres to fall apart and the meat to become more digestible.
5. Overcooking causes proteins to become indigestible.	Overcooked meat is tough and difficult to digest. eg. rasher

Biological functions of proteins	
1. **Structural proteins**	Production of: • Cell membranes ⎫ • Muscle and skin ⎭ Growth and repair
2. **Physiologically active proteins**	Production of: • Hormones • Enzymes • Antibodies • Blood proteins and nucleoproteins
3. **Nutrient proteins**	• Supply body with essential amino acids • Excess protein used for energy

Deamination

Deamination is using protein as a source of energy. Excess protein not required for growth and repair is deaminated in the liver.

▶ The NH_2 group is removed, converted to ammonia then urea and is excreted by the kidneys.

▶ The COOH group is oxidised to produce heat and energy.

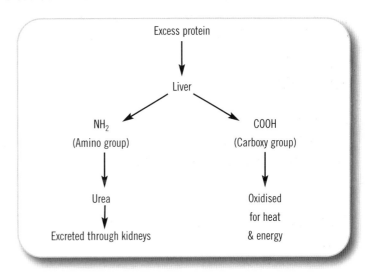

Biological Value of Proteins

Biological value is a measure of the quality of a protein. It is expressed as a percentage determined by the use the body can make of the protein in the food. It is based on the number of essential amino acids present in a protein.

Biological value of proteins	
High biological value proteins (HBV)	**Low biological value proteins (LBV)**
• HBV proteins contain all essential amino acids. • They are also known as complete proteins. • HBV proteins generally come from animal sources, but also from soya beans.	• LBV proteins contain only some of the essential amino acids. • They are also known as incomplete proteins. • LBV proteins generally come from plant sources, but also from gelatine.
HBV foods Eggs 100% Milk 95% Meat/fish 80–90% Soya beans 74%	**LBV foods** Rice 67% Wheat 53% Maize 40% Gelatine 0%

Supplementary/Complementary Value of Protein

Eating two low-biological value protein foods together can ensure that all essential amino acids are obtained. This is of particular importance in the diet of <u>vegetarians</u> where no animal protein is eaten. Beans on toast is an example of proteins supplementing or complementing each other. Beans are high in lysine but low in methionine. Bread (wheat) is low in lysine but high in methionine.

Beans on toast

Energy Value of Protein

Although the primary function of protein is growth and repair, any excess protein is used for energy. <u>1 gram of protein provides 4 kcal (17 kJ)</u>. If enough carbohydrates and fats are not consumed for energy production, protein will then be used for energy. As a general rule protein should make up 15% of the total energy value of the average diet.

Recommended Dietary Allowance (RDA)

The RDA of protein is based on:

1. Body weight   2.   Rate of growth

▶ On average an adult requires <u>1 gram (g) of protein per kilogram (kg) of body weight</u>.

▶ Extra is required during periods of rapid growth, i.e. children and adolescents, during pregnancy and breast-feeding and while convalescing.
recovering

Digestion of Protein

During digestion proteins are hydrolysed to break them down into amino acids. Hydrolysis involves the addition of water and the action of enzymes.

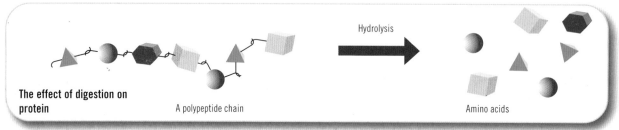

The effect of digestion on protein   A polypeptide chain   Amino acids

Mouth

▶ Food is chewed.

Stomach

▶ Hydrochloric acid denatures protein.

▶ The enzyme rennin converts caseinogen to casein.

▶ The enzyme pepsin converts proteins to peptones.

Small intestine

▶ In the *duodenum* the enzyme trypsin from the pancreas converts peptones to peptides.

▶ The enzyme peptidase from the small intestine converts peptides to amino acids which are now ready for absorption into the bloodstream.

Proteins → Peptones → Peptides → Amino Acids

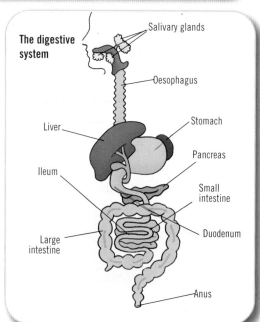

The digestive system

Salivary glands
Oesophagus
Liver
Stomach
Pancreas
Ileum
Small intestine
Duodenum
Large intestine
Anus

Protein digestion summary				
Organ/gland	**Secretion**	**Enzymes**	**Substrate** *what it works on*	**Product**
Stomach	Gastric juice	Rennin Pepsin	Caseinogen Proteins	Casein Peptones
Dueodenum. Pancreas	Pancreatic juice (in the duodenum)	Trypsin	Peptones	Peptides
ileum	Intestinal juice	Peptidase	Peptides	Amino acids

Absorption and Utilisation of Amino Acids

Amino acids are absorbed through the villi of the small intestine into the bloodstream. The portal vein carries them to the liver. In the liver:

(a) They are used to maintain and repair liver cells.

(b) They are sent into the bloodstream to form new cells, repair damaged cells and manufacture hormones, enzymes, antibodies, blood proteins and nucleoproteins.

(c) The excess is deaminated to produce heat and energy.

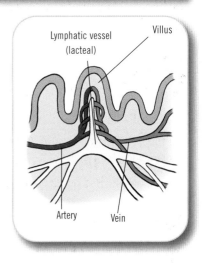

Carbohydrates (1.1.3)
Formation of Carbohydrates

Carbohydrates are produced in plants by a process known as **photosynthesis**:

▶ The roots of plants absorb water from the soil.

▶ Leaves absorb carbon dioxide from the air.

▶ Chlorophyll, the green pigment, absorbs energy from sunlight.

▶ The energy is used to create glucose from carbon dioxide (CO_2) and water (H_2O).

▶ Oxygen is released into the air.

Equation for photosynthesis:

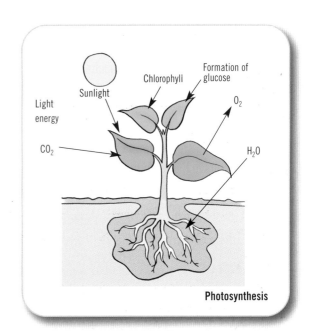

Photosynthesis

$$6CO_2 + 6H_2O + \text{sunlight} \rightarrow C_6H_{12}O_6 + 6O_2$$

Carbon dioxide   Water   Energy   Glucose + oxygen

Elemental Composition of Carbohydrates

Carbohydrates are made up of the elements carbon, hydrogen and oxygen.

Classification of Carbohydrates

All carbohydrates are based on simple sugar units.
Carbohydrates are classified into:

Monosaccharides: 1 sugar unit
Disaccharides: 2 sugar units
Polysaccharides: Many sugar units

Classification of carbohydrates				
Class	**Chemical formula**		**Example**	**Sources**
Monosaccharides (simple sugars)	$C_6H_{12}O_6$		Glucose Fructose Galactose	Fruit Honey/fruit Digested milk
Disaccharides (double sugars)	$C_{12}H_{22}O_{11}$		Sucrose Lactose Maltose	Table sugar Milk Barley
Polysaccharides (complex non-sugars)	$(C_6H_{10}O_5)_n$		Starch Cellulose Pectin Glycogen	Potatoes, cereals Fruit, vegetables Wholegrain cereals Fruit Stored animal starch

Chemical Structure

Monosaccharides

The structure of carbohydrates is based on a sugar unit called a monosaccharide. A monosaccharide has the formula $C_6H_{12}O_6$. The arrangement of the atoms changes with each monosaccharide.

Ring structure of a glucose unit

Disaccharides

Disaccharides are formed when two monosaccharides join together with the elimination of water (condensation reaction). These sugars have the formula $C_{12}H_{22}O_{11}$.

$$C_6H_{12}O_6 + C_6H_{12}O_6 = C_{12}H_{22}O_{11} + H_2O$$

Sucrose = 1 glucose unit + 1 fructose unit
Lactose = 1 glucose unit + 1 galactose unit
Maltose = 1 glucose unit + 1 glucose unit

Polysaccharides

Polysaccharides are formed when many monosaccharides join together with the loss of a water molecule each time. They may be in straight or branched chains. Examples include starch, pectin, cellulose and glycogen. These are complex **non-sugar carbohydrates**. Pectin cellulose and glycogen are also known as **non-starch polysaccharides**. Polysaccharides have the formula $(C_6H_{10}O_5)n$.

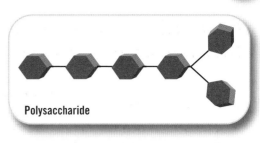

Polysaccharide

Sources of carbohydrates		
Sugar	**Starch**	**Cellulose**
Table sugar	Breakfast cereals	Fruit and vegetables
Biscuits	Potatoes	Wholegrain breakfast cereals
Cakes	Rice	
Sweets	Pasta	Wheat bran
Honey	Flour: bread and cakes	Brown bread
Jam		Wholemeal pasta
Fruit		

Sources of sugar

Biological Functions of Carbohydrates

1. Carbohydrates are used to produce heat and energy.
2. They free protein for its primary function of growth and repair.
3. Excess carbohydrate is converted into glycogen and stored in the liver and muscles as an energy reserve, or converted into fat and stored as adipose tissue which acts as an insulator.
4. Cellulose assists movement of food through the digestive system preventing constipation (See Page **56**).

The Properties of Carbohydrates

Sugar

1. **Solubility:** Sugars are white crystalline compounds which are soluble in water.
2. **Flavour:** Sugars are of varying degrees of sweetness, sucrose being much sweeter than lactose.
3. **Maillard reaction:** Browning occurs when sugars and amino acids react when heated (See Page **10**).
4. **Caramelisation:** When sugar is heated on its own it melts and then caramelises, i.e. changes to a brown syrup (caramel). Eventually it carbonises (burns).
5. **Hydrolysis:** Sugars are capable of hydrolysis. This means that they react with water and enzymes and break down into monosaccharide units, as in digestion.
6. **Inversion:** Sugars are capable of being inverted. Invert sugars are the monosaccharides which result from hydrolysis of disaccharides, e.g. when sucrose is hydrolysed it is inverted to glucose and fructose.
7. **Crystallisation:** This occurs if more sugar is added than can be absorbed by a liquid. Crystal particles are deposited from the solution. Crystallisation is used in the confectionery and sweet industry.
8. **Assists aeration/foaming:** Sugar denatures egg protein allowing aeration to occur (See Page **79**).

Starch

1. **Flavour:** Starch is not sweet in flavour.
2. **Solubility:** Starch is a white powder which is insoluble in cold water.
3. **Gelatinisation:** When starch grains are heated in liquid they swell and burst and absorb the liquid, forming a thickened solution/(sol), e.g. the thickening of soup and sauces with flour. On cooling, this becomes a gel.
4. **Hygroscopic:** Starch absorbs moisture, e.g. biscuits soften if not stored in a sealed container.
5. **Dextrinisation:** When carbohydrate foods are heated, short chains of polysaccharides (dextrins) form, causing the food to brown, e.g. toast.
6. **Hydrolysis:** Starch may undergo hydrolysis (See Page 18).

Sources of starch

Pectin

Pectin is a polysaccharide which occurs naturally between plant cells and in the cell wall of some fruit and vegetables.

Gel formation: Pectin is responsible for the setting of jams and marmalades. Protopectin in under-ripe fruits changes to pectinic acid (pectin) in ripe fruits and eventually to pectic acid in over-ripe fruits.

Pectin extraction

▶ Use a fruit rich in pectin, e.g. apples.

▶ Heat must be applied to extract the pectin.

▶ Acid, e.g. lemon juice, assists in pectin extraction from the fruit.

Culinary functions of carbohydrates			
Sugar	**Starch**	**Cellulose**	**Pectin**
• Sweetens puddings and cakes. • Adds colour, i.e. when brown sugar is used. • Acts as a preservative in jams. • Stabilises egg white foam. • Main ingredient in icings and syrups. • Necessary in yeast fermentation.	• Thickens soups and sauces. • Main ingredient in bread and cakes. • Absorbs water – used in baking powder. • Browning caused by dextrins, e.g. toast.	Adds texture, e.g. breakfast cereals, bread.	Setting agent in jams and jellies.

The effects of heat on carbohydrates	
Moist	**Dry**
• Sugar dissolves easily in warm liquids, e.g. used to sweeten custard sauces or in syrups. • Moist heat causes starch grains to swell and burst and absorb liquids, e.g. flour used to thicken gravy. • Heating fruit in a small amount of water assists the extraction of pectin, e.g. jam-making. • Moist heat causes cellulose to soften, e.g. cooked vegetables.	• Dry heat results in carbohydrate food browning because of the presence of dextrins, e.g. toast. • Dry heat causes sugar to caramelise, e.g. toffee-making. • Dry heat results in the Maillard reaction due to a reaction between carbohydrates and amino acids, e.g. fried potatoes.

non enzymatic browning (handwritten annotation)

Fibre/cellulose (non-starch polysaccharides)

It is recommended that 25–35 g of fibre be included in the daily diet. Research has shown that the average fibre intake still remains below the RDA.

To increase fibre intake:

Sources of fibre

- ▶ Reduce the intake of sugar and refined starch and choose wholegrain bread, pasta, breakfast cereals and brown rice.
- ▶ Add bran to breakfast cereals and homemade breads.
- ▶ Increase the intake of fruit and vegetables.
- ▶ Eat fruit and vegetables with the skin where possible.
- ▶ Increase intake of seeds and nuts.

Approximate dietary fibre content of selected foods			
	Food	**Typical portion (weight)**	**Fibre/portion**
Breakfast cereals	All-Bran	1 medium sized bowl (40 g)	9.8 g
	Weetabix	2 pieces (37.5 g)	3.6 g
	Porridge (milk or water)	1 medium sized bowl (250 g)	2.3 g
	Cornflakes	1 medium sized bowl (30 g)	0.3 g
Bread/rice/pasta	Pitta bread (wholemeal)	1 piece (75 g)	3.9 g
	Pasta (plain, fresh cooked)	1 medium portion (200 g)	3.8 g
	Wholemeal bread	2 slices (70 g)	3.5 g
	Brown rice (boiled)	1 medium portion (200 g)	1.6 g
	White bread	2 slices (70 g)	1.3 g
	White rice (boiled)	1 medium portion (200 g)	0.2 g
Vegetables	Baked beans (in tomato sauce)	Half can (200 g)	7.4 g
	Red kidney beans (boiled)	3 tablespoons (80 g)	5.4 g
	Peas (boiled)	3 heaped tablespoons (80 g)	3.6 g
	Brussel sprouts (boiled)	8 sprouts (80 g)	2.5 g
	Potatoes (old, boiled)	1 medium size (200 g)	2.4 g
	Carrots (boiled, sliced)	3 heaped tablespoons (80 g)	2.0 g
	Broccoli (boiled)	2 spears (80 g)	1.8 g
Vegetables	Pepper (capsicum green/red)	Half (80 g)	1.3 g
	Onions (raw)	1 medium (80 g)	1.1 g
	Tomato (raw)	1 medium/7 cherry (80 g)	0.8 g
Fruit	Avocado pear	1 medium (145 g)	4.9 g
	Pear (with skin)	1 medium (170 g)	3.7 g
	Orange	1 medium (160 g)	2.7 g
	Apple (with skin)	1 medium (112 g)	2.0 g
	Banana	1 medium (150 g)	1.7 g
	Strawberries	7 strawberries (80 g)	0.9 g
	Orange juice	1 small glass (200 ml)	0.2 g
Dried fruit/nuts	Prunes (semi-dried)	3 whole (80 g)	4.6 g
	Almonds	20 nuts (33 g)	2.4 g
	Peanuts (plain)	1 tablespoon (25 g)	1.6 g
	Raisins/sultanas	1 tablespoon (25 g)	0.5 g
Other foods	Quorn (pieces)	1 serving (100 g)	4.8 g
	Sunflower seeds	(20 g)	3.3 g
	Potato crisps (low-fat)	1 bag (35 g)	2.1 g
	Pizza (cheese and tomato)	1 slice, deep pan (80 g)	1.8 g
	Sesame seeds	(5 g)	1.3 g

Energy Value of Carbohydrates

One gram of carbohydrate provides 4 kcal (17 kJ). It is recommended that most of our energy be obtained from carbohydrates (50% of total energy value). Cellulose, as it is not digested by the human body, does not provide calories.

Digestion of Carbohydrates

During digestion, carbohydrates are hydrolysed to break them down into monosaccharides. Hydrolysis involves the addition of water and the action of enzymes.

Polysaccharides → Disaccharides → Monosaccharides

▶ **Mouth:** Food is chewed. The enzyme amylase changes some starch to maltose.

▶ **Stomach:** No carbohydrate digestion takes place.

▶ **Small intestine:** Pancreatic amylase in the *duodenum* changes more starch to maltose.

▶ The intestinal juice contains three enzymes. Maltase changes maltose to glucose. Lactase changes lactose to glucose and galactose. Sucrase changes sucrose to glucose and fructose.

The digestion of carbohydrates is now complete.

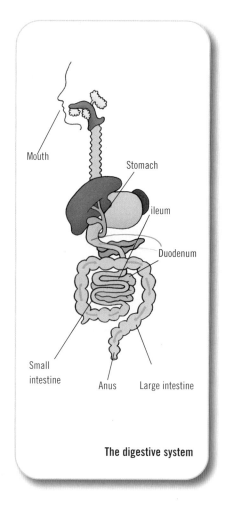

The digestive system

Carbohydrate digestion summary				
Organ/gland	**Secretion**	**Enzymes**	**Substrate**	**Product**
Salivary glands	Saliva	Salivary amylase	Starch	Maltose
Pancreas	Pancreatic juice (in the duodenum)	Amylase	Starch	Maltose
Small intestine	Intestinal juice	Maltase	Maltose	Glucose
		Lactase	Lactose	Glucose and galactose
		Sucrase	Sucrose	Glucose and fructose

Absorption and Utilisation of Carbohydrates

Monosaccharides are absorbed through the villi of the small intestine into the bloodstream. The portal vein carries them to the liver where fructose and galactose are converted to glucose. In the liver:

(a) The glucose is sent into the bloodstream it is oxidised to produce heat and energy.

(b) Some glucose is converted into glycogen and is retained in the liver as an energy reserve.

(c) The excess is converted to fat and stored as adipose tissue.

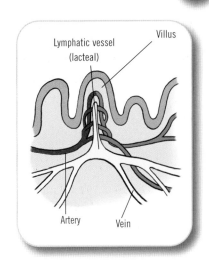

Lipids (1.1.4)

Elemental Composition of Lipids

Lipids are made up of the elements carbon, hydrogen and oxygen in different proportions to carbohydrates.

> **Lipids are fats and oils.**
> Oils – liquid at room temperature.
> Fats – solid at room temperature.

Chemical Structure of Lipids

► Lipids are made up of three fatty acids and a glycerol molecule, referred to as a trigly-ceride.

► Glycerol is an alcohol with three hydroxyl groups (OH).

► A fatty acid attaches itself to each hydroxyl group with the elimination of three water molecules (condensation).

► The fatty acids vary and determine the properties of a lipid.

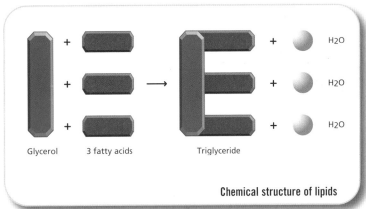

Glycerol   3 fatty acids   Triglyceride

Chemical structure of lipids

Classification of Fatty Acids

Fatty acids are long carbon chains with CH_3 (methyl group) at one end and COOH (carboxyl group) at the other end. The number of carbon atoms differs with each fatty acid, e.g. stearic acid in meat has 18. The chemical formula for fatty acids can be written as $CH_3(CH_2)nCOOH$.

There are three classes of fatty acids: *saturated fatty acids*, *mono-unsaturated fatty acids* and *polyunsaturated fatty acids* (PUFAs).

Saturated fatty acids

▶ Each carbon has a full quota of hydrogen atoms.

▶ There are no double bonds between the carbon atoms of a saturated fatty acid.

▶ Saturated fatty acids are solid at room temperature.

▶ Saturated fatty acids are generally from animal sources, e.g. butyric acid (butter) and stearic acid (meat).

Saturated fatty acid

Mono-unsaturated fatty acids

▶ All carbon atoms are not saturated with hydrogen.

▶ There is one double bond between the carbon atoms of a mono-unsaturated fatty acid.

▶ Mono-unsaturates fatty acids are generally soft/liquid at room temperature.

▶ They generally come from plant sources and fish, e.g. oleic acid (corn oil/olive oil).

Mono-unsaturated fatty acid

Polyunsaturated fatty acids (PUFAs)

▶ All carbon atoms are not saturated with hydrogen.

▶ There is more than one double bond between the carbon atoms of a polyunsaturated fatty acid.

▶ PUFAs are generally soft/liquid at room temperature.

▶ They generally come from plant sources and fish, e.g. linoleic acid (two double bonds), linolenic acid (three double bonds) and. arachidonic acid (four double bonds).

Polyunsaturated fatty acid

Distribution of Saturated, Mono-unsaturated and Polyunsaturated Fatty Acids in Food

No dietary fat is completely saturated or unsaturated but is a mixture of both. The more double bonds a fat has, the greater the degree of unsaturation.

Distribution of fatty acids			
Vegetables oils and shortening	**Polyunsaturated fatty acids**	**Mono-unsaturated fatty acids**	**Saturated fatty acids**
Sunflower oil	66%	20%	10%
Olive oil	8%	74%	13%
Soft tub margarine	31%	47%	17%
Block margarine	18%	59%	19%
Sunflower light	18%	8%	12%
Animal fats			
Tuna fish	37%	26%	27%
Chicken fat	21%	45%	30%
Lard	11%	45%	40%
Butter	4%	29%	62%

Essential Fatty Acids

Essential fatty acids cannot be manufactured in the body, therefore they must be obtained from food. The polyunsaturated fatty acids – linoleic, linolenic and arachidonic acids – are referred to as essential fatty acids. Linoleic is considered to be the most important, as both linolenic and arachidonic acids can be synthesised from linoleic acid.

Functions of essential fatty acids

► These polyunsaturated fatty acids are necessary for the formation of cell membranes and are therefore essential for growth.

► They are also thought to counteract the hardening effect of cholesterol on the arteries, thereby reducing the risk of coronary heart disease.

Cis- and Trans-Fatty Acids

Unsaturated fatty acids may be either cis-fatty acids or trans-fatty acids.

Cis-fatty acids

Polyunsaturated fatty acids are called cis-fatty acids when the hydrogen atoms on either side of the double bonds are both above or both below the carbon chain.

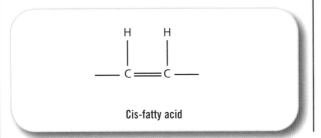

Cis-fatty acid

Trans-fatty acids

Polyunsaturated fatty acids are called trans-fatty acids when the hydrogen atoms on either side of the double bond are on opposite sides of the carbon chain.

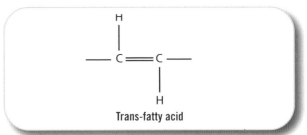

Trans-fatty acid

Significance of trans-fatty acids in the diet

▶ Most unsaturated fatty acids are naturally cis-fatty acids, which are regarded as good because they help to reduce cholesterol.

▶ During processing they may be converted into trans-fatty acid, e.g. by the addition of hydrogen during the production of margarine.

▶ Also when frying in oil the high heat changes the cis-fatty acids to trans-fatty acids.

▶ Trans-fatty acids are regarded as bad, as they are thought to play a role in increasing the incidence of coronary heart disease.

▶ Tests have shown that trans-fatty acids increase the level of low-density lipoproteins (LDL) which deposit cholesterol on the walls of the arteries.

▶ They also reduce high-density lipoproteins (HDL) which remove cholesterol from circulation.

▶ Sources of trans-fatty acids include: hard margarines; crisps; cakes; biscuits; pastries and crackers.

Classification of Lipids

Lipid sources are divided into three groups: animal, plant and marine.

Food companies must include trans-fat content on their nutritional labels.

Classification of lipids by source		
Animal	**Plant**	**Marine**
Meat	Nuts	Salmon
Meat fats, e.g. lard	Nut oils	Mackerel
Butter	Vegetable oils	Trout
Cream	Margarine	Herring
Cheese	Cereals	Sardines
Milk	Soya beans	Tuna
Egg yolk	Avocado	Fish liver oil, e.g. cod liver oil

Omega-3 supplements

Omega-3 Fatty Acids

An omega-3 fatty acid is a particular unsaturated fatty acid with the double bond between the third and fourth carbon atoms.

Oily fish, such as sardines, herring, mackerel and salmon, is the best source of omega-3. It is also present in nuts, seeds and soya beans or as a supplement.

Structure of an omega-3 fatty acid

Benefits: Reduced risk of heart attack, stroke, circulatory diseases and formation of blood clots and certain cancers. It is also associated with healthy brain activity (See Page 71).

Properties of Lipids

1. **Solubility:** Lipids are insoluble in water but soluble in solvents, e.g. petrol and ether. *alcohol*
2. **Affected by heat:** Solid fats melt when heated to 30–40°C. Lipids boil at extremely high temperature (175–195°C). Beyond these temperatures **smoke point** and eventually **flash point** can occur.
3. **Plasticity:** This property relates to whether a lipid is solid, liquid or spreadable. It is determined by the degree of unsaturation. The fewer unsaturated fatty acids present the more solid the lipid. As a result, many unsaturated margarines are spreadable and suitable for creaming.
4. **Rancidity:** This is the spoilage of lipids. There are two types of rancidity:

(a) Oxidative rancidity	(b) Hydrolytic rancidity
• More common. • Oxygen combines with carbon atom at the double bond. • Results in an unpleasant rancid smell. • Aided by light.	• Occurs when enzymes or bacteria hydrolyse lipids, changing them to fatty acids and glycerol. • Results in an unpleasant smell or taste. • Can occur in freezer due to enzymes.

To prevent oxidative rancidity:
(a) Store lipids in cool, dark place.
(b) Wrap well.
(c) Add antioxidants during production. They prevent oxidative rancidity by combining with the oxygen, making it unavailable to attach to the carbon atom.

Examples of antioxidants:
• Vitamins A, C, E
• BHA (Butylated hydroxyanisole)
• BHT (Butylated hydroxytoluene)

Antioxidants are found in:
crisps, biscuits, cooking oils, dairy spreads and stock cubes.

Food containing antioxidant

5. **Hydrogenation:** An unsaturated fatty acid can have hydrogen added in the presence of a nickel catalyst, converting oil into fats. Hydrogenation is used in the production of margarine (See Page 18).

6. **Emulsification:** An emulsion is a colloidal solution formed when two liquids which do not usually mix, e.g. oil and water, are forced to do so. Emulsions may be described as:

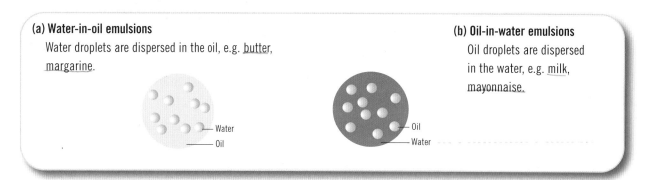

(a) Water-in-oil emulsions
Water droplets are dispersed in the oil, e.g. butter, margarine.
— Water
— Oil

(b) Oil-in-water emulsions
Oil droplets are dispersed in the water, e.g. milk, mayonnaise.
— Oil
— Water

Emulsions may be temporary or permanent

▶ Temporary emulsions are formed by vigorous shaking, e.g. oil and vinegar in a French dressing.

▶ Permanent emulsions are formed with the help of an emulsifier, e.g. lecithin in egg yolk acts as an emulsifier in mayonnaise preventing the vinegar (water) separating from the oil.

Emulsifier/emulsifying agents

An emulsifier is a molecule which has a hydrophilic (water-loving) head and a hydrophobic (water-hating) tail. The hydrophilic head attaches itself to the water molecule and the hydrophobic tail attaches itself to the oil molecule, thereby preventing the two substances from separating. Lecithin is a natural emulsifier. Glycerol monostearate (GMS) is used commercially.

Stabilisers

Stabilisers maintain the emulsion, preventing separation. Examples of stabilisers include pectin, gelatine and gum and they are used in the production of many foods, e.g. ice cream and mayonnaise.

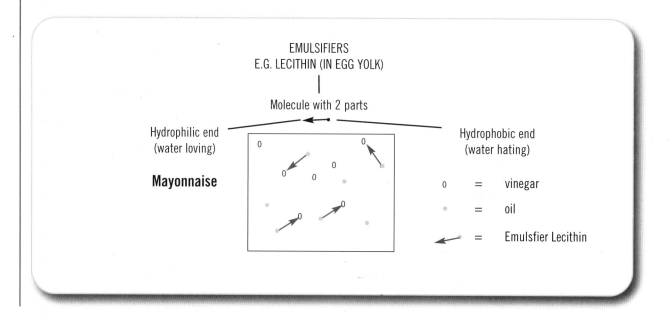

EMULSIFIERS
E.G. LECITHIN (IN EGG YOLK)

Molecule with 2 parts

Hydrophilic end
(water loving)

Hydrophobic end
(water hating)

Mayonnaise

0   =   vinegar
·   =   oil
←   =   Emulsfier Lecithin

Effects of Heat on Lipids

1. Solid fats melt at 30–40˚C.
2. Lipids boil at high temperatures (175–195˚C).
3. **Smoke point:** Fats and oils start to decompose if overheated. The glycerol separates from the fatty acids and changes to acrolein, producing a blue haze (vapour) or smoke while emitting an acrid smell. Smoke point occurs at 200˚C (fats) and 250˚C (oils). The smoke point is lowered if lipids contain impurities like food particles.
4. **Flash point:** Extreme overheating causes the vapour to spontaneously ignite. Flash point occurs at 310°C (fats) and 325˚C (oils).

Biological Functions of Lipids

1. Lipids supply the body with heat and are a concentrated source of energy.
2. Excess lipids are stored as adipose tissue, insulating the body and acting as an energy reserve.
3. Lipids protect the delicate organs of the body, e.g. kidneys, and insulate nerve fibres.
4. Foods containing lipids supply fat-soluble vitamins A, D, E and K.
5. Lipids are a source of essential fatty acids.
6. Foods with lipids are more filling and delay hunger.
7. Some unsaturated fats help lower cholesterol.
8. Omega fatty acids improve brain activity.

Energy Value of Lipids

Lipids supply 9 kcal (37 kJ) per gram. There is a higher proportion of carbon in lipids than in carbohydrates or protein, therefore lipids supply more energy when oxidised in the body. Over-consumption of lipids in Western society has led to an increase in the incidence of obesity and coronary heart disease. Therefore, it is recommended that consumption be reduced to less than 20% of overall energy intake (See Page 41).

Digestion of Lipids

During digestion, lipids are hydrolysed to break them down into glycerol and fatty acids. Hydrolysis involves the addition of water and the action of enzymes.

> Lipids → glycerol + fatty acids

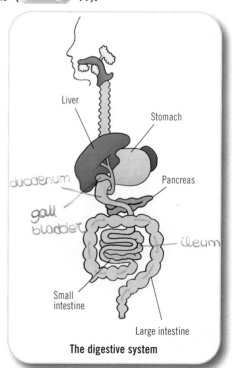

► **Mouth:** Food is chewed.

► **Stomach:** Fats melt.

► **Small intestine:** In the duodenum the enzyme lipase from the pancreas begins the digestion of lipids into fatty acids and glycerol.

► **Bile** produced by the liver and secreted into the *duodenum* emulsifies lipids, aiding their digestion.

► In the *ileum* more lipase from the small intestine continues digestion of lipids into fatty acids and glycerol. This completes the digestion of lipids.

The digestive system

Liver
Stomach
duodenum
Pancreas
gall bladder
ileum
Small intestine
Large intestine

Lipid digestion summary				
Organ/gland	**Secretion**	**Enzymes**	**Substrate**	**Product**
Pancreas	Pancreatic juice (in the duodenum)	Lipase	Lipid	Fatty acids and glycerol
Liver	Bile (in the duodenum)		Lipids	Emulsified lipid
Small intestine	Intestinal juice	Lipase	Lipids	Fatty acids and glycerol

Absorption and Utilisation of Lipids

Fatty acids and glycerol are absorbed through the lacteals in the villi of the small intestine. The lymph system then carries the digested lipids and deposits them into the blood stream at the subclavian vein at the base of the neck.

Digested lipids are oxidised in the muscles and liver and are used:

▶ To produce heat and energy.

▶ In the formation of cell membranes (essential fatty acids).

▶ Excess is stored as adipose tissue, insulating and protecting delicate organs and acting as an energy reserve.

Culinary uses of lipids (See Page **106**)

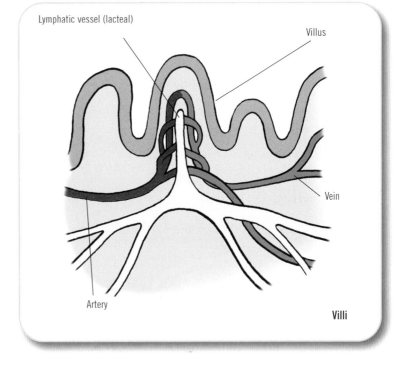

Lymphatic vessel (lacteal)

Villus

Vein

Artery

Villi

Vitamins (1.1.5)

▶ Vitamins are organic compounds which occur naturally in many foods.

▶ They may also be synthetically prepared.

▶ Vitamins are referred to as **micronutrients**.

▶ Vitamins are essential in the diet since most vitamins cannot be synthesised in the body.

▶ Each vitamin is different with its own specific functions.

▶ Deficiency diseases can occur if the diet is lacking in a particular vitamin, e.g. scurvy can develop due to a deficiency of vitamin C.

▶ Many foods such as flour, breakfast cereals and milk are **fortified** with vitamins lost in processing.

▶ Sufficient vitamins are usually supplied by the foods in a balanced diet. Occasionally, it may be necessary or advisable to include extra vitamins in the diet in the form of a vitamin supplement.

▶ The amount of vitamins supplied by foods is difficult to estimate. Factors such as freshness, storage conditions, preparation and cooking methods affect the vitamin content of foods.

▶ Smoking, alcohol and some prescribed medication also have an impact on the amount of vitamins absorbed in the body.

Classification of Vitamins

Vitamins may be classified into two groups:

> • **Fat-soluble vitamins: A, D, E, K** • **Water-soluble vitamins: B, C**

▶ Water-soluble vitamins cannot be stored in the body. If a diet contains more B and C vitamins than is required by the body, the excess is excreted in the urine. Water-soluble vitamins must therefore be included regularly in the diet.

▶ Fat-soluble vitamins may be stored in the body for several months.

▶ If a diet contains too much vitamin A or D, the excess accumulates in the liver causing a harmful condition called **hypervitaminosis**.

▶ Hypervitaminosis occurs very rarely. It is more likely to occur through the over-use of dietary supplements such as cod liver oil (particularly in the diets of babies and young children) than through overeating of foods rich in vitamins A and D.

> Symptoms of hypervitaminosis A include pain in the bones, an enlarged liver, hair loss and even death.

> Hypervitaminosis D causes vomiting, weight loss, kidney damage and could also cause death.

Fat-soluble Vitamins

Vitamin A

Vitamin A is available to the body in two forms:

▶ Pure vitamin A/retinol – found in foods from animals sources.

▶ Beta-carotene/pro-vitamin A – found in plant foods.

Vitamin A/Retinol

Properties	Sources	Functions	Effects of deficiency
• Yellow fat-soluble alcohol. • Insoluble in water. • Soluble in organic solvents. • Heat stable but destroyed by prolonged high temperatures. • Can be destroyed by oxygen when exposed to light and air.	• Halibut and cod liver oil • Margarine • Butter • Cheese • Egg yolk • Oily fish	1. Necessary for the production of rhodopsin (a pigment in the retina which allows the eye to adapt to dim light). 2. Maintains healthy lining membranes, e.g. in the eye, in the respiratory and digestive tracts, thereby helping to prevent entry of micro-organisms. 3. Keeps skin and hair healthy. 4. Helps to regulate growth.	1. Night-blindness – eyes unable to adjust to dim light. 2. Xerophthalmia – an eye infection which may lead to blindness. 3. Reduced resistance to infection. 4. Rough, dry skin (follicular keratosis). 5. Retarded growth.

RDA
Children (1–7 years): 500 µg
Adults: 700 µg
Lactation: 950 µg

Beta-carotene

Beta-carotene, also called pro-vitamin A, is the pigment that gives yellow, orange and red fruit and vegetables their colour. It is found with chlorophyll in plant foods. The strong green colour of the chlorophyll often masks its presence in food. Beta-carotene is a precursor of vitamin A. It can be converted to vitamin A in the intestines.

Beta-carotene

Properties	Sources	Functions	Effects of deficiency
• Bright yellow/orange oil. • Fat soluble. • Insoluble in water. • Generally heat stable. • Effective antioxidant.	• Carrots • Spinach • Tomatoes • Kale • Cabbage • Apricots • Used as a food colouring, e.g. in margarine.	• See also functions for retinol. • Antioxidant which protects the body against free radicals (a by-product of metabolism), helping to prevent conditions such as coronary heart disease and some types of cancer.	Beta-carotene is not an essential nutrient therefore deficiencies do not arise.

RDA
None specified

Vitamin D

There are two forms of vitamin D.

▶ Vitamin D_3 – cholecalciferol – is found mainly in animal foods. It is also created by the action of the sun's ultraviolet light on the skin. The sunlight converts 7-dehydrocholestrol in the skin to vitamin D_3.

▶ Vitamin D_2 – ergocalciferol – is produced by the action of ultraviolet light on fungi and yeasts. It is used in vitamin supplements.

There has been a reoccurrence of rickets in Ireland in recent years. Dark-skinned infants are at high risk of vitamin D deficiency. This has led to a recommendation for a vitamin D supplement for all infants (0-12 months) F.S.A.I. May 07

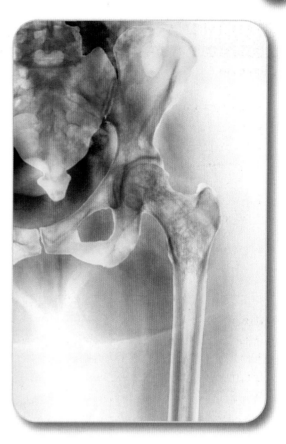

X-ray showing osteoporosis of the hip. The brown patchy area shows reduced bone density

Vitamin D/Cholecalciferol			
Properties	**Sources**	**Functions**	**Effects of deficiency**
<ul><li>White crystalline solid.</li><li>Fat soluble.</li><li>Insoluble in water.</li><li>Most stable vitamin.</li><li>Heat stable – unaffected by cooking or heat treatments, used in food processing.</li><li>Unaffected by oxidation, acids or alkalis.</li></ul> **RDA** Children and adults 10 µg Teenagers 15 µg	<ul><li>Fish liver oils</li><li>Oily fish</li><li>Liver</li><li>Butter</li><li>Margarine</li><li>Eggs</li><li>Fortified milk</li><li>Sunlight</li></ul>	1. Necessary for the absorption of calcium and phosphorous, helping to form and maintain healthy bones and teeth. 2. It regulates the balance of calcium between the blood and the skeleton. 3. Prevents rickets and osteomalacia (see next column). 4. Vitamin D helps maintain strong bones helping to prevent the development of osteoporosis in the elderly.	1. Rickets is a bone disease in children resulting in weak malformed bones. 2. Osteomalacia is a bone disease which occurs in adults, resulting in calcium loss and weaker bones. 3. Tooth decay. 4. Fragile bones and increased risk of bone fractures due to onset of osteoporosis.

Lifelines

Vitamins E and K

Vitamin E/Tocopherol			
Properties	**Sources**	**Functions**	**Effects of deficiency**
• Yellow fat-soluble alcohol. • Insoluble in water. • Heat stable. • Stable to acids. • Unstable to alkalis and ultraviolet light. • Effective antioxidant. **RDA** None specified	• Vegetable oils • Nuts • Seeds • Eggs • Margarine • Cereals • Wheat germ • Avocados	1. Powerful antioxidant. It protects other nutrients, e.g. vitamin A from oxidation in the body (See Page 28). 2. May help prevent coronary heart disease, arthritis and some forms of cancer. 3. May help to prevent eye disease in premature babies.	Rare since there are small amounts of vitamin E in many foods.

Vitamin K/Naphtho-Quinones			
Properties	**Sources**	**Functions**	**Effects of deficiency**
• Fat soluble. • Insoluble in water. • Heat stable. • Depleted by exposure to light. **RDA** None specified	• Liver • Fish • Fish liver oils • Cereals • Green vegetables, e.g. spinach and cabbage • Synthesised by bacteria in the gut.	1. Essential for normal blood clotting.	1. Blood may take longer than normal to clot. 2. Very rare: haemorrhaging – a possibility in newborn babies because the diet lacks vitamin K and gut may not have begun to manufacture vitamin K.

Water-Soluble Vitamins
VItamin C

Vitamin C/Ascorbic acid			
Properties	**Sources**	**Functions**	**Effects of deficiency**
• White crystalline acid. • Sweet/sour taste. • Water soluble. • Very unstable – it is lost during storage, food preparation, cooking and exposure to light and air. • Destroyed by alkalis, by oxidase (an enzyme present in the cell walls of plants) and by dehydration. • Effective antioxidant. **RDA** Children – 45 mg Adolescents and adults – 60 mg Pregnancy and lactation – 80 mg	• **Fruit:** Blackcurrants Kiwis Oranges Grapefruit Strawberries Melons • **Vegetables:** Peppers Cabbage Tomatoes Spinach Broccoli Potatoes	1. Necessary for the production of collagen (connective tissue) which binds the cells of skin and bone. Therefore it is important for growth. 2. Involved in the formation of healthy blood vessels. 3. Helps to prevent bruising and speeds up wound healing. 4. Powerful antioxidant protecting the body. 5. Maintains the immune system by helping white blood cells to fight infection. 6. Necessary for the efficient absorption of iron and calcium.	1. Collagen production will be affected leading to the weakening of body tissue, e.g. skin and blood vessels. 2. Wounds slow to heal, body bruises more easily. 3. Increased susceptibility to infection and illness. 4. Anaemia due to poor iron absorption. 5. Severe deficiency causes scurvy – a disease affecting gums and teeth.

Scurvy

Scurvy is a disease caused by lack of vitamin C in the diet. It was common in the past among sailors whose diet was deficient in fresh fruit and vegetables. Symptoms of scurvy include haemorrhaging under the skin, swollen spongy gums and teeth which are loose and easily lost.

Vitamin B Group

Vitamin B was originally thought to be a single substance. It is now known to consist of at least 12 different vitamins, each with its own role within the body. The vitamin B group/complex includes the following vitamins:

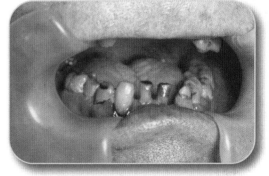

The effects of scurvy

▶ Thiamine (B_1)
▶ Riboflavin (B_2)
▶ Niacin (B_3)
  nicotinic acid
▶ Pyrodoxine (B_6)
▶ Cobalamin (B_{12})
▶ Folate/folic acid

Vitamin B Group/Complex			
Properties	**Sources**	**Functions**	**Effects of deficiency**
Thiamine B$_1$			
• Water soluble. • Very unstable, lost at high temperatures. • Destroyed by alkalis, sulphur dioxide, (preservative) and ultraviolet light. • Lost in milling.	• Wholegrains • Fortified bread • Breakfast cereals • Yeast • Eggs • Potatoes • Small amounts synthesised in intestine.	1. Release of energy from carbohydrate and fat (metabolism). 2. Healthy nerve muscle functioning. 3. Normal growth and development.	1. Rare – mild deficiency causes irritability, fatigue, depression, loss of appetite. 2. Affects growth rate of children. 3. Severe deficiency causes beri-beri, a disorder which affects nerves and muscle function.
Riboflavin B$_2$			
• Water soluble. • Sensitive to light. • Unstable at high temperatures. • Destroyed by alkalis.	• Beef • Offal • Milk • Eggs • Cheese • Fortified cereals • Nuts	1. Release of energy from protein, fats and carbohydrates. 2. Promotes healthy mucous membranes, e.g. in mouth, nose and eyes. 3. Healthy skin, hair and nails.	1. Lack of energy and fatigue. 2. Dermatitis and skin rashes. 3. Sore, cracked lips and tongue. 4. Eye disorders. 5. Retarded growth.
Niacin			
• Water soluble. • Stable to heat. • Stable to acids and alkalis. • Lost in milling.	• Meat • Offal • Bread • Tuna • Nuts • Fortified cereals • Can be synthesised in the body from amino acid tryptophan.	1. Growth. 2. Energy release from food. 3. Healthy functioning of nervous system. 4. Promotes healthy skin.	1. Tiredness, depression and memory loss. 2. If severe, pellagra which causes dementia, dermatitis and diarrhoea.

Beri-beri

Beri-beri is a disease caused by a deficiency of thiamine (B$_1$). It is common in the Far East where polished rice forms the staple diet. The outer layer is removed to improve the texture and shelf-life of the rice. However, this refining process also removes most of the thiamine. Symptoms of beri-beri include loss of appetite, leading to emaciation. The nervous system is affected with muscular weakness and paralysis.

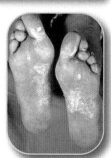

The effects of beri-beri   The effects of pellagra

Pellagra

Pellagra is a disease caused by a deficiency of niacin and tryptophan in the diet. It is associated with poor Third World countries, where the diet consists mainly of maize. While maize contains niacin, it is not readily available to the body. Symptoms of pellagra include dermatitis, diarrhoea, dementia and it can be fatal.

Vitamin B Group/Complex

Properties	Sources	Functions	Effects of deficiency
Pyrodoxine (B₆)			
• Water soluble. • Fairly heat stable but some loss in cooking liquid. • Destroyed by alkalis, ultraviolet light and oxygen.	• Meat • Fish • Offal • Yeast • Green vegetables • Pulses • Nuts	1. Metabolism of proteins, carbohydrates and fats. 2. Involved in production of red blood cells. 3. Maintains a healthy nervous system. 4. Thought to relieve symptoms of premenstrual tension and nausea in early pregnancy.	1. Rare – may cause irritability, depression, dermatitis. 2. May cause convulsions in babies. 3. Premenstrual syndrome. 4. Nausea in pregnancy.
Cobalamin (B₁₂)			
• Water soluble. • Some loss in cooking. • Destroyed by acids, alkalis and ultraviolet light. **RDA** Children 1 μg Teenagers/adults 1·4 μg Pregnancy 1·6 μg Lactation 1·9 μg	• Liver • Meat • Eggs • Milk • Cheese • Fish • Poultry * Only found in animal foods therefore some foods used in vegan diets, e.g. yeast and soya milk, are fortified with B₁₂.	1. Involved in metabolism of fatty acids and folate. 2. Required for the production of red blood cells. 3. Promotes normal growth. 4. Maintains a healthy nervous system.	1. Weakness, fatigue, weight loss. 2. Non-absorption of B₁₂ can cause pernicious anaemia, which results in a decrease in the red blood cell count. 3. Poor growth. 4. Depression and dementia.
Folate/folic acid			
• Water soluble. • Some loss in cooking. • Destroyed by alkalis, exposure to air and ultraviolet light. • Stable to acids. **RDA** Children 200 μg Teenagers/adults 300 μg Pregnancy 500 μg Lactation 400 μg	• Wheat germ and bran • Wholemeal bread • Fortified breakfast cereals/bread • Spinach • Milk • Dietary supplements advisable for pregnant women or women planning pregnancy.	1. Helps to prevent neural-tube defects in the unborn child. 2. Involved with B₁₂ in the formation of red blood cells. 3. Helps maintain the immune system.	1. Increased risk of neural-tube defects, e.g. spina bifida. 2. Anaemia and fatigue in young children and pregnant women.

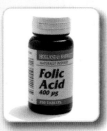

Minerals (1.1.6)

Minerals are inorganic nutrients. The human body requires about 20 mineral elements to protect against diseases. They are required in small amounts. Those required in minute quantities are referred to as *trace elements*.

Minerals	
Major mineral elements	**Trace mineral elements**
Calcium (Ca)	Iron (Fe)
Phosphorus (P)	Zinc (Zn)
Sodium (Na)	Iodine (I)
Potassium (K)	Copper (Cu)
Magnesium (Mg)	Selenium (Se)
Chloride (Cl)	Fluorine (F)

* Copper and Selenium are powerful antioxidants.

Calcium

Calcium is the most abundant mineral in the human body. About 99% is present in bones and teeth, and the remainder in blood, muscles and nerves. Calcification is the term for the hardening of bones and teeth. This is due to the absorption of calcium and phosphorus (calcium phosphate).

Sources of calcium

- ▶ Milk, cheese, yoghurt
- ▶ Canned fish, e.g. sardines, salmon
- ▶ Leafy green vegetables, e.g. cabbage, spinach
- ▶ Sesame seeds
- ▶ Fortified flour
- ▶ Hard water

Calcium content of foods (100 g)	
Cheese	800 mg
Sardines (canned)	550 mg
Milk	103 mg
Bread (white)	100 mg
Spinach	100 mg

> **RDA** Children 800 mg, adolescents 1200 mg
> Adults 800 mg, pregnancy/lactation 1200 mg

Functions of calcium
▶ Calcium plays an important role in the formation of strong bones and teeth.

▶ Calcium is required for blood clotting and to regulate blood pressure.

▶ Calcium is necessary for normal muscle contractions, e.g. regular heartbeat.

▶ Calcium is required for normal nerve function.

Calcium deficiency can cause
▶ Rickets in children and osteomalacia in adults in severe cases.

▶ Osteoporosis in children, teenagers and adults.

▶ Severe osteoporosis in the elderly.

▶ Tooth decay and poor quality teeth.

▶ Poor blood clotting.

▶ Muscular spasms.

▶ Disturbance in functioning of nerve cells.

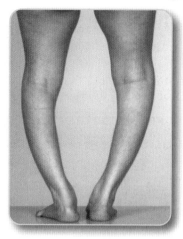

The effects of rickets

Absorption of calcium
Only between 20–30% of calcium in the diet is absorbed. Certain factors may assist or hinder calcium absorption.

Assisting calcium absorption
▶ Sufficient vitamin D in the diet is essential for calcium absorption.

▶ Parathormone, a hormone produced by the parathyroid gland, controls the levels of calcium in the blood.

▶ Oestrogen, a hormone in premenopausal women, promotes calcium absorption.

▶ Phosphorus, which combines with calcium to form calcium phosphate, must be present in the correct proportions.

▶ An acid environment aids calcium absorption. This can be enhanced by combining vitamin C with calcium foods.

▶ Protein is necessary for calcium absorption – the calcium is absorbed into the blood stream by becoming bound to protein.

Hindering calcium absorption
▶ Phytates/phytic acid, present in wholegrain bread and cereals, may combine with calcium, preventing its absorption.

▶ Oxalates/oxalic acid present in rhubarb and spinach may react with calcium inhibiting its absorption.

▶ Tannins in tea and coffee inhibit calcium absorption.

▶ Excess fat – during digestion fatty acids may combine with calcium preventing its absorption.

▶ Excess protein results in calcium being excreted in the urine.

▶ Incorrect calcium/phosphorus ratio inhibits calcium absorption.

▶ Research indicates that over-consumption of soft drinks inhibits calcium absorption.

Iron

Over half of the iron present in the human body is in the blood. The remainder is stored in the liver, spleen and bone marrow, with a small proportion in muscle protein and cell enzymes.

Sources of iron

- ► Liver, kidney, red meat
- ► Wholegrain flour
- ► Dark green vegetables, e.g. spinach, cabbage
- ► Eggs
- ► Cereals

Iron content of foods	
Liver (lamb's, fried)	11 mg
Kidney (pig's, fried)	9 mg
Wholegrain flour	4 mg
Spinach (boiled)	4 mg
Eggs (boiled)	2 mg

RDA
Children 8 mg   Adolescents 14 mg
Adults 10 mg   Pregnancy/lactation 15 mg

Functions of iron

- ► Iron is essential in the formation of the pigment haemoglobin in the red blood cells.
- ► Haemoglobin transports oxygen around the body.
- ► Iron is involved in myoglobin production which carries oxygen to the muscles.
- ► Iron works with enzymes to release energy from food.

Iron deficiency causes

- ► Tiredness, lack of energy.
- ► Muscles tire easily.
- ► Paleness.
- ► Breathlessness.
- ► Anaemia in severe cases.

Anaemia

Anaemia is a disease caused by a shortage of haemoglobin, as a result of insufficient iron in the diet, or an inability to absorb iron. It is more common in females due to menstruation. Symptoms include tiredness, dizziness, headaches, paleness, shortness of breath and loss of appetite.

Absorption of iron

Only about 15% of the iron present in the diet is absorbed. However, the body adjusts and absorbs more in times of special need, e.g. growing children and pregnant women. Certain factors may assist or hinder iron absorption.

Assisting iron absorption

▶ The source of iron – the iron in meat and offal called <u>haem iron is more easily absorbed than non-haem iron</u> from plant sources.

✱ ▶ The presence of vitamin C (ascorbic acid) promotes the absorption of non-haem iron. It reduces <u>ferric iron</u> to the absorbable ferrous state. →same molecule , easier to absorb

▶ Eating animal and plant sources of iron together helps the body absorb more non-haem iron.

Hindering iron absorption

▶ Excess fibre in the diet decreases iron absorption.

▶ Tannins in tea and coffee reduce iron absorption.

▶ Choosing only non-haem sources of iron results in little being absorbed.

▶ Phytates present in wholegrain breads and cereals combine with iron preventing absorption.

▶ Oxalates present in rhubarb and spinach react with iron inhibiting its absorption.

Sources of iron	
Sources of haem iron	**Sources of non-haem iron**
Offal	Eggs
Red meat	Cereals
Meat products	Green vegetables
Chicken	Pulses
	Fish*
	* Although the iron in fish is non-haem iron a property in fish boosts iron absorption.

Mineral elements		
Sources	**Functions**	**Effects of deficiency**
Potassium		
• Pulses, green leafy vegetables • Bananas, oranges • Meat • Milk • Fruit juices, nuts **RDA** 0·8–3·1 g	1. Maintains fluid balance in body tissue. 2. Healthy nerve activity. 3. Normal muscle contractions.	1. Very rare (potassium is present in many foods). 2. Mental confusion. 3. Cardiac arrest. 4. Muscular weakness.
Sodium		
• Table salt • Processed foods • Smoked and cured meat and fish • Meat products • Cheese • Snack foods **RDA** 1.6 g	1. Maintains fluid balance in body tissue. 2. Healthy nerve activity. 3. Normal muscle contractions.	1. Muscular weakness and cramps. 2. Low blood pressure. 3. Loss of appetite.

Mineral elements		
Sources	Functions	Effects of deficiency
Zinc		
• Meat and meat products • Milk • Cereals • Shellfish • Legumes • Seeds **RDA** 7-12 mg	1. Enzyme activity. 2. Protein and carbohydrate metabolism. 3. Normal hormone activity. 4. Healthy skin and hair.	1. Frequent infections. 2. Reduced appetite. 3. Delayed healing. 4. Dry skin.
Iodine		
• Seafood • Cod liver oil • Iodised salt • Vegetables grown in iodine-rich soil **RDA** 70–160 µg	1. Production of thyroid hormone/thyroxine. 2. Regulation of growth and development. 3. Regulates metabolism.	1. Goitre, enlargement of the thyroid gland due to deficiency of thyroid hormones. 2. Retarded mental development. 3. Lethargy. 4. Weight loss.
		The effects of goitre

Retaining Minerals and Vitamins in Fruit and Vegetables

► Choose good-quality fresh foods, avoid prepared produce.

► Buy in small quantities and avoid storing fresh fruit and vegetables for prolonged periods.

► Store fruit and vegetables in a cool, dry, dark place.

► Eat fruit and vegetables raw if possible.

► Avoid peeling fruit and vegetables or peel thinly.

► Prepare food shortly before use.

► Avoid steeping.

► Use a sharp knife to reduce the effect of the enzyme oxidase.

► Begin the cooking of vegetables in boiling liquid.

► Cook for the shortest time possible.

► Cook in the minimum amount of liquid.

► Cover the saucepan.

► Use liquid for sauces or gravy.

► Do not use bread soda to soften green vegetables.

► Serve immediately, avoid keeping warm.

► Avoid reheating.

Water (1.1.7)

Elemental Composition of Water

Water is made up of the elements <u>hydrogen</u> and <u>oxygen</u> in a <u>2:1 ratio</u> – H_2O.

Sources of Water

- ▶ <u>Tap/bottled water.</u>
- ▶ All drinks, e.g. <u>tea, coffee, milk.</u>
- ▶ <u>Fruit</u> and <u>vegetables.</u>
- ▶ Most food, <u>except solid fats</u> and <u>dried foods.</u>

Sources of water

Properties of Pure Water

- ▶ <u>Colourless, odourless, tasteless</u> liquid.
- ▶ Boils at <u>100°C,</u> freezes at <u>0°C.</u>
- ▶ May be <u>solid, liquid</u> or <u>vapour.</u>
- ▶ A <u>solvent</u> – dissolves many substances. *important in laundry & cleaning*
- ▶ Absorbs and <u>retains heat.</u>
- ▶ Is neutral – <u>pH7.</u>

Biological Importance of Water (functions)

- ▶ Essential part of all <u>body tissues and fluids.</u> *makes up every cell in your body*
- ▶ Transportation – the blood transports <u>nutrients, oxygen, carbon dioxide,</u> <u>hormones</u> and enzymes around the body.
- ▶ Involved in <u>hydrolysis</u> during digestion.
- ▶ <u>Distributes heat</u> and <u>controls body temperature.</u>
- ▶ <u>Removes waste</u> through the <u>kidneys.</u> *& sweat*
- ▶ Provides the <u>minerals</u> calcium, flourine.
- ▶ Quenches thirst. *hydrates the body*

RDA = 2·5 litres per day.

Inter-relationship Between Nutrients

- ▶ Vitamin D aids the absorption of calcium.
- ▶ Vitamin C aids the absorption of iron and calcium.
- ▶ Vitamin D, calcium and phosphorus are involved in bone and teeth formation.
- ▶ Vitamin B_6 and B_{12}, folate and iron are involved in the formation of red blood cells.
- ▶ Vitamin K and calcium are important for blood clotting.
- ▶ Vitamin B group is involved in the metabolism of proteins, fats and carbohydrates.

CONTENTS INCLUDE:

▶ Energy – role in the body, energy requirements and energy balance

▶ Dietary guidelines and food tables – information and use

▶ Dietary requirements of different age groups and diet-related health problems

▶ Excesses and deficiencies in the diet and their effects on health and well-being

Diet and Health (1.2)

Health is greatly influenced by the diet. A balanced diet helps to reduce the risk of diet-related diseases and increases the chance of optimum health.

- **Diet:** The food that a person eats.

- **Balanced diet:** A diet containing all of the nutrients in the correct proportions for the needs of the individual.

Energy (1.2.1)

Energy is defined as the body's power for doing work.

The Role of Energy in the Body

▶ Energy is essential for the functioning of internal organs, e.g. heart and kidneys.

▶ Energy is required by the body for all physical activities such as walking and standing.

▶ Energy is involved in the production of heat, which helps to maintain body temperature.

▶ Energy is necessary for growth, therefore it is important during pregnancy for the development of the foetus and for children and adolescents.

▶ Energy plays a role in all cell and nerve activity (metabolism).

Basal Metabolic Rate (BMR)

▶ Basal metabolic rate refers to the minimum amount of energy required to keep internal organs functioning and maintain body temperature.

▶ It is calculated when the body is at complete rest, warm and has been fasting for at least 12 hours.

▶ BMR differs from person to person, but generally accounts for almost two thirds of energy output.

▶ Basal metabolism increases during periods of growth.

▶ Activity increases basal metabolic rate.

▶ As people get older basal metabolism slows down.

Basal metabolic rate per hour	
Males	70 kcal (300 kJ)
Females	60 kcal (250 kJ)
Teenagers	55–70 kcal (250–300 kJ)
Pregnant females	70 kcal (300 kj)

Measuring Energy

Energy that comes from food is measured in kilocalories (kcal) or kilojoules (kJ).

1 kcal = 4·2 kJ

Energy content of foods
1 gram of protein produces 4 kcal (17 kJ)
1 gram of lipids produces 9 kcal (37 kJ)
1 gram of carbohydrates produces 4 kcal (17 kJ)
1 gram of alcohol produces 7 kcal (29 kJ)

> As a general guideline, at least 50% of energy should be sourced from carbohydrates, no more than 35% from fats and 15% from proteins.

Factors Determining Energy Requirements

The amount of energy required is influenced by a number of factors.

► **Age:** Young children and teenagers require a lot of energy for rapid growth and increase in body size. Elderly people's energy requirements fall with decreased activity and decreased basal metabolic rate.

► **Bodyweight/size:** Generally the larger the body the more energy that is required.

► **Gender:** Because of body composition men require more energy than women of equal weight. (Men have a higher proportion of muscle to fat, women have more fat).

► **Occupation:** The more active the occupation the more energy required. A taxi driver would require less energy than a builder.

► **Activity:** The more physically active one is the more energy required. If a person is involved in active sports as a pastime, he/she will require more energy than a person whose pastime is playing computer games.

Daily energy requirements	
Age	Kilocalories
Babies 0–1	800
Children 5–7	1,800
Girls 9–18	2,300
Boys 12–15	2,800
Boys 15–18	3,000
Men (sedentary)	2,700
Women (sedentary)	2,100
Men (active)	3,500
Woman (active)	2,500
Men (elderly)	2,250
Women (elderly)	2,000
Pregnancy and breast-feeding	2,400 to 2,700

► **Pregnancy/lactation:** Women require extra energy during pregnancy and while breast-feeding to allow for growth of the baby.

► **Climate:** A person living in a cooler climate will require extra energy for the production of heat.

► **Health Status:** During illness energy requirements often decrease due to lack of physical exercise. However, injuries such as cuts and burns require extra energy for repair.

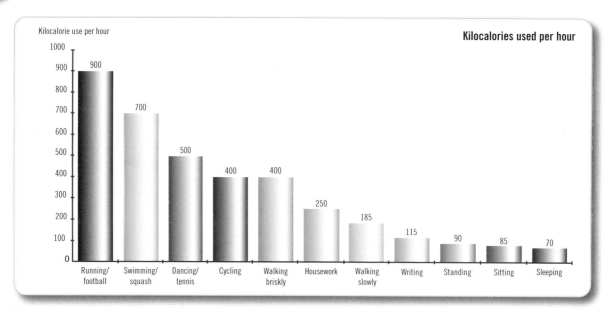

Kilocalorie use per hour

Kilocalories used per hour

Balancing Energy

▶ Energy intake should match energy output. This is known as _energy balance._

▶ If our intake of kilocalories from food exceeds our energy output, we gain weight.

▶ If energy output exceeds energy intake we lose weight.

▶ Balancing energy input with energy output maintains a constant bodyweight.

Dietary Guidelines (1.2.2)
Current Nutritional Guidelines

The nutrition and health of the population of Ireland is the monitored by the Department of Health and Children. This department is supported by:

▶ The HSE (Health Service Executive)   ▶ The Health Promotion Unit

▶ The National Nutritional Surveillance Centre   ▶ The Irish Nutrition and Dietetic Institute

National healthy eating guidelines

1. Eat a variety of different foods, using the food pyramid as a guide.
2. Eat the right amount of food to maintain a healthy weight.
3. Eat five or more portions of fruit and vegetables every day.
4. Eat foods rich in starch: breads, cereals, potatoes, pasta and rice. Aim to have at least six servings a day.
5. Eat plenty of foods rich in fibre: breads and cereals (especially wholegrain) potatoes, pastas and rice; and fruit and vegetables.
6. Reduce the amount of fatty foods you eat, especially saturated fats.
7. Use herbs, spices and black pepper as alternatives to salt to flavour food.
8. Reduce the number of sugary snacks per day.
9. Drink plenty of water.
10. Avoid alcohol. Adults who drink should keep within sensible limits.

DEPARTMENT
OF HEALTH AND
CHILDREN
AN ROINN
SLÁINTE AGUS LEANAÍ

Food Pyramid

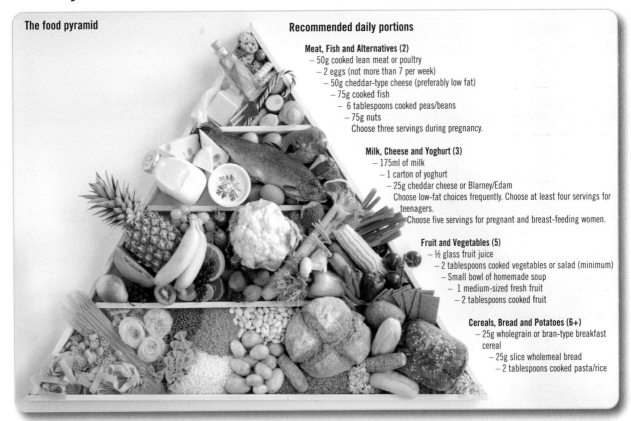

The food pyramid

Recommended daily portions

Meat, Fish and Alternatives (2)
- 50g cooked lean meat or poultry
- 2 eggs (not more than 7 per week)
- 50g cheddar-type cheese (preferably low fat)
- 75g cooked fish
- 6 tablespoons cooked peas/beans
- 75g nuts

Choose three servings during pregnancy.

Milk, Cheese and Yoghurt (3)
- 175ml of milk
- 1 carton of yoghurt
- 25g cheddar cheese or Blarney/Edam

Choose low-fat choices frequently. Choose at least four servings for teenagers.
Choose five servings for pregnant and breast-feeding women.

Fruit and Vegetables (5)
- ½ glass fruit juice
- 2 tablespoons cooked vegetables or salad (minimum)
- Small bowl of homemade soup
- 1 medium-sized fresh fruit
- 2 tablespoons cooked fruit

Cereals, Bread and Potatoes (6+)
- 25g wholegrain or bran-type breakfast cereal
- 25g slice wholemeal bread
- 2 tablespoons cooked pasta/rice

The four food groups

Cereals, bread and potatoes	Milk, cheese and yoghurt
Fruit and vegetables	Meat, fish and poultry

Aim to include three of the four food groups at each meal.

Formulation of Nutritional Guidelines

▶ The dietary practices of the general population are surveyed.

▶ The findings of this research are analysed by nutritional experts.

▶ The areas of dietary practice that require attention are considered in the design of the nutritional guidelines.

▶ *The Healthy Eating Guidelines* are devised to improve the general health of the Irish population.

▶ If followed, they ensure adequate intake of proteins, minerals and vitamins and fibre.

▶ These guidelines help prevent excessive intake of energy, saturated fats, cholesterol, salt, sugar and alcohol.

▶ The possibility of developing conditions such as obesity, high cholesterol levels, high blood pressure and bowel disorders is reduced.

Recommended Dietary Allowances (RDAs)

Recommended dietary allowances (RDAs) are the level of intake of nutrients that are judged to be adequate to meet the nutrient needs of healthy people.

Uses of RDAs

► Providing nutritional information on labels.

► Developing new products in industry.

► Interpreting food consumption records.

► Designing nutritional education programmes.

► Evaluating the adequacy of food supplies in meeting national nutritional needs.

RDAs are revised by nutritionists of the Food Safety Authority of Ireland.

RDA table	
Water	2.5 litres
Protein	30–85 g
Fibre	25–30 g
Potassium	0.8–3.1 g
Sodium	1.6 g
Calcium	800–1200 mg
Vitamin C	45–80 mg
Iron	8–15 mg
Zinc	7–12 mg
Retinol	500–950 µg
Folate	200–500 µg
Iodine	70–160 µg
Vitamin D	10–15 µg
Cobalamin	1–1.9 µg

Lowest threshold intake (LTI)

► LTI is the lowest level of nutrient intake which is required for health.

RDA = Recommended Dietary Allowance
GDA = Guideline Daily amounts

► The majority of people will require more than this amount.

► This reference value is useful in assessing the adequacy of individuals' diets.

Food Composition Tables

► Food tables show the nutrient content of food per 100 g of solids or per 100 ml of liquid.

► Saturated, mono-unsaturated and polyunsaturated fatty acids are usually shown as a percentage of the total fat content.

► The energy value (kcal/kJ) per 100 g is also shown.

► The amount of an average serving may be included.

Uses

► Food tables are used to compile nutritional information labels.

► Design of nutritional guidelines involves the use of food composition tables.

► Food tables may be used to compare different foods in terms of nutrient or energy content.

► These tables are used in order to prescribe diets for conditions such as diabetes or obesity.

Food Composition Table

Food	Inedible waste %	Energy kcal	kJ	Protein g	Fat g	Carbohydrate (as monosaccharide) g	Water g	Calcium mg	Iron mg	Vitamin A retinol equivalent ug	Thiamin mg	Riboflavin mg	Nicotinic acid equivalent mg	Vitamin C mg	Vitamin D ug
Milk															
Cream, double	0	449	1,848	1.8	48.0	2.6	47	65	0	420	0.02	0.8	0.4	0	0.28
Milk, liquid, whole	0	65	274	3.3	3.8	4.8	88	120	0.1	44	0.04	0.15	0.09	1	0.05
Milk dried, skimmed	0	352	1,498	36.0	0.9	53.3	5	1,260	0.5	112	0.30	1.73	9.7	10	0.09
Yoghurt, low-fat, skimmed	0	53	224	5.0	1.0	6.4	86	180	0.1	4	0.05	0.26	1.3	0	0.02
Cheese															
Cheese, cheddar	0	412	1,708	25.4	34.5	0	37	810	0.6	10	0.04	0.50	5.2	0	0.35
Cheese, cottage	0	114	480	15.3	4.0	4.5	75	80	0.4	420	0.03	0.27	3.2	0	0.02
Meat															
Bacon, rashers, cooked	0	447	1,852	24.5	38.8	0	32	12	1.4	27	0.40	0.19	9.2	0	0
Beef, average	17	236	940	16.1	17.1	0	64	7	1.9	0	0.06	0.19	8.1	0	0
Chicken, roast	0	148	621	24.8	5.4	0	68	9	0.8	0	0.08	0.19	12.8	0	0
Ham, cooked	0	269	1,119	24.7	18.9	0	54	9	1.3	0	0.44	0.15	8.0	0	0
Kidney, average	11	89	375	16.2	2.7	0	79	9	6.0	0	0.39	1.90	10.7	12	0
Lamb, roast	0	291	1,209	23.0	22.1	0	54	9	2.1	300	0.10	0.25	9.2	0	0
Pork, average	15	330	1,364	15.8	29.6	0	54	8	0.8	0	0.58	0.16	6.9	0	0
Sausage, pork	0	367	1,529	10.6	32.1	9.5	45	41	1.1	0	0.04	0.21	5.7	0	0
Steak & kidney pie cooked	0	304	1,226	13.3	21.1	14.6	51	37	5.1	0	0.11	0.47	6.0	0	0.55
Fish															
Cod, haddock, white fish	40	76	321	17.4	0.7	0	82	16	0.3	126	0.08	0.07	4.8	0	0
Cod, fried in batter	0	199	834	19.6	10.3	7.5	61	80	0.5	0	0.04	0.10	6.7	0	0
Fish fingers	0	178	749	12.6	7.5	16.1	64	43	0.7	0	0.09	0.06	3.1	0	0
Herring	37	234	970	16.8	128.5	0	64	33	0.8	0	0	0.18	7.1	0	22.20
Salmon, canned	2	155	6648	20.3	8.2	0	70	93	1.4	45	0.04	0.18	10.7	0	12.50
Sardines, canned in oil	0	217	906	23.7	13.6	0	58	550	2.9	90	0.04	0.36	12.4	0	7.50
Eggs															
Eggs, fresh	12	147	612	12.3	10.9	0	75	54	2.1	30	0.9	0.47	3.7	0	1.50
Fats															
Butter	0	731	3,006	0.5	81.0	0	16	15	0.2	140	0	0	0.1	0	1.25
Lard; cooked fat, dripping	0	894	3,674	0	99.3	0	1	0	0	995	0	0	0	0	0
Low-fat spread	0	365	1,500	0	40.5	0	57	0	0	0	0	0	0	0	8.00
Margarine	0	734	3,019	0.2	81.5	0	15	4	0.3	900	0	0	0.1	0	8.00
Oils, cooking and salad	0	899	3,969	0	99.9	0	0	0	0	0	0	0	0	0	0
Preserves etc.															
Chocolate, milk	0	578	2,411	8.7	37.6	54.5	0	246	1.7	6.6	0.03	0.35	2.5	0	0
Jam	0	262	1,116	0.5	0	69.2	30	18	1.2	2.0	0	0	0	10	0
Sugar, white	0	394	1,680	0	0	105.0	0	1	0.	0	0	0	0	0	0
Vegetables															
Beans, canned in tomato sauce	0	63	266	5.1	0.4	10.3	74	45	1.4	50	0.07	0.05	1.4	3	0
Beans, runner	14	23	100	2.2	0	3.9	89	27	0.8	50	0.05	0.10	1.4	20	0
Beetroot, boiled	20	44	189	1.8	0	9.9	83	30	0.7	0	0.02	0.04	0.4	5	0
Brussel sprouts, boiled	0	17	75	2.8	0	1.7	92	25	0.5	67	0.06	0.10	1.0	41	0
Cabbage, green, raw	30	22	92	2.8	0	2.8	88	57	0.6	50	0.06	0.05	0.7	53	0
Cabbage, green, boiled	0	15	66	1.7	0	2.3	93	38	0.4	50	0.03	0.03	0.5	23	0
Carrots, old	4	23	98	0.7	0	5.4	90	48	0.6	2,000	0.06	0.05	0.7	6	0
Cauliflower	30	13	56	1.9	0	1.5	93	21	0.5	5	0.10	0.10	1.0	64	0
Celery	27	8	36	0.9	0	1.3	94	52	0.6	0	0.03	0.03	0.5	7	0
Crisps, potato	0	533	2,222	6.2	35.9	49.3	3	37	2.1	0	0.19	0.07	6.3	17	0
Cucumber	23	9	39	0.6	0	1.8	96	23	0.3	0	0.04	0.4	0.3	8	0
Lettuce	20	8	36	1.0	0	1.2	96	23	0.9	167	0.07	0.08	0.4	15	0
Mushrooms	25	7	31	1.8	0	0	92	3	10	2	0.10	0.40	4.5	3	0
Onions	3	23	98	0.9	0	5.2	93	31	0.3	0	0.03	0.05	0.4	10	0
Peas, fresh or frozen, boiled	0	49	208	5.0	0	7.7	80	13	1.2	50	0.25	0.11	2.3	15	0
Peas, canned, processed	0	76	325	6.2	0	13.7	72	27	1.5	67	0.10	0.04	1,4	0	0
Peppers, green	16	14	59	0.9	0.2	2.2	94	9	0.4	42	0.08	0.03	0.9	91	0
Potatoes, raw	27	76	324	2.1	0	18.0	78	8	0.7	0	0.11	0.04	1.8	8-30	0
Potatoes, boiled	0	80	339	1.4	0	19.7	81	4	0.5	0	0.08	0.03	1.2	4-15	0
Potatoes, roast	0	111	474	2.8	1.0	27.3	64	10	1.0	0	0.05	0.04	2	6-23	0
Sweet corn, canned	0	79	336	2.9	0.8	16.1	73	3	0.1	35	0.06	0.08	0.3	4	0
Tomatoes, fresh	0	12	52	0.8	0	24.	93	13	0.4	117	0.04	0.04	0.7	20	0

Food Composition Table

	Inedible waste %	Energy kcal	kJ	Protein g	Fat g	Carbohydrate (as monosaccharide) g	Water g	Calcium mg	Iron mg	Vitamin A retinol equivalent ug	Thiamin mg	Riboflavin mg	Nicotinic acid equivalent mg	Vitamin C mg	Vitamin D ug
Fruit															
Apples	20	46	297	0·3	0	12·0	84	4	0·3	5	0·04	0·02	0·1	5	0
Apricots, dried	0	182	776	4·8	0	43·4	15	92	4·1	600	0	0·20	3·4	0	0
Bananas	40	76	326	1·1	0	19·2	71	7	0·4	33	0·4	0·07	0,8	10	0
Gooseberries	1	27	116	0·9	0	6·3	87	22	0·4	30	0·04	0·03	0·4	40	0
Grapefruit	50	22	95	0·6	0	5·3	91	17	0·3	0	0·05	0·02	0·3	40	0
Lemons	60	7	31	0·3	0	1·6	91	18	0·1	0	0·02	0	0·1	50	0
Melon	40	23	97	0·8	0	5·2	94	16	0·4	160	0·05	0·03	0·5	25	0
Oranges	30	35	150	0·8	0	8·5	86	41	0·3	8	0·10	0·03	0·3	50	0
Orange juice, canned unconcentrated	0	47	201	0·8	0	11·7	87	10	0·4	8	0·07	0·02	0·2	40	0
Peaches, fresh	13	36	156	0·6	0	9·1	86	5	0·4	83	0·02	0·05	1·1	8	0
Peaches canned (include. syrup)	0	88	373	0·4	0	22·9	74	4	1·9	41	0·01	0·02	0·6	4	0
Pears	25	41	175	0·3	0	10·6	83	8	0·2	2	0·03		0·3	3	0
Pineapples	0	76	325	0·3	0	20·0	77	13	1·7	7	0·05	0·02	0·3	8	0
Plums	8	32	137	0·6	0	7·9	85	12	0·3	37	0·05	0·03	0·6	3	0
Raspberries	0	25	105	0·9	0	5·6	83	41	1·2	13	0·02	0·03	0·5	25	0
Rhubarb	33	6	26	0·6	0	1·0	94	103	0·4	10	0·01	0·07	0·3	10	0
Strawberries	3	26	109	0·6	0	6·2	89	22	0·7	5	0·02	0·03	0·5	60	0
Cereals															
Barley, pearl, dry	0	360	1,531	7·7	1·7	83·6	11	10	0·7	0	0·12	0·08	2·2	0	0
Biscuits, chocolate	0	497	2,087	7·0	24·9	65·3	3	131	1·5	0	0·11	0·04	1·9	0	0
Biscuits, cream crackers	0	471	1,985	18·1	16·2	78·0	4	145	2·2	0	0·22	0·05	2·3	0	0
Biscuits, plain	0	431	1,819	7·4	13·2	73·3	3	126	1·8	0	0·17	0·06	2·0	0	0
Bread, white	0	251	1,068	8·0	1·7	54·3	39	100	1·7	0	0·18	0·03	2·6	0	0
Bread, wholemeal	0	241	1,025	9·6	3·1	46·7	38	28	3·0	0	0·24	0·09	1·9	0	0
Cornflakes	0	354	1,507	7·4	0·4	85·4	2	5	0·3	0	1·13	1·41	10·6	0	0
Crispbread, Ryvita	0	318	1,325	10·0	2·1	69·0	6	86	3·3	0	0·37	0·24	1·3	0	0
Oatmeal	0	400	1,692	12·1	8·7	72·8	9	55	4·1	0	0·50	0·10	2·8	0	0
Rice	0	359	1,531	6·2	1·0	86·8	12	4	0·4	0	0·08	0·03	1·5	0	0
Spaghetti	0	364	1,549	9·9	1·0	84·0	12	23	1·2	0	0·09	0·06	1·8	0	0

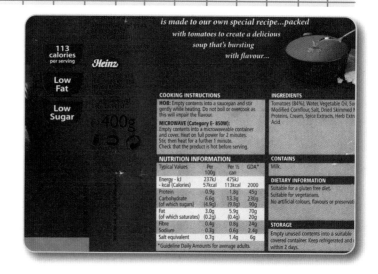

Knowledge of recommended dietary allowances and portion sizes is necessary when using food composition tables.

Dietary and Food Requirements (1.2.3)

Babies

► For the first 4–6 months babies live on either breast milk or formula milk. Although both contain the correct amount of nutrients for the baby, there are many reasons why breast-feeding is recommended.

Reasons to breast-feed
• It allows for bonding between the mother and baby.
• Breast-feeding eliminates the need for sterilising and involves no preparation or cost.
• Antibodies are passed on to the baby which help to build resistance to diseases.
• Breast milk is always at the correct temperature.
• There is less chance of the baby becoming overweight as breast milk has less fat than formula milk.
• Breast-fed babies are less likely to suffer from gastric upset, respiratory and allergic diseases or insulin dependent diabetes.

▶ When formula feeding follow instructions accurately and observe strict hygiene.

▶ After a few months the baby's diet requires vitamin C so fruit juices are often given.

▶ By 4–6 months the baby's reserve of iron is used up and the milk no longer supplies enough nutrients, so solid foods must be introduced. This introduction of solid food is called *weaning*.

▶ Introduce one new food at a time to allow the baby to adjust. Intolerance to certain foods can be recognised.

▶ First foods include sieved or puréed fruit and vegetables, and soft starchy foods e.g. rice and mashed potatoes.

▶ No sugar or salt should be added to baby food.

▶ As the baby grows more energy and protein foods are required, so bread, minced meat and eggs may be added. The four food groups should be included.

Children

Childhood is a very important time in terms of growth and development. It is at this stage that eating habits are established. The diet of children should be highly nutritious.

> Crunchy foods such as rusks and apples help to soothe teething problems.

▶ Protein is important for growth, so foods such as meat, fish, milk, eggs and cheese should be included in the diet.

▶ Calcium, phosphorus and vitamin D are essential for healthy bones and teeth. A diet including milk, cheese, eggs and green vegetables will ensure adequate intake of these nutrients.

▶ A carbohydrate rich diet (containing some cellulose) is necessary as children are active and require plenty of energy foods.

▶ Vitamin C and iron, which are present in fruit, vegetables, meat and fortified foods, contribute to healthy blood and general health of children.

Mother feeding child

- Portions should be small and attractively served.
- Snacks should be nutritious, keeping sweets and 'junk foods' to a minimum to reduce the risk of obesity.
- Avoid adding sugar or salt to children's food, and discourage 'faddy' eating.
- A healthy breakfast including foods from three of the four food groups is important for children.

Adolescents

Adolescence is a time of continued development and rapid growth so a healthy diet is essential.

- Protein, calcium and vitamin D are very important for growth and the development of healthy bones and teeth.
- A calcium rich diet helps to prevent osteoporosis.
- Iron and vitamin C are particularly important in the diet of teenage girls, because of menstruation, to prevent the development of anaemia.
- The amount of energy foods required is determined by how active the teenager is. Over-consumption can lead to obesity.
- High-fibre energy foods should be chosen instead of highly refined or sugary carbohydrates.
- Keeping fatty foods to a minimum may reduce the severity of acne.

Eating Disorders

Anorexia nervosa
Anorexia nervosa is a psychological disorder marked by a refusal to eat enough food to maintain a healthy weight. Appetite is suppressed and the body becomes starved of essential nutrients. Many anorexics retain an intense interest in food while being obsessed with weight loss and body image. They often exercise excessively and may perceive themselves as fat although they are extremely thin.

Anexoria may be triggered by teenage stress i.e. a fear of growing up, difficulty in coping with physical changes or the need to be accepted by peers. Self starvation is an attempt to control one's life.

Symptoms of anorexia include emaciation (abnormal thiness), hair loss, inability to concentrate and the growth of downy body hair. Menstruation stops or does not begin. Death may result due to starvation. Treatment involves medical and psychological intervention.

Bulimia is a psychological disorder where a person binges on food and then uses laxatives or induces vomiting. People with anorexia nervosa often develop this pattern. Sometimes this disorder is not obvious, as the sufferer may not become emaciated. With bulimia a person turns to food when under stress, then feels guilty and tries to remove the calories from the body. They regularly diet, but the food deprivation leads to further bingeing and purging. Symptoms, which are mainly due to vomiting, include tooth decay, irritation of the throat, inflammation of the oesophagus, swollen salivary glands and dehydration. Medical and psychological treatment is necessary.

Girl suffering from anorexia nervosa

Eating disorders are most common among adolescent girls and young women.

Adults

A varied diet will supply all the nutrients required in adulthood.

▶ Protein is important for repair and normal body functioning.

▶ Carbohydrate foods for energy should be rich in fibre and starch and low in sugar.

▶ Choose unsaturated fats to reduce the risk of developing high cholesterol levels.

▶ Include calcium and Vitamin D to prevent bone disease. (osteoporosis)

▶ Iron and vitamin C are important, especially for women, to ensure healthy blood.

▶ Keep salt intake to a minimum to prevent the onset of high blood pressure.

▶ A plentiful supply of vitamin B ensures the release of energy from food.

Manual workers, e.g. builders require more energy than **sedentary workers** such as computer operators. Those involved in active sport may also consume more kilocalories without gaining weight.

Sedentary workers

Manual workers

Pregnancy / Breast-feeding

A healthy diet is very important before pregnancy to reduce the risk of stillbirth and malformation of the baby.

▶ Folic acid (folate) should be included in the diet prior to and during pregnancy to reduce the possibility of neural tube defects e.g. spina bifida in the newborn. It is recommended that folic acid supplements be taken before conception.

▶ During pregnancy, protein, calcium and vitamin D are essential for the baby's development. If calcium intake is not increased it will be obtained from the mother's bones and teeth which may cause osteoporosis in later life.

▶ An increase in iron and vitamin C intake is necessary to ensure healthy blood for both mother and baby.

▶ Fibre should be included in the diet to prevent constipation, which is a common problem during pregnancy.

Pregnant woman eating healthy salad

▶ Fatty acids contribute to the development of a healthy nervous system especially those found in oily fish, egg yolk and liver.

▶ Extra energy (300 kcal daily) supplied by a slight increase of all nutrients will ensure extra minerals and vitamins. Excessive weight gain should be avoided, no more than 12 kg (2 stone) is recommended.

▶ Salt should be avoided as it may lead to high blood pressure and oedema (water retention).

▶ Reduce the risk of salmonella and listeria food poisoning by avoiding raw eggs (mayonnaise), soft cheese and cook-chill foods.

▶ Extra fluids are required for milk production during breast feeding.

> Alcohol and smoking should be avoided completely during pregnancy.

The Elderly

As people age dietary requirements alter slightly.

▶ Elderly people should continue to eat a varied diet with a reduction in energy intake as basal metabolism and activity levels decrease with age.

▶ Easily digested protein foods are important for cell replacement and repair. Include white fish, chicken, eggs and milk in the diet.

▶ Calcium and vitamin D are important to help prevent osteoporosis. Sunshine is particularly important for the elderly.

▶ Vitamin A is important for healthy eyes and skin.

▶ Vitamin C is important for iron absorption, healing and to prevent bed sores.

▶ Iron is essential to prevent anaemia.

▶ Reduce the intake of saturated fats, salt and sugar.

▶ Fibre and plenty of fluids help prevent constipation, which is common among the elderly because of reduced activity.

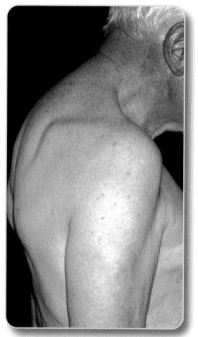
Man suffering from osteoporosis

Dietary problems of the elderly

▶ Loss of appetite and interest in food may result in a poor diet, which could lead to malnutrition.

▶ Reduced income can affect food choices with a possible reduction in protein foods.

▶ Physical disabilities can affect one's ability to shop for, or prepare food. Arthritis and rheumatism are common among the elderly.

▶ Loss of teeth or false teeth can result in difficulty chewing food.

▶ Reduced mental capacity could affect an elderly person's ability to ensure a healthy diet.

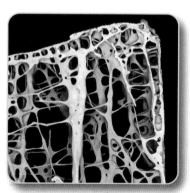
Osteoparotic bone

> **Aids to preventing malnutrition among the elderly**
> • Specialised kitchen gadgets, e.g. tap-turners, electrical can openers.
> (See Page 318)
> • Services such as 'meals on wheels'.
> • Delivery service.
> • Home help.
> • Emergency supplies always in store.

Convalescents

People recovering from illness are referred to as convalescents.

Elderly patient in convalescent home

▶ Follow doctors' instructions.

▶ Energy intake should be reduced during convalescence, as energy expenditure is low.

▶ Plenty of liquids are essential to prevent dehydration especially during a fever.

▶ Foods should be easy to digest and lightly seasoned.

▶ A concentrated supply of protein, minerals and vitamins is necessary to repair damaged tissue, prevent anaemia and for healing.

▶ Fibre is important to prevent constipation, which is more likely because of inactivity.

▶ Hygiene is of particular importance during the preparation of meals for convalescents.

▶ Portions should be small and the foods should be appetising and easy to eat.

Dietary Deficiencies and Excesses

Some dietary deficiency diseases such as scurvy and beri-beri are on the decline. Others such as osteoporosis and anaemia are still prevalent.

Diseases associated with dietary excesses include obesity, cancer, diabetes, cardiovascular disease and bowel disorders. All of these conditions are on the increase, despite the availability of nutritional information. While other factors such as age, weight, gender and lifestyle issues including smoking and high stress levels contribute to the problem, diet plays a very significant role.

Healthy eating guidelines recommend a balanced diet and a reduction in salt, saturated fat and refined carbohydrate. An increase in fibre and foods rich in antioxidants is also advised.

Research has also established inter-relationships between various nutrients that impact on health, e.g. calcium works with phosphorous and vitamin D in bone formation. iron, vit. C

Controlling nutrient intake so that excesses and deficiencies do not occur helps to reduce the risk of diet related disease and to increase the chance of optimum health.

370,000 Irish children are obese
girls overweight   obese   boys over.   obese
11.6%   13%   10.5%   9.2%
1 in 4 nine year olds are overweight/obese

Diet-Related Health Problems
higher % of girls than boys
Obesity

Obesity is a condition in which the body <u>accumulates excess fat</u>. An individual is considered to be obese if <u>his/her weight is 20% or more above the recommended weight</u>. It mainly occurs where more calories are taken in than are 'burned up' by the body over a period of time. <u>The excess energy is stored as fat</u>.

Obesity is one of the most <u>widespread medical problems</u> in the western world, with approximately <u>one-third of adults deemed to be overweight</u>. <u>Obesity among children is also on the increase</u>. Children are consuming increasing amounts of <u>high calorie soft drinks and snack foods</u>. Also, watching TV and playing video games has replaced more physical activities.

It is important to accept that there is <u>no ideal weight</u>. There is however a healthy weight range for height and gender.

Obese teenager

> *22% of 5-12 year olds in Ireland are overweight/obese.*

Causes of obesity

▶ <u>Excessive kilocalorie intake</u>.

▶ <u>Inactive/sedentary lifestyle</u>.

▶ <u>Lack</u> of regular <u>exercise</u>.

▶ <u>Poor food</u> choices – excessive use of processed and fast foods.

▶ <u>Unhealthy eating</u> patterns; the habit of overeating is often established in childhood.

▶ <u>Psychological</u> factors such as <u>depression</u> or <u>boredom</u>.

▶ <u>Hormonal imbalance</u> and some <u>medication</u> may cause weight gain.

Symptoms and health risks of obesity

• <u>Breathing difficulties</u> and excessive tiredness	• <u>Diabetes</u>
• <u>Pain in the back and leg joints</u>	• <u>Gall stones</u>
• <u>High blood pressure</u>	• <u>Strokes</u>
• <u>High cholesterol</u>	• <u>Varicose veins</u>
• <u>Heart disease</u>	• <u>Infertility</u>
• <u>Arthritis</u> – particularly in back and leg joints	• <u>Difficulties in childbirth</u>
• Reduced life expectancy - risk of death from all causes increases as obesity levels rise in men and women of all ages	• Poor self esteem

men   30% healthy   44% overweight   26% obese
women 48% healthy   31% overweight   21% obese

Treatment of obesity

► Obesity is treated by following a balanced, low-calorie diet.

► Increasing exercise also aids weight reduction.

Many overweight people benefit from the support provided by a slimming club.

1 kg per week is the recommended rate of weight loss.

Treatment of childhood obesity may involve:

• Re-educating the family in healthy eating habits.

• Placing more emphasis on physical activity and healthy living in school and at home.

• Regulating television advertisements aimed at children and teens as advertising strongly influences food choices.

• Running national healthy living campaigns.

Dietary guidelines

► Consult a doctor before starting a severe weight reduction programme.

► Establish a regular pattern of balanced meals.

► Eat a wide variety of fresh foods — particularly fruit and vegetables.

► Use low-fat products such as low-fat milk, butter, cheese and yoghurts.

► Choose white fish, poultry and lean meats.

► Grill and steam foods; avoid fried and high calorie snack and fast foods.

► Avoid sugary foods and refined carbohydrates such as biscuits, cakes and pastries. Replace them with high-fibre foods such as wholemeal bread and pasta.

► Replace rich sauces and gravies with low-fat dressings.

► Drink plenty of water and avoid alcohol.

Coronary Heart Disease

The coronary arteries supply oxygenated blood to the heart muscle. Coronary heart disease occurs when fatty substances, including cholesterol, become deposited on the walls of the coronary arteries causing narrowing of the arteries. This gradual blockage or hardening of the arteries is called *atherosclerosis*.

There may be no symptoms of heart disease in the early stages but if the narrowing continues it may have the following effects on the body:

Narrowing of the arteries — atherosclerosis

► *Angina*: If the blood supply is restricted the lack of oxygen causes shortness of breath and severe chest pain. Angina attacks are brought on by exertion and by emotional stress.

► *Heart attack/coronary thrombosis*: A blood clot can develop in a narrowed artery cutting off the oxygen to a part of the heart causing a heart attack.

► *Sudden death* can occur.

Irish men and women have the highest rate of death before the age of 65 from coronary heart disease in the EU. Heart disease is the single largest cause of deaths in Ireland.

Cholesterol

Cholesterol is a soft wax-like substance found in every cell of the body. Most of the cholesterol in the body is synthesised in the liver, the rest is obtained from animal foods. Cholesterol is an essential component in cell membranes, in bile and in some hormones.

There is a direct link between coronary heart disease and the amount of cholesterol in the blood.

Healthy Levels mmo/L*
_____
Total cholesterol - no greater than 5
* millimole per litre

Cholesterol in the blood helps to transport fats around the body. In the blood, cholesterol is bound to certain proteins forming lipoproteins. There are two types of lipoproteins:

- *Low-density lipoproteins* (LDL) found in saturated fats are harmful. They are associated with the build up of cholesterol on the arteries, damaging the blood vessels and causing heart disease.

- *High-density lipoproteins* (HDL) found in unsaturated fats help to remove cholesterol from circulation, thereby reducing the risk of heart disease (See Page 21).

Coronary heart disease	
Risk Factors	
• Males over 45	• Lack of exercise
• Females over 55	• Smoking
• Family history of CHD	• Obesity
• High cholesterol	• Excess alcohol intake
• High blood pressure	• High stress levels
• Diabetes mellitus	• Poor diet

1. There is medical evidence linking salt intake to high blood pressure, heart disease and stroke.
2. According to the Irish Heart Foundation 75-80% of salt consumed comes from processed foods, about 5% occurs naturally in food and 15-20% of salt intake is discretionary.

Lifestyle changes

▶ Follow a low cholesterol, low salt, low sugar diet.

▶ Keep weight within accepted range.

▶ Do not smoke.

▶ Avoid alcohol.

▶ Increase exercise (which lowers LDL's, increases HDL's, and improves circulation).

▶ Try to reduce stress levels.

Dietary guidelines

1. Reduce intake of animal (saturated) fats e.g. butter, cheese, cream or replace with low-fat varieties.
2. Include mono and polyunsaturated oils e.g. corn oil, oily fish and nuts, which help to lower LDL level and counteract hardening of arteries.
3. Increase fibre intake e.g. oats, bran, fruit and vegetables, which also reduces LDL levels.
4. Reduce refined carbohydrate such as cakes and pastry which result in excess production of insulin. (A high level of insulin is thought to contribute to fatty deposits on arteries.)
5. Use fish and chicken as protein sources rather than red meat, which is higher in saturated fat.
6. Reduce salt intake.
7. A range of functional foods which can help lower cholesterol are available (See Page 107).

Osteoporosis

Osteoporosis is a disease which causes the bones to become thin and porous. This loss in bone mass makes the bones fragile and brittle. Osteoporosis is most common in post-menopausal women. (The hormone oestrogen partially protects bone mass in the pre-menopausal years.) Osteoporosis, however, may occur at any age and may affect both sexes.

Osteoporosis is a natural part of ageing, but its effects can be greatly reduced if steps are taken in earlier life. Bone mass peaks between the ages of 25 and 35. If sufficient calcium and vitamin D is included in the diet of teenage girls and young women it reduces the risk of bone disease in later years.

Risk factors

Some individuals are more likely to develop bone disease due to:

1. **Gender:** Females are more likely than males to develop bone disease. Post-menopausal women are most at risk.
2. **Age:** Risk increases as men and women get older.
3. **Heredity:** Family history of osteoporosis increases risk.
4. **Weight:** People who have considerably reduced their weight may also have lost bone mass. Anyone with a current or past eating disorder such as anorexia is at high risk of developing bone disease.
5. **Diet:** Lack of calcium and vitamin D in the diet.
6. **Lack of exercise:** Insufficient weight-bearing exercise.

> ### Signs/Symptoms of Osteoporosis
>
> - Fragile, brittle bones.
> - Bone fractures – particularly in hip, wrist and spine.
> - Curved/humped back and rounded shoulders.
> - Loss in height.
> - Neck and back pain.
> - Medical evidence of loss in bone mass.
> - Osteoporosis is known as the 'Silent disease' as there are usually no signs/symptoms before bones begin to break.

To reduce risk

▶ Increase intake of calcium, phosphorus and vitamins D, and C which aid calcium absorption.

▶ Dairy products such as milk and yoghurt are good sources of calcium. Sometimes calcium supplements are recommended.

▶ Balance protein intake – too much or too little has an impact on bone density.

▶ Fish oils, evening primrose oil and soya foods are thought to help preserve bone mass.

▶ Reduce salt and caffeine intake which are linked to a decrease in bone density.

▶ Do not smoke and avoid alcohol.

▶ Exercise – weight-bearing exercise such as walking is best.

Osteoporosis can cause a humped back

> Osteoporosis affects 1 in 5 men and 1 in 2 women over 50 and can affect teenagers and children.

Bowel Disorders

Bowel disorders such as constipation, haemorrhoids, diverticular disease, cancer and irritable bowel syndrome are becoming increasingly common in western society. This increase has been linked to diets deficient in fibre.

Bowel disease	
Disorder	**Symptoms/effects**
1 Constipation	Infrequent bowel movements. Faeces hard, small and difficult to expel.
2. Haemorrhoids	Painful swollen veins on anus, which may cause itching and blood loss.
3. Diverticular disease	Distended pockets filled with food waste and bacteria form in the bowel wall causing pain and sometimes blood loss. Diverticulitis develops when these areas become inflamed/infected.
4. Irritable bowel syndrome (IBS)	Bowel does not function as it should, resulting in painful cramping and bloating, diarrhoea or constipation. While it is painful it does not damage the bowel.
5. Bowel cancer	Common disorder of the colon and rectum in both males and female. It can lead to anaemia due to blood loss and there is a danger that it could spread to surrounding areas. Very curable if diagnosed at an early stage.

Non-starch polysaccharides/dietary fibre

▶ Non-starch polysaccharides (NSP) are complex carbohydrates such as cellulose, which occur in plant foods.

▶ They are present in the cell walls of plants helping to form the structural framework of plants.

▶ Non-starch polysaccharides are indigestible and so are unchanged when they enter the bowel.

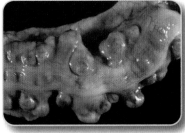

Diverticular disease

▶ They have the ability to absorb water making the waste in the bowel soft and large. This stimulates contractions in the walls of the bowel (peristalsis) helping food to move more quickly through the body. This quicker transit time is thought to play a role in reducing the incidence of bowel disorders. Fibre is therefore an essential component of a healthy diet.

To reduce risk of bowel disorders

1. Follow a high-fibre diet (See Page 17).
2. Exercise – lack of physical activity increases the risk of bowel cancer.
3. Drink more water to assist the passage of fibre through the digestive system.

RDA 25-35 g of fibre every day.

Benefits of a diet rich in fibre

▶ Fibre adds bulk to the diet giving a feeling of fullness without adding calories.

▶ It helps to speed up movement of food through the intestines helping to prevent bowel disorders.

▶ Fibre slows the release of glucose into the bloodstream, which is beneficial to individuals who suffer from diabetes mellitus.

▶ Research has shown that a high-fibre diet helps to lower blood cholesterol, thereby reducing the risk of coronary heart disease.

Diabetes

Diabetes mellitus is a common disorder caused by a deficiency in the production of insulin by the pancreas or by the ineffectiveness of the insulin produced. As a result, the glucose in the blood cannot be taken up by the muscles and other body cells for the production of energy. This results in a high concentration of glucose in the blood, which damages many organs such as the eyes and the kidneys.

Diabetes is a chronic disease which is on the increase worldwide. This increase is due mainly to sedentary lifestyles and unhealthy diets leading to obesity.

Injecting insulin

There are two forms of diabetes:

Type 1: Insulin dependent	Type 2: Non-insulin dependent
• Pancreas fails to produce insulin. • More likely to occur in children and adolescents. • Controlled by diet and insulin injections.	• Body unable to respond properly to insulin produced in pancreas. • More common (90% of all diabetes worldwide) occurs mainly in adults over 40 who are overweight. Incidence is increasing in children due to obesity. • Controlled by diet alone or by diet and tablets, which control blood sugar levels.

Symptoms of diabetes

Symptoms vary in severity from mild to more pronounced. They include:

- ▶ Excessive thirst.
- ▶ Weight loss.
- ▶ Blurred vision.
- ▶ Frequent urination.
- ▶ Tiredness.

Approximately 200,000 Irish people have diabetes.

Symptoms may be completely absent so that the diabetes does not become obvious until complications arise. Possible complications include:

- ▶ Blindness/visual impairment resulting from damage to blood vessels in the retina.

- ▶ Kidney failure due to high level of blood glucose and high blood pressure.

- ▶ Heart disease and strokes – risk is increased by smoking, high blood pressure, high blood cholesterol and obesity.

Treatment of diabetes

Treatment aims are to eliminate symptoms and prevent long-term complications. Diabetics are advised to follow a healthy eating plan and an exercise routine, so that weight is kept within acceptable limits. Some diabetics need oral medication or insulin injections.

Dietary guidelines

1. Eat regular balanced meals helping to avoid hypoglycaemia (low blood sugar) which could result in coma. Hyperglycaemia (raised blood sugar) is also dangerous and can lead to coma.

2. It is recommended that diabetics follow a low glycaemic index (GI) diet.

3. Try to eat a similar amount of starchy foods e.g. bread or rice each day.

4. Increase the intake of high-fibre foods such as wholegrain cereals, vegetables and fruits.

5. Avoid using too much salt, which increases blood pressure.

6. Reduce sugar intake – use low-sugar foods, artificial sweeteners and diabetic food and drinks.

7. Reduce fried and fatty foods to reduce the risk of heart disease and stoke.

Diabetic foods

The **glycaemic index** rates carbohydrates according to their effect on blood glucose levels. High GI foods release glucose quickly causing a rapid rise in blood glucose levels, to which the body needs to react with insulin. Low GI foods are more beneficial because they release glucose slowly over several hours so less insulin is required.

Dental Disease

Two of the most common forms of dental disease are:

▶ Dental caries/tooth decay.

▶ Periodontal disease which affects the gums and tissues surrounding the teeth.

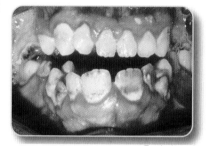
Tooth decay

Both of these conditions are caused by plaque. Plaque consists of a mixture of saliva, food particles and streptococcal bacteria, which forms a coating on the teeth. If it is allowed to remain on the teeth, the bacteria react with the food particles producing acid. The acid attacks the tooth enamel weakening it and eventually causing cavities. Bacteria may then enter the dentine and pulp cavity causing intense pain and abscesses may develop.

Research has identified sugar as the main cause of tooth decay since it produces the most acid in the mouth. The more often sugar is eaten, the more acid attacks the teeth must endure, increasing the risk of decay.

Every litre of fizzy drink contains 100 g of sugar and 476 million litres are consumed in Ireland each year.

If plaque is allowed to accumulate at the gum-line and between the teeth it can calcify (harden) and may not be removed by normal brushing. This build-up (tartar) may cause inflammation of the gums leading to periodontal disease.

To reduce intake of sugary foods:
• Replace sugar-rich snack foods with fruit, vegetables and nuts.
• Artificial sweeteners may be used instead of sugar.
• Be aware of other terms used on food labels which indicate sugar content e.g. sucrose, glucose, maltose.
• Drink water in preference to fizzy drinks and be aware of the sugar content of fruit juices.
• Choose wholegrain, less refined breakfast cereals instead of more processed varieties which have sugar added.

Fluoridation

*ppm = parts per million

Fluoridation is the practice of adding fluorine to drinking water. Fluorine is a mineral which helps to prevent tooth decay. It hardens tooth enamel by combining with the calcium phosphate in the teeth. It is added in strictly monitored amounts (1 ppm)* to water supplies in Ireland. (Over 1.5 ppm may cause teeth to become discoloured.) Fluoridation is currently under investigation. Some research has linked it to an increased incidence of conditions such as cancer and osteoporosis, making it a possible health risk.

To prevent dental disease:
1. Avoid sugar.
2. Brush teeth at least twice a day – if possible after each meal.
3. Floss daily to help prevent gum disease.
4. Use and drink fluorinated tap water and use a fluoride toothpaste.
5. Have regular dental check-ups.
6. Sealant may be applied to the biting surface (fissures) of molars helping to prevent the onset of dental caries particularly in children's teeth.

Teeth covered in tartar

Coeliac Disease/Condition

It is estimated that one in 300 Irish people have Coeliac disease.

Coeliac disease is a chronic disease caused by an intolerance to gluten. Gluten is a protein found in wheat, rye and barley. Some coeliacs may also be sensitive to oats. If gluten is eaten it damages the gut causing flattening of the villi (finger-like projections which line the gut wall). This results in a decreased surface area for the absorption of nutrients in particular lipids, vitamins and minerals. People with undiagnosed coeliac disease can suffer from a wide range of symptoms and can experience nutritional deficiencies.

Symptoms of coeliac disease

- Weight loss.
- Fatigue and lethargy.
- Bloating and abdominal pain.
- Retarded growth in children.
- Nausea, vomiting, diarrhoea.
- Vitamin and mineral deficiency diseases e.g. anaemia.

Gluten-free products for coeliacs

Treatment and dietary guidelines for coeliac disease
A strict, life-long, gluten-free diet must be followed.
1. Exclude all foods which contain gluten.
2. Corn and rice or any products made from these cereals may be included in the diet.
3. A range of gluten-free products are available e.g. gluten-free bread, flour and biscuits.
4. Base diet on foods which are naturally gluten free i.e. fresh meat, fish, cheese, eggs, vegetables and fruit.
5. Look for the gluten-free symbol when food shopping.

Sources of gluten
- Bread, pasta cakes, biscuits, crackers, pastry, pizza bases.

  Also, convenience foods such as:
- Sauces, soups
- Sausages, hamburgers and foods covered in batter/breadcrumbs
- Foods containing bread stuffing

Vegetarian Diets

Vegetarian diets consist wholly or mainly of foods from plant sources. Vegetables, fruit, cereals, legumes, nuts and seeds are the staple foods in the diet. Vegetarian diets may be classified as follows:

> ▶ *Vegan/strict vegetarian diet:* Excludes all foods of animal origin such as meat, poultry, fish, eggs and all dairy products.

> ▶ *Lacto-vegetarian diet:* Excludes meat, fish and poultry but includes dairy products.

> Lacto-ova-vegetarian: excludes meat, poultry and fish but includes eggs and dairy products.

> Pesco-vegetarians eat fish but not meat.

> Pollo-vegetarians do not eat meat or fish but eat chicken.

Reasons for choosing vegetarianism

People may choose to follow a vegetarian diet for a number of reasons.

> ▶ *Cultural:* Vegetarianism may be the traditional diet of a particular area or country.

> ▶ *Religious:* Some religious communities, such as Hindus, Muslims and Jews, place restrictions on consumption of meat and animal products, e.g. Jews are not allowed to eat pork.

> ▶ *Health:* Vegan and vegetarian diets are becoming an increasingly popular option for the health conscious, i.e. high in fibre, low in cholesterol.

> ▶ *Moral:* People may dislike the thought of killing animals for food, or may disapprove of some of the practices involved in rearing animals for food.

> ▶ *Financial:* Vegetarian dishes are cheaper to produce, ingredients tend to be less expensive and cooking time is usually short.

> ▶ *Tradition:* Vegetarianism may be the traditional diet of a family, setting eating patterns for later life.

Benefits of vegetarian diets

1. Vegan diets lack saturated fat, thereby reducing the risk of cholesterol-related problems such as coronary heart disease.
2. Reduced incidences of intestinal disorders such as gall stones and bowel disease.
3. Obesity is less likely to occur.
4. Lower incidence of diabetes.
5. Vegans consume less sodium in food and therefore tend to have lower blood pressure.

> Note: It is difficult to identify the benefits of diet alone. Many vegans tend to be health conscious, avoiding smoking, excessive alcohol or over-eating i.e. their healthy lifestyle has an impact on their general wellbeing.

Planning vegetarian diets

1. Plan diet carefully to meet nutritional needs, particularly of children and teenagers.
2. Use a wide variety of plant foods in order to supply all essential nutrients.
3. Diet should not be too bulky so that children in particular consume enough calories needed for energy and growth.
4. Vegetable protein foods such as TVP, quorn, nuts, beans and peas are good alternatives to animal protein foods.
5. Mix cereals and legumes, e.g. beans on toast, to improve the quality of protein in the diet.
6. Soya milk, soya yoghurt and tofu may be used instead of dairy products.

Vegetarian dish

Nutrients for a healthy diet

There is a danger, particularly in strict vegan and vegetarian diets, of deficiencies in the following nutrients. Careful planning can reduce the risk.

Nutrients for a healthy vegetarian diet		
Nutrient	**Problem**	**To overcome**
Protein	Plant proteins are of low biological value except soya beans. **(Complementary/Supplementary Value of Proteins** See Page **12).**	Diet should contain a combination of whole grains, soy protein, legumes, quorn, seeds and nuts eaten over the course of the day.
Calcium	Lacto-vegetarians obtain sufficient calcium from dairy products. It is more difficult in a vegan diet to supply enough calcium particularly for growing children and teenagers.	• Use fortified products such as breakfast cereals, white flour, soya milk. • Good plant sources include sesame seeds, broccoli, cabbage, spinach, beans and almonds.
Iron	Iron in meat is more easily absorbed than iron from plant sources.	• Good plant sources of iron include beans, chickpeas, avocado, dark green vegetables, dried fruit and cereals, e.g. oats. • Foods rich in vitamin C aid iron absorption.
Zinc	Dairy products and eggs are good sources of zinc for lacto-vegetarians. Vegans must obtain zinc from plant sources.	• Good plant sources of zinc include wheatgerm, whole grains, nuts, seeds and beans
Vitamin D	Best sources of vitamin D are animal foods, many of which are excluded from vegan and vegetarian diets.	• Margarine and some breakfast cereals may be fortified with vitamin D. • Vitamin D supplement may be necessary in vegan diets. • Sunshine is also a source.
＊Vitamin B_{12}	There is sufficient B_{12} in eggs and dairy products for lacto-vegetarians. Vitamin B_{12} is not present in plant foods.	• Use fortified products such as breakfast cereals, soya milk and TVP. • Supplements may be advisable in some cases.

key for vegans

CONTENTS INCLUDE:

- ▶ Meat
- ▶ Fish
- ▶ Eggs
- ▶ Cereals
- ▶ Milk and milk products
- ▶ Cheese
- ▶ Alternative protein foods
- ▶ Vegetables
- ▶ Nuts
- ▶ Fruit
- ▶ Fats and oils

Meat

Meat is the flesh or muscular tissue of animals and birds. It varies in flavour, texture and composition according to species, breed, feeding and rearing methods. Ireland produces high quality meat – in particular beef, lamb, pork, bacon and poultry for the home and export market.

Classification of meat

Carcass meat	Poultry	Game (wild animals and birds)	Offal (edible internal organs)
Beef, veal (cattle) Pork, bacon, ham (pig) Lamb, mutton (sheep)	Chicken Turkey Duck Goose	Pheasant Snipe Deer (venison) Rabbit Hare	Heart Liver Kidney Tongue

Average composition of carcass meat

Protein	Fat	Carbohydrate	Vitamins	Minerals	Water
20–30%	10–30%	0%	1.5% Niacin, B_1, B_2, B_6, B_{12}	Iron Zinc Potassium Phosphorous Sulphur	50–60%

Nutritive Value of Meat

Protein: Meat is a good source of high biological value protein. Myosin, actin and globulin are present in the meat fibres. The connective tissue contains collagen and elastin.

Fat: Fat content varies depending on the type of meat, the cut of meat and the method of cooking used. For example, skinless chicken fillets are low in fat. Pork and lamb have a much higher fat content. Any fat present is saturated fat.

Carbohydrate: There is no carbohydrate present in carcass meat. Liver may contain traces of glycogen.

Vitamins: Meat is a good source of the B group vitamins, niacin, thiamine (B_1), riboflavin (B_2), pyridoxine (B_6) and cobalamin (B_{12}). Small amounts of vitamins A and D are present in liver.

Minerals: Red meat and offal are very good sources of iron. The iron present is easily absorbed by the body (haem-iron). Small amounts of potassium, zinc, phosphorous and sulphur are also present in meat.

Water: Meat contains a high proportion of water. Water content varies, meat with a high fat content has less water than leaner cuts.

Dietetic Value of Meat

► Meat is an excellent source of high biological value protein essential for growth. It is therefore valuable in the diets of pregnant women, children and teenagers.

► Meat supplies the mineral iron in a form which can be easily absorbed in the body, helping to prevent anaemia.

► Because the fat in meat is saturated, people with high cholesterol or heart conditions should reduce their intake of red meat.

► Meat lacks carbohydrate, calcium and vitamin C and therefore should be combined with foods rich in these nutrients in order to balance the diet.

► Meat is readily available and may be prepared and cooked in a wide variety of ways adding interest to the diet.

► Some meat is relatively cheap, e.g. offal or minced meat, yet is very nutritious.

Structure of Meat

Lean meat consists of bundles of tiny fibres. The fibres contain water, proteins (such as actin and myosin) minerals and extractives. The walls of the muscle fibres are made of a connective tissue called elastin. Bundles of fibres are held together by collagen, another type of connective tissue. 'Invisible' fat is present in varying amounts i.e. fat cells are distributed between the fibres (marbling). 'Visible' fat may be seen under the animal's skin as a layer of adipose tissue or surrounding internal organs such as the kidneys.

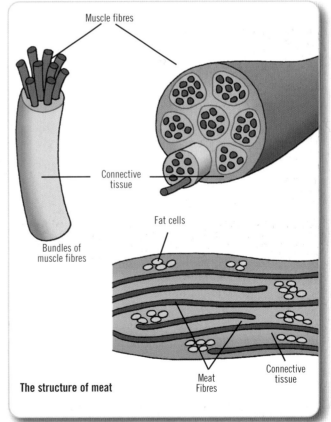

The structure of meat

Extractives

Extractives are substances, e.g. lactic acid, which are dissolved in the water in meat fibres. They give meat its distinct flavour. They stimulate the secretion of saliva and gastric juice thereby aiding digestion.

Causes of toughness in meat

▶ **Age**: Meat from older animals has longer, coarser, muscle fibres and more connective tissue present. It therefore tends to be tougher meat.

▶ **Activity**: Meat from the more active parts of the animal, such as the neck or leg, tends to be tougher also due to the development of longer, thicker fibres and more connective tissue.

▶ **Treatment before and after slaughter**: Prior to slaughter animals are rested to allow glycogen to build up in the animal muscle. After death the glycogen gradually breaks down to lactic acid, which has a tenderising effect on meat protein. Animal carcasses should be hung for a specific period of time to allow this tenderising to take place. Failure to hang carcasses in carefully monitored conditions for the correct length of time results in tougher meat.

▶ **Incorrect method of cooking**: Tough cuts of meat which are cooked by an unsuitable method such as grilling or frying will undergo further toughening.

> Traditional butchers allow beef carcasses to hang for 14–21 days; lamb carcasses require seven days.

Tenderising meat

Meat can be tenderised in a number of ways:

1. **Meat tenderisers**, e.g. papain which contain proteolytic enzymes, may be sprinkled on meat before cooking. These enzymes help to break down meat fibres making them more digestible.
2. **Mechanical breakdown** – pounding meat such as steak with a meat hammer or piercing with knives helps to tenderise it.
3. **Mincing** also helps to break up the fibres of tougher cuts of meat.
4. **Marinating** meat in a mixture of oil, wine, lemon juice/vinegar and flavourings prior to cooking has a tenderising effect on meat.
5. **Slow moist methods of cooking** such as stewing may be used to tenderise meat.

Meat hammer

Buying Meat

1. Buy meat from reliable premises, which sell good quality meat and where a strict code of hygiene is observed.
2. Meat should be moist looking with a fresh smell. It should have a good colour characteristic of the type of meat (e.g. beef is dark red with creamy yellow fat) with no excess juices running from the meat.

> Bord Bía provides Quality Assurance Schemes for beef, lamb, pig meat and poultry. The scheme aims to maintain high standards of food safety and hygiene in meat production and processing. This logo serves to reassure consumers regarding the quality of meat on sale.
>
> QUALITY
> ASSURANCE SCHEME
> BORD BIA
> ORIGIN-IRELAND

3. Avoid uneconomical cuts with large amounts of bone, gristle or visible fat.
4. Choose a cut which suits the chosen method of cooking.
5. Remember that cheaper cuts of meat and offal can be as nutritious as more expensive cuts.

Storing meat

1. Remove wrapping, place in a bowl or on a plate, cover loosely with grease-proof paper/foil to allow air circulation.
2. Refrigerate raw meat as soon as possible after purchase.
3. Place in a refrigerator on a shelf below any cooked foods to avoid cross-contamination.
4. Use within 2–3 days (use offal and minced meat on day of purchase).
5. Store pre-packed/vacuum-packed meats in original wrapping, and observe any instructions on the label.

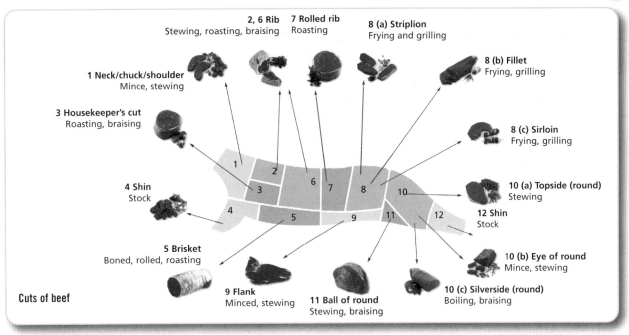

2, 6 Rib
Stewing, roasting, braising

7 Rolled rib
Roasting

8 (a) Striplion
Frying and grilling

8 (b) Fillet
Frying, grilling

1 Neck/chuck/shoulder
Mince, stewing

3 Housekeeper's cut
Roasting, braising

8 (c) Sirloin
Frying, grilling

4 Shin
Stock

10 (a) Topside (round)
Stewing

12 Shin
Stock

5 Brisket
Boned, rolled, roasting

10 (b) Eye of round
Mince, stewing

Cuts of beef

9 Flank
Minced, stewing

11 Ball of round
Stewing, braising

10 (c) Silverside (round)
Boiling, braising

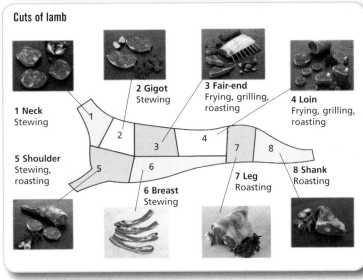

Cuts of lamb

1 Neck
Stewing

2 Gigot
Stewing

3 Fair-end
Frying, grilling,
roasting

4 Loin
Frying, grilling,
roasting

5 Shoulder
Stewing,
roasting

6 Breast
Stewing

7 Leg
Roasting

8 Shank
Roasting

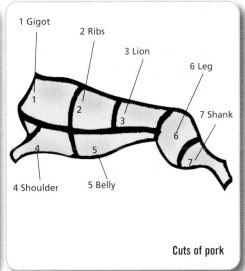

1 Gigot

2 Ribs

3 Lion

6 Leg

7 Shank

4 Shoulder

5 Belly

6

7

Cuts of pork

Effects of Cooking on Meat

The way in which the colour, flavour, texture and nutritive value of meat are affected by cooking depends on:

- ▶ Method of cooking (dry/moist).
- ▶ Cooking time and temperature.
- ▶ Quality of meat being cooked.

Effects include:

1. Meat protein coagulates causing the fibres to shrink. The meat decreases in size and some juices are lost.
2. Collagen is converted to gelatine in moist heat, this causes the fibres to loosen and fall apart, making the meat more digestible.
3. The fat melts, moistening the leaner meat and adding flavour.
4. Colour changes from red to brown due to denaturation of myoglobin.
5. Flavour develops due to presence of extractives which are squeezed out of the fibres.
6. B group vitamins and some minerals may be destroyed or lost into the cooking liquid.
7. Bacteria are destroyed.
8. Over-cooking causes the meat to become tough and indigestible and causes further shrinkage.

Meat Processing

Method/Processing	Effects	Examples
1. **Freezing** • Meat is prepared (i.e. bone removed, fat trimmed) then frozen and stored at -18°C. • May be done in the home or commercially.	• Quick freezing ensures minimum nutrient loss and has little effect on the quality of the meat. • Some extractives and B vitamins are lost through drip loss when thawed. • Fats may go rancid and freezer burn may occur if meat is badly wrapped. (See Page 177).	Cuts/joints of beef, pork, lamb
2. **Vacuum packing** • Meat is boned and sealed into polythene bags. • Once opened, meat must be treated as fresh. • Note modified atmosphere packaging may be used to prolong shelf life (See Page 154).	• Nutritive value texture and flavour unaffected.	Bacon, rashers
3. **Curing and Salting** • The meat is injected with a solution of preserving salts, e.g. sodium chloride and potassium nitrate (saltpetre). • The meat is then soaked in brine for 3-4 days to develop colour. • The meat is stored for 5-6 days to develop flavour. • May be smoked or left unsmoked.	• Little effect on the nutritive value other than an increase in sodium. • Change in colour and flavour. • Smoking produces a characteristic colour and flavour.	Bacon, ham
4. **Canning** • Meat is heated to a high temperature, cooled quickly and sealed in sterile cans.	• Some loss of vitamin B due to high temperatures used. • Long shelf-life but once opened must be treated as fresh.	Corned beef, ham, meat stews and pies
5. **Dehydration** • Small pieces of meat are freeze dried (See Page 184) and used in packet soups and dehydrated ready meals.	• Loss of B vitamins • Long shelf-life, but once rehydrated treat as fresh.	Packet soups, ready meals

Meat Products

1. *Fresh sausages*
   Raw meat (usually pork), filler (rusk), fat, water and flavourings are filled into a casing (synthetic collagen).

2. *Cooked sausages,* e.g. frankfurters, black and white pudding
   Similar ingredients to above but fillers may differ (e.g. oatmeal is used in black pudding). Other ingredients are used to impart a distinct flavour, e.g. pigs' blood is used in black pudding.

3. *Dried sausages,* e.g. salami, pepperoni
   Meat is cured, minced and mixed with other ingredients, e.g. garlic, and then dried.

Meat and meat products

4. **Beef burgers**
   Minced beef, fat, onions, breadcrumbs/rusks and seasonings are mixed and moulded into shape.

5. **Cold cooked meats,** e.g. corned beef, luncheon meat. Made from a mixture of meat, fillers and flavourings used mainly for packed lunches and salads.

6. **Pâté**
   A mixture of chopped meat and liver, fat and flavouring is puréed together to form a smooth paste.

7. **Meat extractives,** e.g. stock cubes, gravy mixes
   Made from meat juices which are dried and mixed with ingredients such as cornflour, salt, yeast extract and flavour enhancers are used to add flavour to soups, stews and gravies.

8. **Gelatine**
   Gelatine is used to set dishes such as soufflés, cheesecakes and mousses. It is extracted from the bones and hooves of animals which have been purified and dried. Gelatine is colourless, odourless and tasteless. It can absorb large quantities of hot water to form a solution. When the solution cools it sets as a gel (gelation).

Stock cubes and gravies

Pâté

Using gelatine
- Use 15 g gelatine to 500 ml liquid.
- Add to cold/warm (not boiling) water.
- Dissolve by stirring in a bowl over gently simmering water.
- Use when solution is clear.

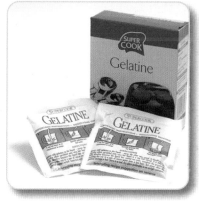
Gelatine

Offal

Offal is the term used to describe the edible internal organs of animals. Examples includes liver, kidney, heart, tongue and oxtail. Offal should be used while it is very fresh and firm with no unpleasant smell. It is a good source of protein, iron and vitamin B complex. Liver is also a source of vitamins A and D. Offal may be fried or grilled (e.g. liver, kidney) or used as an ingredient in a dish, e.g. steak and kidney pie, or oxtail soup.

Poultry

The term poultry refers to domesticated fowl such as chicken, duck, turkey and goose.

Nutritive Value of Poultry

Protein	Fat	Carbohydrate	Vitamins	Minerals	Water
Poultry are an excellent source of high biological value protein.	Fat content varies. White chicken and turkey meat are low in fat. The dark meat and the skin contain more fat. Duck and goose have a much higher fat content.	None present.	Some B group vitamins present.	Less iron than red meat, small amounts of calcium phosphorous and zinc present.	Varies depending on fat content.

Dietetic Value of Poultry

► The protein present in poultry is easy to digest because there is less connective tissue than in red meat, so it is useful in the diets of children, the elderly and convalescents.

► The low-fat content of skinless chicken breasts makes poultry suitable for low calorie and low cholesterol diets.

► Poultry combines well with a variety of ingredients to produce a wide range of dishes but the recipe or method of cooking chosen may significantly increase the fat content.

► Poultry should be combined with carbohydrate and foods rich in vitamins and minerals to produce a balanced meal.

► Poultry is a relatively inexpensive tasty meat.

Buying Poultry

► Buy from a reliable source.

► Check the expiry date on the packaging.

► Bird should be fresh, i.e. no unpleasant smell; moist, with no discolouration.

► Breast should be firm and plump.

► Frozen poultry should be frozen solid.

Storing poultry

Store fresh poultry as for meat (See Page 64). Frozen poultry should be placed in a freezer as soon as possible after purchase.

Cooking Poultry

Poultry can be a source of salmonella bacteria, therefore it must be carefully prepared and cooked to avoid danger of food poisoning.

1. Thaw frozen poultry completely before cooking.
2. Remove giblets.
3. Carefully wash hands and any equipment used in the preparation to avoid cross-contamination of bacteria.
4. Cook poultry thoroughly and do not cook stuffing in the cavity.
5. Cool any leftovers quickly. Cover and store in fridge and use up within two days.

Effects of cooking on poultry (Meat See Page 65)

Processing of Poultry

▶ Poultry is available whole (fresh/frozen), boned and rolled, jointed and in fillets.

▶ Processed poultry products include chicken nuggets, burgers and chicken kiev or ready meals such as chicken curry and sweet and sour chicken.

Poultry products

Fish

The consumption of seafood in Ireland is low when compared with other European countries. In recent years the greater availability of fresh fish, the wide range of consumer ready products and a greater knowledge of the health attributes of fish oils have all contributed to a steady increase in fish as part of the Irish diet.

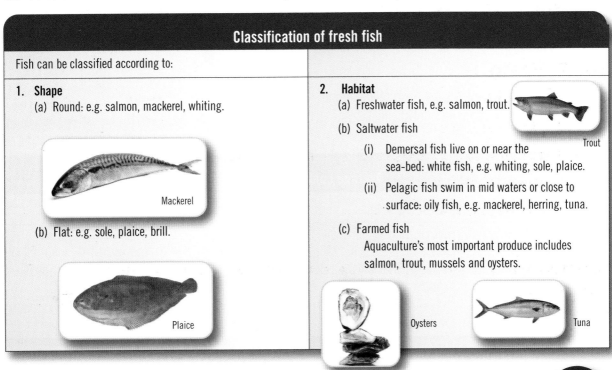

Classification of fresh fish

Fish can be classified according to:

1. **Shape**
   (a) Round: e.g. salmon, mackerel, whiting.

   Mackerel

   (b) Flat: e.g. sole, plaice, brill.

   Plaice

2. **Habitat**
   (a) Freshwater fish, e.g. salmon, trout.

   Trout

   (b) Saltwater fish
      (i) Demersal fish live on or near the sea-bed: white fish, e.g. whiting, sole, plaice.
      (ii) Pelagic fish swim in mid waters or close to surface: oily fish, e.g. mackerel, herring, tuna.

   (c) Farmed fish
      Aquaculture's most important produce includes salmon, trout, mussels and oysters.

   Oysters

   Tuna

Nutritive Value

This is the most commonly used method of classification when studying food science.

(a) White fish – round and flat

e.g. cod, haddock, whiting, coley (smoked pollack), monkfish, hoki, plaice, sole (lemon/black), turbot, halibut.

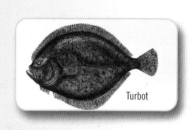

Turbot

(b) Oily fish – round

e.g. mackerel, herring, salmon, tuna, trout, swordfish.

Mackerel

(c) Shellfish

(i) Molluscs – hard outer shell and no legs, e.g. mussels, oysters, scallops, clams, cockles, periwinkles.

(ii) Crustaceans – segmented shells with legs and claws, e.g. prawns, shrimps, crabs, lobsters, crawfish.

Lobster

Structure of Fish

Fish flesh is composed of bundles of short fibres called myomeres held together by thin layers of connective tissue (collagen). The fibres are arranged in broad vertical bands. The fibres of fish are shorter than those of meat. There is less connective tissue and no elastin present, therefore fish is more tender and easier to digest than meat and cooks more quickly.

The fibres of shellfish are a little more coarse than those of white and oily fish causing shellfish to be more difficult to digest.

A waterproof scaly skin covers the flesh of white and oily fish, a shell encloses the flesh of shellfish.

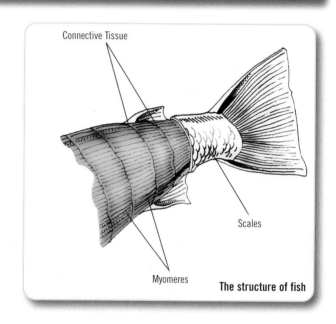

Connective Tissue

Scales

Myomeres

The structure of fish

Average composition of fish			
White	**Oily**	**Shellfish**	**Breaded fish (plaice)**
Protein: 17%	Protein: 18%	Protein: 16%	Protein: 13%
Fat: 0.5%	Fat: 15%	Fat: 3%	Fat: 9%
Carbohydrate: 0%	Carbohydrate: 0%	Carbohydrate: 0%	Carbohydrate: 16%
Minerals: 1%	Minerals: 2%	Minerals: 2%	Minerals: 1%
Vitamin B Group: 1%	Vitamins A, D, B: 2%	Vitamin B Group: 1%	Vitamins B Group:1%
Water: 80.5%	Water: 63%	Water: 78%	Water: 60%

Nutritive Value of Fish

Omega-3 fatty acids present in oily fish
EPA – eicosapentaenoic
DHA – docosahexaenoic

Protein: Fish is an important source of high biological value protein, containing almost as much as meat. Collagen, actin and myosin are proteins present in fish.

Fat: The fat of white fish is stored in the liver. As the liver is removed in fish preparation white fish does not contribute to fat in the diet. The fat in oily fish is unsaturated and present in the flesh. Consumption of oily fish is important to ensure adequate intake of polyunsaturated fatty acids especially omega-3 fatty acids (See Page 23). Shellfish contains a small amount of cholesterol and may contribute to cholesterol build up.

Carbohydrate: As fish does not contain carbohydrate it is usually served with a carbohydrate food such as potatoes, pasta or rice.

Vitamins: Fish contains useful amounts of the B group vitamins necessary for release of energy from food and a healthy nervous system. Vitamins A and D are found in oily fish. Molluscs supply vitamin A. Oysters contain vitamin C. Fish liver oils, e.g. cod and halibut liver oils are rich in vitamins A and D.

Minerals: Fish is a good source of iodine, phosphorus, flourine and zinc. Canned fish, because the bones are eaten, e.g. sardines, are an excellent source of calcium. Shellfish and sardines are particularly high in iron.

Water: White fish contains a high proportion of water and is therefore low in kilocalories. Oily fish, because of the fat content, has less water.

Dietetic Value of Fish

► Fish is an important source of high biological value protein, vitamin B and iodine.

► White fish contains practically no fat making it ideal for slimmers and is an easy to digest protein food.

► The fat in oily fish is unsaturated and contains omega-3 fatty acids which help to reduce the risk of heart disease and cancer.

► Fish is very easy to digest and is therefore suitable for children, the elderly and convalescents.

► There is a wide variety of fish available and many different cooking methods may be used.

► Some fish is inexpensive yet nutritious e.g mackerel and herring.

► Fish is available processed, e.g. canned and frozen when not in season.

► Because fish is tender it cooks quickly saving time and fuel.

Spoilage of Fish

Fish is an extremely perishable food. It must be kept 'on ice' and used or processed as quickly as possible after being caught. Spoilage occurs due to:

1. **Oxidative rancidity:** Oily fish have a shorter shelf-life because the oils in the fish react with oxygen in the atmosphere causing the fish to become rancid.

2. **Enzymes:** Naturally present enzymes cause deterioration of fish flesh, even at low temperatures.

3. **Bacteria:** While fish are being caught they struggle. This struggling uses up the stored glycogen in the muscle. The result is that little or no lactic acid is produced to preserve the fish. Bacteria therefore cause rapid deterioration of fish flesh. A strong smelling nitrogen compound called trimethylamine is produced.

Buying Fresh Fish

▶ Fish must be absolutely fresh (see below).

▶ Buy from a clean, reliable source:
  - the fish is stored on ice in a chilled display unit
  - there is a quick turnover, good value, and knowledgeable and helpful staff.

▶ Buy fish in season when they are cheapest, taste better and are at their nutritional best.

▶ Choose medium sized fish for best flavour.

▶ Fresh fish can be bought whole, in fillets, in cutlets, in steaks, or as tailpieces.

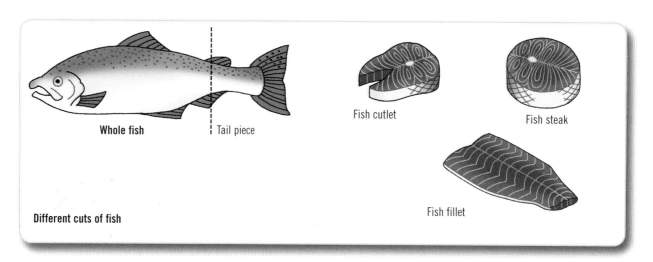

Whole fish   Tail piece   Fish cutlet   Fish steak   Fish fillet

Different cuts of fish

Fresh fish		
Whole fish	**Shellfish**	**Cuts of fish**
• Bright bulging eyes. • Glossy bright red or pink gills. • Shiny moist skin with scales tightly adhered. • Firm elastic flesh. • Inoffensive, slight sea smell.	• Heavy for their size. • Molluscs – shells should be closed or close when handled. • Crustaceans – should be alive.	• Firm, elastic moist flesh. • Flesh – transparent or translucent appearance. • No discolouration. • Inoffensive, slight sea smell.

Processed fish		
Frozen Fish	**Canned fish**	**Smoked fish**
• Frozen solid. • Packaging intact. • Use within expiry date.	• No bulges or dents in cans. • No leaks. • Use within expiry date.	• Glossy firm flesh. • Not sticky. • Fresh smoky odour. • If vacuum packed – stored below 2°C. Packaging not damaged or blown. • Use within expiry date.

Storing fish			
Fresh fish	**Frozen fish**	**Smoked fish**	**Shellfish**
• Remove wrapping, rinse and cover loosely with foil. • Refrigerate as soon as possible after purchase. • Store on a bed of ice. • Store as close to ice box as possible. • Replace ice as it melts. • Use within 1–2 days of purchase.	• Carry from shop in a cooler bag. • Place in freezer immediately. • Use within recommended time. • If beginning to thaw do not refreeze. Use immediately.	• Do not ice smoked fish. • Store hot smoked and cold smoked fish separately. • Store in a refrigerator. • Use within expiry date.	• Mussels, oysters etc. should be washed and placed in the bottom part of the fridge. • Cover with clean damp tea towel. • Do not place in water.

Preserving/Processing Fish

Fish can be preserved by freezing, canning or smoking.

Freezing

Freezing is a very effective method of preserving fish. The cold temperature inactivates micro-organisms thereby preventing microbial spoilage.

Fresh fish is commercially 'blast frozen' at −30°C (See Page 182) retaining the colour, flavour, texture and nutritive value of the fish.

Because oxidative rancidity may occur and enzyme activity continues while frozen, use oily fish within three months of freezing. White fish should be used within six months.

Processed fish

Fish can be frozen whole, in fillets, in cutlets or steaks. It may be coated in breadcrumbs or batter, or may be in a sauce.

Canning

Salmon, sardines, tuna, mackerel and crab are examples of canned fish. Fish may be canned in oil, brine or sauce. The extreme heat involved in the canning process kills the micro-organisms and the sealing of the can prevents re-entry preserving the fish.

Although there is some loss of thiamine during canning, vitamins A and D are provided by fish canned in oil, and all canned fish provides calcium as the softened bones are consumed.

Smoking

Salmon, trout, kippers (herring), coley (pollack), cod and mackerel are examples of fish that are preserved by smoking. The chemicals creosote and formaldehyde in the smoke, prevent the growth of micro-organisms on the fish flesh thus preserving the fish.

The fish is first salted using either dry salt or brine. It is then smoked using a cold smoking or hot smoking technique. Both techniques involve exposing the fish to smoke rising from smouldering wood chips. In cold smoking, the temperature of the fish does not exceed 27°C, so the fish requires further cooking. Haddock and herrings are often cold smoked.

When fish is hot smoked the temperature is gradually increased to 80°C. Hot smoked eel, mackerel and salmon can be eaten without further cooking.

Smoking not only preserves the fish but gives it its distinctive flavour, colour and sheen, and increases its sodium content.

Effects of Cooking on Fish

1. Micro-organisms and parasites are destroyed.
2. The protein coagulates and some shrinkage occurs.
3. Collagen changes to gelatine and the fish flakes easily.
4. Flesh changes from translucent to opaque.
5. There is some loss of B group vitamins.
6. Minerals, vitamins and extractives dissolve into cooking liquid.
7. Overcooking results in the flesh becoming dry and rubbery.

Preparation of Fresh Fish for Cooking

Remove scales

Cut off head, tail and fins

Slit underside and remove insides

Wash fish

Preparing fish for cooking

Filleting fish	
Fish can be filleted before it is cooked. This means removing the bones from the fish.	
Round fish	**Skinning fish fillets**
1. Cut down the back of the fish from head to tail, keeping the knife on the backbone. 2. With the knife against the bone cut downwards along the ribs, gradually paring away fish. 3. Repeat with the second fillet (two fillets in all).	1. Place fillet, skin side down, on a work surface. 2. Grasp the fillet firmly at the tail end and, holding the knife blade flat, work the knife in between the flesh and the skin. 3. Carefully slide it down the length of the fillet to remove the skin in one piece.

Cooking Fish

► Cook fish when absolutely fresh.

► Wash and dry fish before cooking.

► Fish cooks very quickly – overcooking causes it to break apart.

► When fish is cooked its transparent colour becomes opaque and breaks apart easily.

Salmon steaks grilled on a barbecue

Suitable methods for cooking fish

► *Frying:* Shallow or deep. Fish is usually coated (see below).

► *Grilling:* Suitable for fish fillets, steaks, cutlets or small whole fish.

► *Poaching:* Simmer fish gently in liquid (water, milk, wine, stock). Do not boil.

► *Steaming:* Steam fish in a steamer.

► *Baking:* Whole fish fillets, steaks or cutlets, often stuffed.

► *Stewing:* Cook fish in a sauce, e.g. curry sauce.

► *Reheating:* Fish pies or cakes can be reheated.

► *Microwave:* Suitable for fish fillets, steaks and cutlets.

► *Barbecuing:* Suitable for fish fillets, steaks and cutlets.

Cod in parsley sauce

Coatings, sauces and garnishes for fish

► *Coatings:* Seasoned flour, egg and breadcrumbs, egg and oatmeal (for herring), batter.

► *Sauces:* Cheese sauce, parsley sauce, Hollandaise sauce, egg sauce, tartare sauce, tomato sauce.

► *Garnishes:* Lemon slices, parsley (chopped/sprigs), cucumber twists, grated cheese, tomato lilies, peas.

Fish with lemon slices

Fish dish garnished with lemon slices and parsley

Eggs

Eggs are a <u>nutritious</u>, <u>versatile</u> and <u>widely available</u> food which <u>cook quickly</u> and are a <u>suitable food for all age groups</u>.

Structure of Eggs

Eggs are composed of <u>three main parts</u>: the <u>shell</u>, the <u>white</u> and the <u>yolk</u>.

Shell – 10%

The outer shell forms a <u>hard protective layer</u>. It is composed mainly of <u>calcium carbonate</u>. This inedible shell is <u>porous</u> and <u>varies in colour from white to brown</u>, which does <u>not affect the nutritive value of the egg</u>. On the inside of the shell is a <u>thin membrane</u> which encloses the white and yolk and leaves an <u>air space</u> at the wider end of the egg. As an egg stales the <u>air space becomes larger</u> as air, <u>bacteria</u>, <u>flavours</u> and <u>odours pass through the porous shell</u>.

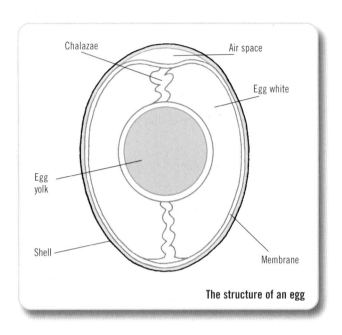

The structure of an egg

Egg white – 60%

Egg white is a <u>viscous, colourless liquid</u>. It is composed of <u>water</u>, <u>proteins</u> (<u>ovalbumin</u> and <u>globulin</u>) <u>minerals</u> and <u>vitamins</u>. The jelly-like white becomes <u>thin and watery</u> as the egg gets stale.

Egg yolk – 30%

The yolk of the egg is <u>held in position</u> by <u>string-like structures called chalazae</u>. It is the <u>most nutritious part of the egg</u> containing <u>proteins</u> (<u>vitellin</u> and <u>livetin</u>), <u>saturated fat</u>, <u>cholesterol</u>, <u>lecithin</u>, <u>vitamins A</u> and <u>D</u> and some <u>minerals</u>.

Average composition of egg		
Whole Egg	**White**	**Yolk**
Protein: 13%	Protein: 12%	Protein: 16%
Fat: 12%	Fat: 0·25%	Fat: 32%
Carbohydrate: 0%	Carbohydrate: 0%	Carbohydrate: 0%
Vitamins A, D, B: 1%	Vitamins B Group: 0·5%	Vitamins A, D, B: 1·5%
Minerals: 1%	Minerals: 0·75%	Minerals: 2%
Water: 73%	Water: 86·5%	Water: 48·5%

Nutritive Value of Eggs

Protein: Eggs are an excellent source of <u>high biological value protein</u>. The main proteins present are <u>albumin</u>, <u>globulin</u>, <u>vitellin</u> and <u>livetin</u>. Eggs provide protein in a form which is <u>easy to digest</u>.

Fat: Almost <u>one-third</u> of the egg yolk is <u>made up of fat</u>. It is <u>saturated fat</u>, present in a <u>fine emulsion</u>, because of the emulsifier lecithin. This makes the <u>fat easy to digest</u>. <u>Cholesterol</u> is also present in egg yolk.

Carbohydrate: Eggs do not contain carbohydrates, so they are usually served with a carbohydrate food, e.g. scrambled egg on toast.

Vitamins: Fat soluble vitamins A, D, E and K are present in the yolk. Beta-carotene gives the yolk its yellow colour. B group vitamins B_1, B_2, B_{12} and niacin are also present in the yolk, but to a greater extent in the white. Eggs are deficient in vitamin C.   *(B3)*

Minerals: Eggs are an important source of calcium, iron, phosphorus and sulphur.   *non haem iron source*

Water: Most of the water is present in the egg white.

Dietetic Value of Eggs

▶ As eggs contain high biological value protein they are important in the diets of all groups, especially lacto-ovo vegetarians who eat dairy products and eggs.

▶ Eggs are an easily digested food which make them important for children, elderly and convalescents.

▶ The saturated fat and cholesterol present in eggs may cause cholesterol problems so intake should be restricted by those on low-fat/cholesterol diets.

▶ Eggs are deficient in carbohydrate so they should be served with a high fibre carbohydrate food.

▶ Eggs are a good source of minerals: calcium, phosphorus, sulphur and iron. But as vitamin C is required to absorb iron it is important to include it in the meal, e.g. serving orange juice before eggs at breakfast.

▶ Eggs are a very nourishing food yet low in kilocalories (150 kcal approx.), making them important in low kilocalorie diets.

▶ Eggs are readily available, relatively cheap and a very versatile food.

Selection of Eggs

1. Buy fresh eggs – check best before date.
2. Eggs should be heavy for their size and the shell should feel rough.
3. Ensure that there are no cracks or breakages.
4. Check carton for information, e.g. size, class and quality.
5. Free-range eggs are more expensive than mass-produced eggs.

Labelling Regulations for Eggs

Egg packs must declare the following information on the outside of the pack in clearly visible and legible type:

▶ The name, address and number of the packer.

▶ The quality of the eggs i.e. class A, B (class A must indicate farming method, e.g. free range).

▶ Class A eggs must also indicate the size: XL (extra large), L (large), M (medium) or S (small).

▶ Class A must show the best before date.

▶ Advice to consumers on storage instructions.

▶ The number of eggs in the pack.

Grading of Eggs

Eggs are graded according to:	
(a) size	**(b) Class/quality**
XL L M S	A Fresh eggs B For use in industry

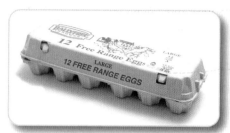

Eggs are graded according to size

Quality Assured eggs

Some European countries, including Ireland, have an EU-approved salmonella plan, i.e. Quality Assurance Scheme. The purpose of the Egg Quality Assurance Scheme is to ensure best practice at all stages of egg production, thereby minimising food safety risks. Under this plan:

► All egg producing farms are monitored and tested by the Department of Agriculture, Fisheries and Food.

► All hens are tested and certified salmonella free.

► Only heat-treated feed is used.

► Management systems must ensure that all eggs are fully traceable.

► If the specific requirements are met the producer is awarded the Quality Assurance (QA) mark from An Bord Bia which will appear on the packaging and on the egg.

► Each egg carries the QA logo, the code and the best before date.

Egg Quality Assured symbol

Salmonella = food poisoning bacteria (**See Page** 173).

Storage of eggs

1. Eggs should be stored in the refrigerator to prevent rapid deterioration.
2. Store eggs with pointed end downwards to prevent chalazae from breaking and to keep the egg yolk intact.
3. As shells are porous, store eggs away from strong-smelling foods.
4. Eggs should be used at room temperature, remove from fridge one hour prior to use to prevent the shell cracking (when boiling) or curdling.
5. Use within recommended time.

> **Tests for freshness**
>
> 1. Egg should be heavy for their size, and have a rough shell.
> 2. Fresh eggs sink in water, stale eggs float.
> 3. When deshelled, fresh eggs have a well-rounded yolk and jelly-like white; whereas stale eggs have a flat yolk and a watery white.

Staling of eggs

Eggs deteriorate quickly if not refrigerated. Washing increases the rate of staling. As eggs become stale the air space increases in size. Very stale eggs will smell strongly of hydrogen sulphide. Eggs can be preserved by freezing (deshelled) and as dried egg (used in cake mixes).

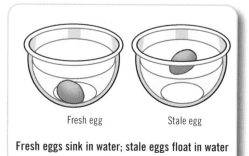

Fresh egg   Stale egg

Fresh eggs sink in water; stale eggs float in water

Properties of Eggs

Eggs have three main properties which are responsible for their many culinary uses: coagulation, emulsification and aeration.

1. Coagulation

The protein in eggs coagulates or sets during cooking. Egg whites coagulate at temperatures between 60°C and 65°C. Yolks coagulate between 65°C and 70°C. Coagulation is an example of protein denaturation. Examples of foods using egg coagulation properties are boiled, fried, poached and scrambled egg, omelettes, custards, and dishes where egg is used for binding, e.g. burgers, and for coating, e.g. fish coated with egg and breadcrumbs.

> *Always add hot liquid to cold eggs and not the other way around, e.g. when making a custard.*

Overcooking causes the egg proteins to clump together squeezing out the water. This is known as *curdling*.

2. Emulsification

Egg yolk contains the natural emulsifier lecithin which binds oil and water together. (**Properties of Lipids,** (See Page **24**) This property is used in the production of mayonnaise (oil, egg yolk and vinegar), hollandaise sauce (vinegar and butter) and cake-making (sugar and fat).

3. Ability to entrap air (aeration/foam formation)

Whisking eggs introduces air (the addition of sugar aids aeration). The heat produced by the friction slightly coagulates the protein around the air bubbles. Cooking further coagulates the protein. This aeration property is used in the production of meringues, soufflés and sponge cakes.

Culinary uses of eggs	
1. As a food, e.g. boiled, scrambled.	6. As an emulsifier, e.g. mayonnaise.
2. To enrich, e.g. rice pudding.	7. To aerate, e.g. sponge, meringue.
3. To bind, e.g. burgers, fishcakes.	8. To glaze, e.g. scones, pastry.
4. To coat, e.g. fish.	9. To garnish, e.g. slices of hard-boiled egg on salads.
5. To thicken, e.g. custard, quiche.	10. To clarify, e.g. clarifying homemade stock with egg whites.

Effects of Cooking on Eggs

1. Protein coagulates causing the egg to solidify.
2. Pathogenic bacteria, e.g. salmonella are destroyed by heat.
3. Heat causes loss of B group vitamins especially thiamine.
4. The egg white changes from transparent to opaque.
5. Egg white becomes insoluble when heated.
6. Overcooking or cooking at a very high temperature causes eggs to curdle.
7. Eggs become tough and difficult to digest if overcooked.
8. A reaction between iron and sulphur causes a green ring to form around the yolk if overcooked.

Frying egg

Milk

Milk, because it contains all six nutrients, is an ideal food for babies in the first months of life. It is also a valuable food in adult diets, although it is lacking in iron and vitamin C. Cows supply most of the milk consumed in Ireland.

Average composition of milk		
Whole milk	**Skimmed milk**	**Human milk**
Protein: 3.5%	Protein: 3.5%	Protein: 2.5%
Fat: 4%	Fat: 0.2%	Fat: 3.5%
Carbohydrate: 4.5%	Carbohydrate: 5%	Carbohydrate 6%
Vitamins A, D, B: 0.3%	Vitamin B: 0.2%	Vitamins A, B, C, D: 1%
Minerals: 0.7%	Minerals: 0.6%	Minerals: 0·5%
Water: 87%	Water: 90%	Water: 86.5%

Nutritive Value of Milk

Protein: Milk is a good source of high biological value protein. The proteins present are caseinogen, lactoalbumin and lactoglobulin.

Fat: Milk contains saturated fat, which is present in the form of tiny droplets making it easy to digest.

Carbohydrate: Milk contains lactose, a disaccharide also called milk sugar. It lacks starch and cellulose.

Vitamins: Milk is a very good source of vitamin A. It is also a good source of riboflavin and contains small amounts of niacin and thiamine. However, thiamine is destroyed by heat treatment. Milk contains traces of vitamin D. Any vitamin C present in raw milk is lost in processing.

Minerals: Milk is an excellent source of calcium. It also contains phosphorous and minute quantities of other minerals such as potassium and magnesium. Milk is lacking in iron.

Water: Milk contains a very high proportion of water.

Dietetic Value of Milk

Other sources of milk include: goats, sheep, camels, buffaloes and soya beans.

▶ Milk is relatively cheap, readily available in a variety of types and supplies a range of nutrients in an easily digested form.

▶ Milk is the sole food of babies supplying all nutrients essential for growth i.e. protein, calcium, phosphorous, vitamins A and D. This also makes it a valuable food in the diets of pregnant women, children and teenagers.

▶ Milk is also available fortified with vitamins A and D, calcium and omega–3 fatty acids.

▶ Milk should be combined with foods rich in starch, fibre, vitamin C and iron in order to balance the diet.

▶ Individuals who follow a low cholesterol or low kilocalorie diet can opt to use low-fat or skimmed milk.

▶ Milk is a very versatile food with many culinary uses.

Effects of Heat on Milk

▶ The protein coagulates forming a skin on the surface of milk.

▶ Bacteria are destroyed by boiling.

▶ Some B vitamins are lost.

▶ Flavour is altered slightly due to caramelisation of the lactose.

Different types of milk

Processing of Milk

Milk undergoes processing to:

1. **Improve flavour** and make it more palatable (homogenisation).
2. Heat treatments **destroy bacteria** making it safe for human consumption and increase its shelf-life.

Homogenisation

Process

▶ Milk is heated to 60°C, then forced under pressure through tiny valves or holes. This breaks up the fat globules into smaller fat droplets.

Effects

▶ The smaller more uniform fat droplets are distributed through the milk. They remain suspended in the milk and do not coalesce on the surface as they would in unhomogenised milk.

▶ Milk is creamier with a better flavour.

Heat Treatments

Pasteurisation	
Process	**Effects**
Milk is heated to 72°C for 15 seconds then it is cooled rapidly to below 10°C.	• Pathogenic bacteria are destroyed. • Some souring bacteria are destroyed so the milk will stay fresh for at least five days. • No noticeable change in texture or flavour. • Loss of vitamin C and thiamine.

Sterilisation	
Process	**Effects**
Milk is homogenised, sealed into bottles, and heated to 110°C for approximately 30 minutes, then cooled.	• Milk will remain in good condition (unopened) for weeks. • All micro-organisms are destroyed. • Flavour altered. • Loss of vitamin C and B group.

Ultra-heat heated (UHT) – also known as long-life milk	
Process	**Effects**
Milk is heated to 132°C for 1–3 seconds by pouring it over a heated surface. It is then cooled to 10°C and packed in sterile containers.	• Slight change in flavour. • Loss of vitamin C and B. • All bacteria are destroyed so the milk keeps (unopened) for several months without refrigeration.

Evaporated milk

Process	Effects
1. Milk is pasteurised, evaporated to half its volume, then homogenised. 2. Milk is sealed into cans and sterilised at 115°C for 20 minutes.	• Vitamins C and B group lost. • Flavour altered. • Bacteria destroyed. • Very long shelf-life (unopened).

Condensed milk

Process	Effects
1. Milk is pasteurised and 15% sugar is added. 2. Milk is evaporated to one-third of its volume, cooled and sealed into cans. (It does not require prolonged sterilisation because of preservative effect of added sugar.)	• Loss of vitamin C, vitamin B group. • Increase in carbohydrate (sugar). • Flavour altered. • Bacteria destroyed. • Very long shelf-life (unopened).

Dried or dehydrated milk (whole or skimmed milk may be dried)

Whole/skimmed milk may be dried.

Process

Milk is homogenised, pasteurised then evaporated to 60% of its original volume. It is dried by one of the following methods:

1. Roller drying Milk is poured over heated revolving rollers and is scraped off as it dries. The milk powder is cooled and packed into airtight containers.	**The effects of roller drying:** • The high temperature destroys some amino acids. • Loss of vitamin B. • Bacteria are destroyed. • Flavour altered. • Does not reconstitute easily.
2. Spray drying Milk is sprayed into a hot air chamber. The droplets dry to a fine powder as they fall. The dried milk is cooled and packed in airtight containers.	**The effects of spray drying:** • Some amino acids and vitamin B are lost. • Bacteria are destroyed. • Better flavour than roller dried milk and reconstitutes more easily.

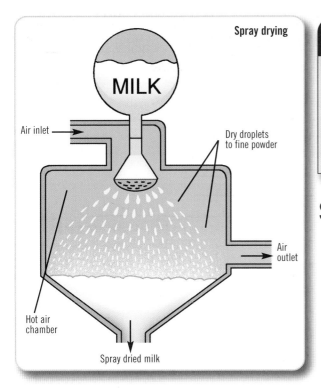

Spray drying

Air inlet

MILK

Dry droplets to fine powder

Air outlet

Hot air chamber

Spray dried milk

Culinary uses of milk

Drinks:	Milk shakes, drinking chocolate.
Puddings and sweets:	Rice pudding, caramel custard.
Sauces:	Parsley sauce, cheese sauce.
Soups:	Mushroom soup, vegetable soup.
Baking:	Scones, bread.
Savoury dishes:	Quiche, pancakes.

Storing Milk

▶ Check 'best before' date and use milk in rotation.

▶ Never mix milks of different date stamping.

▶ Store in refrigerator, preferably in original container.

▶ Keep milk covered and away from strong smelling foods.

Souring/Spoilage

Souring occurs when lactic acid bacteria break down the lactose in milk to form lactic acid. This gives milk an unpleasant taste and causes it to curdle.

Curdling

Curdling occurs when the protein (caseinogen) separates from the liquid part of the milk. Curdling of milk may occur during food preparation/cooking because of:

▶ The addition of acid, e.g. lemon juice to milk.

▶ Heat, e.g. adding milk to very hot coffee.

▶ The addition of enzymes, e.g. rennet which is added to milk during cheese-making.

Milk Quality

In Ireland:

1. Cattle are routinely tested for TB, a disease which can be transmitted to humans through milk.

2. All farms which supply milk for public consumption are registered and are subject to inspections.

3. Dairies must adhere to strict codes of hygiene when transporting, storing and processing milk.

4. Milk is sampled and tested for a variety of factors, including microbial contamination and the presence of antibiotic residues.

5. All milk on sale has been heat-treated.

> Legislation governing all aspects of milk production and processing is based on an EU directive. It is enforced mainly by the Department of Agriculture, Fisheries and Food.

These precautions are necessary because milk, which contains nutrients important for human health, can also be an ideal medium for the growth of micro-organisms. Disease-causing organisms, which may be transmitted in unpasteurised milk, include salmonella, campylobacter and e-coli 0157, all of which are destroyed or inactivated by pasteurisation. Therefore, the sale of raw (unpasteurised) cows milk is prohibited in Ireland.

Butter

Butter is a milk product. It is a water in oil emulsion made from pasteurised cream.

Average composition of butter					
Protein	Fat	Carbohydrate	Vitamins	Minerals	Water
1%	82%	0.5%	0.5% A, D	2%	14%

Nutritive Value of Butter

Protein: Very small amount of high biological value protein present.

Fat: Butter is a concentrated source of fat. The high proportion of saturated fatty acids, e.g. butric acid, may contribute to an increase in cholesterol.

Carbohydrate: Only traces of lactose remain after churning.

Minerals: Salt added during manufacture results in the presence of sodium and chlorine. Only traces of calcium and phosphorous remain.

Vitamins: Butter supplies vitamin A and small quantities of vitamins D and E.

Water: Butter contains little water.

> By law, butter must contain a minimum of 80% fat and a maximum of 16% water.

> Butter-milk is an acidic liquid used in bread-making (a by-product of butter production).

Storage (See Page 23)

Butter should be well wrapped and refrigerated to prevent oxidative rancidity. Remove from the fridge shortly before use to soften slightly.

Butter Production

Butter is made from cream containing 35–40% milk fat.

1. Cream is pasteurised then chilled to 10–15°C.
2. It is churned (agitated) until the fat particles coalesce into granules separating from the butter-milk which is drained off.
3. Salt is added and the butter is 'worked' to distribute the salt. Working also influences the keeping quality, texture and colour of the butter.
4. Butter is weighed and packed.

Different types of butter

Types of butter	
Type	**Use**
1. **Butter** contains approximately 2% salt.	• Baking, table use.
2. **Unsalted butter** has no salt added during manufacture.	• Low sodium diets, baking.
3. **Spreadable butter.** After churning the butter is agitated to break up the fat and make it spreadable.	• Sandwiches.
4. **Reduced-fat butter** contains approximately 40% fat.	• Low kilocalorie diets.
Butter is unsuitable for frying because it begins to decompose at a relatively low temperature.	

Cream

Cream is an oil in water emulsion.

Production

Milk is heated to 50°C. It is then subjected to centrifugal force which separates the upper cream layer from the lower layer of skimmed milk. The cream is heat-treated using pasteurisation, sterilisation or ultra-heat treatment.

Nutritive Value of Cream

Cream is high in saturated fat. Small amounts of protein and carbohydrate are present. It also contains some calcium and traces of vitamins A and D.

Types of cream	
Standard cream	30-40% fat
Double cream	48% fat
UHT/long-life cream	40% fat
Sour cream (lactic acid)	18% fat
Cream is also available frozen, whipped and in aerosol form.	

May be used instead of cream:

- Crème fraiche (18% fat) is a mixture of soured cream and yoghurt or buttermilk.
- Greek yoghurt (10% fat) is a thick creamy yoghurt.

Different types of cream

Yoghurt

Production

1. Whole, low-fat or skimmed milk is homogenised.

2. It is pasteurised at 90°C to destroy all bacteria, then cooled to 37°C.

3. A culture such as *lactobacillus bulgaris* is added to the milk which is then incubated for 6–8 hours to allow fermentation to occur. During this time the lactose changes to lactic acid and the milk proteins coagulate. This thickens the yoghurt and gives it a distinct flavour.

4. The yoghurt is cooled and other ingredients like sweeteners, colours, flavours, fruit and nuts are added to it.

5. The yoghurt is packaged for sale.

Different types of yoghurt

Nutritive Value of Yoghurt

Protein: Yoghurt contains a small quantity of high biological value protein. Some yoghurts contain extra milk solids which further enhance the protein content.

Fat: Fat content varies depending on milk used.

Carbohydrate: Carbohydrate content is influenced by the addition of sugar and fruit.

Vitamins: Yoghurt contains small amounts of vitamin A and the vitamin B group.

Minerals: Yoghurt is a good sources of calcium.

Dietetic Value of Yoghurt

► Yoghurt is an economical and easily digested source of protein, calcium and vitamin A, suitable for growing children, teenagers and pregnant women.

► It is a convenient and versatile food useful in packed lunches, as a snack or dessert.

► Low-fat yoghurts are a useful substitute for cream in low cholesterol and slimming diets.

► It is nourishing food requiring no preparation making it useful for convalescents and elderly people.

► Yoghurt is available in a wide range of flavours, textures and energy contents to suit all tastes.

Yoghurt may be:
- full fat, low fat or diet (0% fat).
- thick and creamy, liquid drink or frozen.
- natural or contain added ingredients, e.g. fruit.

Culinary uses of yoghurt

► On its own.

► Dip or salad dressing.

► Ingredient in savoury dish, e.g. curries.

► Instead of cream in desserts.

► Yoghurt drinks and smoothies.

Bio-yoghurts contain additional bacteria cultures such as lactobacillus casei, which manufacturers claim support the natural bacteria in the intestine and help to regulate digestion.

Cheese

Cheese is a concentrated form of milk. It is a very nutritious, versatile and relatively inexpensive food, which does not require cooking, and it is available in many different varieties. The milk from cows, goats and ewes may be used in cheese production.

Classification of cheese (by method of production)			
Hard cheese	**Semi-hard cheese**	**Soft cheese**	**Processed cheese**
Cheddar	Edam	Brie	Cheese slices
Cheshire	Gouda	Camembert	Cheese spreads
Emmenthal	Blarney	Mozzarella	Calvita
Parmesan	Stilton	Cottage cheese	Galtee
Kilmeaden	Roquefort	Cream cheeses	Smoked cheese
	Gruyère	Ricotta	
	Halloumi	Feta	

Examples						
Italian	**Irish**	**British**	**Swiss**	**Dutch**	**Greek**	**French**
Mozzarella	Kilmeaden	Cheddar	Emmenthal	Edam	Feta*	Roquefort
Parmesan	Wexford	Cheshire	Gruyère	Gouda	Halloumi	Brie

*Traditionally made using ewes' milk.

Cultured cheeses		
Cheeses with internal mould (these are blue-veined cheeses)	**Cheeses with external mould**	**Cheeses with holes**
Stilton Roquefort Gorgonzola	Camembert Brie Mozzarella	Emmenthal (starter culture produces CO_2 during fermentation and maturation resulting in the formation of holes)

Other types of cheese

▶ Vegetarian cheese uses a non-animal rennet.

▶ Low-fat cheese is produced from skimmed milk, e.g. cottage cheese.

▶ Farmhouse cheeses are produced on a small scale rather than in a factory (See Page **145**).

▶ Fromage frais is a blend of soft cheeses.

▶ Processed cheese involves the addition of other ingredients.

Different types of cheese

Production of Cheese

All cheeses have the same basic method of production as cheddar cheese.

1. A culture of lactic acid bacteria is added to pasteurised milk. This changes lactose to lactic acid giving flavour and acting as a preservative.
2. The milk is heated to 30°C and rennet is added. The rennet contains the enzyme rennin which coagulates milk protein (changing caesinogen to caesin).
3. After 30–45 minutes the mixture has separated into curds (solids) and whey (liquid). The curds contain most of the nutrients: protein (caesin) fat, fat-soluble vitamins, some thiamine and calcium. The whey contains mainly water with water-soluble vitamins and some milk protein.
4. The curds are chopped releasing more whey, which is drained off. (At this point cottage cheese is produced.)
5. The curds are heated to 35–40°C to squeeze out more whey and to achieve the correct consistency (scalding).
6. The curds are cut into blocks and piled on top of each other. This process is known as *cheddaring* and completes the drainage of whey.
7. The blocks are further cut and 2% salt is added to improve flavour and keeping qualities.
8. The salted curds are placed into moulds and pressed for a number of hours (longer pressing produces harder cheeses). The moulds may be sprayed with hot water to form a protective rind.
9. The cheese is removed from the moulds, date stamped and stored for 3–12 months. Ripening occurs which allow flavour, texture and smell to develop due to enzymatic and bacterial action.
10. The cheese is graded, packed and sold.

Processed Cheeses

Processed cheese is a cheese product. It is made from chopped ripened cheese with salt, water, whey powder, dried milk and emulsifiers added. This mixture is heated and mixed. Colourings, such as annato, and flavourings (e.g. herbs, meat flavouring) may be added. It is packed into blocks, slices or triangles. Because of the added water the nutritive value is decreased.

Average composition of cheese	
Cheddar	**Cottage**
Protein: 27%	Protein: 14%
Fat: 33%	Fat: 4%
Carbohydrate: 0%	Carbohydrate: 1.5%
Vitamins A, B: 1%	Vitamins A, B: 1.5%
Minerals: 4%	Minerals: 1%
Water: 35%	Water: 78%

Processed cheese

Nutritive Value of Cheese

Protein: Cheese is an excellent source of high biological value protein – caesin (soft cheese contains less protein than hard).

Fat: The fat in cheese is saturated. Hard cheeses are very high in fat, but contain considerably less fat if made using skimmed milk.

Carbohydrate: Cheese lacks carbohydrate as the lactose in the milk is converted to lactic acid. Therefore, cheese is often served with a carbohydrate food, e.g. cheese sandwiches.

Vitamins: Cheese is a good source of vitamin A (retinol and beta-carotene) and B$_2$ (riboflavin). It also contains some vitamin D, but is deficient in vitamin C.

Minerals: Cheese is an excellent source of calcium. Because of the salt added during production, cheese contains sodium.

Water: The water content of cheese varies depending on the type of cheese. The harder the cheese the lower the water content.

Low fat cheddar cheese contains 20% fat.

One litre of milk produces 100g of cheese.

Dietetic Value of Cheese

► Cheese is very important for its protein and calcium content, making it an ideal food for children, adolescents, and pregnant and lactating women.

► Because of the vast variety of cheeses available there is always one to suit different tastes.

► As there is no waste and no cooking necessary cheese is a reasonably inexpensive food within everybody's means.

► Cheese is a very versatile food which can be used in many tasty dishes.

► Cheese is generally high in saturated fat, so consumption must be reduced by those with cholesterol problems.

- Because of the high fat content, some cheeses are very high in kilocalories, so consumption must be limited by those on slimming diets.

- The amount of fat in cheese makes it a difficult food to digest, it is best used in small amounts, especially by children and the elderly.

- Soft cheeses should be avoided during pregnancy to reduce risk of listeria food poisoning (**See Page** **173**).

Buying and Storage of Cheese

- Freshly cut cheese should be purchased in small amounts and used within days (2–3 for soft cheeses).
- Check the date stamp. Use before expiry date.
- Vacuum-packed cheeses should be fully sealed.
- Cheese should be sealed well after opening and stored in the refrigerator.
- Blue-veined cheeses require air circulation therefore store in a polythene box.
- All cheeses should be used at room temperature; remove from fridge one hour before use.

Uses of cheese

- As a snack, e.g. with crackers.
- In sandwiches – plain or toasted.
- As a main ingredient, e.g. in lasagne, pizza and quiche.
- As a filling, e.g. in omelettes, baked potatoes.
- In salads – grated or sliced.
- In sauces, e.g. cheese sauce over vegetables.

- In dips, e.g. cream cheese mixed with herbs.
- In baking, e.g. cheese pastry or cheese biscuits.
- As a dessert – cheesecake.
- To end a meal – cheeseboard.
- As a garnish, e.g. grated cheese on soup or gratin dishes.

Effects of cooking on cheese:

- Protein coagulates and shrinks.
- Fat melts but no loss of nutritive value occurs.
- There is a colour change as the cheese browns.

- Cheese becomes hard, tough and indigestible if reheated or overcooked.
- Overcooking causes the fat to separate and the cheese becomes stringy; it will eventually cause the cheese to burn.

Cheese products

To aid digestion of cheese	Cheese products
• Use low-fat cheese. • Use uncooked or cook for a short time. • Grate or slice thinly. • Add in at end of cooking time (e.g. in cheese sauce). • Acid seasoning aids digestion, e.g. mustard.	• Processed cheeses • Cheese dips • Cheese strings • Petit filous (fromais frais)

Alternative Protein Foods

Alternative protein foods are also known as <u>novel</u> (new) <u>protein foods</u>. There are two main sources of protein alternatives which are derived from non-animal sources:

1. Those <u>processed from plant</u> foods.
2. Those <u>processed from micro-organisms</u>.

1. Protein Alternatives from Plants

The most widely used novel protein foods are made from <u>soya beans. Soya beans are a legume</u>.

Soya protein

Unlike other plant proteins, which have a low biological value, soya beans contain <u>high biological value protein</u>. When compared with beef, soya beans compare very favourably. Beef is higher in the <u>amino acid methionine</u> but there is no other significant difference.

Average composition of soya beans					
Protein	**Fat**	**Carbohydrate**	**Vitamins**	**Minerals**	**Water**
43%	20%	21%	B Group: 1%	Calcium and iron: 1%	14%

Nutritive value of soya beans

Protein: Soya beans are an important source of <u>high biological value protein</u>, although the <u>methionine content is low</u>.
Fat: The oil in soya beans is <u>polyunsaturated, linoleic acid</u> making up 50% of the <u>fatty acid content</u>.
Carbohydrate: <u>Less than one-third of soya beans</u> is carbohydrate in the form of <u>starch and fibre</u>.
Vitamins: Some <u>B group vitamins</u> are present in soya beans.
Minerals: The minerals <u>calcium</u> and <u>iron</u> are present in useful amounts.
Water: Soya beans contain <u>little water</u>.

Soya protein products include:

▶ <u>TVP: Textured vegetable protein</u> used as an alternative to meat.
▶ <u>Tempeh:</u> A <u>fermented soya product</u> used as a meat substitute.
▶ <u>Tofu: Soya bean curd</u> (soya cheese).
▶ <u>Soya milk.</u>
▶ <u>Soya yoghurts.</u>

Textured vegetable protein
Production
1. Soya beans are <u>de-hulled</u> and the <u>oil is extracted</u>.
2. The beans are <u>ground into flour</u> and some <u>carbohydrate is removed</u>.
3. <u>Vegetable oil, flavouring, seasoning and nutritive additives</u> (B_{12}, methionine and iron) are added.
4. The <u>mixture is then heated and extruded through a nozzle</u> causing expansion and the formation of texture.
5. The mixture is then chopped (cubes) or <u>minced, then dried and packed</u>.

Soya products

To use TVP:

▶ Steep TVP in water (15–30 min).

▶ Add drained TVP to a sauce 15 minutes before the end of cooking time to heat it through.

Advantages of TVP

▶ Cheaper than meat.

▶ Nutritionally comparable to meat.

▶ Practically no saturated fat present.

▶ Little preparation required.

▶ Short cooking/heating time.

▶ Useful source of fibre.

▶ No shrinkage occurs.

Disadvantages of TVP

▶ Inferior to meat in flavour.

▶ Extra flavouring required.

▶ Texture different to meat.

Other soya products:

▶ Miso-soya bean paste (condiment)

▶ Soya oil

▶ Soya sauce (condiment)

▶ Soya flour

2. Protein Alternatives from Micro-organisms

Micro-organisms such as yeast, fungi, bacteria and algae are currently being developed as sources of edible protein. They grow rapidly and can be grown in an inexpensive medium, e.g. industrial or agriculture waste and therefore are cheap to produce. The resulting protein is called *mycoprotein*.

Production of mycoprotein (also known as 'single cell protein')

1. Fungus cells are fermented under ideal conditions for growth.
2. The cells are harvested from the fermenter, filtered and drained.
3. The resulting sheet of mycelia is bound together with egg albumin.
4. Flavourings and colourings may also be added.
5. The mycoprotein is then textured to resemble meat.
6. It is then sliced, diced or shredded and steamed to set the binder.
7. The mycoprotein is then used in the production of mycoprotein foods.

Quorn

Quorn is a mycoprotein product. It may be sold chilled in chunks or minced like TVP. It is also used in prepared meals, e.g. Quorn oven bake fillets, curries, burgers.

Nutritive value of mycoprotein

Protein: Similar protein content to meat with less methionine.

Fat: Mycoprotein is low in fat and contains no saturated fat.

Carbohydrate: It is a good source of fibre.

Vitamins: Some B group vitamins are present.

Minerals: Zinc is also present but mycoprotein is low in iron.

Water: It is low in water.

Quorn products

Cereals

Cereals are the grains of cultivated grasses. They form the major part of carbohydrate intake in the diet, providing about one-third of all energy. The most popular cereals are wheat, oats, maize and rice, with barley and rye used to a lesser extent.

Structure of the Cereal Grain

All cereal grains are similar in structure to the wheat grain.

Wheat

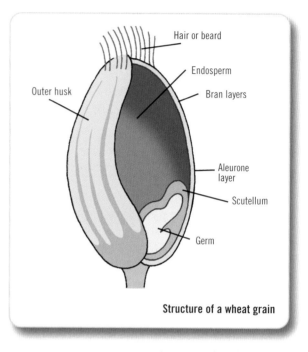

Structure of a wheat grain

Structure of the Wheat Grain

The wheat grain is an oval-shaped grain about 1 cm x 0.5 cm. The grain is enclosed in a loose outer inedible husk which is removed during threshing. It has a tuft of hair at one end which is called the *beard*. The grain is composed of three main parts.

1. **The bran layers – 14% of the whole grain**
    The bran layers consist largely of cellulose with valuable amounts of B group vitamins, calcium, iron and phosphorous.

2. **The endosperm – 84% of the grain**
    The major part of the wheat grain is the endosperm. It is composed mainly of starch, the protein gluten and some B group vitamins. The outer layer of the endosperm is called the aleurone layer which is rich in protein.

3. **The germ – 2% of the grain**
    Although accounting for only a small proportion of the total grain, the germ, which is situated at the base of the grain is very nutritious. It is made up of protein, fat, B group vitamins, vitamin E and iron. The thin layer separating the germ from the endosperm is called the scutellum.

Average composition of wheat					
Protein	Fat	Carbohydrate	Vitamins	Minerals	Water
12%	2%	72%	B and E: 1%	Calcium and iron: 1%	12%

Nutritive Value of Cereals

Protein: The protein in cereals is low biological value protein as lysine threonine and tryptrophan are present in reduced amounts. Gluten is the main protein in wheat and rye.

Fat: All the fat of cereals is present in the germ. As it is polyunsaturated fat cereals supply essential fatty acids.

Carbohydrates: The principal nutrient in cereals is carbohydrate, most of which is starch (64%). The remainder (8%) is cellulose, which is removed in the production of white flour.

Vitamins: Cereals are an important source of B group vitamins especially B_1, B_2 and niacin. Processing removes many of these vitamins. The germ contains vitamin E.

Minerals: The minerals present in cereals are calcium, iron and phosphorus.

Water: As the water content is quite low, cereals keep well.

> *Gluten is the protein present in wheat flour which* <u>*gives*</u> *<u>elasticity</u>.*
> *It allows dough to stretch before it sets in the oven.*

Dietetic Value of Cereals

- ▶ As cereals are composed mainly of starch they are an important energy food for all groups.
- ▶ Wholegrain cereals provide valuable amounts of fibre essential in all healthy diets.
- ▶ A considerable amount of B group vitamins, calcium and iron are provided by wholegrain cereals.
- ▶ Any fat present is unsaturated, therefore does not contribute to cholesterol build up, but is a source of essential fatty acids.
- ▶ Cereals are an inexpensive, readily available food which are very versatile.
- ▶ Gluten cannot be digested by coeliacs, who must therefore avoid wheat, oats, barley and rye.
- ▶ <u>Phytates</u> present in wholegrain cereals inhibit calcium and iron absorption.
- ▶ Deficiency diseases such as beri-beri and pellagra may occur when polished rice (vitamin B removed) and maize (lacking in tryptophan) are the staple diets (See Page 32). See Page 32

Buying/Storage of Cereals

Cereals for home use (e.g. flour, pinhead oatmeal, polished rich, breakfast cereals) have been processed to some degree.

- ▶ Packaging should be secure.
- ▶ Check the date stamp.
- ▶ Store in a cool dry area.
- ▶ When opened – seal well or store in an airtight container.
- ▶ Use within the recommended time.
- ▶ Wholegrain cereals, e.g. brown flour, deteriorate faster because of the fat content in the germ.

Types of Wheat

Spring wheat is sown in March and harvested in September. It is grown in climates with cold winters and hot summers, e.g. North America. It is fast-growing wheat which has a high gluten content.

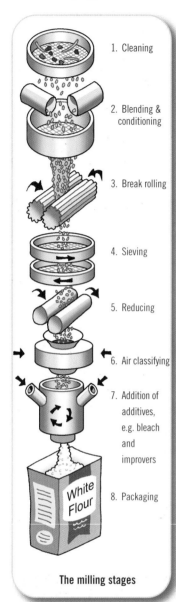

1. Cleaning
2. Blending & conditioning
3. Break rolling
4. Sieving
5. Reducing
6. Air classifying
7. Addition of additives, e.g. bleach and improvers
8. Packaging

The milling stages

Winter wheat is sown in autumn and harvested in late summer. It is more suitable to climates with milder winters, e.g. Ireland and England. The slower growth produces a wheat with a lower gluten content. Plain flour is made from a blend of both types of wheat.

Flour Milling

Milling is the term used to describe the processing of wheat to produce flour.

Milling stages
Preparation
▶ *Cleaning:* A series of sieves remove any stones, straw, soil and dust from the wheat grains, which are then washed.
▶ *Conditioning:* This process ensures that the grains have the correct moisture content making it easier to mill.
▶ *Blending:* Blending involves mixing different wheats together to form a 'grist'.

Milling
▶ *Break rolling:* Ridged rollers revolve at high speed in opposite directions, peeling open the grain, releasing the endosperm without breaking the bran layer into tiny fragments. Wholegrain flour has been produced at this stage.
▶ *Sifting and purifying:*
  • The opened grain passes through a series of rotating sieves which separate the grain into bran, germ and rough endosperm (semolina).
  • Air is blown through the grain separating the lighter bran from the heavier endosperm.
  • The bran and germ are sold as products themselves and are used in the production of breakfast cereals.

▶ *Reducing:* The rough endosperm is ground down further by a set of smooth 'reducing rollers'.
▶ *Air classifying:* This process lightens the flour.
▶ *Addition of additives:* The nutritive additives calcium and B vitamins, bleaching agents and improvers (to improve the quality of the gluten, e.g. vitamin C) are added.
▶ *Packing:* Flour is weighed and packed.

Effects of Processing

▶ Wholegrain flour has more protein than white as the aleurone layer and the germ are removed in the production of white flour.
▶ White flour is deficient in fibre and has a greater proportion of starch than wholegrain.
▶ As the germ is removed in the production of white flour no fat remains, which allows for longer storage.

Types of flour		
Flour	**Extraction Rate**	**Description**
Stoneground flour	100%	Full grain ground between stones instead of rollers.
Wholegrain flour	100%	None of the grain removed.
Wheatenmeal (brown) flour	85%	A lot of bran removed.
White flour (plain or cream)	Less than 75%	Bran and germ removed.
Self-raising flour	Less than 75%	White flour with raising agent added.
Strong flour		High gluten content suitable for yeast baking.
Gluten-free flour		Gluten removed – suitable for coeliacs.
High-ratio flour	Less than 50%	Soft, finely milled flour used by confectioners.

> Extraction rate refers to the percentage of the grain used in producing the flour which affects the nutritive value.

Effects of Heat on Cereals

▶ Moist heat causes starch grains to swell and burst and absorb liquids, e.g. rice pudding.

▶ Dry heat causes starch grains to swell, burst and absorb fat, e.g. popcorn, pastry-making.

▶ Cellulose is softened.

▶ Starch becomes more digestible.

▶ Protein coagulates in dry heat setting bread and cakes.

▶ Dextrinisation and caramelisation occur causing surface browning of bread and cakes.

▶ Heat causes loss of some B group vitamins.

Different types of pasta

Cereal Products

Main cereal products include flour, pasta and breakfast cereals.

Breakfast cereals

Pasta: Pasta is made from a high gluten wheat called durum wheat. The rough endosperm (semolina) is mixed with water, salt, oil, eggs and possibly coloured with tomato purée or spinach. The dough is formed into many different shapes. It is available fresh but usually sold dried.

Breakfast cereals: There are a wide variety of breakfast cereals available made from a range of cereal grains. Some are flaked, some shredded and others are puffed. Other ingredients, e.g. nuts, sugar, fruit or honey may be added. Breakfast cereals are often fortified with vitamins and minerals. The nutrient content is largely dependent on the ingredients.

Other cereals

Rice: Rice contains less protein, fat and minerals than other cereals. It is a commonly used food which is available in many varieties and is usually polished (bran removed).

Varieties of rice

Short grain rice (Carolina rice): Round grains used for puddings.

Medium grain rice (Italian rice): Longer, narrower grain grown in Italy and used in risottos and salads.

Long grain rice (Patna rice): Long thin grains used for savoury dishes, e.g. accompaniment to curry.

Brown rice: Only some of the bran is removed. Used as long grain rice but takes longer to cook and is more nutritious.

Basmati rice: Long grain rice grown in India. Used in savoury dishes and noted for its flavour, texture and aroma.

Rice products

- ▶ Prepared rice meals, e.g. frozen risotto.
- ▶ Easy cook rice – steam treated to cook more quickly.
- ▶ Rice Krispies breakfast cereal.
- ▶ Cans and cartons of rice pudding.
- ▶ Rice cakes.
- ▶ Rice flour – thickening agent.
- ▶ Rice paper – edible.

Cereal products

Cereal products	
Cereals	**Products**
Oats	Pinhead oatmeal, oatflakes, flapjacks.
Maize (corn)	Popcorn, cornflakes, cornflour.
Barley	Pearl barley, barley water.
Rye	Rye bread, Ryvita.
Wheat	Flour, pasta, couscous (crushed semolina steamed over a flavoursome broth or stew).

Vegetables

Vegetables are a versatile, wholesome and nutritious food which add colour, flavour and texture to the diet. They are a valuable source of minerals, vitamins, antioxidants and fibre which play a significant role in maintaining good health.

Classification of vegetables

Green vegetables	Roots and tubers	Pulse vegetables	Fruit vegetables	Bulbs	Stems	
Spinach Cabbage Kale Brussel sprouts Broccoli (flowers) Cauliflower (flowers)	Carrots Parsnips Turnips Beetroot Radishes Potatoes (tuber)	Peas Lentils Beans, e.g. runner, French, kidney and broad	Tomatoes Cucumber Peppers Courgettes Marrow Aubergines	Onions Shallots Leeks Garlic	Celery Asparagus	Mushrooms and truffles are classified as fungi.

Average composition of vegetables

Vegetable	Protein	Fat	Carbohydrate	Vitamins	Minerals	Water
Green	3%	0%	3%	A, B_6, folate C,	Calcium, iron potassium	90–95%
Root	2%	0%	5–20%	A, C	Calcium, iron	70–90%
Pulses	2–8%	0%	3–20%	A, B_1, B_2, B_6, C	Calcium, iron potassium	75–90%
Fruits	1%	0%	2–5%	A, C	Calcium, iron	90–95%

Nutritive Value of Vegetables

Protein: Roots, greens and fruits contain small quantities of low biological value protein. Pulses are a better source of protein. One exception, soya beans, supply high biological value protein (See Page 11).

Fat: Vegetables are lacking in fat. Exceptions include olives and soya beans which contain polyunsaturated fat.

Carbohydrate: Vegetables, particularly pulse vegetables, are among the best sources of cellulose in the diet. Pulses, root vegetables and potatoes contain a high proportion of starch. Small amounts of sugar are found in some vegetables such as carrots, beetroot and onions.

Vitamins: Vegetables are an excellent source of beta-carotene (pro-vitamin A), vitamin C and some vitamin B group. Dark green vegetables such as spinach, cabbage and yellow/orange or red coloured vegetables such as peppers and carrots are the best sources of beta-carotene.

Most fresh young vegetables contain some vitamin C. Leafy greens and fruit vegetables such as tomatoes and peppers are the best sources. Potatoes are an important source of vitamin C in the Irish diet. Vitamins B_1, B_2 and B_6 are found in pulse vegetables. Mushrooms are a good source of B_2 and niacin. Leafy greens such as spinach supply folate.

Minerals: Vegetables supply small quantities of calcium and iron. Root vegetables and leafy greens are the best sources of calcium. Dark green vegetables are important as a source of iron in the diet. Vegetables contain traces of other minerals such as potassium, zinc and iodine.

Water: All vegetables contain a high proportion of water.

Note: **Oxalates** (found in spinach), **phytic acid** (found in pulses) and **cellulose** may inhibit the absorption of some of the calcium and iron in vegetables.

Dietetic Value of Vegetables

1. Vegetables are an invaluable source of vitamins, minerals and fibre.
2. Vegetables supply the antioxidants beta-carotene and vitamin C, which play a role in preventing diet-related health problems such as cancer and heart disease.
3. Vegetables are lacking in fat and low in kilocalories yet are filling and are therefore useful in low cholesterol and slimming diets.
4. Pulse vegetables are an important source of protein in vegan diets.
5. Vegetables are very versatile and can be prepared and cooked in a wide variety of ways adding colour, flavour and texture to the diet.
6. When in season vegetables are cheaper and more readily available. However, a wide variety of fresh vegetables are available all year round.
7. Since vegetables are lacking in vitamins D and B_{12} vegans need to supplement their diet with these vitamins.

Buying Vegetables

To obtain vegetables which are at their best in terms of appearance, flavour, texture and nutritive value:

▶ Buy fresh, good quality vegetables in usable quantities.
▶ Buy when in season while produce is plentiful.
▶ Choose loose or netted vegetables.
▶ Avoid washed produce or vegetables which are pre-packed in plastic.
▶ Select medium sized vegetables (best flavour) with no bruising or discolouration.

Look for the following characteristic signs of freshness in each class:

Green	Roots and tubers	Pulses	Fruits	Stems	Bulbs
• Crisp green leaves. • Closely packed head. • No evidence of insects or slugs.	• Firm and heavy in relation to size. • Correct colour. • No excess soil.	• Full, firm pods. • Heavy for size. • Not discoloured or shrivelled.	• Bright colour. • No mould growth. • Medium sized.	• Correct colour. • Any attached leaves un-withered. • Crisp looking stalks.	• Medium size. • Firm. • No mould growth.

Storing of Vegetables

Badly, or incorrectly stored fresh vegetables deteriorate quickly in terms of flavour, texture and nutritive value. To maintain good quality:

1. Store vegetables in a cool, dark and ventilated place.
2. Remove from plastic bags and store loosely in a vegetable rack or in the salad drawer of the refrigerator.
3. Store salad vegetables in sealed plastic bags in the refrigerator.
4. Remove any spoiled/damaged vegetables from stored produce.
5. Use up quickly after purchase.

Preparing Vegetables

Care must be taken during preparation to minimise the loss of vitamins and minerals, in particular vitamin C which is easily destroyed.

To reduce vitamin loss:

1. Prepare vegetables shortly before cooking.
2. Avoid peeling or scrape thinly.
3. Use a sharp knife.
4. Do not steep in water.

> An enzyme *oxidase* is released from the cell walls of fruit and vegetables when cut. Oxidase destroys vitamin C. Vitamin C is also destroyed or lost by exposure to oxygen, light, alkalis and certain metals, such as brass and copper, or by steeping in water.

Cooking Vegetables

Vegetables which are badly cooked lose colour, flavour and texture. Their mineral and vitamin content is greatly depleted. To avoid this:

1. Eat vegetables raw where possible.
2. Cook quickly in the least amount of water.
3. Cover with a lid.
4. Use cooking liquid for soups, sauces, stocks and gravies.
5. Do not use alkalis (e.g. bread soda) to soften greens.
6. Avoid using copper or brass saucepans.
7. Steaming, pressure cooking and microwave cooking are conservative methods of cooking vegetables (i.e. keep vitamin and mineral loss to a minimum).
8. Avoid over-cooking – serve vegetables 'al dente', i.e. a slightly crunchy texture.

Effects of Cooking on Vegetables and Fruit

1. Vegetables and fruit absorb water and swell.
2. Cellulose softens and starch grains burst so vegetables and fruit become more digestible.
3. Some loss of minerals and vitamins, which may be destroyed by high temperatures, or may leach into cooking liquid.
4. Enzymes are denatured and micro-organisms are destroyed.
5. Overcooking causes loss in colour, flavour and texture, and destroys vitamin C.

Processing of vegetables and fruit			
Method	**Suitable vegetables**	**Suitable fruit**	**Effects**
Freezing	Carrots Turnip Peas Sweetcorn Broccoli	Blackcurrants Apples Raspberries Rhubarb	• Enzymes and micro-organisms inactivated. • Change in texture due to blanching prior to freezing. • Little change in nutritive value, colour or flavour.
Canning	Peas Beans Carrots Corn	Pears Peaches Strawberries Mandarins	• Change in colour, flavour and texture. • Loss of vitamins and minerals due to heat involved. • Enzymes and micro-organisms destroyed. • Fruit canned in syrup has a higher sugar content. Vegetables canned in brine have a higher sodium content.
Dehydration	Peas Beans Lentils Potatoes	Raisins Sultanas Currants Figs	• Loss of water and water-soluble vitamins. • Enzymes and micro-organisms inactivated. • Change in texture. • Dried fruit is high in sugar.
Irradiation (See Page 184)	Onions Potatoes	Rhubarb Dried fruit	• Destroys enzymes and micro-organisms. • Prevents sprouting and decay and prolongs shelf-life. • Resembles fresh in terms of flavour and texture. • Some vitamin loss.

> Herbs, spices and vegetable seasonings are currently the only foods on the EU permitted list.

EU Grading of Vegetables and Fruit

All fruit and vegetables on sale in Ireland must be labelled and graded according to EU directives.

All produce must be:
- ► Sound (in good condition).
- ► Relatively clean – no excess soil.
- ► Free from chemicals, e.g. pesticides
- ► No evidence of disease/pests.
- ► Graded according to size.

► Classed according to quality into one of the following:
  Class extra: Very high-quality, unblemished produce.
  Class I: Good-quality produce – uniform size and shape with no defects.
  Class II: Marketable quality but with minor defects.
  Class III: Marketable but poorer quality. Defects in shape, size and colour.

> **Labelling must show:**
> * Quality/class
> * Packers name and address
> * Country of origin.

Legumes or Pulses

Legumes or pulses are the edible seeds of leguminous plants. Peas, beans and lentils which grow as seeds inside pods are referred to collectively as legumes or pulses. Usually only the seeds are eaten, but sometimes the pod is also edible as in green beans and mangetout peas.

Humus = chickpea paste/dip

Nutritive Value of Pulses

Protein: Pulses are a good source of low biological value protein. (Soya beans supply high biological value protein.)

Fat: Pulses are deficient in fat (except soya beans which contain 20% fat).

Carbohydrate: Pulses contain some starch and more fibre than any other type of vegetable.

Vitamins: Fresh and frozen peas and beans are a source of vitamin C, thiamine, riboflavin and niacin. Dried and tinned pulses lack vitamin C.

Minerals: Pulses contain small quantities of calcium and iron.

Water: Water content varies depending on type of pulse vegetables.

Storage of dried pulses	Preparation/Cooking
Dried pulses may be stored in airtight containers, out of direct sunlight for up to six months.	• Soak overnight to rehydrate and to shorten cooking time. • Rinse thoroughly. • Boil rapidly for ten minutes to destroy toxins on skins of some types of beans (e.g. kidney beans). • Simmer until soft (30–50 minutes).

Different types of pulses

Nuts

Nuts are defined as fruit consisting of a hard shell which surrounds an edible kernel. Peanuts, walnuts, brazil nuts, hazelnuts and almonds are popular examples.

Nuts are a source of iron and calcium

Nutritive Value of Nuts

Protein: Valuable source of low biological value protein.

Fat: Most nuts are high in polyunsaturated fats and are therefore high in kilocalories.

Carbohydrate: Good source of cellulose (especially peanuts and hazelnuts).

Vitamins: Small amounts of vitamin B.

Minerals: Source of iron and calcium.

Water: Low – generally around 5%.

Dietetic Value of Nuts

► Valuable source of protein in vegan diets.

► Add texture and variety to diet.

► Useful ingredient in a range of sweet and savoury dishes.

► Keep well.

► Available whole, chopped, flaked, ground.

Culinary Uses of Nuts

► Vegetarian main course dishes, e.g. casseroles, nut cutlets, stir-fries.

► Ingredient in biscuits, cakes, sweets.

► Salads, e.g. waldorf salad.

► Toppings, e.g. sprinkled on desserts.

► Snacks and packed lunches.

► Almond paste.

Fruit

Fruits, like vegetables, are valuable for their vitamin, mineral, anti-oxidant and fibre content. They also contribute colour, flavour and texture to the diet.

Fruits are a valuable source of vitiamins and minerals

Classification of fruit				
Citrus fruits	**Hard fruits**	**Stone fruits**	**Berries**	**Others**
Oranges	Apples	Plums	Strawberries	Bananas
Mandarins	Pears	Peaches	Blackberries	Kiwis
Lemons		Nectarines	Raspberries	Grapes
Limes		Cherries		Rhubarb
Grapefruit		Avocados		Melon

Average composition of fresh fruit					
Protein	**Fat**	**Carbohydrate**	**Vitamins**	**Minerals**	**Water**
0.5%	0%	5–10%	A, C	Calcium Iron	80–90%

Nutritive Value of Fruit

Protein: All fruit is deficient in protein.

Fat: Fruit, with the exception of avocados, is lacking in fat.

Carbohydrate: Fruit contains sugar, starch, cellulose and pectin in varying amounts. Sugar is present in all fruit in the forms of glucose, sucrose and fructose. Starch is present in under-ripe fruit such as bananas. Cellulose is present in the cell walls of fruit. Pears, apples, oranges and melons are particularly good sources of dietary fibre.

Health experts recommend that we include five or more portions of fruit and vegetables in the daily diet.

Vitamins: Fruit is a valuable source of vitamin C. Blackcurrants, strawberries, citrus fruit and kiwis are rich in vitamin C. Yellow, orange and red coloured fruit such as apricots and peaches are a good source of pro-vitamin A (beta-carotene).

Minerals: Small amounts of calcium and iron are present in fruit. Bananas are a useful source of potassium.

Water: All fruit contains a high percentage of water.

Best fruit sources of vitamin C	
Blackcurrants	200 mg
Strawberries	60 mg
Oranges	50 mg
Melon	50 mg
Grapefruit	40 mg

Citrus fruits are a good source of of vitamin C

Dietetic Value of Fruit

► A wide variety of fresh fruit is available throughout the year adding colour, flavour and texture to the diet.

► Fruit which is high in water and fibre and low in fat, is very useful in low kilocalorie, low cholesterol diets and high-fibre diets.

► The vitamin and minerals in fruit help to maintain health. The anti-oxidant properties of beta-carotene and vitamin C are particularly beneficial in helping to prevent disease.

► Fruit may be used (cooked/uncooked) as an ingredient in a wide range of sweet and savoury dishes.

► Fruit is a useful snack food. It is relatively cheap, requires little preparation and is a cool and refreshing alternative to less healthy snack foods.

Like vegetables, fruit will deteriorate quickly in terms of texture, flavour and nutritive value if it is incorrectly or badly handled during purchase, storage or preparation.

To maintain good quality

Buying fruit

► Buy when in season.

► Buy in usable quantities.

► Choose good quality, ripe fruit.

► Avoid fruit pre-packed in plastic.

► Fruit should be firm, correct colour with no discolouration or mould growth.

Storing fruit

► Store in a cool dark ventilated place.

► Use up quickly after purchasing.

► Remove from bags and store loosely.

► Remove any spoiled or damaged fruit from stored produce.

Preparing fruit

► Wash fruit before use to remove any traces of chemicals (see note).

► Eat raw where possible.

► Avoid peeling or peel thinly.

► Avoid steeping in water.

Effects of cooking (See Page 99)

Ripening of fruit

Fruit undergoes a natural process of growth, ripening and eventually decay. Ripening begins during growth. When the fruit is harvested ripening continues. Unripe fruit is unappealing and less palatable than ripe fruit.

A series of changes occurs during ripening:

- ▶ Enzymes convert starch to sugar (fructose) making the fruit sweet and juicy.

- ▶ Insoluble protopectin found in between the cell walls in fruit converts to soluble pectin.

- ▶ Ethylene gas which promotes ripening is produced in some fruit.

- ▶ The fruit develops its characteristic colour, flavour and odour.

> Note: Under-ripe fruit may be sprayed with ethylene gas. This speeds up the ripening process. The ripening process may also be delayed by spraying the fruit with a combination of oxygen and carbon dioxide. This facilitates transport and increases shelf-life.

Decay of fruit

Once ripe, fruit will only remain wholesome for a limited period of time before decay sets in. Softer fruits with thin skins tend to decay more readily than hard fruits with tougher skins, which can remain in good condition for months. Decay occurs as follows:

> Fruit, due to its high acidity and lack of protein, is not usually subject to bacterial growth.

- ▶ Fruit suffers water loss and shrinkage as a result of ageing during storage.

- ▶ Bruises and soft spots develop on badly handled hard fruit.

- ▶ Eventually decay occurs due to continued enzyme activity and attack of micro-organisms.

- ▶ Juices released onto the surface of fruit encourage mould and yeast growth, which break down and rot the fruit.

Processing of fruit (See Page **100)**

Organic Produce

Organically produced fruit and vegetables are cultivated without the use of artificial fertilisers or chemicals. Currently there are approximately 320 producers of organic fruit and vegetables in Ireland. Consumer demand for organic produce is on the increase with growing awareness of the possible risks associated with the over-use of chemical pesticides, growth promoters and preservatives.

Organic food

Organic produce is grown on a less intensive basis. Farming practices used must comply with organic standards for soil cultivation, fertilisers, pest, weed and disease control. Organic certification in Ireland can only be obtained from one of three organic certification organisations recognised by the Department of Agriculture, Fisheries and Food. They are:

- ▶ The Irish Organic Farmers and Growers Association

- ▶ Organic Trust Ltd.

- ▶ Demeter Standards (Biodynamic Agriculture Association)

Produce that carries symbols from any of these organisations indicates that it is good quality, organically-grown produce. Organic farming is more labour intensive with lower crop yields, therefore food produced organically tends to be more expensive.

Organic Trust symbol

Fats and Oils

Fats and oils (lipids) are obtained from plant and animal sources.

Classification of fats	
Animals (saturated fat)	**Plant (mainly unsaturated)**
Suet Dripping Lard Butter Eggs Cream Cheese **Polyunsaturated fat** Oily fish Fish liver oils, e.g. cod and halibut liver oil	• Vegetable oils, e.g. olive, corn and soya oils • Margarine • Nut oils, e.g. ground nut, almond and walnut oil, peanut butter • Seed oils, e.g. cottonseed, sunflower seed and rapeseed oil

Visible and invisible fats	
Visible fats	**Invisible fats**
Fats/oils which are clearly visible in food. Examples: butter, margarine, vegetable oil, meat fat.	Fats and oils which are not clearly visible because they are combined with other nutrients in food. Examples: lipids in cheese, eggs, milk, oily fish, nuts, pastry.

Average composition of fats and oils							
Fats	**Protein**	**Fat**	**Carbohydrate**	**Vitamins**	**Minerals**	**Water**	**Energy/kcal per 100 g**
Butter	0.5	82	0.5	A, D (trace)	Calcium	14	731
Lard	0	99.3	0	A (trace)	0	1	894
Margarine	0.2	81.5	0	A, D	Calcium	18	734
Salad/cooking oil	0	99.9	0	0	0	0.1	899
Low-fat spread	0	40.5	0	A, D (trace)	0	57	365

Nutritive Value of Fats and Oils

Protein: Butter and margarine contain traces of protein. Most fats and oils are deficient in protein.

Fat: Fat content varies from around 82% fat (butter) to 99.9% fat (salad and cooking oils). Low-fat margarines and dairy spreads contain approximately 40% fat.

Carbohydrate: Fats and oils are deficient in carbohydrate.

Vitamins: Butter and dairy spreads contain traces of the fat soluble vitamins A and D. Margarine is fortified with vitamins A and D.

Minerals: Traces of calcium are present in butter and margarine.

Water: Varies in proportion to fat content.

Dietetic Value of Fats and Oils/Contribution to the Diet

(See Biological Functions of Lipids and Energy Value of Lipids (**See Page** 25)

- ► Heat and energy.
- ► Protection of delicate organs.
- ► Supply essential fatty acids.
- ► Insulation/energy reserve.
- ► Source of fat-soluble vitamins.
- ► Add flavour to food.

Meat fats			
Suet:	Adipose tissue under skin and surrounding delicate organs in animals.	**Use:**	Ingredient in pastries, steamed puddings and mincemeat.
Lard:	Pig fat which has been rendered.	**Use:**	Pastry-making, frying.

Vegetable Oils

Vegetable oils are obtained from a range of plants which are rich in oil including:

- ▶ Cereals, e.g. maize.
- ▶ Seeds, e.g. sesame, sunflower, rapeseed.
- ▶ Olives.
- ▶ Nuts, e.g. coconuts, almonds, walnuts.
- ▶ Soya beans.

Coconut

Walnut

Soya beans

Processing

1. Sources of vegetable oil such as seeds (e.g. rapeseed, sesame seeds), nuts and cereals are cleaned, crushed and heated.
2. Oil is extracted and is refined to remove impurities.
3. It is bleached and filtered to produce a clear liquid and deodorised to remove odours.
4. It is packaged in plastic or glass bottles for sale.

Margarine

Margarine is a water-in-oil emulsion originally developed as a butter substitute. Manufacture is based on the principle of hydrogenation, i.e. the conversion of oil into solid fat by the addition of hydrogen.

Manufacture of margarine

1. **Oil extraction:** Oils from various sources are extracted and refined. Oils may come from vegetable sources (e.g. soya, sunflower, rapeseed); animal sources (e.g. beef fat) and marine sources (e.g. whale oil).
2. **Hydrogenation:** Hydrogen is forced through the oil. One molecule of hydrogen is absorbed by each double bond in the unsaturated fatty acids of the oil converting them to saturated fats.

   $$- CH = CH - + H_2 \rightarrow - CH_2 - CH_2 -$$

   Hydrogenation is carried out in the presence of a nickel catalyst which speeds up the hardening.
3. **Blending:** Different oils are blended together. Choice of oils depends on the desired properties of the final product in terms of plasticity, creaming shortening properties, low cholesterol etc.
4. **Other ingredients added:** Water or skimmed milk, salt, flavouring, colours are added and the product is fortified with vitamins A and D.
5. **Emulsification:** An emulsifying agent such as lecithin is added. The oil and the water-based ingredients are mixed together in a machine called a votator until they form an emulsion. This emulsion is cooled and kneaded until the texture is smooth.
6. **Packaging:** The margarine is weighed, wrapped and labelled.

Types of margarine	
Block margarine	**Soft margarines**
• Foil/waxed paper wrapping. • Made chiefly from vegetable oils, but may contain marine and animal oils. • High in saturated fat. **Uses:** Spreading, baking, frying.	• Packaged in plastic tubs. • Contain vegetable oil, whey/buttermilk and water. • High in saturated fat (slightly less than block margarine due to higher water content). **Uses:** Spreading, baking, frying.

Dairy Spreads

A wide range of dairy spreads and butters are available to the Irish consumer. These include:

▶ **Low-fat dairy spreads,** e.g. Dairygold Light, Avonmore Extra Light
These spreads contain approximately half the fat of butter (38–40%). Chief ingredients include water, vegetable oil and milk proteins. Emulsifiers, stabilisers, salt, colouring and vitamins A, D and sometimes E are also present. These dairy spreads are low in saturates and high in mono-unsaturated fatty acids. They are not suitable for baking or frying due to high water content.

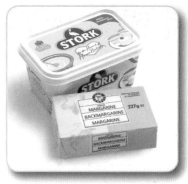

Block and soft margarine

▶ **Spreadable low-fat butters,** e.g. Connaught Gold
Ingredients include water, cream, milk protein and salt. Potassium sorbate (preservative) beta-carotenes and vitamins A, D and E are present. Spreadable butters contain approximately 7% protein and 40% fat, and are unsuitable for baking or frying.

Functional dairy spread

▶ **Functional dairy spreads,** e.g. Benecol, Flora Pro-Active
These spreads have been medically proven to reduce cholesterol levels in the body. Ingredients include sunflower oil, vegetable oil, buttermilk, plant stanol ester (12%), water and salt. Emulsifiers, stabilisers, carotene, vitamins A and D are also present. The plant sterols (stanol ester) prevents the absorption of cholesterol in the small intestine so that it is excreted from the body. There are no hydrogenated fatty acids and virtually no trans-fatty acids present. They can be used for spreading and are also suitable for baking or frying.

> Inclusion of plant stanol ester in the diet over a period of time will cause a gradual reduction in blood cholesterol levels, with a subsequent reduction in the risk of heart disease.

Storage of Fats and Oils

Rancidity or spoilage (See Page 23) may occur if fats or oils are incorrectly stored:

> Antioxidants added during manufacture to some fats and oils help to prevent rancidity (See Page 23).

▶ Store oils in a cool, dry, dark cupboard.
▶ Butter, margarine and dairy spreads should be stored in a fridge.
▶ Keep fats covered to prevent the absorption of surrounding flavours or odours.
▶ Observe best before date.

Culinary uses of fats and oils

1. Spreading and adding flavour to food, e.g. vegetables.
2. Frying: Vegetable oils are suitable for shallow and deep fat frying due to their high boiling points.
3. Shortening: the fat inhibits the formation of long protein strands in the pastry resulting in a short crumbly texture.
4. Creaming: Useful for baking, i.e. Madeira and all-in-one mixes.
5. Anti-staling: Fats improve the keeping quality and therefore the shelf-life of bread and cakes.
6. Emulsions: Fats and oils are capable of forming an emulsion with water, e.g. mayonnaise.

CONTENTS INCLUDE:

- ▶ Management and planning of meals
- ▶ Food preparation and cooking processes
- ▶ Selection, use and care of food preparation and cooking equipment

- ▶ Recipe balance and adaptation
- ▶ Aesthetic awareness of food
- ▶ Sensory analysis in the evaluation of food products and dishes

Meal Management and Planning (1.3.3)

Careful advance planning can contribute to the success and enjoyment of a meal. When planning meals there are many factors that should be taken into account.

1. **Nutrition:** All meals should be well balanced, containing all the nutrients in the correct proportion for the needs of the individual. Include three of the four food groups.

2. **Current dietary guidelines:** Reduce fat and salt; increase fibre and water (See Page 42).

3. **People for whom the meal is being prepared:** The requirements of a school-going child will differ from those of a manual worker **(see Chapter 2)**.

4. **Special diets:** e.g. coeliacs or vegetarians require certain modifications to be made when meal planning.

5. **Introduce variety:** Use different flavours, colours, textures, cooking methods and temperatures.

6. **Time:** The amount of time available to prepare, cook and serve the meal must be considered, e.g. a beef stew cannot be ready in one hour, a stir-fry might be a better choice.

7. **Knowledge and skills:** An experienced cook can afford to be more adventurous by choosing dishes that are more complicated.

8. **Budget:** Certain ingredients, e.g. fillet steak, are more expensive than others. Many tasty dishes can be produced using less expensive meat, e.g. minced beef.

9. **Availability of foods:** Foods are more available when in season. Certain ingredients may only be available in specialist shops, e.g. health food stores.

10. **Equipment available:** Equipment can speed up preparation and cooking times. Always read a recipe first to ensure that all necessary equipment is available.

Other factors to consider
- Number of guests.
- The occasion.
- Time of year.
- Type of meal, e.g. buffet, breakfast.

Food Preparation and Cooking Processes (1.3.4)

Food Preparation

Physical and chemical changes can occur while food is being prepared.

Physical Changes

- ▶ Increase in size – dried fruit and vegetables absorb water when soaked, e.g. prunes, dried peas or beans.
- ▶ Thickening, e.g. cream thickens when whipped as air becomes entrapped.
- ▶ Loss of nutritive value, e.g. water-soluble vitamins and some minerals leach into water if vegetables are steeped in water.
- ▶ Tenderising, e.g. meat is tenderised by mincing or pounding as fibres are broken up.

Chemical Changes

- ▶ Colour change, e.g. apples and bananas go brown as enzymes present react with the air (enzymatic browning).
- ▶ Nutrient loss, e.g. preparation of vegetables with blunt knives releases the enzyme oxidase which destroys vitamin C.
- ▶ Tenderising, e.g. commercial tenderisers contain enzymes which tenderise meat.
- ▶ Increase in size, e.g. yeast dough doubles in size as enzymes produce CO_2.

Reasons why food is cooked

1. To destroy pathogenic micro-organisms, thereby making food safer.
2. To destroy enzymes, thereby lengthening the shelf-life of food.
3. To make food more palatable and digestible, e.g. meat and starch.
4. To improve the appearance, e.g. red meat becomes an appetising brown colour.
5. To develop flavours, e.g. extractives are released from meat fibres, thereby improving the taste.
6. To stimulate the digestive juices.
7. To destroy naturally occurring toxins in particular foods, e.g. kidney beans.
8. To allow ingredients to be combined, e.g. a stew.

Cooking of Food

Physical and chemical changes occur while food is cooking.

Physical changes

- ▶ Tenderising, e.g. meat is more tender because collagen changes to gelatine.
- ▶ Texture change, e.g. cell walls in fruit and vegetables soften.
- ▶ Bacteria are destroyed because high temperatures kill micro-organisms.
- ▶ Nutrient loss, e.g. water-soluble vitamins and some minerals dissolve into cooking liquid.
- ▶ Foods solidify, e.g. because of protein coagulation, foods such as eggs harden.
- ▶ Thickening, e.g. heat causes starch grains to swell and burst and absorb liquids and flour thickens sauces.
- ▶ Shrinkage, e.g. meat becomes smaller because protein coagulates and shrinks.

Chemical changes
Non-enzymatic browning includes:

▶ *The Maillard reaction*: A colour change occurs as a result of a reaction between amino acids and carbohydrates. It is evident in roast potatoes and bread.

▶ *Caramelisation*: When sugar is heated above dissolving point it goes brown, e.g. in toffee-making.

▶ *Dextrinisation*: When heating starchy foods long starch chains break down into shorter chains called dextrins, e.g. toasted bread.

Dextrinisation causes bread to turn brown

Heat causes the protein in the egg to coagulate

Underlying Principles of Cooking Food

All cooking methods involve heat. The heat must be transferred from the heat source to the food. There are three methods of heat transfer: *conduction*, *convection* and *radiation*.

Conduction

Conduction is a method of heat transfer that involves the passing of heat from one molecule to the next. Conduction is used in boiling, stewing and frying. The ring of the cooker heats the pan. This in turn heats the liquid or fat. Then the food which is in the liquid or fat also gets hot. Saucepans and frying pans are good conductors of heat.

Convection

Convection involves the transfer of heat by currents in air or liquid. It is based on the principle that hot air or liquids rise when heated and fall on cooling. Convection is used in oven cooking, e.g. baking and in boiling (with conduction).

Radiation

Radiation involves the transmission of heat directly from the heat source to the food. Grilling involves radiation.

Most cooking methods involve more than one method of heat transfer. For example:

Boiling = conduction and convection

Grilling = radiation and conduction

Roasting = conduction and convection

Methods of cooking

Moist methods	Dry methods	Frying
Boiling	Baking	Dry frying
Stewing	Grilling	Shallow frying
Steaming	Roasting	Deep-fat frying
Poaching	Barbecuing	Stir-frying
Braising	*Microwave cooking* (See Page 116)	
Pressure cooking		

Conduction

Convection

Radiation

Choosing a method of cooking

Consider

1. Ingredients available.
2. Experience of cook.
3. Time available.
4. Equipment.
5. Desired result.
6. Fuel economy.
7. Retention of nutrients.

Possible advantages and disadvantages of cooking methods

Advantages	Disadvantages
• Needs little attention.	• Needs constant attention.
• Quick.	• Slow.
• Clean.	• Spatters grease.
• Food remains moist and juicy.	• Food may dry out.
• Vegetables and meat can be cooked together.	• Little flavour added.
• Cooking liquid may be used.	• Flavour, minerals and vitamins lost into the cooking liquid.
• Ideal for tough cuts of meat.	• Not suitable for tough cuts of meat – expensive.
• Only one pot used, saving fuel, space and washing-up.	• Takes time to prepare.
• Nourishing method as juices are served as part of the food.	• Lacks texture.
• Digestible method.	• Danger of overcooking.
• Little loss of nutrients.	• Not suitable for large cuts of meat.
• Little preparation required.	• Greasy, indigestible and high in calories.
• Attractive appearance and taste.	• Unsuitable for large numbers.
• Less greasy.	• Shrinkage occurs.

111

Methods of cooking

Boiling

Definition	Suitable foods
Boiling is cooking food by conduction and convection in bubbling liquid (100°C) in a covered saucepan on the hob. Simmering is cooking food in liquid at 90°C. **Guidelines** • Ensure that the liquid is bubbling at all times. • Vegetables require only a small amount of liquid in a tightly covered saucepan. • Use the cooking liquid to make soups, sauces and gravies. • Cook for the shortest possible period.	• Meat, e.g. bacon • Eggs • Pasta, rice • Vegetables, e.g. potatoes, cabbage, turnips, carrots  

Stewing

Definition	Suitable foods
Stewing is a slow method of cooking food by conduction and convection, using gentle heat in liquid in a covered container on a hob or in an oven. **Guidelines** • Bring it to the boil and then reduce the heat. • Maintain a temperature between 80° and 90°C to prevent meat from becoming tough and vegetables and fish from falling apart. • Cover to prevent the evaporation of liquid. • Pressure cookers greatly reduce stewing times.	• Tougher cuts of meat, e.g. mutton/shin beef and fish • Vegetables, e.g. potatoes, celery, onions, carrots • Fruit, e.g. rhubarb, apples, prunes  

Steaming

Definition	Suitable foods
Steaming is a slow method of cooking by the steam rising from boiling water. Food can be steamed: (a) Between two plates over a saucepan of boiling water. (b) In a covered bowl standing in a saucepan of boiling water. (c) In a steamer over a saucepan of boiling water. (d) On a trivet or raised separator in a pressure cooker. **Guidelines** • A tightly fitting lid must be used to prevent steam escaping. • Liquid must be boiling before putting food on to steam. • Food must not come in to contact with the water.	(a) Chicken or fish fillets (b) Plum pudding, canary pudding (c) Vegetables, e.g. potatoes, spinach (d) Vegetables   

Methods of cooking	
Poaching	
Definition	**Suitable foods**
Poaching is cooking food gently in liquid which is slightly below simmering, i.e. 85°C. Poaching can be done in a saucepan on the hob or in a casserole dish in the oven. **Guidelines** • The liquid should be barely moving, not bubbling. • Only suitable for delicate foods requiring gentle cooking.	• Fish • De-shelled eggs • Fruit, e.g. pears
Braising	
Definition	**Suitable foods**
Braising is cooking meat in a small amount of stock. Meat is placed on a base of diced sautéed vegetables, called a mirepoix. Braising combines stewing and steaming and is carried out in a covered saucepan on the hob. **Guidelines** • Use only enough stock to cover the vegetables. • Food may be browned under the grill or in a hot oven before serving.	• Root vegetables, e.g. onions, carrots • Chicken • Offal • Tougher cuts of meat e.g. beef, lamb

Pressure Cooking

Definition: Pressure cooking is a fast moist method of cooking food at high temperatures in a pressure cooker. It can be used for boiling, stewing or steaming.

Working principle
Water normally boils at 100°C. If pressure is increased it boils at a higher temperature. The pressure inside a pressure cooker is increased by preventing the steam from escaping thereby increasing the boiling temperature, which results in food cooking more quickly (**one-third** of normal cooking time).

Structure of a pressure cooker
A pressure cooker is a heavy gauge saucepan with a locking lid. A rubber gasket forms a seal between the saucepan and the lid. A raised separator basket keeps food out of the liquid (older pressure cookers had a trivet). A vent on the lid is sealed using weights or a dial to prevent steam from escaping.

Pressure cooker

Guidelines for pressure cooking

▶ Never overfill (see manufacturers instructions).

▶ Steam should be escaping in a steady stream before weights/pressure are applied.

▶ Time cooking accurately, as high temperatures may easily result in overcooking.

▶ Pressure must have reduced before attempting to remove the lid.

Weights/Pressure	Water boiling temperature
5 lbs (2.25 kg)/low	108°C
10 lbs (4.50 kg)/medium	115°C
15 lbs (6.75 kg)/high	122°C

Suitable foods/processes:
- Stocks and soups
- Vegetables, e.g. potatoes, pudding
- Jam-making
- Stews
- Bottling

Methods of cooking – continued

Baking

Definition	Suitable foods
Baking is a dry method of cooking food by convection currents in an oven. **Guidelines** • Make sure that the oven is fully preheated before cooking. • The steam produced in the oven helps to prevent food from drying out: tinfoil or greaseproof paper may also be used. • Avoid opening the oven door while baking breads and cakes.	• Bread, cakes, tarts, biscuits • Vegetables, e.g. potatoes and tomatoes • Fish fillets, cutlets, steaks • Desserts, e.g. apple crumble, Eve's pudding  

Grilling

Definition	Suitable foods
Grilling is a fast method of cooking food by radiant heat under a grill. **Guidelines** • Make sure that the grill is preheated. • The high heat seals the surface of the food preventing nutrient loss. • Use tongs to turn the food. • This method of cooking is only suitable for thin pieces of food.	• Steaks, chops, rashers, sausages, liver, kidney • Fish • Tomatoes  

Methods of cooking

Barbecuing

Definition	Suitable foods
Barbecuing is cooking food by radiant heat on a grid over burning charcoal. **See guidelines for grilling.**	• Meat, e.g. steaks, sausages • Fish, e.g. mackerel • Vegetables, e.g. potatoes and peppers

Roasting

Definition	Suitable foods
Roasting is cooking food in a little fat in a roasting tin in the oven. **Pot roasting** is cooking food in a little fat in a saucepan on the hob. **Spit roasting** is roasting food on a rotating spit under a grill or in an oven. **Guidelines** • Preheat the oven. • Cooking time of meat depends on weight. • Baste the food every 30 minutes. • Use the cooking juices to make gravy. **Quick roasting** 230°C/Gas 7 for 20 minutes, 190°C/Gas 5 for remainder of time. Suitable for tender meats. Beef 20 mins per 500 g + 20 mins Lamb 25 mins per 500 g + 20 mins Pork 30 mins per 500 g + 30 mins **Slow roasting** 175°C/Gas 4 for all of cooking times. More suitable for less tender cuts. Beef 35 mins per 500 g Lamb 35 mins per 500 g Pork 50 mins per 500 g	• Meats, e.g. beef, pork, chicken, turkey • Vegetables, e.g. potatoes, parsnips   

Frying

Definition	Suitable foods
Dry frying is cooking fatty foods by conduction in a frying pan on the hob. **Shallow frying** is cooking food in hot fat. **Deep-fat frying** is cooking food immersed in hot fat using a deep-fat fryer. **Guidelines** • When frying always preheat the fat/oil (wok is heated before oil is added). • Food can be coated before frying. • Turn food regularly using food tongs. • Drain food before serving. • Frying requires constant attention.	• Meat, e.g. rashers, sausages, chops, burgers, chicken joints • Fish, e.g. mackerel, fish fingers • Eggs • Onion rings, chips • Mushrooms • Doughnuts

Microwave Cooking

Microwave cooking is a very fast method of cooking food by conduction in a microwave oven. The heat is generated within the food by electromagnetic waves, which are radiated into the food. These waves cause the molecules within the food to vibrate creating heat (**See Page** 258).

Guidelines for using microwave ovens

▶ Time food accurately and follow the instructions. Cooking time is affected by:
  (a) Food composition, e.g. foods containing fat and sugar cook very quickly.
  (b) Size and shape, e.g. small thin pieces of food cook faster than large thick pieces.
  (c) Density – light open food, e.g. bread and cakes, cook faster than dense foods such as potatoes.
  (d) Temperature – the cooler the food at the beginning of the cooking time, the longer it will take to cook.
  (e) Amount of food – a larger quantity of food takes longer to cook.

▶ Cover food to prevent spatters and retain steam, thus cooking food faster and keeping it moist.

▶ Turn or stir food regularly to ensure even cooking.

▶ Pierce skins of potatoes, tomatoes and sausages to prevent bursting.

▶ Arrange food, e.g. potatoes in circles with thickest part facing outwards.

▶ Only use suitable containers – do not use metal in microwave ovens.

▶ Allow standing time after the microwave oven has been turned off. During this time food continues to cook as vibration continues until food begins to cool.

Suitable foods/cooking processes for microwave ovens:

▶ Defrosting food, e.g. meat, bread.

▶ Reheating food, e.g. lasagne, apple crumble.

▶ Cooking food – see recipe book supplied with microwave.

▶ Melting chocolate.

▶ Heating water and milk.

Microwave

Unsuitable foods/cooking processes in microwave ovens:

▶ Pastries.

▶ Meringues.

▶ Deep-fat frying – danger of fat overheating.

▶ Unsuitable for large quantities of food which would take too long to cook.

Effects of cooking

Moist methods

Effects on nutritive value	Effects on palatability
• Loss of vitamins B and C and some minerals into cooking liquid.	• Cellulose is softened and becomes more digestible. • Collagen changes to gelatine, making meat more digestible. • Mixing of flavours make food more appetising.

Dry methods

Effects on nutritive value	Effects on palatability
• Loss of vitamins B and C because of high temperature. • Grilling causes loss of fat. • Shrinkage causes meat juices to be squeezed out resulting in some loss of nutrients. • Use of juices to make gravy helps retain nutrients.	• Dry heat results in appetising crispy food. • Grilling results in loss of fat and therefore loss of some flavour. • Aromas produced during cooking add to the palatability of food.

Frying methods

Effects on nutritive value	Effects on palatability
• Generally fat is added. • Coating food adds nutrients, e.g. egg and breadcrumbs add protein and carbohydrate.	• Food becomes more greasy and therefore more difficult to digest. • Fried foods tend to be full of flavour.

Microwave cooking method

Effects on nutritive value	Effects on palatability
• Rapid cooking helps retain nutritive value.	• Foods cooked in a microwave remain soft and moist. • The use of a grill/crisper adds to the palatability of food.

Soups

Soups are a versatile food which may be used in a variety of ways in the diet including:

► A lunch dish with sandwiches or brown bread.

► A nourishing snack between meals.

► A course in a dinner menu.

Soup

Soups are included in the diet:

► To provide nourishment. Soups made from fresh ingredients are a source of vitamins, minerals and fibre and are free from artificial colours, flavours and preservatives.

► Soups provide warmth on cold days.

► They add variety to the diet.

► Soups vary greatly in consistency, texture and flavour. Some are served chilled, e.g. gazpacho, but most are served hot.

► Soups can stimulate appetite and aid digestion when used as a starter.

► Vegetable soups made without the addition of fat or thickening agents are useful to add bulk to low-cholesterol or slimming diets.

Stock

Stock is the liquid in which meat or fish bones, vegetables and herbs have been gently simmered over a period of time (2–3 hours). Stock is valued for its flavour rather than its food value. It is used as a flavoured base for soups and sauces.

> Stock may be stored in refrigerator for 2–4 days or may be frozen for 3 months.

Rules for stock-making

1. Use fresh, preferably raw ingredients.
2. Do not use starchy or fatty foods, milk or green vegetables, which would cause the stock to sour more readily.
3. Use a heavy-based saucepan or pressure cooker.
4. Simmer gently. Rapid boiling clouds the stock.
5. Skim stock frequently to remove scum and fat which would cause cloudiness.

Commercial stocks

A range of stocks in granule or cube form is available commercially. Flavours include beef, chicken, fish, vegetable and herbs, e.g. garlic and parsley. Commercial stocks are high in salt. Other ingredients include flour, hydrogenated vegetable oil, dehydrated chicken fat, concentrated vegetable extracts, lactose, starch, flavouring and colouring. Dried organic stocks are also available.

Stock cubes

Characteristics of well-made soup

▶ Good flavour – main ingredient(s) should predominate.

▶ Good colour, no film of grease.

▶ Correct texture and consistency.

▶ Well seasoned.

▶ Served very hot or chilled.

> Soup-making is speeded up by using a food processor in the preparation, and a pressure cooker in the cooking.

> The food value of a soup depends on the range and quality of the ingredients used.

Classification of soup	
Thick soups	**Thin soups**
• **Purées** are soups which are thickened by liquidising or sieving the cooked ingredients, e.g. carrot and orange soup. • **Thickened soups** are soups which are thickened with a liaison (thickening agent) such as cornflour or flour, e.g. mushroom soup.	• **Clear soups** are soups based on a well-flavoured, clarified stock, e.g. consommé. • **Broths** are clear soups which contain finely chopped meat or vegetables, e.g. mutton broth.

Liaisons/thickening agents

Liaisons are used to thicken soups and to hold ingredients in suspension. Examples of liaisons include: flour, cornflour, arrowroot, roux (equal amounts of fat and flour) or cereals such as pearl barley.

Preparation and cooking of soups

Guidelines:

► Use fresh, good-quality ingredients.

► Dice/finely chop ingredients to extract maximum flavour.

► Use fresh stock if possible.

► Simmer soup gently to develop flavour.

► Blend thickening agents well.

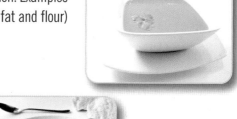

Different types of soup

Garnishing soup

> **Convenience soups**
> Soups are available dried, tinned and chilled in cartons.

Serving soups

Garnishes are used to make the soup look more attractive. Soup is often served with an accompaniment.

Garnishes

Soured/whipped cream

Yoghurt, crème fraîche

Chopped parsley, chives, mint

Finely grated orange or lemon rind

Croutons – fried cubes of bread

Grated cheese, e.g. Parmesan, Gruyère

Vegetables, e.g. julienne strips of carrot on consommé; cucumber slices on gazpacho

Crispy pieces of fried bacon/rashers

Accompaniments

Bread, e.g. brown soda bread, sage and onion bread, garlic bread, French bread

Rolls or dinner buns

Melba toast (very thin slices of toasted bread)

Sauces

A sauce is a flavoured liquid: it can be sweet or savoury.

> The food value of a sauce depends on the ingredients used.

- ► Sauces form part of a dish, e.g. chicken curry.
- ► Sauces can be used to coat food, e.g. cauliflower with cheese sauce.
- ► Sauces may also be served separately as an accompaniment, e.g. apple crumble and custard sauce.

Sauces are used to:

- ► Add flavour and variety.
- ► Complement texture.
- ► Moisten food.
- ► Counteract high fat content of some foods, e.g. apple sauce and pork.
- ► Improve appearance, add colour.
- ► Improve nutritive value.
- ► Bind ingredients together (panards).

Classification of sauces	
Sauces may be loosely classified as follows:	
Roux sauces:	White sauce, parsley sauce, béchamel sauce, brown sauce
Egg-based sauces:	Custards, hollandaise, mayonnaise
Sweet sauces:	Chocolate sauce, butterscotch sauce, caramel sauce
Fruit sauces:	Apple sauce, cranberry sauce, jam sauce, redcurrant sauce
Cold sauces:	Mint sauce, horseradish sauce, French dressing
Miscellaneous sauces:	Bread sauce, tomato sauce, black-bean sauce, barbecue sauce

Chocolate sauce

Apple sauce

Mint sauce

Preparation and cooking of sauces

Guidelines:

- ► Use correct proportions of ingredients.
- ► Follow recipe accurately.
- ► Ensure that sauce is of the correct consistency.
- ► Season well and taste before serving.
- ► Serve hot sauces hot, serve cold sauces chilled.

Tomato sauce

Roux sauces

A roux sauce consists of equal amounts of flour and fat and varying amounts of liquid.

Basic roux sauces				
Flour		**Fat**	**Liquid**	
Pouring	25 g	25 g	500 ml	
Stewing	25 g	25 g	375 ml	
Coating	25 g	25 g	250 ml	
Binding (panard)	25 g	25 g	125 ml	

Method

1. Melt the fat in a saucepan, add the flour and cook gently for 1 minute.
2. Remove from the heat and cool slightly.
3. Add the liquid gradually, stirring well between each addition.
4. Return to the heat and stir until sauce boils, then simmer gently for 5 minutes.
5. Adjust seasoning.

The liquid used in a white sauce is usually milk, in a brown sauce the roux is allowed to brown slightly before adding the liquid, which is usually brown stock.

A good roux sauce should:

▶ Be a good colour.

▶ Be the correct texture and consistency.

▶ Be grease-free, well cooked and well flavoured.

A sauce may be made before it is needed. Dampened greaseproof paper can be pressed down on the surface to prevent a skin forming. Reheat when required.

Variations on the basic white sauce

▶ **Parsley sauce:** Add 1 tablespoon of chopped parsley.

▶ **Cheese sauce:** Add 50 g grated cheese and $1/4$ teaspoon of mustard.

▶ **Mushroom sauce:** Add 50 g chopped sautéed mushrooms.

▶ **Béchamel sauce:** Milk and vegetables, e.g. – onion, carrot, celery – and flavourings such as bayleaf, peppercorns, salt are brought to the boil, then set aside to infuse for 30 minutes. The milk is strained and used to make a roux sauce.

Presentation/serving sauces

1. Sauces may be served hot/cold as part of a dish or separately in a sauce boat.
2. Sauces may be served over foods such as fish or poultry or they may be poured onto serving dish/plate with the food placed on top.
3. Sweet sauces, e.g. coulis or chocolate sauces, served with desserts can be used to great effect to make the dish attractive and aesthetically pleasing.

Pastry

Pastry is a mixture of flour, fat and water. Richer pastries may contain other ingredients such as egg yolk or sugar.

Ingredients for pastry-making	
Flour • Plain flour rather than self-raising is used in pastry-making. • Strong flour is suitable for richer pastries, e.g. flaky.	**Water** • Cold water is used for pastry. • Water should be added carefully until a stiff pastry is formed. • Lemon juice may be added to the water to soften the gluten, making pastry more elastic.
Fat • Butter, margarine and lard are commonly used in pastry-making. • Oil may be used in some all-in-one shortcrust pastry recipes. • Suet is used in suetcrust pastry.	**Raising agents** • Air is the only raising agent used in some pastry, e.g. shortcrust. • Self-raising flour may be used for suetcrust pastry or baking powder can be added. • Steam acts as a raising agent in choux pastry and in rich pastry.

Classification of pastry		
• Shortcrust pastry Variations: Cheese pastry, wholemeal pastry	• Apple tart • Bakewell tart • Quiche	
• Rich shortcrust pastry/ biscuit pastry/flan pastry	• Mince pies • Sweet or fruit flans • Lemon meringue pie	
• Rough puff pastry	• Sausage rolls • Steak and kidney pie • Cream horns	
• Puff pastry	• Vol-au-vents • Cream horns • Mille feuilles (iced jam and cream slices)	
• Flaky pastry	• Vol-au-vents • Eccles cakes (dried fruit and butter wrapped in pastry) • Cream horns	
• Choux pastry	• Éclairs • Profiteroles • Gougére (ring of choux pastry with a filling)	
• Suetcrust pastry	• Jam roly-poly • Steamed puddings • Dumplings	
• Filo pastry	• Apple strudel • Spring rolls • Baklava (sweet nut and pastry dish)	

Preparation

Good pastry has a crisp, light and flaky texture and is golden brown in colour. Best results are achieved by following some basic guidelines.

Rules for pastry-making

1. Weigh ingredients accurately.
2. All utensils and ingredients must be cold (exception hot pastries).
3. Introduce air by sieving flour, rubbing in fat, kneading, folding and lightly rolling pastry.
4. Mix with a knife and avoid over handling.
5. Roll lightly – avoid over-stretching pastry.
6. Some pastry needs to be refrigerated between rollings to prevent shrinkage in the oven.

Cooking

1. Bake pastry in a pre-heated hot oven for the first 10 minutes to allow starch grains to burst and absorb the melted fat.
2. Reduce heat for the remainder of the cooking time to allow food to cook through.
3. If the oven is too cool the pastry will be heavy and greasy; if the temperature is too high for too long the surface will burn while the inside remains uncooked.

> If a recipe states 250 g of pastry this refers to the amount of flour used. The other ingredients may need to be modified accordingly.

> **Baking blind**
> Baking blind means baking a pastry case without any filling. Prod the base with a fork, place greaseproof paper on the base and cover with a layer of rice or dried beans to prevent the pastry from rising. Bake for 15 minutes at 200°C. Remove paper and rice and bake for a further 5 minutes.

Baking blind

Raising Agents

Raising agents are used to aerate baked products, making them light and improving the texture and palatability.

Classification of raising agents

1. **Mechanical:** Air
2. **Chemical:** Bread soda and baking powder
3. **Biological:** Yeast

air   baking powder
"ABBY" – yeast
bread soda

> Air is used as a raising agent in sponge mixtures, pastry and batters.

Mechanical raising agents

Air is introduced mechanically/physically into a mixture by:

- ► Sieving dry ingredients, e.g. flour.
- ► Rubbing in fat.
- ► Creaming fat and sugar.
- ► Whisking eggs and sugar.
- ► Folding and rolling, e.g. rough puff pastry.
- ► Beating, e.g. batter.

> Steam is a raising agent in some types of pastry, e.g. choux.

Chemical raising agents

Chemical raising agents are based on the chemical reaction between an acid, an alkali and a liquid, resulting in the production of a gas (carbon dioxide).

acid + alkali + liquid = CO_2

Raising agents

Bread soda

Bread soda = <u>bicarbonate of soda (alkali)</u>. Used in soda bread, gingerbread.

> **Bread soda**
> Bicarbonate of soda + buttermilk/sour milk
> (alkali)　　　　　　　(acid + liquid) ⟹　CO_2

Self-raising flour contains baking powder.

Baking powder

Baking powder = <u>bicarbonate of soda (alkali)</u>, <u>cream of tartar (acid)</u> and <u>maize starch (to absorb any moisture and to prevent a reaction between the acid and alkali before use)</u>. Used in bread, cakes, scones, muffins and biscuits.

> **Baking powder**
> Bicarbonate of soda + cream of tartar + milk/water ⟹　CO_2
> (alkali)　　　　　　(acid)　　　　　(liquid)

The heat of the oven causes the <u>carbon dioxide</u> to <u>expand and rise</u>, pushing up the mixture. The heat of the oven also <u>sets the gluten</u>.

Biological raising agents

Baker's <u>yeast</u> (Saccharomyces cerevisiae) is used as a <u>raising agent</u>.

Types of yeast	
Fresh yeast	**Fast-action dried yeast**
• Soft, putty-like texture. • Compressed into blocks and crumbles easily. • Creamy colour and 'beery' smell. • Blend with liquid before adding to flour.	• Granules of dehydrated active yeast and improvers, e.g. ascorbic acid (vitamin C), that speed up fermentation. • Sold in pre-packed airtight sachets. • Added directly into flour.
Storage • Refrigerator 1–2 weeks. • Freezer 3 months.	**Storage** • Up to 1 year.

Different types of yeast

Rules for use of yeast

1. Use the <u>correct</u> amount of <u>good-quality</u> yeast.
2. Use <u>strong</u> flour.
3. <u>Weigh ingredients accurately</u>.
4. <u>Avoid adding too much salt/sugar (retards fermentation)</u>.
5. Ingredients and utensils should be <u>warm</u>.
6. Knead well to <u>develop gluten</u>.
7. Allow to <u>prove/rise</u> until <u>double its size</u>.
8. Bake in a <u>hot oven</u>.

Chorleywood process
This involves the addition of vitamin C to the yeast mixture. Vitamin C strengthens gluten, making it more elastic, and it speeds up fermentation.

Proving
Allowing the dough to expand and rise in warm, moist conditions.

Physical and chemical changes that occur during bread-baking

1. Gluten becomes elastic when moistened, allowing the dough to rise when the CO_2 expands.
2. Enzymes present in flour and yeast bring about fermentation in yeast cookery.
3. Fermentation, which occurs best at 26°C during proving, ceases when the oven temperature reaches 54°C because the yeast is killed.
4. Water, alcohol and some carbon dioxide escape from the mixture.
5. Starch grains absorb water, swell and gelatinise, causing the bread structure to become firmer.
6. Coagulation of gluten begins at 74°C and continues until baking is complete.
7. Maillard's reaction occurs between the carbohydrate and proteins present, contributing to the browning of the crust.
8. Surface starch changes to dextrin, forming a crust on the bread.

> **Note: If using a breadmaker follow the instructions accurately for best results.**

Fermentation of yeast

Fermentation is the breakdown of a substance by micro-organisms such as yeast and bacteria. During fermentation yeast feeds on sugar in warm, moist conditions to produce carbon dioxide, alcohol and energy.

$$\text{Yeast} + \underset{\text{glucose}}{C_6H_{12}O_6} + \text{moisture} + \text{warmth} \longrightarrow \underset{\substack{\text{carbon} \\ \text{dioxide}}}{2CO_2} + \underset{\text{alcohol}}{2C_2H_5OH} + \text{energy}$$

Fermentation is based on a series of enzymic reactions. The enzymes involved are present in flour and yeast. Diastase is the enzyme in flour; maltase, invertase and zymase are present in yeast.

Fermentation occurs in stages

1. Diastase in flour converts starch to maltose.
2. Maltase in yeast converts maltose to glucose.
3. Investase in yeast converts sucrose to glucose and fructose.
4. Zymase in yeast ferments the glucose and fructose to CO_2 and alcohol.

During proving the carbon dioxide expands and raises the dough. When placed in a hot oven the yeast is killed, the alcohol evaporates and the gluten sets. Surface starch changes to dextrin, forming a brown crust on the dough.

Food Preparation and Cooking Equipment

A growing range of electrical food preparation and cooking appliances is available to today's consumer.

Selection of appliances

1. ***Cost:*** Consider the price of the appliance and the running cost. Installation and maintenance costs may also be a factor.
2. ***Need:*** An appliance should only be purchased if it will be used on a regular basis. Otherwise it just takes up valuable kitchen space.

Cooker

3. **Quality:** Choose a reliable brand. Electrical appliances should carry a manufacturers guarantee. Also look for a safety symbol (See Page 273).

4. **Time saving:** Many food preparation appliances are time saving. However, time taken to assemble and also to dismantle and clean the appliance after use should be a consideration.

5. **Use:** Many modern appliances are multi-purpose. Extra features and attachments should not make an appliance too complicated for the consumer to use with ease.

6. **Energy saving:** All appliances should be environmentally friendly and should be energy efficient. Some larger appliances such as fridges are graded according to energy efficiency (See Page 282).

7. **Design:** Ultimately the style, design and colour of the appliance must appeal to the consumer and will have an impact on choice.

Food preparation appliances	Cooking equipment
Blenders	Cookers
Liquidisers	Kettles
Food mixers	Contact grills
Food processors	Sandwich toasters
Juice extractors	Bread makers
Carving knives	Microwave ovens
Fridges	Deep-fat fryers

Safe use of preparation and cooking equipment

▶ Manufacturers instructions should be read in detail prior to first use and should be adhered to at all times.

▶ Electrical appliances should never be overrun or overfilled.

▶ Attachments should be inserted correctly and should only be used for the purpose intended.

▶ Only use electrical appliances which are in good working order.

▶ Be careful to avoid contact between water and electrical equipment. Always disconnect after use.

▶ Extra care is necessary when using or cleaning appliances which have blades, e.g. liquidisers, blenders and carving knives.

Care of food preparation and cooking equipment

▶ Disconnect all equipment before cleaning.

▶ Dismantle the appliance and wash all detachable parts in warm, soapy water.

▶ Use a soft brush to remove any food particles.

▶ Rinse and dry thoroughly.

▶ Wipe the body of the appliance and flex with a damp cloth.

▶ Store appliances unassembled in a dry, ventilated cupboard.

Non-electrical food preparation equipment

Kitchen utensils may be made from a range of materials including plastic, wood, glass and metals such as tin and stainless steel.

General guidelines		
Selection	**Safe use**	**Care**
• Buy good-quality and well-designed equipment. • All materials should be non-toxic, durable and rust-proof. • Equipment should be safe to use, e.g. well-balanced, heat-resistant handles, etc. • Utensils should be easy to handle and comfortable to use. • Materials used should be stain resistant and easy to clean.	• Care should be take when using sharp equipment. • Handles should be firmly attached and heat resistant. • Handles of pots and pans should be turned inwards while on the cooker. • Avoid sudden changes of temperature when using pyrex and glass utensils.	• Wash the equipment in warm, soapy water. • Avoid harsh abrasives, steep and use a soft brush to remove baked on food. • Rinse thoroughly to remove traces of cleaning agents. • Do not use metal utensils on non-stick ware. • Wood and plastic utensils should not be subjected to direct heat or very high temperatures.

Recipe Balance and Adaptation

Many basic recipes can be modified without interfering with quality. Recipes may need to be adapted for a variety of reasons:

▶ To make the dish more nutritious in line with healthy-eating guidelines (See Page 42), e.g. to increase fibre.

▶ To increase or decrease quantity (most standard recipes cater for four adults).

▶ To accommodate individuals on special diets, e.g. coeliac.

▶ To economise by substituting expensive ingredients with less expensive ones, e.g. margarine instead of butter.

▶ To add variety to a basic recipe such as a stir-fry.

Adapting a recipe in accordance with healthy-eating guidelines

Quiche Lorraine
Ingredients
Pastry
150 g plain flour
pinch of salt
75 g margarine
squeeze of lemon juice
cold water

Filling
2 eggs
200 ml milk/cream
salt and pepper
25 g butter
75 g streaky bacon
100 g Cheddar/Gruyère cheese

Modified Ingredients
Pastry
75 g plain flour
75 g wholemeal flour
75 g Benecol/Flora pro-active
squeeze of lemon juice
cold water

Filling
2 eggs
200 ml low-fat milk
pepper
pinch of nutmeg
25 g polyunsaturated oil
50 g lean bacon
1 onion
50 g mushrooms
1 small tomato
25 g green pepper
75 g low-fat Cheddar cheese

The recipe was modified to make it more nutritious by:

Modifications	Healthy-eating guidelines
• Omitting the salt.	• Reduce salt.
• Using a functional dairy spread (suitable for baking) in the base. • Using a polyunsaturated oil to sauté filling ingredients. • Reducing the quantity of bacon and using lean instead of streaky rashers. • Using low-fat milk instead of cream. • Using low-fat cheese.	• Reduce fat/cholesterol.
• Using half wholemeal and half plain flour.	• Increase fibre.
• Introducing extra vegetables.	• Eat a variety of fresh foods. • Increase fruit and vegetables in the diet.

Some recipes may need to be modified to reduce sugar content.
Reduce sugar by:
► Reduce quantity or omit sugar from recipe (not always possible).
► Use fruit juice to sweeten food, e.g. fruit salads and flans.
► Add dried fruit such as raisins, dates, figs to baked food, e.g. fruit crumble, tarts.
► Use an artificial sweetener, e.g. Canderel.

Aesthetic Awareness of Food

All five senses are involved in the appreciation of food: sight, hearing, smell, taste and touch.

Appearance and Colour

▶ Sight is used to judge and evaluate the appearance and colour of food. The appearance of a food takes into account the size, shape and the surface appearance, together with the presentation of a food.

▶ The colour of a food relates to the actual colour, e.g. green peas, but also any colour change caused by cooking and any colour added by garnishing or decorating.

▶ Appearance and colour may often be used to determine the freshness of a food, e.g. wizened carrots/green oranges.

▶ Certain flavours are associated with certain colours, e.g. strawberry-red, lime-green.

▶ We expect certain foods to have a definite appearance and colour, e.g. mould is acceptable in Stilton cheese but not in bread; green is an appetising colour for many vegetables but never associated with meat.

▶ Colour may be lost in processing and replaced with artificial colours to make the food acceptable to the consumer, e.g. canned peas and smoked fish.

Appearance
Burnt
Clear/cloudy
Foamy
Fresh
Grained
Greasy
Moist
Opaque
Powdery
Shiny
Smooth
Thick
Translucent
Watery

Attractively presented buffet

Flavour

The flavour of food is determined by the senses: smell, taste and mouth feel.

Smell (olfactory sense)

► Smell is used to evaluate the aroma of food.

► The nasal cavity has tiny smell receptors. To detect a smell a substance must be in a gaseous state.

► Smell is very important in the enjoyment of food. It can make it more appetising and intensify the flavour.

► Smell may also be used to determine freshness, rancidity or a poisonous food.

Taste

► Taste is detected by the taste buds on the edges of the tongue.

► Substances must first be dissolved before they can be tasted (e.g. sugar crystals). The saliva dissolves and dilutes food, and it also controls the temperature of food.

► Processing of food may result in loss of flavour. Natural and artificial flavours are often used as a replacement. Monosodium glutamate is commonly used to enhance the flavour of processed foods.

Mouth feel

► The nerves in the skin of the mouth are stimulated by thermal or chemical reaction, e.g. coldness of ice-cream or the burning sensation of chilli.

► See mouth-feel descriptors under Texture below.

Texture

► The texture of food refers to its consistency as detected by sight and mouth feel.

► Variety of textures is important in meal planning, e.g. lasagne accompanied by a crisp green salad.

► Texture is very important in the appreciation of bland-flavoured foods, e.g. crisp lettuce.

► Mouth feel of many processed foods is improved by the addition of additives (physical conditioning agents).
  • Modified starch increases smoothness.
  • Humectants such as glycerol retain moistness (cakes).
  • Gums add creaminess (dried soups).

Sound

► Sound is detected by one's sense of hearing. It is perceived during preparation and consumption of a food.

► Certain sounds are associated with certain foods, e.g. sizzling of bacon, popping of corn, crunch of vegetables.

► Sound may be used to determine the freshness of a food, e.g. crunch of vegetables, crispiness of potato chips.

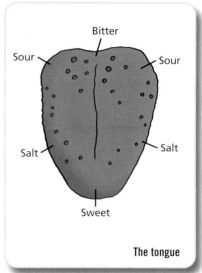

The tongue

Flavour/Taste	Smell
Acidic	Acidic
Bitter	Aromatic
Bland	Burnt
Creamy	Fresh
Piquant	Fruity
Salty	Pungent
Sharp	Roasted
Smoky	Smoky
Sour	Sour
Spicy	Spicy
Sweet	Strong
Tangy	
Tasteless	

Texture	Sound
Brittle	Bubbling
Chewy	Crackly
Coarse	Crunchy
Crunchy	Fizzy
Dry	Grating
Fibrous	Sizzling
Fizzy	Snapping
Flaky	
Grainy	
Greasy	
Lumpy	
Moist	
Mushy	
Powdery	
Smooth	
Soft	
Spongy	
Sticky	

Sensory Analysis

Sensory analysis is a scientific discipline used to evoke, measure, analyse and interpret reactions to those characteristics of foods and materials as they are perceived by the senses of sight, smell, taste, touch and hearing. The five senses – sight, smell, taste, touch and hearing – are involved in the sensory analysis of a food. The properties of the food being analysed are referred to as the ***organoleptic properties,*** i.e. flavour, texture, appearance, aroma and aftertaste. One or more senses is involved in assessing each property. For example, appearance is determined by sight, whereas flavour is determined by both smell and taste.

Uses of sensory analysis

► Developing new products.
► Evaluation of products and dishes.
► Testing of modified recipes.

Sensory-analysis tests

Three different types of tests are used in sensory analysis. Each type has a different aim.

1. **Preference tests:** To determine which product is preferred, or if a product is acceptable.
2. **Difference tests:** To determine if a difference can be detected
3. **Descriptive tests:** To rank the organoleptic properties of a product.

Controlling tests

In order to acquire accurate results, testing conditions must be strictly controlled.

(a) Timing of tests: It is preferable to carry out tests in mid-morning or mid-afternoon as tasters have better taste sensitivity at these times.
(b) Tasters must avoid consuming strongly flavoured foods for at least 30 minutes before tests.
(c) Temperature of all food samples must be the same.
(d) All samples should be equal in quantity.
(e) Rinsing water must be provided for each taster.
(f) Sample containers must be identical in colour, size and shape.
(g) Coding of samples must not appear to give any information about the tests, e.g. do not use 1, 2, 3 or A, B, C.
(h) Sequencing of samples must be well planned.

Sequencing options

1. Random – used for large number of samples.
2. Balanced – used in triangle test (see below) Here every possible order
   occurs an equal number of times, e.g. ○○△, ○△○, ○△△, △○○, △○△, △△○
   ○ = control and △ = sample).
3. Using a combination of random and balanced sequencing.

Preference Tests

(a) **Paired Preference Test:** Two samples are presented. Tester identifies which is preferred.

(b) **Hedonic Ranking Test:** One or more samples are ranked on a verbal scale (a 5, 7 or a 9 point), or on a facial scale. This test indicates the degree of liking a product.

Five-point verbal scale

1. Like a lot.
2. Like a little.
3. Neither like or dislike.
4. Dislike a little.
5. Dislike a lot.

.... Like a lot

.... Like a little

.... Neither like nor dislike

.... Dislike a little

.... Dislike a lot

Difference Tests

(a) **Simple Paired Test:** Two samples are presented. Tester states whether they are the same or different.

(b) **Paired Comparison Test:** Pairs of samples are presented. The tester states the difference between the samples (based on one characteristic per pair), e.g. which is sweeter, more salty, tougher. (May be used when comparing homemade and commercial products.)

(c) **Triangle Test:** Three samples are presented, two are identical. The taster identifies the sample that is different. (May be used to compare two brands of a product, or to distinguish slight difference, e.g. less sugar.)

Descriptive tests

(a) **Ranking Test** – used to sort a choice of foods (2–12 samples) in order. Foods may be ranked:
   (i) by preference (hedonic ranking) *or*
   (ii) according to a particular characteristic, e.g. colour, flavour or shape.

(b) **Rating Test** – used to find out:
   (i) how much a person likes or dislikes a food (hedonic rating scale) *or*
   (ii) to compare two or more foods for different aspects of quality using a 5, 7 or 9 point scale.

A descriptive test is an example of a grading or quality test.

Presentation of results

The results of all tests must be presented and analysed in order to determine what changes are required for a product.

Results may be presented on:

(a) A pie chart.

(b) A histogram.

(c) A star diagram.

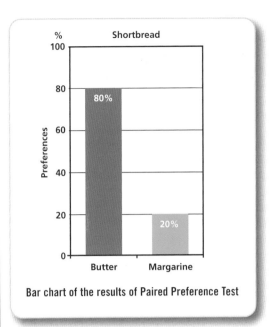

Bar chart of the results of Paired Preference Test

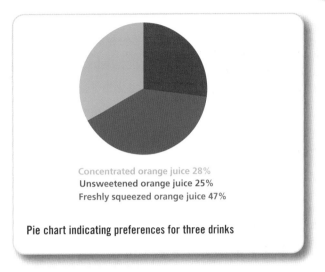

Concentrated orange juice 28%
Unsweetened orange juice 25%
Freshly squeezed orange juice 47%

Pie chart indicating preferences for three drinks

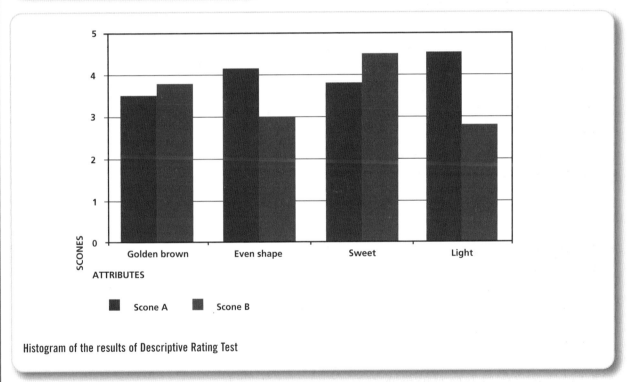

Histogram of the results of Descriptive Rating Test

Star diagrams

The star-diagram method of presenting results is often used by the food industry to illustrate the results of descriptive tests.

This form of presentation:

▶ Allows for easy comparison of products.

▶ Includes many qualities in one diagram.

▶ Enables a product profile to be written.

Using a star diagram

1. Draw a graph with eight lines (see example). The more lines, the more detailed the profile.
2. Label each line with a sensory descriptor of the food/product, e.g. sweet, crispy.
3. Each line of the graph is marked with a scale of 1 to 5.
4. As the food or product is tested, each descriptor is ranked from 0–5.
5. Each score is marked on the graph and joined by lines to form a star.

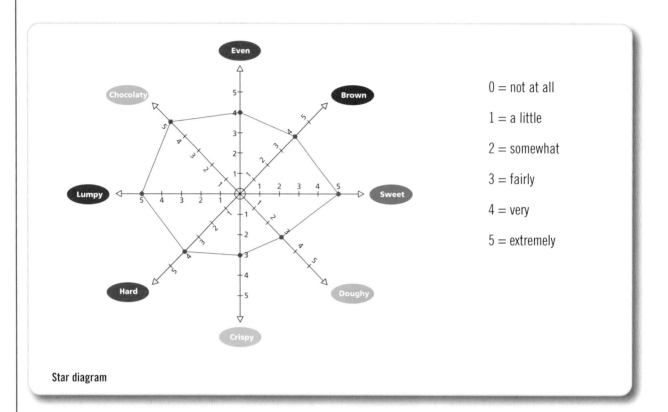

0 = not at all

1 = a little

2 = somewhat

3 = fairly

4 = very

5 = extremely

Star diagram

Profile of a Chocolate Chip Cookie

The chocolate chip cookie is fairly crispy and fairly doughy. It is extremely sweet and very brown. It is very even and extremely chocolaty. It is extremely lumpy and very hard.

Uses of descriptive/grading/quality tests

► Testing the shelf-life of a product.

► Quality control during production.

► In the development of new products.

► Dealing with consumer complaints.

CONTENTS INCLUDE:

▶ Analysis of the Irish diet in relation to current dietary guidelines

▶ Changes in food and eating patterns in the Irish diet from the beginning of the twentieth century

▶ Structure of the Irish food industry

▶ Role of small businesses

▶ Career opportunities in the food industry

The Irish Diet (1.2.4)

Diet-related information is gathered through national nutrition surveys. Slán (Survey of Lifestyle, Attitudes and Nutrition) was conducted in 1998, 2002 and 2007.

National Nutrition Surveillance Centre

The National Nutrition Surveillance Centre was set up in 1992. Its functions include:

▶ Collecting information on and examining trends in the Irish diet.

▶ Observing how those trends impact on health and advising health planners accordingly.

▶ Establishing how these trends relate to other socio-economic factors such as poverty.

Dietary Habits of the Irish Population

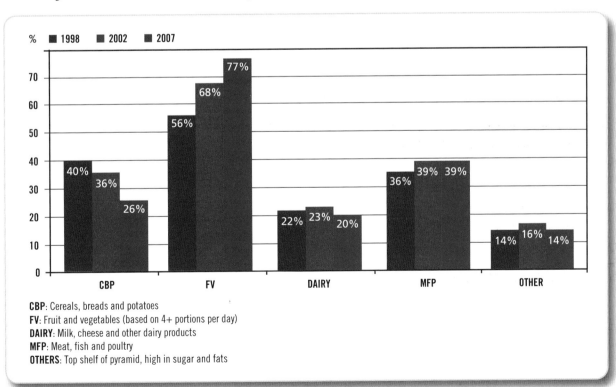

CBP: Cereals, breads and potatoes
FV: Fruit and vegetables (based on 4+ portions per day)
DAIRY: Milk, cheese and other dairy products
MFP: Meat, fish and poultry
OTHERS: Top shelf of pyramid, high in sugar and fats

The results from the Slán Survey above show the percentage of all respondents consuming the recommended number of servings from each shelf of the food pyramid

135

Irish dietary habits	
Cereals, bread and potatoes	There has been a reduction (10%) in the number of individuals consuming the recommended six or more daily servings of cereal, bread and potatoes.
Fruit and vegetables	Survey indicates an increase in the number of people consuming four or more portions of fruit and vegetables. (65% are consuming the recommended 5+ portions daily)
Milk, cheese and yoghurt	The survey shows a slight decrease in the consumption of dairy products.
Meat, fish and poultry	The percentage of people consuming the recommended number of portions of meat, fish and poultry has remained the same.
Others	The vast majority (86%) are consuming more than three items from this category per day.

Food Pyramid

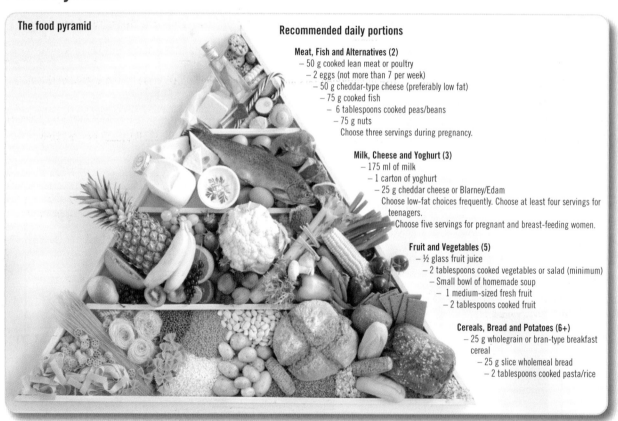

The food pyramid

Recommended daily portions

Meat, Fish and Alternatives (2)
– 50 g cooked lean meat or poultry
– 2 eggs (not more than 7 per week)
– 50 g cheddar-type cheese (preferably low fat)
– 75 g cooked fish
– 6 tablespoons cooked peas/beans
– 75 g nuts
Choose three servings during pregnancy.

Milk, Cheese and Yoghurt (3)
– 175 ml of milk
– 1 carton of yoghurt
– 25 g cheddar cheese or Blarney/Edam
Choose low-fat choices frequently. Choose at least four servings for teenagers.
Choose five servings for pregnant and breast-feeding women.

Fruit and Vegetables (5)
– ½ glass fruit juice
– 2 tablespoons cooked vegetables or salad (minimum)
– Small bowl of homemade soup
– 1 medium-sized fresh fruit
– 2 tablespoons cooked fruit

Cereals, Bread and Potatoes (6+)
– 25 g wholegrain or bran-type breakfast cereal
– 25 g slice wholemeal bread
– 2 tablespoons cooked pasta/rice

Findings Slán '07	
1. **Enjoy a variety of foods using the food pyramid as a guide.**	While Irish people eat a variety of foods from each food group, they do not always adhere to the recommended portion size or number of portions.
2. **Maintain a healthy weight.**	Only about one in three Irish adults maintain a healthy weight. 38% of Irish adults are classified as overweight. 23% are obese. Obesity levels have increased across all age groups including children. The high incidence of overweight and obesity in Ireland poses a major health risk.
3. **Eat five or more portions of fruit and vegetables every day.**	65% of those surveyed are consuming the recommended 5 portions of fruit and vegetables daily.
4. **Eat six or more servings of cereals, bread and potatoes every day.**	There was an overall decrease in the number of people consuming the recommended six or more portions from this food group.
5. **Eat fibre rich foods.**	Many Irish adults consume less than the daily recommended 25–35 g of fibre daily. A decline in consumption of complex carbohydrates has led to a decrease in fibre intake. However, the increasing fruit and vegetable intake should help to counteract this trend.
6. **Reduce intake of foods high in fat – particularly saturated fat.**	Use of saturated fats and the consumption of fried foods has decreased in recent years.
7. **Reduce salt intake.**	A large proportion of the population consumes more than the recommended limit of 6 g of salt per day.
8. **Reduce sugar intake.**	86% of those surveyed consume at least 3 servings per day from the top shelf of the pyramid which includes foods high in sugar, salt and fat and lacking in other nutrients. Ireland is one of the highest consumers of sugar in the EU.
9. **Keep alcohol within sensible limits. (Weekly limits: women 14 units, men 21 units.)**	8% of respondents consumed more than the weekly limits for alcohol. Health campaigns promote moderation in alcohol consumption to reduce the level of alcohol-related health problems.

Changes in Food and Eating Patterns in the Irish Diet from Beginning of the Twentieth Century

Changes in food and in eating patterns in the Irish diet from the beginning of the twentieth century have been influenced by a number of factors including:

▶ Developments in agricultural practices and food processing.

▶ Improvements in transport and services such as water and electricity.

▶ A growing range of new foods, culinary skills and cooking methods due to increased travel and migration.

▶ An increase in diet-related research leading to the availability of more nutritional information.

Irish obesity statistics		
SLÁN 2007		
Gender	Overweight	Obese
Men	44%	22%
Women	31%	23%
Total	38%	23%

Early 1900s

▶ During the early 1900s, potatoes, homemade bread and porridge continued to be staple foods in the Irish diet.

▶ Sugar consumption increased greatly in the early 1900s.

▶ Fat consumption increased in line with an increased consumption of meat (e.g. pig meat and poultry) and dairy products.

▶ World War I led to widespread unemployment and food shortages and to a marked increase in food prices.

▶ Deficiency diseases such as anaemia were common. *vitamin C- seasonal fruit*

▶ In the 1930s the Irish diet was still relatively low in fat and high in carbohydrate and there was little variety in the daily diet. Food was wholesome, plain and generally unprocessed.

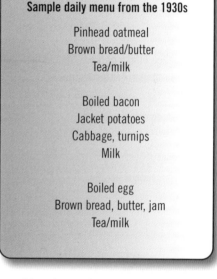

Sample daily menu from the 1930s

Pinhead oatmeal
Brown bread/butter
Tea/milk

Boiled bacon
Jacket potatoes
Cabbage, turnips
Milk

Boiled egg
Brown bread, butter, jam
Tea/milk

▶ Shop-bought foods were becoming more accessible and were often considered superior to homemade foods.

▶ World War II brought food shortages (e.g. white flour was scarce) and rationing of foods such as sugar and tea.

▶ By the middle of the century imported fruit, such as bananas and oranges, became more widely available.

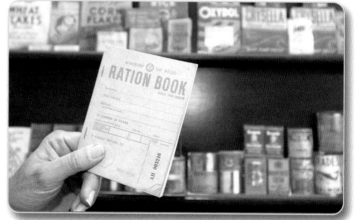

There was rationing during and after World War II

1950s onwards

▶ From the 1950s onwards white bread and tea became part of the Irish diet.

▶ While bacon and eggs became a popular dish among the middle classes, oatmeal and various corn and meal mixes were still widely consumed.

▶ Shop-bought foods were considered a glamorous novelty and there was a demand for packet and tinned produce such as corned beef and custard.

▶ Rural electrification in the 1950s and 1960s meant that perishables could be refrigerated.

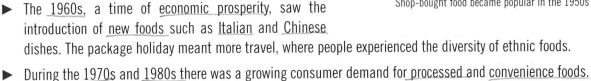
Shop-bought food became popular in the 1950s

▶ The 1960s, a time of economic prosperity, saw the introduction of new foods such as Italian and Chinese dishes. The package holiday meant more travel, where people experienced the diversity of ethnic foods.

▶ During the 1970s and 1980s there was a growing consumer demand for processed and convenience foods. Many of the first convenience foods were lacking in fibre, vitamins and minerals and often high in sugar, salt, saturated fat and additives.

▶ The intake of meat and dairy produce such as beef, pork, poultry, cheese and yoghurt increased greatly in the late 1900s while consumption of potatoes and bread decreased.

Comparison of average daily nutrient intake per capita per day 1948/2007			
1948		**2007**	
Energy/kcal:	3,105	Energy/kcal:	2,384
% Protein energy:	13	% Protein energy:	16
% Fat energy:	29	% Fat energy:	36
% Carbohydrate energy:	58	% Carbohydrate energy:	48

The higher energy intake in 1948 can probably be attributed to:
- More physical labour.
- Few labour saving devices.
- Less transport.
- Poor quality housing – lacking heating and insulation.

Early twenty-first century

▶ Eating patterns have changed due to lifestyle changes. Meals tend to be irregular, with the main meal in the evening and individual family members often eating at different times.

▶ A variety of foods and cooking methods are replacing more traditional ones. Rice, pasta and couscous are now commonly eaten instead of potatoes. A range of breads, for instance, ciabata and flavoured breads are readily available. Microwave foods and barbecued foods frequently form part of the diet.

▶ Irish eating patterns are influenced by other cultures through TV programmes, holidays abroad and the influx of immigrants from other countries into Ireland in recent times.

► People are <u>shopping</u> in a more <u>price-conscious way</u> and <u>competition</u> between <u>supermarkets</u> is currently <u>forcing down food prices.</u>

► People are more <u>nutritionally aware</u> and <u>shop for food</u> in a more <u>health conscious way.</u> They <u>demand</u> more detailed <u>information,</u> <u>read nutritional labels</u> and <u>compare</u> and <u>contrast</u> different <u>foods</u> in an effort to <u>follow healthy eating guidelines.</u>

► There is a <u>growing demand</u> for <u>processed foods,</u> such as <u>take-away foods</u> and convenience meals.

It is evident that some <u>progress</u> has been made <u>towards</u> <u>improving the Irish diet.</u> However, more <u>change</u> is <u>necessary</u> to <u>reduce the growing risk</u> posed by <u>diet-related conditions.</u>

Aspects of malnutrition currently identified					
	Low Fibre Intake	High Saturated Fat Intake	Low Iron Intake	Low Calcium Intake	Rising Level Of Obesity
Causes	• Insufficient <u>whole grains,</u> <u>fruit</u> and <u>vegetables.</u> • <u>Over-consumption</u> of <u>convenience foods.</u>	• Diet high in animal fats. • Over-consumption of fried foods, take-aways and processed foods.	• Diet lacking in iron rich foods. • Poor absorption.	• Not including 3 portions of dairy. • Insufficient Vitamin D. • Poor absorption.	(See Page 52).
Effects	• <u>Bowel disorders</u> (See Page 56).	• Weight gain, obesity, high cholesterol, coronary heart disease, diabetes.	(See Page 36).	• Osteoporosis, Osteomalacia, Dental Decay, Rickets.	(See Page 52).
Corrective measures	• Reduce refined carbohydrates. • Increase wholegrains, fruit, vegetables, nuts, seeds and water.	• Follow low cholesterol diet. • (See Page 54).	• Include haem iron/mix haem and non-haem sources. • Increase Vitamin C. • Avoid excess fibre phytates and oxalates.	• Eat 3 portions dairy daily. • Include Vitamin D and Vitamin C. • Avoid phytates, oxalates, excess fat, excess protein and caffeine.	(See Page 53).

The Irish Food Industry (1.3.1)

Regulation of the Irish food industry is primarily the responsibility of the Department of Agriculture, Fisheries and Food. However, other government departments and agencies also play a key role.

Irish food agencies and their functions	
Department of Agriculture/Fisheries and Food	• To develop all aspects of the agriculture, food, fisheries and forestry sectors. • To contribute to a vibrant rural and coastal economy. (See Page **194**)
Department of Health and Children	• To develop food safety policies and health promotion strategies which are implemented by the HSE. (See Page **194**)
The Food Safety Authority of Ireland (FSAI)	(See Page **193**)
An Bord Bia (Irish Food Board)	• To promote Irish food, drink and horticulture industries at home and abroad. • Provides quality insurance scheme for the meat, eggs and horticulture sectors.
An Bord Iascaigh Mhara (BIM)	• To promote and develop all aspects of Irish mariculture on national and international levels. • To encourage the public to consume more fish through advertising campaigns.
Teagasc	• To research into agriculture and food production (Food Research Centre). • To provide advice and training on all aspects of farming including environmentally friendly farming (Rural Environmental Protection Scheme, REPS).
Enterprise Ireland	• To promote the development of industry in Ireland by advising and supporting individuals who are setting up or expanding small businesses. • To provide equipment grants and start up finance for Irish food businesses.

Structure of the Irish Food Industry

► Agriculture and food are central to the Irish economy.

► The agri-food and drinks sector is valued at €8.16 billion.

► The Irish food industry is divided into nine key areas or sectors.

► It accounts for 10.5% of Ireland's exports and 8.2% of total employment.

Ireland is currently the 4th largest exporter of food and drink in Europe.

Source: Irishfoodmagazine.com

The Irish food industry is divided into nine key areas

1. Dairy and ingredients
2. Beef
3. Sheep and sheepmeat
4. Pig meat
5. Poultry
6. Seafood
7. Edible horticulture
8. Beverages
9. Prepared consumer foods

Major Food Exports

Ireland exports food and drinks to over 170 countries worldwide. Most of Ireland's food and drinks exports however go to countries within Europe.

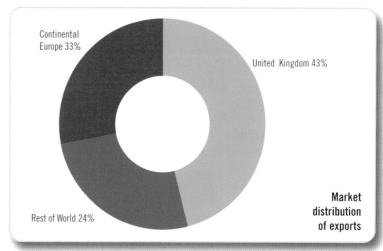

Continental Europe 33%
United Kingdom 43%
Rest of World 24%

Market distribution of exports

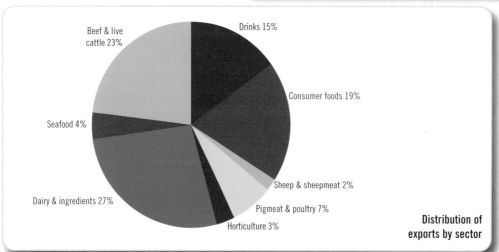

Beef & live cattle 23%
Drinks 15%
Consumer foods 19%
Sheep & sheepmeat 2%
Pigmeat & poultry 7%
Horticulture 3%
Dairy & ingredients 27%
Seafood 4%

Distribution of exports by sector

Major food exports		
Dairy and ingredients	27%	• Include butter, cheese, cream, milk powder, dairy spreads, yoghurt, ice cream and infant formula. • Over 80% of Irish dairy production is exported.
Beef & live cattle	23%	• Ireland is the largest net exporter of beef and beef products in the northern hemisphere. • 90% of Irish beef output is exported to over 60 countries worldwide.
Prepared consumer foods/ready meals	19%	• Ready meals, pizzas, luxury chocolate, confectionery, sauces, relishes and mustards. • Ireland exports a wide range of convenience foods.
Beverages	15%	• Whiskey, cream liqueurs, Guinness, beer, cider and water.
Pigmeat & poultry	7%	• Over half of Irish pigmeat production is exported primarily to the EU, US and Japan. The UK is the main market. • Ireland exports small quantities of chicken and ostrich meat. (Market share is slowly increasing.)
Seafood	4%	• Shellfish, i.e. oyster, mussels, fresh fish, i.e. salmon and trout, processed fish, i.e. smoked salmon.
Edible horticulture	3%	• Potatoes, soft fruit, root vegetables, mushrooms and cereals.
Sheep & sheepmeat	2%	• Irish lamb is exported mostly within the EU. France is the chief market.

LOVE
IRISH
FOOD

LoveIrishFood.ie
A new organisation of food producers. The aim is to safeguard the
future of food and drink manufacture in Ireland by
encouraging consumers to buy Irish-made food and drinks.

Major Food Imports

Ireland imports many of the same foods that it exports, e.g. meat, fish, dairy and cereals. Food is imported when Irish produce is out of season when there are insufficient home produced goods to meet consumer demands and for economic reasons. Other major imports are listed below.

Major food imports				
Type of food	**Country of origin**		**Type of food**	**Country of origin**
Fruit			**Miscellaneous**	
Melons	Spain		Tinned tomatoes	Italy
Oranges	Spain		Tea	Sri Lanka and Kenya
Pineapples	Costa Rica		Coffee	Colombia, Costa Rica and Kenya
Apples	South Africa			
Kiwi fruit	Chile		Dried pasta	Italy
Grapes	Mexico		Soya sauce	Hong Kong (China)
			Olive oil	Italy and Spain
			Bottled water	France
			Cheeses	France, Netherlands, Italy and Denmark
Vegetables				
Chilli peppers	Zambia		**Herbs**	
Green beans	Egypt		Coriander	Israel
Sugar snaps	Kenya		Basil	Israel
Spinach	Spain			
Peppers	Spain			

The role of small food businesses and home enterprises

► One of the fastest growing sectors in Ireland's agri-food industry is the area of ***speciality foods***.

► Speciality foods are foods mainly produced in limited quantities by small businesses or home enterprises using non-industrial traditional skills.

► Such foods include a growing range of products such as cheeses, chutneys, relishes, jams, sauces, breads, biscuits, smoked fish and cured meat products.

► Many small food businesses are based in rural areas where their role is:
  1. to produce good quality speciality foods.
  2. to provide employment for relatively small numbers of people.
  3. to promote the area in which they are based, since many of them export their produce.
  4. to enhance Ireland's reputation as a producer of high quality food and drink.

Investigation of a Local Food Industry

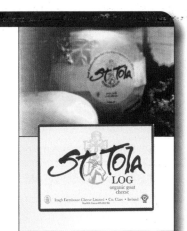

Company name: Inagh Farmhouse Cheese Ltd.
Address: Inagh, Co. Clare.
Product type:
A range of farmhouse cheeses including:
St. Tola Log – a gourmet soft goat cheese.
St. Tola Crottin – smooth, textured buttons of goat cheese.
St. Tola Hard Cheese – a hard cheddar type of goat cheese.
St. Tola Feta.
Brand name: St. Tola Organic Goat Cheese

When was the business set up?
2000

Why was it set up in Inagh?
To make alternative use of the family farm by transferring the business from a retired couple in the locality.

Who are the main suppliers?
The company's own goat herd supplies most of the milk. The remainder is sourced from a local organic supplier.

How many people are employed and what positions do they hold?
Four full-time: two farmers, two people in cheese production.
Two part-time: one on the farm and one in sales and administration.
Two seasonal: both in cheese production.

What type of aid or grant was/is available?
The Clare Enterprise Board Feasibility Grant. The Leader Capital Grant and the Bord Bia Marketing Grant.

What type of research was carried out?
We carried out a feasibility study. This was to see if there was room for expansion of the existing business, which we took over in 2000.

Have there been changes in any area since establishment?
We are now fully certified as organic. Our product range has increased. Our animal breeding programme has improved.

Where do you market your product?
Locally and nationally and in Britain and Germany. The products are marketed mainly in the hotel and restaurant sector and speciality food shops and high quality supermarkets, e.g. *Superquinn*, Ireland, and *Fresh and Wild*, London.

What packaging style is used?
We use environmentally friendly packaging made from recyclable material: cheese paper and cardboard boxes.

How do you market/promote your product?
By attending trade fairs and exhibitions. By entering cheese competitions. By doing promotions with our wholesale customers. Through in-store tastings and dairy promotions with restaurant and hotel associations.

What type of quality control is used?
HACCP (Hazard Analysis Critical Control Point) system.

Approximate annual turnover?
The approximate annual turnover is €450,000.

Have you received any awards?
St. Tola Organic Goat Cheese has won several awards including
- British Cheese Awards – gold and silver
- Irish Farmhouse Cheese Competition – First Prize
- Great Taste Awards – gold and international awards.

Career Opportunities in Food and Related Industries

A wide variety of certificate, diploma and degree courses are available in all areas of food and agriculture including:

Teagasc/Agricultural Colleges

▶ Farm management courses

▶ Horticultural courses

Universities

▶ Degree courses in human nutrition, dietetics, food science, food technology, food business.

Institutes of Technology (ITs)

▶ Certificate and diploma courses in food science and technology, nutrition and dietetics, hotel management and catering.

▶ Fáilte Ireland courses.

Teacher Training College (St Angela's, Sligo)

▶ Home Economics (degree course)

Fáilte Ireland– run in ITs and Fáilte Ireland Centres

▶ Training for jobs such as chef, waiter, receptionist, and for work in hospitality tourism and hotel management.

Career openings in food and related industries	
Areas of work	**Examples of career opportunities**
Supplying/Producer	Farmer, fisherman, horticulturist, butcher/abattoir worker, baker/confectioner/cheesemaker
Promotion	Marketing, advertising organisations, e.g. Bord Bia, BIM
Retailing	Retailer, demonstrator (food promotions), distributor (in shops)
Catering	Chef, waiter/waitress, restaurateur.
Food technology	Food technologist, product developer, food technician
Dietetics/nutrition research	Nutritionist, dietician, food technician
Food safety	Environmental health officer, microbiologist, public analyst

CONTENTS INCLUDE:

▶ Identification of the range of processed/convenience foods available

▶ Packaging of food including evaluation of materials used and their impact on the environment

▶ Evaluation of food labelling as a source of consumer information

▶ Study of food additives including legal control

▶ Identification of contaminants that may enter the food chain

Processed Foods

Processed foods are foods that have been altered in some way by the manufacturers. The degree of processing varies greatly. Most of the foods we use have been processed to some extent. The range of processed foods includes milk, cheese, yoghurt, ice cream, butter, margarine, dairy spreads, oils, flour, pasta, rice, breads, cakes, biscuits, breakfast cereals and convenience foods.

Reasons Why Food Is Processed

Food is processed:

1. To extend the shelf-life, e.g. pasteurisation of milk.

2. To make food safe to eat, e.g. freezing fish for long term storage.

3. To create new food products, e.g. cheese, yoghurt.

4. To ensure variety and choice throughout the year, e.g. canned and frozen varieties of out of season foods.

5. To allow for the **fortification** of foods, e.g. calcium added to flour (See Page 157) .

6. To save time, energy and fuel, e.g. convenience foods.

Processed foods

Convenience Foods

Advantages of convenience foods

► Save time, labour and fuel.

► Require little cooking skill.

► Little or no waste.

► Many are fortified with minerals and vitamins.

► Easy to store.

► Wide variety available.

Disadvantages of convenience foods

► More expensive.

► Many contain additives.

► Often low in fibre.

► High in salt, sugar and fat.

► Inferior in taste, colour and texture when compared with fresh version.

Classification of convenience foods	
Frozen foods	Chicken, fish, vegetables, fruit, meals, e.g. chicken curry.
Dried foods	Milk, sauces, soups, potatoes, cake mixes, TVP.
Canned/bottled foods	Fish, vegetables, soup, fruit, jams, pickles.
Cook-chill foods	Fresh pastas, cartons of soup and sauces, portions of quiche, lasagne (ready meals).
Instant foods	Prepared salads, sausage rolls, breakfast rolls, pizzas, take-aways, e.g. burgers and chips.

Using Convenience Foods

► Always follow the directions on the pack.

► Use them in combination with fresh foods.

► Make use of convenience foods in complicated dishes, e.g. use frozen pastry for Bakewell tarts.

Functional Foods

The term 'functional food' is used to describe any food that contains an added ingredient that gives the food health promoting properties beyond its nutritive value.

Functional foods			
Ingredients	**Examples**	**Claimed health benefits**	
Plant sterols (stanol ester)	Benecol, Flora Pro-Active	Reduces risk of cardiovascular disease.	
Probiotics	Bio-yoghurt	Improves the functioning of the digestive system.	
Omega-3 fatty acids	Milk	Reduces risk of heart disease and cancer.	
Folic acid	Bread and breakfast cereal	Reduces risk of neural tube defects, e.g. Spina Bifida in newborn babies	

Profile of three types of processed foods

1. ***A food that undergoes extensive processing:***, e.g. milling of wheat to produce flour (See Page **94**).

2. ***A food that is processed to extend shelf-life:***, e.g. processing of milk (See Page **81**).

3. ***Added value foods:*** result from the processing of raw materials to produce a product of higher economic value, e.g. processing milk to produce cheese (See Page **87**), the production of margarine (See Page **106**) or the production of cook-chill foods.

Cook-chill Foods

All cook-chill meals are prepared from a recipe, e.g. lasagne (See Page **200**) and processed as follows:

Cook-pasteurise-chill method

▶ The cooked portion of food is put into a container.

▶ A partial vacuum is formed and the container is heat sealed.

▶ It is then pasteurised at 80°C for 10 minutes.

▶ The food is then rapidly chilled to 3°C and stored at temperatures between -1°C and 3°C.

▶ Food is transported in cold conditions and stored in chilled cabinets.

▶ Shelf-life is between 2–3 weeks.

Genetically Modified Foods

▶ Genetically modified foods are foods that have had their DNA altered. The DNA in the genes of plants and animals is responsible for the characteristics of the plant or animal, e.g. size, colour or speed of ripening.

▶ By isolating the gene responsible for a particular characteristic, it can be introduced into another animal or crop, e.g. lobster genes can be transferred into a tomato to intensify the redness of the tomato.

▶ Rigorous testing is carried out before any genetically modified food receives approval. There is very restricted use of modified food crops in Ireland. No GM whole foods have been approved. However, processed foods sold on the Irish market include various types of GM ingredients, e.g. GM maize starch, GM potato starch, GM soya.

▶ EU regulations state that manufacturers must label any food where the GM ingredient constitutes more than 0.9% of total ingredients.

GM labelled food

The **E.F.S.A.** = European Food Safety Authority.
The **F.S.A.I.** = Food Safety Authority of Ireland.
Monitor GM foods on the Irish market.

Packaging

Functions of packaging

Food products are packaged for the following reasons:

1. To protect the product ensuring that it reaches the consumer in optimum condition.
2. For convenience in the transport, storage and selling of the product.
3. To preserve food, thereby preventing waste and food poisoning.
4. For marketing purposes – to make goods more attractive to the consumer.
5. To carry information about the product, i.e. food labelling.

Properties of food packaging	
• Safe/non-toxic	• Easy to open and reseal if necessary
• Reasonably strong	• Attractive
• Hygienic	• Economical
• Biodegradable (capable of decomposing) or recyclable	• Odourless

Materials used in packaging	
Materials used	**Examples of use**
Metals (aluminium, tin, plated steel) Food cans Aluminium cans Foil containers Aluminium foil wrap Foil bags Aerosols	Fruit, fish Soft drinks Take-aways, Ready meals Frozen vegetables Whipped cream
Glass Jars Bottles	Mayonnaise, sauces Soft drinks, olive oil
Paper Plain paper, Waxed paper, Waxed/laminated cardboard, cartons Greaseproof paper Cardboard	Sugar, flour Bread Milk, orange juice Sausage rolls Egg boxes, cereal boxes
Plastics Polythene bags Plastic cartons/boxes PET (polyethylene terephthalate) bottles Polystyrene	Dried pasta, seeds Yoghurt, dairy spreads Soft drinks Take-aways, e.g. pizza

Suitability for Purpose

Metal

Advantages

- Protects food totally, i.e. impervious to moisture, gases and micro-organisms.
- Tins and cans are easy to stack and store.
- Suitable for heat treatment.
- Tins are lacquered to prevent reaction with the food.

Disadvantages

- Metal is heavy, increasing transport costs.
- Metal is expensive to produce.

> 100 million aluminium cans are sold in Ireland each year. Recycling aluminium saves 95% of the energy used to produce cans from raw materials.

Impact on Environment

- Limited and non-renewable resource.
- Non-biodegradable but recyclable.
- Recycling saves raw materials and energy and reduces the impact production has on the environment in terms of air pollution and use of clean water.

Glass

Advantages

- Hygienic and protects food very well.
- Rigid containers which are available in a variety of colours, shapes and sizes.
- Transparent and resealable.
- Easy to stack.
- Suitable for heat treatment.
- Does not react with food.
  can be recycled

Disadvantages

- Heavy to transport.
- Breakable.
- Costly to produce.

Impact on Environment

- Reusable and 100% recyclable.
- Numerous bottle banks throughout the country.
- May be recycled many times with no loss in quality.
- Recycling saves energy, raw materials and reduces production and landfill costs.
- Careless disposal can be dangerous

> Recycling one glass bottle saves enough energy to power a computer for 25 minutes.

> Every home in Ireland produces on average one tonne of domestic waste every year, half of which could be effectively recycled. One-third of this wastage is packaging.
>
> Careless disposal of even a small proportion of packaging materials contributes significantly to environmental pollution and litter. The growing waste problem also increases the need for costly landfill sites.

Paper

Advantages
- Biodegradable.
- Low cost.
- Easy to open.
- Lightweight.
- May be printed upon.
- Waxed paper is waterproof and may be heat sealed.
- Waxed cartons are suitable for packaging sterilised foods.

Disadvantages
- Plain paper – not suitable for all foods.
- Does not reseal well.
- Not very strong and disintegrates when wet.

Impact on Environment
- Biodegradable and recyclable.
- Recycling conserves trees, saves energy and reduces disposal costs.

17 trees must be felled to produce one tonne of paper.

Plastic

Advantages
- Strong and moisture proof.
- Convenient and easy to handle.
- Lightweight and flexible.
- Heat sealable.
- Relatively low cost. *? price of oil*
- Suitable for frozen foods.
- Variety of weights and thicknesses.
- May be printed upon.

Disadvantages
- Evidence that some plastics may contaminate foodstuffs with carcinogenic substances when used in microwave cooking.

Impact on Environment
- Non-biodegradable and can persist in the environment for many years.
- Made from crude oil which is a limited and non-renewable resource.
- Only limited amount recycled in Ireland because procedure is costly and time consuming and facilities are limited.
- Plastic packaging (as litter) is a major environmental hazard.

Millions of PET bottles are sold in Ireland each year. PET bottles can be recycled as fibre for the textile industry.

Consumer Responsibility

To reduce the impact of packaging materials on the environment consumers should:

► Reduce, reuse and recycle where possible.

► Avoid buying products with excess packaging.

► Buy loose rather than pre-packed fruit and vegetables.

► Compact cartons and plastic bottles before placing in recycling bin.

► Compost organic packaging, e.g. cardboard.

► Buy products in recycled packaging.

The plastic bag levy introduced in March 2002 discourages the use of plastic bags, estimated to be 1.26 billion bags per year.

Recycle = to convert waste to reusable material.

Food Labelling

Functions

1. To inform the consumer about the nature and properties of pre-packed foods.
2. To provide the consumer with information on areas such as genetically modified ingredients, saturated fats and food allergies.
3. To provide instructions for safe storage, use and cooking of food.
4. To enable the consumer to make informed food choices.

Food labelling regulations

All pre-packed foodstuffs for sale in Ireland must adhere to EU legislation with regard to food labelling. The Food Safety Authority of Ireland (FSAI) has overall responsibility for enforcement of these regulations in Ireland.

Labelling information must be:

▶ Clear, unambiguous and not misleading.

▶ Indelible, clearly legible.

▶ Easy to see, i.e. not obscured in any way.

▶ Written in English (includes any food imports sold in Ireland).

The essential information that must be present on the packaging of pre-packed foods is as follows:

1. Name under which the product is sold.
2. List of ingredients in descending order of weight (additives including flavourings and sweeteners must be included).
3. Quantity of certain ingredients, e.g. quantity of beef in beef burgers.
4. Net quantity in metric units, i.e. kilograms/litres.
5. Date of minimum durability, i.e. date until which a food remains wholesome (when correctly stored).

   The 'best before date' is used on non-perishable foods with a long shelf-life.

   The use by date is used on highly perishable foods, which are likely after a short period of time to constitute a danger to health.
6. Any special storage conditions or instructions for use.
7. Name and address of manufacturer, packager or seller within the EU.
8. Place of origin of food where its absence might mislead the consumer.
9. Instructions for use where necessary.
10. Beverages with more than 1.2% alcohol by volume must display alcoholic strength.
11. Indication if the food has been subjected to irradiation (See Page 184) contains genetically modified ingredients or has been packaged in a modified atmosphere.

Irradiation symbol

Genetically modified ingredient

Modified atmosphere packaging (MAP)
- ► Some foods such as raw and cooked meats are packed in a modified atmosphere.
- ► These foods must be labelled "packaged in a protective atmosphere".
- ► This means that the composition of the gas in the package is different from that of air.
- ► Gases such as CO_2, O_2 and N_2 (inert gas) are used to inhibit microbial growth and prolong shelf-life of food.
- ► Foods packed in a modified atmosphere must be refrigerated and should be eaten within 48 hours of opening.

Claims on food
1. A claim is a declaration regarding the properties of a food stuff.
2. Claims must not be false or misleading.
3. A claim on the label of a fortified food must be substantiated by the manufacturer.
4. If a nutritional claim is made about a particular ingredient in a food product, the quantity of that ingredient must be stated on the label, e.g. low fat butter – 39% fat.
5. Medicinal claims that a food has a property for treating, preventing or curing human disease are prohibited.

Nutritional labelling
Nutritional labelling supplies the consumer with information regarding the energy value and the nutrient content of the food. Amounts of protein, fat, saturates, carbohydrate, sugar, fibre and sodium may be indicated.

Nutrient content must be stated per 100 g/100 ml to allow for comparison between products. Nutrient content per serving may also be stated.

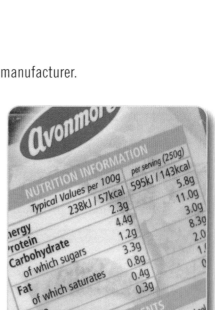
Nutritional labelling

Non-packaged food labelling
The following information must be displayed on or near the food:
- ► Name of food.
- ► Country of origin.
- ► Class.
- ► Variety.
- ► Unit price/price per kilogram.

Price labelling
By law the price must be displayed on the foodstuff or on a shelf or notice nearby. Pre-packed foods of varying weights, e.g. rashers, cheese, must show the unit price and price per pack. The unit price must be clearly displayed near fruit and vegetables sold loosely. Itemised receipts showing product, brand and price are a useful source of consumer information when comparing shopping costs.

Unit pricing

Food Additives (1.3.6)

Definition

Additives are substances intentionally added to foods to improve the colour, flavour, keeping qualities, nutritive value or physical condition (texture) of the food.

Classification

• Colourings	• Preservatives
• Flavourings	• Nutritive additives
• Sweeteners	• Physical conditioning agents

Colourings (E100–199)

Classification	Examples	Use	Origin	Functions
Natural	Chlorophyll – green	Tinned vegetables	Plants	• To improve appearance.
	Carotene– yellow, orange	Soft drinks	Carrots	• To replace colour lost in processing.
	Cochineal – red	Red colouring jellies	Cactus insects	
	Caramel – brown	Gravies, sauces	Heated carbohydrates	• To satisfy consumer expectations, e.g. orange juice should be orange.
Synthetic	Tartrazine – yellow	Soft drinks	Coal tar	
	Red (E128)	Sausages	Coal tar	
	Green (E142)	Sweets	Coal tar	• To give colour to foods which would be colourless, e.g. ice pops.
	Amaranth – purple red	Blackcurrant products	Coal tar	

Note: Colourings are not permitted in fresh meat, fish, poultry, fruit, vegetables or in baby food.

Flavourings

Classification	Examples	Use	Origin	Functions
Natural	Sugar	Jams, breakfast cereals, tinned beans, in cooking	Sugar cane, beet	• To add flavour to food.
	Salt	Cheese, butter, meat products, in cooking	Sodium chloride	
	Spices	Meat products, sauces, in cooking	Roots and seeds of plants	
	Herbs	In cooking, stock cubes	Leaves of plants	• To replace flavours lost in processing.
Artificial	Esters, e.g. Ethyl acetate / Amyl acetate	Rum flavouring / Pear flavouring	Chemical reactions resulting from heating acetic acid and ethyl alcohol	
	Aldehydes, e.g. Benzaldehyde (almond/ cherry flavour) / Maltol (freshly baked smell)	Sweets, essence / Bread and cakes	(as above) / Tree bark	
Flavour enhancers (E600–699) (tasteless additives that intensify the flavour of food)	Monosodium glutamate	Chinese food, dried soups, stock cubes, crisps	Glutamic acid (amino acid)	• To enhance the flavour of food.

Sweeteners E900-E999

Classification	Examples	Use	Origin	Functions
Natural	Fructose	Tinned peas	Fruit	• To sweeten food.
	Table sugar	Biscuits, cakes, sweets, canned vegetables/fruit	Sugar beet, sugar cane	
	Glucose syrup	Tinned fruit, jelly	Fruit, honey	
Artificial • Intense sweeteners – used in small amounts as they are many times sweeter than sugar – low in kcal	Aspartame (Nutrasweet, Canderel)	Soft drinks, confectionery, Sweetening tablets	Dipeptide (aspartic acid and phenylalanine) (100–200 times sweeter than sugar)	• Intense sweeteners used in slimming and low-calorie foods.
	Saccharin (Hermesetes)	Sweetening tablets Soft drinks, cider	Coal tar (500 times sweeter than sugar)	
• Bulk sweeteners – used in large amounts as they have the same sweetening strength as sugar – high in kcal	Sorbitol	Diabetic foods, sugar-free confectionery	Lichens (algae and fungi)	• Sorbitol is used in the production of diabetic foods as it does not require insulin.
	Manitol	Sugar-free chewing gum, sweets, ice cream	Lichens	

Note: Sweeteners may not be used in foods for infants or young children.

Preservatives E200–E299

Classification	Examples	Use	Origin	Functions
Natural	Sugar	Jams, sweets	Beet/cane	• Prevent the growth of micro-organisms thereby preventing food spoilage. • Provide greater variety of food in the diet.
	Salt	Bacon, pickles	Sodium chloride	
	Vinegar	Pickles, chutney	Fermentation of yeast, alcohol fermentation	
	Alcohol	Essence, cakes		
	Smoke	Fish, meat	Burning wood	
Artificial	Sulphur dioxide	Dried fruit and vegetables, sausages, fruit juices	Laboratory produced chemicals	• Reduce the risk of food poisoning. • Extend shelf-life
	Sorbic acid	Soft fruit, fruit yoghurts and processed cheeses		

Note: Preservatives are not permitted for use in baby foods.

Antioxidants E300–E399

Classification	Examples	Use	Origin	Functions
(prevent reaction with oxygen): Natural	Vitamin C (Ascorbic acid)	Fruit drinks	Fruit and vegetables	• Reduce waste. • Prevent oxidation.
	Vitamin E (Tocopherol)	Vegetable oils	Nuts and seeds	
Artificial	Butylated hydroxyanisole (BHA)	Stock cubes Cheese spread	Laboratory produced chemicals	
	Butylated hydroxytoulene (BHT)	Chewing gum		

Note: Antioxidants (BHA/BHT) are not permitted for use in baby foods.

Nutritive additives/nutritional supplemented/fortified foods

Supplements	Examples of fortified food	Added nutrients
Some foods have extra nutrients added in during processing. These are referred to as 'fortified' foods. **Food fortification** may: • Replace nutrients lost in processing. • Increase the nutritional value. • Increase sales. • Imitate another food (e.g. TVP which is used instead of meat).	Margarine Flour Milk Low-fat milk Fruit drinks TVP Dried potato Breakfast cereals	Vitamins A and D Vitamins B, Calcium Calcium Vitamins A and D Vitamins C, B_2, B_{12}, folic acid B_{12}, methionine, iron Vitamins C B_1, B_2, B_6, B_{12}, folate, iron

Physical conditioning agents				
Classification	Examples	Use	Origin	Functions
Emulsifiers E400 —E449	Lechitin	Mayonnaise, hollandaise sauce, biscuits	Egg yolk Commercially produced from soya beans and maize	• To form emulsions. (See Page 25)
	Alginates	Ice cream, jellies	Sea weed	
Stabilisers	Guar gum	Confectionery	Guar plant	• To stabilise emulsions.
	Carageenan	Ice cream	Sea weed moss	
Polyphosphates	Magnesium Carbonate	Salt – anti-caking agent, cake mixes	Chemically produced	• To prevent lumping.
Pectin		Jams/jellies	Fruit	• To aid setting of jams/jellies.
Humectants	Sweeteners sorbitol and mannitol	Confectionery, sweets	Lichens	• To absorb water vapour from the air and prevent foods from drying out.

Advantages of additives	Disadvantages of additives
• Preservatives prolong the shelf-life of food. • Preservatives reduce the risk of food poisoning. • Preservatives prevent waste. • Colourings make food more appetising. • Flavourings improve the taste of food. • Physical conditioning agents improve the texture of foods. • Nutritive additives increase the nutritive value of food. • Additives allow for the provision of a variety of foods. • Additives ensure consistent quality.	• Some people react to additives such as tartrazine, a food colouring, with side effects such as migraine, rashes and hyperactivity. • Little is known about the cumulative effects or the effects of the combination of additives consumed (cocktail of additives). • Bulking agents may deceive the consumer. • Some additives destroy nutrients, e.g. sulphur dioxide destroys vitamin B. • Some sweeteners, e.g. saccharin, leave a bitter aftertaste.

Legal control of use of additives

► The use of food additives is controlled by EU legislation and all EU countries share the same list of permitted additives.

► Additives undergo stringent testing by the ESFA (European Food Safety Authority) before approval for use in food.

► Each approved additive (except flavourings) is assigned an E number according to its function.

► The E number, or name of the additive, must be listed on a food label.

► Additives must be used in the smallest possible amount at which they are effective and *must not* be used –
  – to disguise faulty processing.
  – mislead the consumer.
  – if they present a hazard to the health of the consumer.

► In Ireland the FSAI has overall responsibility for monitoring the safe use of additives in food.

Contaminants

Contaminants are substances that enter food either unintentionally or illegally at various stages of food processing. They are generally harmless in small amounts but consumption may result in damage to the body. Continuous testing is carried out to monitor levels of contamination.

Quality control testing

Effects of contaminents on humans		
Contaminant	**Food source**	**Effects**
Pesticides	• Crops (cereals, fruit and vegetables) sprayed with insecticides, herbicides and fungicides. • Water contaminated with run offs from crops.	• Respiratory problems. • Heart and circulatory problems. • Affects nervous systems. • Can cause cancer.
Antibiotics	• Meat from animals and poultry treated with antibiotics to cure disease / prevent infection. • Milk from treated animals.	• Builds up resistance to antibiotics. • Can cause allergies.
Metals, e.g. Lead and Cadmium	Transferred to food from: • Soil • Water • Food Containers • Cooking Equipment	• Stomach Cramps. • Damage to kidneys and liver. • Effects immune system and nervous system.
Chemicals, e.g. Dioxins	Transferred to food by air/soil/water from industrial burning of hydrocarbon fuels.	• Can cause cancer. • Damage to immune system.

Other contaminants include:

▶ Plastic chemicals from packaging.

▶ Formaldehyde from treated paper packaging.

▶ Foreign bodies, e.g. hair due to carelessness.

▶ Chemicals, e.g. growth promoters – illegally used in meat production.
  – Cancer causing chemicals formed on food due to smoking and barbecuing.

▶ Micro-organisms (See Page 171).

Farmer spraying pesticide in an orchard

Chapter 7 | Microbiology

The Study of Micro-organisms

Microbiology is the study of micro-organisms or microbes. Micro-organisms are tiny living organisms that are found everywhere but cannot be seen with the naked eye.

Micro-organisms are classified into three groups:

1. **Fungi:** Moulds, yeast and large fungi.

2. **Bacteria:** Such as salmonella and E. coli.

3. **Viruses:** Such as those which cause influenza, mumps and hepatitis.

In the study of food, the emphasis is placed on fungi and bacteria.

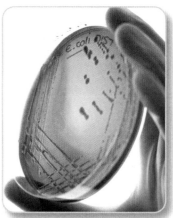

E. coli bacteria in a petri dish

Terminology of micro-organisms

- Parasites: Micro-organisms that feed on living matter (animals/humans).
- Saprophytes: Micro-organisms that feed on dead organic matter (food/soil).
- Psychrophiles: Micro-organisms that thrive at low temperatures from −5°C to 20°C.
- Mesophiles: Micro-organisms that thrive at temperatures between 20°C and 45°C.
- Thermophiles: Micro-organisms that thrive at higher temperatures 45°C–75°C.
- Aerobic: Micro-organisms that require oxygen.
- Anaerobic: Micro-organisms that can thrive without oxygen.
- Facultative: Micro-organisms that adapt to aerobic or anaerobic conditions.
- Unicellular: Micro-organisms made up of a single cell.
- Multicellular: Micro-organisms made up of many cells.
- Pathogens/pathogenic bacteria: Bacteria that cause diseases.
- Non-pathogens: Bacteria that do not cause diseases.

Optimum Temperature: Temperature at which micro-organisms grow best.

How microbes feed/multiply/contaminate food

Micro-organisms, secrete enzymes into their source of food. These enzymes break down the food source into simple soluble compounds. These simple compounds are then absorbed through the cell wall of the microbe providing nourishment for growth/multiplication.

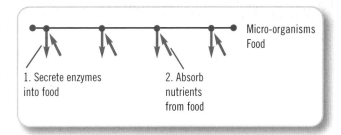

Micro-organisms
Food

1. Secrete enzymes into food

2. Absorb nutrients from food

Fungi

▶ Fungi are simple plants that cannot manufacture their own food, as they do not contain chlorophyll.

▶ Parasitic fungi feed on living matter, e.g. athlete's foot or ringworm on humans and animals.

▶ Saprophytic fungi feed on dead matter, e.g. mucor on bread or mushrooms on soil.

A highly magnified picture of the fungus which causes athlete's foot

Classification of fungi

▶ Moulds

▶ Large fungi (mushrooms)

▶ Yeast

Or as follows:

Class	Examples
Phycomycetes	Mucor and rhizopus (moulds)
Ascomycetes	Aspergillis and penicillium (moulds)
Basidiomycetes	Large fungi (mushrooms)
Saccharomycetes	Yeast

A highly magnified picture of sparangium bread mould

Moulds

The basic unit of all moulds is a mould spore. There are many mould spores present in the atmosphere but in order for them to develop into moulds certain conditions are necessary.

Conditions necessary for the growth of moulds

1. ***Food:*** Most moulds are saprophytes. They will grow on many different foods, particularly bread, fruit, jam and cheese.

2. ***Warmth:*** Most moulds are mesophiles (optimum temperature range 20°C–45°C). Freezing (–18°C) inactivates mould growth. Temperatures below 15°C including fridge temperature (below 5°C) retard mould growth. Cooking temperatures above 75°C destroy moulds.

3. ***Moisture:*** Moulds require moisture for growth. They grow best in moist humid conditions and on foods with water present in liquid form. Therefore, frozen foods are not a suitable medium.

4. ***Oxygen:*** As moulds are aerobic they grow on the surface on solid foods, e.g. jam and throughout open structure foods, e.g. bread (see note).

5. ***pH level:*** Moulds favour slightly acidic conditions (pH 4–6). Extreme conditions, which are very acidic or alkaline, inhibit the growth of moulds.

6. ***Time:*** Moulds require time to multiply.

Preventing food spoilage by moulds

► Store perishable food in the fridge.

► Ensure that storage presses are clean and dry.

► Many foods are preserved in vinegar, e.g. pickles.

► Other foods are preserved by drying which removes moisture or in cans removing oxygen.

► Use food within the recommended time.

► Cook food at high temperatures to destroy moulds.

► Handle fruit and vegetables with care to avoid bruising.

> Note: Although mould may only appear to affect the surface of a food, harmful mycotoxins can be produced and pass into the remainder of the food. Therefore, it is important that none of the mouldy food is consumed.

Structure of moulds

► Moulds are multicellular fungi that can be seen on food.

► Each mould begins as a single spore which lands on a suitable medium, e.g. surface of the food.

► If conditions are favourable, the spore develops a thin, thread-like filament called a hypha, which grows down into the food and absorbs nutrients.

► The hypha, as it grows, branches into many hyphae, which become intertwined to form a furry mass called a mycelium.

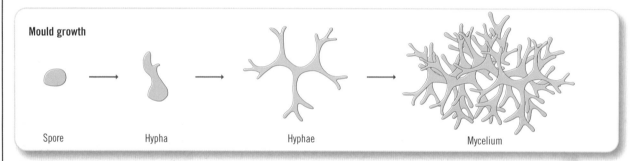

Mould growth

Spore   Hypha   Hyphae   Mycelium

Reproduction of moulds

Moulds reproduce both (a) Asexually and (b) Sexually.

(A) Asexual reproduction

When the mycelium is well established and the conditions remain favourable for growth, asexual reproduction occurs as follows:

► A hypha grows upwards from the mycelium on the surface of the food.

► A structure develops on the tip of the hypha inside which new spores develop. This structure may be in one of two forms:

   (i)   Sporangium – round ball-like structure.

   (ii)   Conidium – arranged as a chain of spores (conidia).

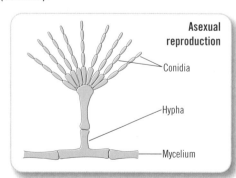

Asexual reproduction

Conidia

Hypha

Mycelium

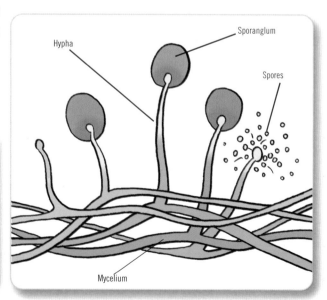

Hypha

Sporangium

Spores

Mycelium

► When this structure is fully developed the sporangium bursts releasing the spore into the atmosphere, or the conidia break off releasing the spores into the atmosphere.

► If the spore then finds suitable conditions new mould growth begins.

(B) Sexual reproduction

► Two hyphae grow toward each other.

► The two hyphae fuse together.

► The dividing wall breaks down and zygospore containing spores develops.

► The thick wall of the zygospore protects the internal spores in unfavourable conditions.

► Under suitable conditions, the spores develop hyphae which grow out of the zygospore.

► A sporangium or conidia develops on the top of each hypha.

► On ripening the spores are released into the atmosphere.

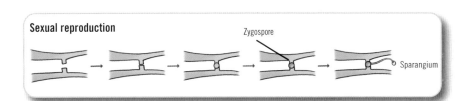

Sexual reproduction — Zygospore — Sparangium

► If these spores find suitable conditions new mould growth begins.

Classification of moulds

Classification of moulds			
Classification	**Examples**	**Description**	**Grows on**
Phycomycetes • Favour optimum temperature range of 30°C–40°C. • Reproduce sexually and asexually. • Hyphae develop sporangia.	Mucor	• Saprophytic mould. • Reproduces sexually and asexually. • White hyphae. • Grey sporangia.	• Bread, other starchy foods, e.g. grain • Meat • Soil
	Rhizopus	• Saprophytic mould. • Reproduces asexually. • Fluffy white mycelium. • Black pin-head sporangia.	• Bread • Vegetables (soft rot) • Berries, fruits (soft rot) • Soil
Ascomycetes • Favour lower optimum temperatures of 20°C–25°C. • Reproduce asexually only. • Hyphae develop conidia.	Penicillium	• Saprophytic mould. • Green-blue mould with a powdery texture. • Used in the production of blue-veined cheese. • Used in the production of antibiotics.	• Cheese • Bread • Fruit
	Aspergillis	• Saprophytic mould. • Occurs as black mould and greenish mould.	• Dried fruit, • Fruit, vegetables (black-rot) • Grain

Basidiamycetes – Large Fungi (Mushrooms)

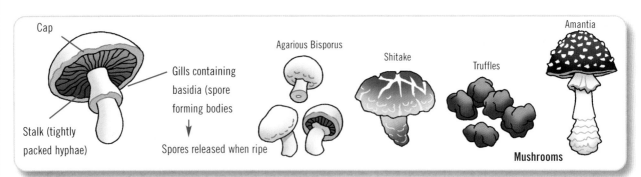

Cap

Gills containing basidia (spore forming bodies)

↓

Spores released when ripe

Stalk (tightly packed hyphae)

Agarious Bisporus

Shitake

Truffles

Amantia

Mushrooms

- ► Mushrooms are large fungi visible to the naked eye.
- ► They grow in the same way as moulds, beginning as a single spore.
- ► The spore develops hyphae which form the mycelium.
- ► Millions of tightly packed hyphae grow upwards from the mycelium as the stalk.
- ► A cap forms on top.
- ► The underside of the cap contains gills.
- ► Between the gills are spore-forming bodies called basidia.
- ► When the mushroom is fully ripe the basidia release the spores into the atmosphere.
- ► If the spores land on a suitable medium (e.g. soil) and conditions are favourable they repeat the cycle.

A spore print is visible if an open-capped mushroom is left on a white sheet of paper overnight

There are several varieties of mushrooms including:

Agaricus Campestris	– edible field mushrooms (button, shitake, oyster)
Agaricus Bisporus	– commercially produced mushrooms
Truffles	– pungent wild fungus regarded as a food delicacy, grows underground
Amanita	– poisonous mushrooms

Saccharomycetes – Yeast

Yeast is a unicellular saprophytic fungus, present in the air and on the surface of fruit. Yeast causes spoilage of fruit, jam, honey, fruit juice, wine and meat. *Saccharomycetes cerevisiae* is used in the production of foods such as bread, beer, wine and vinegar.

Conditions favouring the growth of yeast
1. *Food:* Yeast feeds on carbohydrate foods.
2. *Warmth:* Yeast flourishes at temperatures between 25°C–30°C. Yeast is killed at temperatures above 60°C. Low temperatures inactivate yeast.
3. *Moisture:* Yeast requires moisture for growth.
4. *Oxygen:* Yeast is a facultative organism so can live with or without oxygen.
5. *pH level:* Yeast favours an acid environment.
6. *Time:* Yeast requires time to grow.

Structure of yeast

Yeast cells are oval shaped. They have a thin outer wall enclosing granular cytoplasm. Each yeast cell also has a nucleus and vacuoles which store food reserves in the cell.

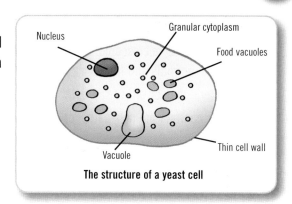

The structure of a yeast cell

Yeast reproduction (budding)

Yeast cells reproduce asexually by a process called *budding*.

► Under favourable conditions a yeast cell develops a bud (bulge).

► The nucleus of the yeast cell moves towards the bud.

► The nucleus then divides into two.

► A wall develops which divides the bud from the parent cell.

► The bud then separates from the parent cell.

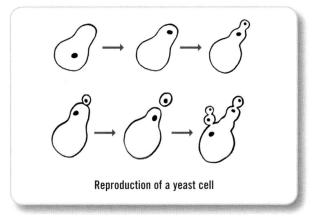

Reproduction of a yeast cell

A chain of yeast cells may form during rapid growth, when a bud develops its own bud, before it has broken away from the parent cell.

Preventing food spoilage by yeast

► Handle fruit with care to avoid bruising.

► Weigh sugar accurately for preserves.

► Store jams/marmalades covered, in cool conditions.

Fungi	
Advantages/benefits	**Disadvantages/harmful effects**
• Some are edible, e.g. mushrooms, truffles. • Fungi are involved in the decomposition of organic matter. • Moulds are used in cheese production. • Moulds are used in the production of antibiotics, e.g. penicillin. • Novel protein foods, e.g. Quorn, are produced by fermenting fungi. • Yeast is used in bread-making and in brewing. • Yeast is a rich source of vitamin B and is used in the production of food supplements.	• Fungi causes spoilage of food. • Some fungi, e.g. amanita are poisonous. • Fungi cause plant diseases, e.g. potato blight. • Some human diseases, e.g. athlete's foot and ringworm, are caused by fungi.

Bacteria

▶ Bacteria are microscopic unicellular organisms that are present everywhere: in the air, water, soil, on plants, animals and humans.

▶ Bacteria may be either saprophytic or parasitic.

▶ Many bacteria are non-pathogenic but some are pathogenic.

Conditions required for the growth of bacteria

1. *Food:* Saprophytic bacteria include those present in soil and food and cause decomposition. Parasitic bacteria cause diseases in humans, plants and animals.

2. *Correct Temperature:* Bacteria have a wide temperature range. Some are psychrophiles, e.g. listeria. Some are thermophiles, e.g. some clostridia bacteria. Most bacteria are mesophiles. Temperatures between 70°C–100°C destroy most bacteria. Temperatures above 121°C are required to destroy bacterial spores. Freezer temperature (-18°C) inactivates bacteria while cold temperatures (4°C) slow down bacterial growth.

3. *Moisture:* Bacteria require moisture in liquid form. Moist foods, e.g. milk, fish, meat, stews and cream are an ideal medium for bacterial growth.

4. *Oxygen:* Most bacteria are aerobic, e.g. E. coli. Some are anaerobic, e.g. clostridium botulinum while others such as salmonella are facultative.

5. *pH level:* Bacteria thrive best in neutral or slightly alkaline condition. Extremely acidic or alkaline conditions inhibit the growth of bacteria.

6. *Time:* In ideal conditions bacteria will double in number every 20 minutes.

Structure of a bacterial cell

▶ Bacteria have a rigid outer cell wall.

▶ Inside the cell wall is the cell membrane enclosing a colourless liquid called cytoplasm.

▶ The cytoplasm contain nuclear material and ribosomes which synthesise protein.

▶ Some bacteria are encased in a gel-like protective layer called a capsule and some have hair-like structures called flagellae, which assist movement.

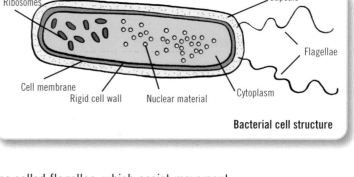

Bacterial cell structure

Reproduction/growth of bacteria

▶ Bacteria reproduce asexually by a process known as **binary fission**.

▶ If conditions are suitable a mature bacterial cell duplicates its nuclear material and the remaining cell divides forming two cells.

▶ The rapid growth ceases as bacteria compete for food, oxygen, moisture and space.

▶ Waste toxins build up in the medium preventing growth and causing the death of the bacteria.

This division can occur every 15–20 minutes resulting in over one million bacterial cells in five hours.

Large groups of bacteria are known as 'colonies'.

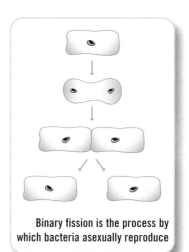

Binary fission is the process by which bacteria asexually reproduce

Spore-forming bacteria

► If conditions become unfavourable for bacterial growth bacteria die, but some bacteria are capable of forming spores.

► The spores which develop within the bacterial cell are referred to as endospores.

► Endospore forms and grows.

► Endospore develops a tough protective protein wall.

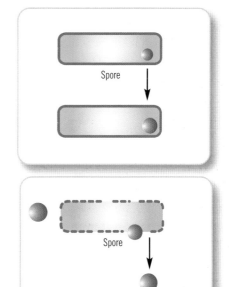

► Parent cell disintegrates.

► Spore is released.

► These spores can remain dormant for months or years, until conditions are suitable and the spores then germinate into new bacterial cells.

► Bacilli and clostridia bacteria have the ability to form spores, which are highly resistant to heat, cold and disinfectants.

► Ordinary cooking temperatures do not destroy bacterial spores. Moist temperature of 121°C for 15 minutes or dry temperature of 150°C for one hour is necessary in order to destroy these bacterial spores.

Toxins

During rapid growth, some bacteria produce waste products called toxins. These toxins or poisons are a frequent cause of food poisoning, and may be produced in two different ways: exotoxins and endotoxins.

Exotoxins	Endotoxins
• Produced outside the bacterial cells as they grow in the food.	• Produced within the bacterial cells as they grow.
• Produced both before and after the food is eaten.	• Released when the bacteria die.
• Causes toxic food poisoning (See Page 172):	• Cause infectious food poisoning (See Page 172),
Examples: Staphlococci and clostridium botulinum.	**Examples:** Salmonella, listeria.

Classification of bacteria

Bacteria are classified by (a) *shape* or (b) *gram staining.*

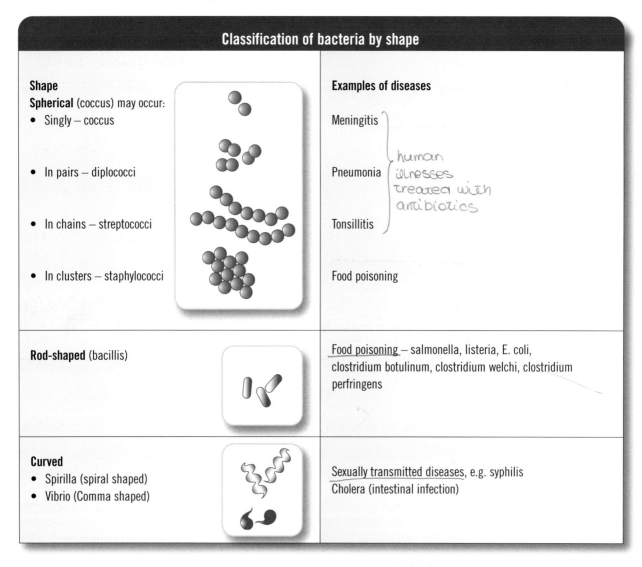

Classification of bacteria by shape		
Shape **Spherical** (coccus) may occur: • Singly – coccus • In pairs – diplococci • In chains – streptococci • In clusters – staphylococci		**Examples of diseases** Meningitis Pneumonia Tonsillitis human illnesses treated with antibiotics Food poisoning
Rod-shaped (bacillis)		<u>Food poisoning</u> – salmonella, listeria, E. coli, clostridium botulinum, clostridium welchi, clostridium perfringens
Curved • Spirilla (spiral shaped) • Vibrio (Comma shaped)		<u>Sexually transmitted diseases</u>, e.g. syphilis Cholera (intestinal infection)

Classification by gram staining

Bacteria may be classified as (a) gram-positive or (b) gram-negative using a gram stain test:

Gram-positive bacteria	Gram-negative bacteria
• Cell wall is one thick layer. • No flagellae. • Spore forming. • Low resistance to antibiotics. **Examples:** Streptococci, clostridia	• Cell wall is two thin layers. • Flagellae present. • Non-spore forming. • High resistance to antibiotics. **Examples:** E. coli, salmonella

Bacteria	
Advantages/benefits	**Disadvantages/harmful effects**
• Harmless bacteria are used in food production, e.g. cheese, yoghurt and vinegar. • Bacteria are involved in the break down of waste matter. • Bacteria produce vitamins B and K in the intestines. • Bacteria are used in the production of food supplements.	• Bacteria can contaminate food and cause food poisoning. • Other human diseases, e.g. pneumonia, cholera, tonsillitis are caused by bacteria. • Bacteria cause diseases in animals, e.g. brucellosis. • Food spoilage may be caused by bacteria, e.g. souring of milk. • Some plants are damaged by bacteria, e.g. apple scab. • Bacteria cause tooth decay.

Preventing food spoilage by bacteria (See Page 189).

Uses of micro-organisms in food production		
Food	**Micro-organism**	
Cheese	Bacteria	(See Page 87)
Yoghurt	Bacteria	(See Page 85)
Bread	Yeast	(See Page 124)
Mycoprotein	Fungi	(See Page 91)
Vinegar	Yeast and bacteria	(See Page 169)

Vinegar

Vinegar is the acidic liquid obtained from the fermentation of alcohol. The alcohol is first produced by yeast fermenting carbohydrates (fruit in wine, grain in beer). This alcohol is then further fermented by the addition of acetic acid bacteria. Wine vinegar is based on wine, malt vinegar is based on beer, and cider vinegar is based on cider.

Different types of vinegars

Vinegar is used as:
• A preservative
• An ingredient in salad dressing
• A marinade
• A condiment

CONTENTS INCLUDE:

▶ Food spoilage including moisture loss, enzymatic spoilage and microbial spoilage

▶ Food-borne diseases and food poisoning bacteria

▶ Principles and methods of food preservation

Food Spoilage (1.3.8)

The main causes of food spoilage are:

▶ Moisture loss ▶ Enzyme action ▶ Micro-organism contamination.

Moisture Loss

Moisture loss mainly affects fruit and vegetables. After harvesting, fruit and vegetables can no longer absorb moisture from the soil. Moisture loss through skins and leaves results in shrinkage, wrinkling of the skin and a limp appearance. *dry mandaring, wrinkly apple*

Enzyme Action

Enzymes are organic catalysts which are naturally present in foods. They cause spoilage of food in the following ways:

(a) Ripening

▶ Certain enzymes present in fruit and vegetables are responsible for their ripening.

▶ During the ripening process starch in under-ripe fruit is converted to sugars.

▶ There is also a colour change, e.g. green under-ripe oranges change to an orange colour.

▶ Texture changes during ripening, e.g. hard, under-ripe bananas become softer and easier to digest.

▶ The enzymes continue to work after ripening, resulting in over-ripe fruit, e.g. unappetising black bananas, at which stage food spoilage has occurred.

Ripening oranges

(b) Browning/Enzymic browning

Certain food such as bananas, apples and potatoes turn brown when the cut surface releases oxidase and is exposed to the air.

(c) Enzyme deterioration

Enzymes naturally present in fish cause deterioration even at low temperatures. *oily fish even in the freezer*

170

Control of enzymatic spoilage of food

▶ Enzymes are inactivated by **heat**, therefore browning and ripening can be stopped by cooking the food, e.g. boiling potatoes or stewing apples.

▶ As **cold** temperatures slow down enzymatic action, food is stored at low temperatures to lengthen shelf-life.

▶ **Blanching** of vegetables before freezing prevents enzymatic spoilage of frozen foods (See Page 177).

▶ The addition of **acids** inactivates enzymes as they work better in neutral conditions, e.g. lemon juice may be added during the preparation of apples to prevent browning.

▶ The **preservative** sulphur dioxide is an used in dried fruit, vegetables and fruit juices to control enzymatic spoilage of food.

Apples turn brown when the flesh is exposed to the air

Microbial Contamination

Yeasts, moulds, (fungi) and bacteria are the principal micro-organisms responsible for food spoilage. Food is an ideal medium for microbial growth as it provides the necessary nutrients and moisture, the pH is suitable, oxygen is often available and food if not correctly stored may be at the optimum temperature for micro-organisms to grow.

Rotting apple

Spoilage	
Fungal spoilage	**Bacerial spoilage**
• Mainly spoil the exterior of foods. • The spoilage is usually visible therefore the food is seldom consumed. • It is rarely responsible for food poisoning. • However, certain mycotoxins, e.g. alfatoxin produced by the aspergillus flavus mould on grains and nuts, have been associated with liver cancer.	• Some bacteria produce toxins within the food. • Spoilage is not visible and these toxins often result in food poisoning when the contaminated food is consumed. • Souring bacteria spoil milk, cream and yoghurt.

Food Poisoning/Food-borne Diseases

Food poisoning is caused by eating food which contains harmful substances. There are three types of food poisoning – based on the substances present in the food.

1. **Chemical food poisoning:** Chemicals present (such as in antibiotics and metals) can cause illness.

2. **Biological food poisoning:** Natural substances present in some foods are poisonous, e.g. oxalic acid in rhubarb leaves, solanine in green potatoes.

3. **Bacterial food poisoning:** Caused by the presence of pathogenic bacteria in food.

Symptoms of food poisoning

Food poisoning symptoms include: nausea, vomiting, abdominal cramps, diarrhoea, fever and loss of appetite. Food poisoning can be very serious among more **vulnerable** groups, e.g. infants, pregnant women and the elderly.

Bacterial food poisoning

There are two types of bacterial food poisoning:

1. **Toxic** food poisoning

2. **Infectious** food poisoning

Types of food poisoning	
Toxic Food Poisoning	**Infectious Food Poisoning**
• Illness caused by eating foods containing **exotoxins** produced outside bacteria cells as they grow in food. • Exotoxins may be produced before or after food is eaten. • Exotoxins are difficult to destroy (require boiling for 30 mins). • If not destroyed cause toxic food poisoning. • Short incubation period – within 2 hours. • Staphylococcus aureus and clostridium botulinium are examples of toxic food poisoning bacteria.	• Illness caused by eating food containing large numbers of pathogenic bacteria which produce **endotoxins** within bacteria cells as they grow in food. • Endotoxins are released when the bacteria die. • Endotoxins and the bacteria which produce them are easy to destroy (normal cooking temperatures and correct reheating procedures). • If not destroyed cause infectious food poisoning. • Long incubation period (over 12 hours). • Salmonella and listeria are examples of infectious food poisoning bacteria.

High risk foods

The foods most susceptible to bacterial contamination are the liquid protein foods: milk, cream, meat, poultry, fish, egg, meat dishes, e.g. pies, gravies, soups and stocks, egg dishes such as custards and mayonnaise, and reheated dishes.

Common strains of food poisoning bacteria				
Infectious Food Poisoning Bacteria				
Description	Source/habitat	Environmental factors	High risk foods	Incubation, duration, symptoms
Salmonella • Rod-shaped. • Gram negative. • Non-spore forming. • Causes infectious food poisoning. • Highly contagious.	• Found in the intestines of humans and animals. • Human and animal waste. • Unwashed hands.	• Facultative bacteria. • Optimum temperature of 37°C.	• Meat, poultry, eggs, fish. • Any food handled by an unhygienic worker.	• Incubation period: 12–36 hours. • Duration: 1–7 days. • Symptoms: nausea, vomiting, abdominal cramps, diarrhoea and fever.
Listeria monocytogenes: • Rod-shaped. • Gram positive. • Spore forming. • Causes infectious food poisoning.	• In soil. • Human and animal waste.	• Facultative bacteria. • Optimum temperature of 30°C but continue to grow at temperatures as low as 4°C and up to 43°C. • Slightly acidic conditions. • High moisture content. • Tolerates salt.	• Raw meat and poultry. • Unpasteurised milk and soft cheeses. • Paté and cooked poultry. • Raw vegetables, pre-packed salads, coleslaw. • Cook-chill foods.	• Incubation period: up to 70 days. • Duration: several days. • Symptoms: fever, diarrhoea, meningitis in new born babies, possible miscarriage or premature births, septicaemia, possible death.
E. coli 0157 (Escherichia coli): • Rod-shaped. • Gram negative. • Causes infectious food poisoning. • Non spore-forming	• In intestines of humans and animals. • Human and animal excreta. • Contaminated water supply. • Unwashed hands.	• Aerobic bacteria. • Widespread in nature. • Optimum temperature range 30–40°C.	• Unpasteurised milk. • Raw meats. • Undercooked meats. • Minced meat.	• Incubation period: 12–24 hours. • Duration: 1–5 days. • Symptoms: abdominal cramps, fever, nausea, bleeding bowel, diarrhoea. • In serious cases: kidney failure and death.

Incubation: period of time between ingesting bacteria and developing the symptoms.

Salmonella

Duration: the length of time for which the symptoms last.

Common strains of food poisoning bacteria				
Toxic Food Poisoning Bacteria				
Description	Source/habitat	Environmental factors	High risk foods	Incubation, duration, symptoms
Clostridium botulinum: • Rod-shaped. • Gram positive. • Spore forming. • Causes toxic food poisoning (botulism).	• In soil and decaying matter.	• Anaerobic bacteria. • Optimum temperature 30–37^{0}C. • Slightly acid conditions. • Requires temperature of 121^{0}C for 15 minutes for destruction.	• Low acid canned foods, e.g. fish (faulty processing). • Vacuum-packed foods. • Smoked fish. • Unpasteurised cheese.	• Incubation period: 12–36 hours. • Duration: often death in 1–8 days. • Symptoms: headache, diarrhoea, double vision, slurred speech, paralysis of throat and possible death. • Recovery is very slow (months) if antidote is administered.
Staphylococcus aureus: • Spherical in shape, found in clusters. • Gram positive. • Non-spore forming. • Causes toxic food poisoning.	• In nose and throat and on infected skin, e.g. boils. • Unwashed hands.	• Facultative bacteria. • Optimum temperature 30–40°C.	• Unpasteurised milk. • Cold meats. • Cream • Custard • Ice cream	• Incubation period: 3–6 hours. • Duration: up to 24 hours. • Symptoms: vomiting, cramps and diarrhoea.

Food Preservation (1.3.9)

Correct storage and cooking of food prevents food spoilage in the short-term. For long term storage it is necessary to preserve food. Preservation removes one or more of the conditions favourable for enzyme activity and microbial growth and therefore prevents food spoilage.

Methods of preservation	
Home	**Commercial**

• Freezing.
 • Heat treatments
  – jam making
  – chutney making.
 • Chemical preservation
  – jam and chutney making, pickling.
 • Drying/dehydration.
	• Freezing.
	 • Heat treatments
	  – Canning/bottling
	  – Pasteurisation, sterilisation, UHT **(See Chapter 3 Milk)**.
	 • Chemical preservation.
	 • Dehydration.
	 • Fermentation.
	 • Irradiation.

Principles of preservation

1. Preservation prevents enzyme activity in food.
2. It inhibits the growth of microbes, often destroying them.
3. Preservation prevents microbes from re-entering by sealing the food.
4. It maintains as much nutritive value, colour, flavour and texture of the fresh food as possible.

Home Preservation

Advantages of home preservation

1. It saves money – home-made preserves, e.g. jams and chutneys are generally less expensive than the commercially produced variety.
2. It avoids waste – a plentiful supply of garden produce, e.g. fruit/vegetables may be preserved to prevent spoilage.
3. Preservation can make 'out of season' foods available, e.g. frozen rhubarb at Christmas.
4. Preserved foods provide variety in the diet and are convenient and handy in emergencies.
5. Some methods, e.g. freezing are simple yet very effective methods of preservation.

Freezing

Underlying principle of freezing

▶ Freezing involves the use of very low temperatures which are generally unsuitable for enzyme activity and microbial growth. Micro-organisms are inactivated not killed.

▶ During freezing moisture is converted to ice, making it unavailable to micro-organisms thereby preventing microbial multiplication.

▶ Wrapping of the food prevents the re-entry of micro-organisms and helps to maintain colour, flavour and texture.

Quick and slow freezing

Quick freezing	Slow freezing
• Food is frozen quickly at −25°C in the fast-freeze section of a freezer.	• Food is frozen at temperatures between 0°C and −18°C, e.g. in the ice box of a fridge or in the storage section of a freezer.
• Small ice crystals form within the food, causing less damage to the cell walls of the food.	• Large ice crystals form causing more damage to the cell walls.
• Nutritive value, texture, colour and flavour are better retained on thawing than with slow freezing.	• Greater loss of nutritive value, texture, colour and flavour on thawing.

Effects of quick and slow freezing

Food Cell

Slow freezing

Frozen   Thawed

Quick freezing

Frozen   Thawed

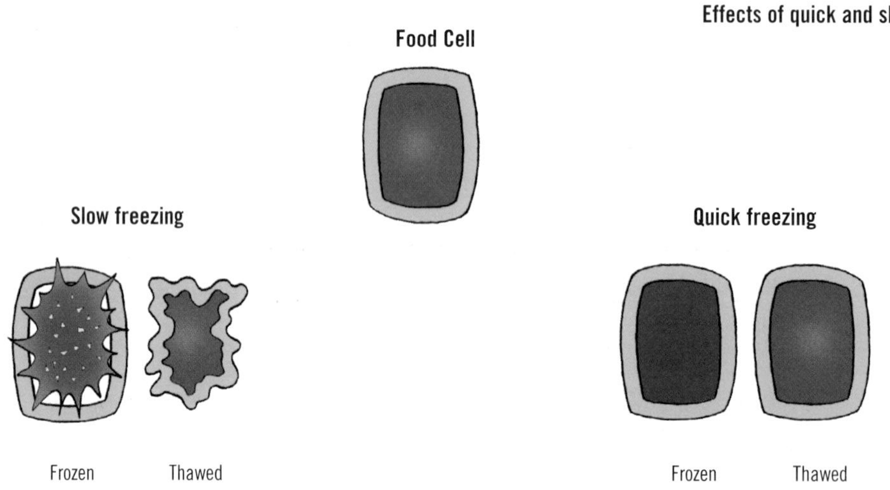

Freezing

Advantages	Disadvantages
• Simple, safe method of preserving food.	• Initial cost of freezer and running costs (1 unit of electricity per week per 15 litre capacity).
• Suitable method of preserving for a variety of foods.	• Packaging is required for freezing food.
• Best method for retaining nutritive value, texture, colour and flavour of food.	• Effective freezing requires following the rules from preparation to thawing of food.
• Prevents waste as leftovers can be frozen.	• Defrosting of freezer takes time and effort.
• Bulk cooking and freezing saves time and fuel.	• Space required for a freezer.
• Frozen food is available for emergencies.	

Freezing	
Suitable foods	**Unsuitable foods**
• Fruit and vegetables. • Meat/fish, both raw and cooked. • Baked foods, e.g. bread, scones, cakes. • Pastry and dough. • Soups and sauces. • Cooked meals, e.g. quiche, lasagne, shepherd's pie.	• Whole eggs unless deshelled. • Some vegetables, e.g. lettuce, cucumber, whole peppers. • Some fruit, e.g. melons, .pears, bananas. • Mayonnaise.

General Rules for Freezing Food

Preparation

▶ Turn on the <u>fast-freeze button 3–4 hours in advance</u> of freezing food.

▶ Only freeze $\frac{1}{10}$ of the capacity of the freezer in any 24-hour period.

▶ Choose <u>best quality fresh food </u>for freezing.

▶ <u>Freeze</u> foods in <u>usable quantities/portions.</u>

▶ <u>Cool</u> all foods <u>before freezing.</u>

▶ Open-freeze foods that <u>will stick together,</u> e.g. prawns.

▶ <u>Blanch vegetables before freezing</u>. Even freezing temperatures do not totally inactivate enzymes; therefore blanching of vegetables before freezing prevents enzymatic spoilage of frozen food.

Packaging suitable for freezer use

Packaging

▶ Seal foods well in packaging removing as much air as possible.

▶ Use moisture proof, vapour proof and strong packaging.

▶ Allow space for liquids to expand.

▶ Label all foods with name, quantity and date of freezing.

> *Blanching*
> • 5 litres of boiling water per 500 g of vegetables.
> • Time from when water and vegetables begin to boil.
>
> *Equipment*
> • Large saucepan
> • Wire basket
> • Large bowl

Freezing food

▶ Place food in fast-freeze section of freezer in contact with sides or base of compartment.

▶ Leave for the recommended time – up to 24 hours.

▶ Remove frozen food from fast-freeze section and place in storage section.

▶ Open-frozen foods can now be packed into containers.

▶ Turn off fast-freeze button.

> **Freezer burn:** if protein food is not properly wrapped freezer burn may result, causing the food to toughen, discolour and dry out.

Storage

- ▶ Store similar food together.
- ▶ Store only for recommended time (see chart).
- ▶ Use in rotation.
- ▶ Keep the freezer filled to reduce running costs.
- ▶ Avoid opening the door unnecessarily or leaving it open for a length of time.

Label and date food that is to be frozen

Thawing

- ▶ Read commercially-frozen food packs, as many do not require thawing before cooking.
- ▶ Vegetables should be cooked directly from frozen.
- ▶ Foods that require thawing, e.g. meat should be thawed slowly and completely in the refrigerator or use a microwave oven.
- ▶ Never refreeze thawed food and use up quickly as microbial growth is reactivated on thawing.
- ▶ Be careful of drips from thawing meat, poultry and fish as they can easily contaminate other foods.
- ▶ Foods like bread and cakes can be thawed at room temperature.

Packaging materials for freezing	Characteristics of packaging for freezing
• Strong, polythene, sealable freezer bags. • Polythene boxes. • Aluminium containers. • Aluminium foil. • Cling film. • Freezer papers. • Waxed cartons.	• Strong. • Vapour proof. • Water proof. • Grease proof. • Easy to use. • Sealable.

Freezing carrots

Method

1. Prepare carrots by washing, removing tops and tails and peeling thinly.
2. Cut into required shapes – circles or strips.
3. Blanch carrots by boiling for 4 minutes to inactivate enzymes, then plunge into ice-cold water for a further 4 minutes to stop cooking.
4. Drain well and pack in usable quantities into polythene bags or boxes.
5. Label and date.
6. Place in pre-cooled, fast-freeze section of the freezer.
7. When fully frozen remove to the storage area of the freezer and turn off the fast-freeze button.
8. Use within the recommended time.

Effects of freezing (See Page 176)

Recommended storage time for frozen foods

Food	Time
Chicken	12 months
Vegetables	12 months
Beef	12 months
White fish	6 months
Pastry (cooked)	6 months
Lamb	6 months
Oily fish	4 months
Soups, sauces	3 months
Minced meat	3 months
Casseroles	2 months
Bread	1 month

Heat Treatments

Fruit and vegetables can be preserved in the home by using very high temperatures. Jam-making, chutney-making and bottling involve using heat to preserve foods. A chemical preservative such as sugar or vinegar is also used.

Jam-making

Jam is fruit that is boiled with a high proportion of sugar.

Underlying principle

▶ Jam-making involves using very high heat to kill any microbes and enzymes in the fruit and to soften the fruit.

▶ A high proportion of sugar (65%) is used in jam-making which acts as a preservative (see below) and helps the jam to set.

▶ Pectin and acid also help the jam to set.

▶ Sealing prevents re-entry of micro-organisms.

Sugar as a preservative

The sugar dissolves in the water of the fruit forming a concentrated solution. Water is then drawn from any microbial cells by osmosis to equalise the solution thereby dehydrating the microbial cells causing death.

Ingredients for jam

Fruit: Use good quality, ripe, acidic fruit with a high proportion of pectin.

Sugar: Measure the sugar accurately as it acts as a preservative and a sweetener. Sure-set sugar is a preserving sugar. Large sugar crystals are coated with pectin and acid. It has a shorter boiling time and as it is purer than ordinary granulated sugar, it produces less scum while boiling.

> **Test for pectin**
> Add 1 tablespoon of boiled fruit to 3 tablespoons of methylated spirits and mix.
>
> **Result**
> 1 clot = high pectin content.
> 2-3 medium clots = medium pectin content.
> 3+ clots = low pectin content.

Acid: Acid is necessary to draw out the pectin from the fruit. As many fruits are acidic no extra acid needs to be added, but some recipes include lemon juice. Acid also results in a better colour and flavour and helps to prevent crystallisation.

Pectin: Pectin is a polysaccharide present in the cell walls of ripe fruit. Some fruits are richer in pectin than others so it may be necessary to combine fruits in order to achieve a good set, e.g. blackberry and apple jam. Liquid pectin is also available.

Sure-set sugar and pectin

Pectin content		
High	**Medium**	**Low**
Apples	Apricots	Cherries
Blackcurrants	Blackberries	Late blackberries
Gooseberries	Plums	Pears
	Raspberries	Strawberries

Characteristics of a good jam	
• Clear • Bright colour • Fruity flavour	• Well set • Keeps for one year

Equipment

▶ Large heavy-based stainless steel saucepan

▶ Long handled perforated spoon

▶ Sugar thermometer

▶ Measuring jug

▶ Jam jars

▶ Jam covers: wax discs, cellophane covers, elastic bands and labels.

The wax side of the disc is placed on hot jam causing the wax to melt forming an airtight seal. The cellophane shrinks slightly around the jar on cooling which also acts as a sealant.

Equipment needed for jam-making

Stages in jam-making

1. **Weigh** and measure ingredients accurately.

2. **Jars:** Use sound jars that have been washed and sterilised in the oven.

3. **Preparation of fruit:** Wash, peel, remove stones and chop if necessary.

4. **Cooking fruit:** Grease the base of the saucepan to prevent sticking and reduce scum. Follow the recipe, allowing the fruit to simmer gently to soften and release pectin.

5. **Addition of sugar:** Pre-warm in a low oven. This makes the sugar dissolve more quickly. Add to the stewing fruit, stirring until all the sugar has dissolved.

6. **Boiling:** When the sugar is fully dissolved bring the jam to the boil and boil rapidly, stirring occasionally. Boil until the setting point is reached. (**Setting Tests** See Page 181)

7. **Potting:** Skim jam and pour into the sterilised jars filling them to within 5 mm of the top.

8. **Cover** immediately with waxed discs removing any air with the back of a spoon. Wipe the outside of the jars and apply the cellophane cover and elastic bands.

9. **Label** with the name of the jam and date.

10. **Store** in a cool, dry, dark and well-ventilated press.

Problems when jam-making		
Crystallisation	Crystal particles of sugar deposited from jam.	**Possible cause** • Too much sugar used. • Sugar not fully dissolved before boiling. • Jam not boiled for long enough. • Insufficient acid.
Jam not set	Watery consistency.	• Insufficient pectin. • Incorrect amounts of sugar or acid. • Potted before setting point was reached.
Fermentation	Breakdown of jam by micro-organisms producing CO_2, alcohol and an 'off' flavour.	• Too little sugar. • Poor quality fruit. • Too little boiling.

Setting tests		
1. Wrinkle test	When you think the jam is ready, put a teaspoon of jam on a cold plate. Let it cool for 1–2 minutes. Push jam with your finger – if it wrinkles it is ready.	
2. Flake test	Lift out some jam with a clean, dry wooden spoon. Allow to cool slightly. Turn spoon and allow the jam to run off. If it forms into wide flakes, it is ready. If it trickles off into a thin stream it is not.	
3. Thermometer test	Use a sugar thermometer – it will read 105°C (220°F) when it is ready to pot.	

Chutney-making

Chutney is boiling fruit, vegetables or a mixture of both with sugar and vinegar and spices.
Chutney should be thick in consistency with a good colour and a mellow flavour.

Underlying principle

▶ The high temperature used destroys any microbes and enzymes in the fruit/vegetables.

▶ The sugar preserves the chutney by dehydrating the microbial cells.

▶ The vinegar acts as a preservative by lowering the pH level which prevents microbial growth.

▶ Sealing prevents re-entry of micro-organisms.

Different types of chutney

Equipment

Use the same type of equipment as when making jam. Use a wooden spoon as metal reacts with the vinegar. The cellophane covers allow evaporation so it is better to use plastic-lined, metal screw tops.

Making chutney
Follow the recipe and store for a few months to allow flavour to mellow.

Different types of pickles

Chemical Preservation

Chemical Preservation		
Method of preservation	**Chemical used**	**Principle**
Jam making	Sugar	Sugar and salt form a concentrated solution which dehydrates microbial cells.
Chutney making	Sugar and vinegar	
Pickling	Salt and vinegar	Vinegar lower pH to to unacceptable level for microbial growth.

Dehydration

Drying is rarely used as a method of home preservation. Herbs can be dried by tying them in bundles and allowing them to dry in a hot press for some days. The herbs are then preserved as both micro-organisms and enzymes require moisture and are inactivated without it.

Dried herbs

Commercial Preservation
Commercial Freezing

Underlying principle
The underlying principles of commercial freezing are the same as those for home freezing (See Page 175).

Different methods are used in commercial freezing including:

Commercial freezing	
Method	**Use**
1 Blast freezing Food is subjected to a blast of cold air as it passes through a tunnel on a conveyor belt.	• Most common method. • Used for foods such as vegetables and meat.
2 Plate or contact freezing Food is pressed between two cold metal surfaces.	• Thin pieces of food such as burgers, fish fingers, flat pieces of meat and fish.
3 Flow freezing Food is frozen by freezing air blown from underneath which keeps the food moving and prevents it from sticking together.	• Small pieces of food such as peas or corn.

(Effects of freezing See Page 185)

Commercial Heat Treatments

▶ Canning/bottling.

▶ Pasteurisation, sterilisation and UHT of milk are outlined in **Chapter 3**.

Canning/bottling

The canning process destroys micro-organisms and enzymes by using very high temperatures. The food is then stored in an airtight container to prevent re-entry of micro-organisms. Canned food include fruit, vegetables, meat, fish and soup:

Canning process

▶ The food is prepared.

▶ Vegetables are blanched and fish and meat are cooked.

▶ The lacquered cans are filled with food and syrup, brine, oil or sauce.

▶ The air is then removed from the can.

▶ The cans are hermetically sealed (air-tight seal).

▶ The can and contents are sterilised.

▶ Cans are then cooled and labelled.

> Cans with bulges or dents should never be used.

> Remove food from can on opening and use up quickly.

Canning factory

High/low acid foods

▶ The method of canning differs for food depending on its acid content.

▶ High acid foods such as fruit, require fast heat treatment – usually less than 30 minutes at 100°C.

▶ Low acid foods such as meat, fish and vegetables, require a higher temperature for longer: 115°C for over 30 minutes.
(Effects of canning on food `See Page` **185).**

> Bottling is very similar to canning except glass jars are used. Air is eliminated and a vacuum is created on cooling, preventing re-entry of micro-organisms. Examples of bottled foods include vegetables and sauces, e.g. ketchup, mayonnaise.

Aseptic canning

▶ Aseptic canning involves sterilising the food and the can separately at ultra-high temperatures.

▶ The sterilised food is then put into the sterile can and the can is hermetically sealed, cooled and labelled.

▶ The extreme heat results in a short processing time with greater retention of food quality and is a more suitable method for large cans.

Chemical Preservation

Chemical preservation involves the addition of preservatives to food, which prevent enzyme activity and microbial growth (**Preservatives** `See Page` **157).** The most commonly used preservatives include sugar, salt, sulphur dioxide, sorbic acid, antioxidants, alcohol and acids.

Underlying principle

▶ Most chemical preservatives work by dissolving in the water of the food cells forming a concentrated solution. Microbial cells are then dehydrated by osmosis and thus destroyed.

▶ Alcohol denatures the protein in the bacterial cells.

▶ Acids lower the pH level to an unacceptable level for microbial growth and enzyme activity.

Dried foods

Dehydration

Underlying principle

As microbes require moisture for growth, dehydration of the food ensures that microbial growth is prevented. Commercial dehydration methods include:

1. Spray drying: Used for eggs and milk (See Page 82).
2. Roller drying: Used for milk, dried potato, breakfast cereals, baby food.
3. Sun drying: This method of drying is used in very hot climates. It is used to dry fruit, e.g. figs and sultanas, and sun-dried tomatoes.

Accelerated freeze drying (AFD)		
Process	**Advantages**	**Uses**
• During AFD, food is first frozen at very low temperatures. • The tiny ice crystals are then evaporated in a vacuum chamber. • This process is known as sublimation, i.e. the solid ice is changed to vapour without going through a liquid state.	• The resulting foods are lightweight. • Food retains more flavour and shape • Foods have a longer shelf-life than other methods of drying.	• Coffee, dried fruit and vegetables, dried meat and fish.

Effects of drying (See Page 185)

Fermentation

▶ Fermentation is the breakdown of substances by micro-organisms such as yeast and bacteria.

▶ Fermentation is used on a method of preservation in yoghurt where lactose converted to lactic acid by bacteria acts as a preservative.

▶ The production of vinegar and alcohol (beer, wine) is based on fermentation.

▶ Yeast used in bread-making also involves fermentation.

Irradiation

Principle

Food is preserved by being exposed to radiation which:

1. Destroys pathogenic and spoilage micro-organisms.
2. Kills parasites, e.g. insects.
3. Stops ripening and sprouting in fresh foods.

Irradiation symbol

► Irradiation is used in the preservation of over 60 food types (e.g. fruit, vegetables, cereals) in at least 40 countries worldwide. However dried herbs, spices and vegetable seasonings are the only irradiated foodstuffs currently authorised across the EU.

► There are no food irradiation facilities in Ireland. Any irradiated foods/ingredients on the Irish market are imported.

► Any irradiated foods must be clearly marked 'irradiated'. It may also carry the 'radura' symbol.

Irradiation	
Advantages	**Disadvantages**
• Destroys food poisoning bacteria and parasites. • Increases shelf-life. • Slows down ripening and sprouting of fruit and vegetables. • Has little effect on the colour, flavour and texture of the food. • Eliminates need for chemical preservatives.	• Not suitable for foods with a high fat content, which may become rancid. • Loss of vitamins. • High levels of radiation are necessary to destroy some micro-organisms. • Public concern over the use of radiation in food production. • The use of radiation may be misused, i.e. to disguise poor manufacturing techniques.

Effects of Preservation on Food

Freezing

► Microbial growth is prevented.

► Blanching stops enzyme activity and results in loss of vitamin B_1 and C.

► Thawing may result in further loss of vitamin B_1 and C.

► Slow freezing results in loss of texture and nutrients on thawing.

► Poorly wrapped protein foods may develop freezer-burn.

Canning

► Microbial growth and enzyme activity are prevented.

► Heat sensitive B vitamins and vitamin C are destroyed.

► The food is already cooked.

► There is loss of colour, flavour and texture.

► Foods canned in brine, oil and syrup have salt, fat and sugar added respectively.

Tomatoes drying in the sun

Drying

► Microbial growth is prevented.

► Water is removed.

► Water-soluble vitamins B and C are removed.

► Food changes shape and weight.

For a comparative evaluation of foods that have been preserved by different methods **see workbook.**

CONTENTS INCLUDE:

- ► National and European food legislation
- ► Safe food preparation
- ► The HACCP System
- ► ISO 9000

- ► The role of national agencies in food preparation

Food Legislation (1.3.7)

Food safety and hygiene in Ireland is governed by national and European legislation. It includes the following regulations/acts which serve to protect the consumer from any food related risk to health.

Food Hygiene Regulations (1950–89)

These regulations protect the consumer by:

- ► Prohibiting the sale of food which is diseased, contaminated or otherwise unfit for human consumption. *points*
  HACCP - hazard analysis of critical control
- ► Requiring that precautions are taken at all stages – such as importation, processing and distribution – to prevent contamination of food.
  health inspector
- ► Ensuring that food premises maintain hygienic conditions regarding equipment, food waste, water supply etc.
- ► Ensuring that food handlers observe food hygiene and safety rules and adhere to a HACCP system (See Page 191).

Under this legislation those in breach of the law, or regarded as a possible threat to public health, risk prosecution or closure.

European Communities (Hygiene of Foodstuffs) Regulations 2006

1. These regulations lay down general hygiene requirements for food premises.
2. Under this legislation foodstuffs deemed to be unsafe can be seized and destroyed and food premises which pose a threat to public health may be closed.

Sale of Food and Drugs Acts 1875, 1879, 1899, 1936

These acts protect the consumer against adulteration and fraud. Under these acts, it is an offence to:

1. Mix, colour or stain a food with any ingredient which would render the food a danger to human health, e.g. the addition of colouring to raw minced meat is illegal.
2. Sell any food which is not of the nature and quality demanded by consumers, e.g. it is illegal to inject bovine protein into chicken breasts with the purpose of increasing weight.

Health Acts

The Health Acts of 1947, 1953 and 1970 and the European Communities (Health Act 1947) Regulations 1991 enable regulations to be made to:

► Prevent danger to public health arising from the importation, manufacture, distribution and sale of food.

► Control compositional standards for foods which are of special importance to public health, e.g. dairy spreads.

Labelling Regulations

► General labelling regulations which apply to foodstuffs sold in Ireland are laid down in the European Communities (labelling, presentation and advertising of foodstuffs) Regulations 2002.

► Nutrition labelling is governed by The Health (nutrition labelling for foodstuffs) Regulations 1993 (national legislation) and by an EU directive (1990) (**Food Labelling** See Page 153).

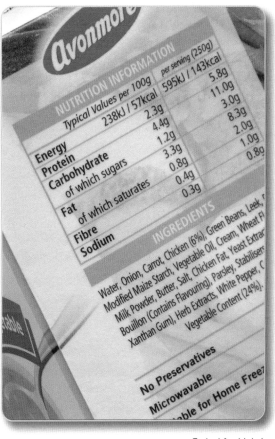

Typical food label

Food Safety and Hygiene

Food which is not stored, handled or cooked properly may quickly become a hygiene hazard.

Contamination may occur when:

1. Food is prepared by unhygienic food handlers.

2. Food is in contact with dirty utensils, equipment, work surfaces or cloths.

3. Bacteria are transferred from raw to cooked food.

4. There is poor temperature control during storage, preparation, cooking and reheating of food.

5. Food preparation areas are of poor structural standard, making it difficult to maintain acceptable standards of hygiene and safety.

Food handlers must observe food hygiene rules

Safe Food Preparation

Safe food preparation which minimises the risk of food poisoning involves the areas of:

▶ Personal hygiene.

▶ Kitchen hygiene (structure and procedures).

▶ Food hygiene (preparation, cooking, reheating and storage).

Chefs preparing food should wear protective clothing

Personal hygiene

Food handlers should observe strict hygiene:

1. Wash hands thoroughly using hot water and disinfectant soap, particularly:
   - Before handling food.
   - When switching from raw to cooked food preparation.
   - After using the toilet.
   - After handling waste and pets.
   - After coughing, sneezing, or blowing nose.
2. Keep nails short, clean, and remove jewellery.
3. Cover cuts with a brightly coloured waterproof dressing.
4. Avoid coughing or sneezing over food and do not smoke in food preparation areas.
5. Hair should be neat and tidy. Cover with a hat or a hairnet, tie back long hair.
6. Do not dip fingers into food. If tasting food use a clean spoon each time.
7. Avoid touching hair and face while preparing food.
8. Wear protective clothing such as an apron.
9. Do not prepare or cook food if suffering from illness or an infectious disease such as food poisoning.

Kitchen hygiene structure	Kitchen hygiene procedures
Hygiene and safety should be priorities in the design and layout of food preparation areas: 1. Flooring, walls, ceiling and work surfaces should be easy to clean, non-absorbent surfaces with no joints or crevices which could harbour microbes or insects. 2. A good lighting system is essential to illuminate all working areas and to facilitate cleaning. 3. An effective system of ventilation is necessary to reduce condensation and discourage microbial growth. 4. A clean water supply and effective drainage system is essential to maintain good hygiene. 5. A kitchen should be constructed so that there is no access for pests such as mice and cockroaches, e.g. around water pipes.	1. Floors and work surfaces should be washed and disinfected regularly. 2. Cloths should be washed, disinfected and changed frequently. Different cloths should be used for different purposes. 3. All equipment should be thoroughly washed and stored in clean, dry cupboards. 4. Pets should not be allowed in the kitchen during food preparation. 5. Bins should be kept clean, covered and disinfected and should be emptied regularly. 6. Clean all cutting surfaces and chopping boards immediately after use. Use separate surfaces for preparing raw and cooked meats. 7. Food storage areas should be well monitored and cleaned regularly.

Hygiene	
Food hygiene: preparation	**To avoid the risk of contamination during food preparation:**
The risk of cross-contamination is highest during food preparation because the food comes into contact with hands, utensils, work surfaces and equipment – any of which may transfer harmful bacteria onto the food. There is also a risk that raw food may contaminate cooked food. Contamination may also occur during preparation if the food is at room temperature for a considerable length of time (danger zone 6°–63°C).	1. Keep the danger-zone time to a minimum. 2. Prepare high-risk foods just before they are ready to be cooked. (High-risk foods include meat, poultry, fish, eggs and dairy products, all of which are especially vulnerable to bacterial growth.) 3. Prepare raw and cooked food separately to avoid cross-contamination. 4. Thoroughly wash fruit and vegetables and prepare separately from meat. 5. Avoid handling food during preparation.

Food hygiene: cooking

Cooking can destroy most bacteria if the food has reached a high enough temperature and if that temperature is maintained for the recommended period of time. Temperature and cooking time vary depending on the type of food.

To prevent contamination of food during cooking:
1. Keep cooking utensils clean and in good condition.
2. Frozen meat and poultry must be fully thawed before cooking.
3. Cook poultry, meat and fish thoroughly, e.g. the centre of a meat joint must reach a temperature of 82°C and that temperature must be maintained for 20 minutes.
4. When cooking stews and gravies stir frequently to ensure that the food is heated through. Maintain a temperature above 73°C and serve as soon as possible when cooked.
5. Cook made-up dishes such as meat pies thoroughly, because there is a risk of cross-contamination between the different ingredients.
6. Avoid handling cooked foods.

Reheating cooked food

Reheating cooked food creates a potential hygiene risk because it may result in food being warmed to a temperature, which suits bacterial growth, but not high enough to destroy the bacteria.

Ideally, food should be eaten immediately after cooking. Since this is not always practical, the following rules apply to reheating foods:

1. Leftovers should be cooled quickly, covered and stored in a refrigerator. Use within two days.
2. Heat food quickly to reduce the time spent in the danger zone.
3. Heat to 100°C and simmer for 10 minutes to destroy bacteria.
4. Never reheat food more than once.
5. If using a microwave oven follow manufacturers instructions to ensure that the food has been heated to the correct temperature for the right length of time.

Safe food storage		
Food type	**Risk/hazard**	**Correct storage**
Dry goods	• Bacterial contamination. • Pests.	• Store food in a cool, dry, well-ventilated storeroom. • Use food in rotation. • Use original container or other suitable container.
Fresh fruit and vegetables	• Bacterial contamination, e.g. E. coli. • Mould growth. • Enzyme activity. • Pests.	• Store correctly according to class. (See Page 99).
Chilled foods	• Multiplication of bacteria. • Some mould growth.	• Store below 4°C. • Check date stamp. • Use foods in rotation. • Do not over-pack fridge – allow air circulation. • Cover all food. • Store raw foods below cooked foods. • Never place warm food in a fridge.
Frozen food	• Multiplication of bacteria if correct temperature (−18°C) is not maintained.	• Place in freezer as soon as possible after purchase. • Freeze fresh foods at −25°C, store at −18°C • Keep accurate records and use food in rotation. • Never refreeze thawed foods.

Hazard Analysis Critical Control Points (HACCP)

HACCP is a food safety system which identifies and controls hazards that could pose a threat to the safe production of food.

Hazard

In the food industry, a hazard can be described as anything that could contaminate food or cause harm to the consumer. Hazards may be divided into three groups:

Hazards		
Microbiological contamination	**Chemical contamination**	**Physical contamination**
Bacteria	Cleaning agents	Metal particles
Moulds	Pesticides	Human hairs
Yeast	Commercial oil	Glass
	Unauthorised food additives	Wood splinters

The HACCP has seven main components

1. *Identify the hazards* that might occur during food production and estimate the risk of each hazard to the consumer.
2. *Determine critical control points,* i.e. any stage during the food production where lack of control would result in risk to food safety, e.g. purchasing, storage, preparation, cooking and serving of food.
3. *Set critical control limits*, e.g. fridge temperature must be below 4°C.
4. *Monitor critical limits*, e.g. fridge temperature is checked morning and evening seven days a week (written record kept). ·
5. *Take corrective action* when monitoring indicates that *critical limits* have not been met, e.g. fridge temperature registering above 4°C on a regular basis, the refrigeration company may need to be contacted.
6. *Establish an effective recording system* at each critical control point.
7. *Review the system* occasionally to check that it is working effectively.

Setting up an HACCP system

1. To set up an HACCP system first choose a HACCP team. The members should be familiar with the food processes involved and should have been trained in food hygiene.
2. The team draws up a flow chart showing all aspects of the food production from raw material to the consumer.
3. The team identifies all potential hazards throughout the food operation.
4. A risk assessment is carried out to determine how likely it is that a problem might occur. Risks are estimated as high, medium or low.
5. The team decides what control measures should be taken at certain stages (critical control points) of the food operation to remove or reduce any physical, chemical or microbial risk.
6. For each critical control point the team decides:
   ▶ What is to be done.
   ▶ When it is to be done.
   ▶ Who is to do it.

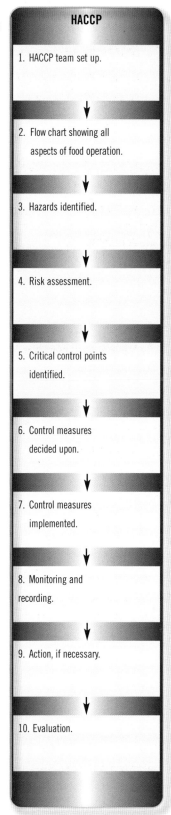

HACCP

1. HACCP team set up.

2. Flow chart showing all aspects of food operation.

3. Hazards identified.

4. Risk assessment.

5. Critical control points identified.

6. Control measures decided upon.

7. Control measures implemented.

8. Monitoring and recording.

9. Action, if necessary.

10. Evaluation.

Example of a simple HACCP system – lasagne		
Step	**Possible hazards**	**Control measures**
1. Purchase of ingredients	• Minced meat may be contaminated with food poisoning bacteria. • Fresh vegetables may be subjected to mould growth or insect damage. • Perishable ingredients may be incorrectly stored in shop.	• Buy ingredients from reputable food suppliers. • Examine vegetables thoroughly on purchase, buy loose produce. • Check dates and note storage temperature of chilled foods at point of purchase.
2. Transport and delivery of food	• Rise in temperature leading to growth in food poisoning bacteria. • Cross contamination between meat and vegetables.	• Wrap foods well and transport in suitable containers. • Store at suitable temperature as soon as possible after purchase.
3. Storage prior to use	• Growth of food-poisoning bacteria and toxins on meat. • Cross-contamination between meat and other perishables.	• Store food covered and in suitable containers. • Store at correct temperature. • Place foods in separate areas of the fridge.
4. Preparation of lasagne	• Contamination of high-risk foods. • Cross-contamination. • Growth of food-poisoning bacteria.	• Observe good personal hygiene. • Surfaces and equipment must be clean. • Prepare raw and cooked foods separately. • Limit the time food is at room temperature.
5. Cooking	• Survival of food-poisoning bacteria.	• Cook meat sauce thoroughly, stirring frequently to ensure even temperature throughout. • Cook lasagne at correct oven temperature for recommended length of time.
6. Serving	• Growth of any surviving food-poisoning bacteria. • Contamination from serving utensils, food handlers, raw foods, e.g. side salad.	• Serve quickly to prevent cooling. • Serve correctly prepared accompanying salad as soon as possible after removing from the fridge.

Benefits of the HACCP system

► It focuses the attention of management on food safety issues.

► Potential hazards are identified and control measures are set in place, thereby reducing the risk of problems occurring.

► HACCP increases awareness among food workers of food safety and hygiene.

► Records that are kept can be used as evidence that all reasonable precautions are being taken to ensure safe food, and that food safety legislation is observed (relevant in a possible court case).

► Records also enable food safety officers to get a more informed overview of food hygiene practices within a food business.

ISO 9000

► ISO (The International Organisation for Standardisation) is an association that sets standards for quality in industry.

► The National Standards Authority of Ireland provides an IS quality scheme for food companies (IS 343).

► If the company's food safety is up to standard the company is awarded the NSAI Food Safety Management Mark which is independent evidence that their food safety system is operating effectively.

National Food Safety Agencies

Several government departments and agencies deal with food safety including:

1. The Food Safety Authority of Ireland
2. Department of Agriculture, Fisheries and Food
3. Department of Health and Children
4. HSE – the Health Service Executive
5. Public analyst laboratories
6. National Consumer Agency
7. Local Authorities

The Food Safety Authority of Ireland (FSAI)

The FSAI is an independent, statutory body set up in 1999 to protect public health and consumer interests in the area of food hygiene and safety. It is responsible for the enforcement of all food legislation in Ireland which it does through a number of agencies including the HSE, the Department of Agriculture, Fisheries and Food and the local authorities.

Role / functions

► To take all reasonable steps to ensure that food produced, distributed or marketed in Ireland meets the highest standards of food safety and hygiene.

► To advise Ministers, regulators, the food industry and consumers on food safety issues.

▶ To co-ordinate and deliver food safety services through the various agencies involved.

▶ To ensure that food companies comply with legal standards, are implementing good codes of hygiene and are committed to the production of safe food.

▶ To take action when a food premises is in breach of legislation, e.g. Issuing Improvement Notices and Closure Orders.

▶ To co-ordinate rapid alert systems enacted if a food product presents a serious risk to the consumer.

Improvement Notice
Issued when a premises or practise will or is likely to pose a risk to public safety and hygiene.

Closure Order
Issued if there is or there is likely to be a grave and immediate danger to public health at/on food premises. All or part of the premises may be closed immediately

One such alert occurred in December '08. Pork and pork products were withdrawn from the market amid fears of dioxin contamination.

Department of Agriculture, Fisheries and Food

Role in food safety

▶ Plays a major role in ensuring the highest possible standards of food safety and consumer protection in Ireland.

▶ Monitors food safety in the following areas—
   1. **Meat and meat products**
      Supervise larger abattoirs and meat processing plants producing for home and export market.
   2. **Milk and milk products**
      Inspect milk-processing plants and monitor operational hygiene.
   3. **Eggs and egg products**
      Enforce a range of EU egg regulations.
   4. **Pesticides**
      Various food such as fruit,vegetables and cereals are continually monitored for pesticide residues.

▶ Enforces EU legislation controlling the import of foods of animal origin from countries outside the EU.

▶ Ensures that all cattle in Ireland are registered and fully traceable. There are also traceability systems in place for pigs and sheep.

Department of Health and Children

The Department of Health and Children is responsible for the development of food safety legislation and policies.

DEPARTMENT
OF HEALTH AND
CHILDREN
AN ROINN
SLÁINTE AGUS LEANAÍ

Health Service Executive

Environmental Health Officers (EHOs) implement legislation in relation to food hygiene and safety including:

▶ The inspection of retail and catering establishments.

▶ Responsibility for food safety at major public gatherings, e.g. concerts and sports events.

▶ Monitoring legislation dealing with food and nutrition labelling, additives and contaminants.

▶ Investigating incidences of food-borne illness (Medical Officers and laboratory staff are also involved).

▶ Responding to rapid alerts: recalling, withdrawing and destroying foodstuffs when necessary.

Public Analyst Laboratories

▶ Public Analyst Laboratories work with EHOs sampling and assessing foods for bacteriological safety.

▶ They analyse foods to monitor compliance with food legislation and labelling in terms of additives and GMOs (genetically modified organisms, etc.).

▶ They also analyse food and water samples for the general public (a fee is charged for this service).

National Consumer Agency

▶ The National Consumer Agency enforces the European Communities (Labelling Presentation and Advertising of Foodstuffs) Regulations 2002 in relation to pre-packed foods.

▶ It visits and investigates food premises to ensure full compliance with food labelling legislation.

▶ The Agency acts on consumer complaints regarding food labelling advertising.

national **consumer** agency
gníomhaireacht náisiúnta **tomhaltóirí**

Local authorities

Veterinary officers monitor abattoirs and meat processing plants, which supply meat to the domestic market.

The Department of the Environment, Heritage and Local Government

The Department of the Environment, Heritage and Local Government monitors the safety of tap and bottled water.

'Safe Food' (Food Safety Promotion Board)

The Food Safety Promotion Board was set up under the British Irish Agreement Act in 1999.

▶ Its role is to educate and inform the general public on food safety and food-borne disease.

▶ It runs food safety campaigns through TV, radio and print-media advertising and by issuing information leaflets.
www.safefoodonline.com

Chapter 10 | Practical Coursework/Recipes

CONTENTS INCLUDE:

▶ **Areas of practice for practical coursework**
▶ **Recipes**
▶ **Food composition tables**
▶ **Herbs and spices**

Practical Coursework

There are five areas of practice:		Assignments
A	Application of nutritional principles	2
B	Food preparation and cooking processes	1
C	Food technology	1
D	Properties of a food	1
E	Comparative analysis	1

Students are required to complete **five assignments** – one assignment each from areas A, B, C, and D + one other assignment from either area A or area E.

Area of practice		Examples
A	To apply knowledge of nutritional principles to the planning of meals for various age groups/special diets.	Diets for children, adolescents, the elderly. Low-fat, low salt diets. High fibre foods. Diabetic, coeliac.
B	To acquire new culinary skills and to use and evaluate modern items of equipment.	Yeast, pastry, gelatine, food processor, wok, microwave oven.
C	To study simple food processing procedures that can be carried out in the home/commercially.	Making jam, chutney, ice-cream, mincemeat.
D	To understand the properties of foods and the scientific principles that apply in the making of specified dishes.	Gelatinisation, caramelisation, emulsification, coagulation.
E	To learn to critically evaluate dishes using sensory analysis skills.	Product/recipe development, comparative testing of different versions of the same product.

Recording Criteria for Food Studies assignments shown overleaf.

For sample food studies assignment (See Page 440).

Recording Criteria for Practical Food Studies Assignments
(to be applied in conjuction with the specific requirements of the assignment)

| **Investigation: Analysis/Research = 30 marks** |

Area of Practice A: Application of Nutritional Principles
- Investigation of nutritional needs
- Identification and application of appropriate meal planning guidelines
- Suitable dishes/modified dishes
- Chosen dish/es (name and source of recipe) and selection criteria

Area of Practice B: Food Preparation and Processes – New skills/equipment
  (each point may not be relevant)
- Brief description of the item of equipment in terms of types and use / brief description of new skill concerned
- Suitable dishes illustrating improved efficiency using this equipment / suitable dishes illustrating use of skill concerned
- Understanding of the key points essential to making a dish using the equipment / the skill concerned
- State chosen dish (name and source of recipe) and selection criteria

Area of Practice C: Food Technology
- Investigate the method of processing and the principles involved
- Identify suitable foods/dishes appropriate to the assignment
- State chosen foods/dishes and selection criteria
- Suggested packaging/containers/labelling

Area of Practice D: Properties of a Food
- Definition of a particular property
- Suitable dishes illustrating that property
- Understanding of associated principles
- State chosen dishes and selection criteria

Area of Practice E: Comparative Analysis including Sensory Analysis
- Investigation, description and possible outcomes of the intended testing technique
- Investigation of foods/recipes appropriate to the assignment
- Selected dishes / foods and selection criteria
- Identification of the conditions to be controlled during the testing

| **Preparation and Planning = 6 marks** |

- Resources (ingredients incl. costing, key equipment)
- Work plan

| **Implementation = 28 marks** |

- Procedure followed while carrying out practical including food preparation processes / testing procedures used
- Key factors considered when making the dishes / conducting tests
- Safety and hygiene issues relevant to the dishes / foods

| **Implementation = 16 marks** |

Evaluate the assignment in terms of:
- Implementation
- The specific requirements of the assignment

Recipes
Starters

Possible properties/processing methods are included for some recipes.

Savoury Puffs

Ingredients

175 g puff pastry
8 slices of salami
25 g grated Cheddar cheese
beaten egg, to glaze
parsley to garnish

Method

1. Preheat oven to 200°C (400°F, Gas Mark 6).
2. On a floured surface, roll out the pastry thinly.
3. Using a 10-cm fluted cutter, cut out 8 circles of pastry.
4. Lay a slice of salami in the middle of each pastry circle.
5. Put a little cheese on each slice of salami.
6. Beat egg and brush around edges of pastry.
7. Fold the pastry circle in half and press the edges firmly to seal.
8. Brush each puff with beaten egg.
9. Bake in the oven for 15 minutes until well-risen and golden brown.
10. Serve garnished with parsley.

Shortening

Garlic Mushroom and Chicken Vol-au-vents

Ingredients

2 cooked chicken breasts
1 small onion
1 tbsp oil
125 ml cream
salt and pepper
6 vol-au-vent cases

100 g mushrooms
1 clove of garlic
125 ml milk
1 tsp cornflour dissolved
in 1 tbsp water

Method

1. Preheat the oven and cook the vol-au-vent cases according to the instructions on the packet.
2. Dice the chicken and mushrooms.
3. Peel and chop the onions and garlic.
4. Heat the oil and sauté the onions and garlic for 2 minutes. Add mushrooms and cook for 5–7 minutes.
5. Add the milk and cream and bring to the boil.
6. Add the blended cornflour. Bring back to the boil. Reduce heat and simmer for 5 minutes.
7. Add the diced chicken and heat through and season to taste.
8. Spoon mixture into the cooked vol-au-vent cases and place lids on the cases.
9. Serve warm with a green salad.

Gelatinisation

Soups

Cream of Celery Soup

Ingredients

300–375 g chopped celery	several sprigs of parsley
1 potato, sliced	1 bay leave
25 g flour	pinch of thyme
1 large onion, chopped	salt and pepper
1 rasher	cooking oil
500 ml water (or white stock)	
500 ml milk	

Garnish

4–6 tbsps cream
paprika
croutons

Method

1. Chop the rasher and sauté.
2. Add the celery, potato and onion. Cook together for 4–5 minutes, stirring constantly to prevent browning.
3. Sprinkle in the flour and cook gently for 1 minute.
4. Add the stock water, stir and bring to the boil.
5. Reduce the heat, add the bay leaf, parsley sprigs and thyme. Simmer for 20–30 minutes, or until the vegetables are tender.
6. Blend the soup until smooth. Reheat gently.
7. Add milk and seasoning. Reheat gently.
8. Serve with a spoonful of cream, a dusting of paprika and croutons.

Gelatinisation

Vegetable Soup

Ingredients

a mixture of vegetables:	25 g butter or margarine
(400–500 g), e.g.	25 g flour
1 medium potato	1 litre stock
1 medium parsnip	125 ml milk
1 leek	chopped parsley
1 medium onion	
1 medium carrot	
2 sticks celery	
1 tbsp frozen peas	

Method

1. Prepare and dice the vegetables.
2. Melt the margarine, sauté the vegetables for 5 minutes.
3. Add stock and seasoning, bring to the boil, simmer until vegetables are soft, about 40 minutes.
4. Blend the flour with a little cold milk, add to the soup and boil for 2–3 minutes.
5. Stir in the remaining milk and heat without boiling.
6. Serve in a warmed soup tureen.
7. Garnish with cream and chopped parsley.

Gelatinisation

Main Courses

Spaghetti Bolognese

Ingredients – Bolognese Sauce

450 g of minced beef
1 tbsp oil
1 onion chopped
3–4 slices of streaky bacon, finely chopped
2 tbsp tomato purée
1 tsp basil or mixed herbs
400 g tin tomatoes
2 cloves of garlic, crushed
salt and black pepper
(extra vegetables may be added)

Method

1. Heat the oil. Add the bacon and cook until crisp.
2. Add the onion and garlic and cook until the onion is soft.
3. Stir in the meat and fry until brown.
4. Add the tomatoes, purée, herbs, salt and pepper.
5. Bring to the boil, reduce the heat and simmer gently for 15–20 minutes.

To cook the spaghetti, place in a large saucepan of boiling water to which a little oil and salt has been added. (The oil will prevent the spaghetti from sticking together.) Bring the water back to the boil and cook for 8–10 minutes. As soon as the pasta is cooked drain it in a colander.

To Serve: Pour the bolognese sauce over the spaghetti. Sprinkle with parmesan cheese and parsley to garnish.

Lasagne

Ingredients

Bolognese sauce (as opposite)
12 sheets lasagne
Cheese sauce

Ingredients – Cheese Sauce

25 g flour
25 g margarine/butter
375 ml milk
salt and pepper
75 g cheddar cheese, grated

Method

1. Melt the margarine or butter.
2. Add flour and cook for 1 minute over gentle heat.
3. Remove from the heat and gradually add the milk mixing well between each addition.
4. Season with salt and pepper.
5. Cook the sauce stirring continuously until it boils. Simmer for 2–3 minutes.
6. Remove from the heat and stir in half the cheese.

Method for Lasagne

1. Spread a layer of bolognese sauce over the base of a greased pie dish.
2. Cover with sheets of lasagne.
3. Pour a layer of cheese sauce over the lasagne.
4. Repeat until all the meat sauce, lasagne and cheese sauce are used.
5. Sprinkle the remaining cheese on top.
6. Bake at 190°C (Gas Mark 5) for 30–40 minutes.
7. Garnish with tomato and parsley.
8. Serve with green salad and garlic bread.

Gelatinisation

Chilli Con Carne

Ingredients

400 g minced beef	2 onions (chopped)
1 green/yellow pepper	1 can of tomatoes
(chopped)	1 tbsp tomato purée
1 can of red kidney beans	2 garlic cloves
1–2 tsps chilli powder	(crushed)
salt and pepper	olive oil

Method

1. Prepare all vegetables according to kind.
2. Heat the oil in a large saucepan.
3. Add the onions, garlic, meat and peppers and fry for 2–3 minutes, until the meat is brown.
4. Add the chilli powder, purée and tomatoes.
5. Season and bring to the boil and simmer for 30–40 minutes.
6. Add the beans and cook for a further 5 minutes.
7. Serve on a bed of rice. Garnish with parsley and cayenne pepper.

Beef Stroganoff

Ingredients

500 g sirloin fillet steak
2–3 onions, sliced
150 g mushrooms, sliced
salt and black pepper
125 ml cream
juice of $\frac{1}{2}$ lemon
cooking oil

Method

1. Heat the oil and fry the onions over a gentle heat until golden brown. Lift out and keep warm.
2. Fry the mushrooms, remove from the pan and keep warm with the onions.
3. Increase the heat, add the oil and fry the steak strips for about 3–4 minutes. Fry the meat in two or three lots so that the temperature is not lowered too much.
4. Return all the meat to the pan, season well.
5. Add onions and mushrooms and stir together.
6. Mix the cream and lemon juice, add to the pan and heat through.
7. Serve on a bed of boiled rice.
8. Garnish with parley and cayenne pepper.

* marinade to tenderise and improve flavour

Marinating

Paprika Chicken

Ingredients

400 g chicken breasts	450 ml chicken stock
200 g pasta shapes	50 g onions
50 g mushrooms	100 ml soured cream
50 g onions	$\frac{1}{2}$ green pepper, $\frac{1}{2}$ red pepper
2 tsps paprika	salt and pepper
	2 tbsps oil

Method

1. Peel and chop the onion, slice the peppers and mushrooms.
2. Cut the chicken into bite-sized pieces.
3. Heat the oil and fry the onion.
4. Add the chicken, mushrooms and paprika and fry for 2 minutes.
5. Stir in stock and seasoning, bring to the boil. Add the peppers and pasta and cover.
6. Simmer gently for about 20 minutes, until chicken and pasta are tender.
7. Stir in soured cream.
8. Serve in the casserole dish.
9. Garnish with a sprinkle of paprika and serve with a green salad.

Gelatinisation

Baked Liver and Bacon

Ingredients
250 g lamb's liver
2–3 streaky rashers
125 ml stock

Stuffing
50 g breadcrumbs
1 tsp chopped parsley
1 slice finely chopped onion
salt and pepper
13 g melted margarine
a little stock to bind

Method

1. Wash and dry the liver. Cut into slices 1 cm thick. Place on a greased tin.

2. Make the stuffing by mixing all the stuffing ingredients together and place a little on each slice of liver.

3. Remove rind from the rashers and cut into two.

4. Arrange the rasher slices on the stuffing.

5. Pour a little stock into the tin, cover with foil and bake in a moderate oven, 190°C (375°F, Gas Mark 5) for 30 minutes.

6. Garnish with parsley. Serve with baked potatoes and other vegetables such as carrots and broccoli.

Curry Sauce

Ingredients
2 onions chopped
1 small cooking apple
(peeled and chopped)
1 tbsp curry powder
(or to taste)
25 g flour
1–2 tsps chutney

1–2 tsps lemon juice
25 g sultanas (optional)
250–370 ml stock
1 tsp tomato purée
salt
1 tbsp oil

Method

1. Heat oil. Add onion and fry for 1–2 minutes. Reduce heat.

2. Add curry powder and flour, cook gently for 1–2 minutes, stirring all the time.

3. Slowly add stock and continue to stir until it comes to the boil.

4. Add the chopped apple to the sauce, together with the chutney, lemon juice, tomato purée, sultanas and salt.

5. Simmer gently for 20 minutes stirring now and then.

This sauce can be used with 500 g of cooked fish or meat, e.g. chicken, beef or lamb (diced), or a selection of cooked vegetables. Add to cooked sauce and reheat thoroughly.

Gelatinisation

Creamy Smoked Haddock

Ingredients

400 g smoked haddock

5 peppercorns

250 ml milk

1 small onion (sliced)

200 ml crème fraîche

6 spring onions (trimmed and sliced)

3 tomatoes (chopped)

bay leaf

salt and pepper

Method

1. Place the haddock in a saucepan with the bay leaf, milk, peppercorns and onion.

2. Cover, bring to the boil and simmer for 5 minutes.

3. Remove fish from the saucepan.

4. Reduce the milk by simmering for 2–3 minutes uncovered.

5. Strain the milk and return to saucepan.

6. Add the crème fraîche and seasoning and bring to the boil stirring occasionally.

7. Return the fish to the sauce with tomatoes and spring onions.

8. Heat through and serve with creamed potatoes. Garnish with lemon and parsley.

Cod and Tomato Bake

Ingredients

400–500 g cod (or any white fish)

1 tbsp chopped parsley

1 onion

1 tin chopped tomatoes

1 green pepper (optional)

$1/2$ tsp oregano

salt and pepper

1 tbsp oil

2 tbsps brown breadcrumbs

50 g grated cheese

Method

1. Preheat oven to 180°C (350°F, Gas Mark 4).

2. Wash and dry fish (skin if necessary). Place in an ovenproof dish.

3. Peel and chop the onion. Wash, de-seed and chop the pepper.

4. Heat the oil in a small saucepan. Sauté onions without browning, for 1 minute. Add tomatoes, peppers, herbs and seasoning. Cook gently for 5 minutes.

5. Prepare the breadcrumbs, grate the cheese and mix together.

6. Pour the tomato mixture over fish. Sprinkle with breadcrumbs and cheese.

7. Bake for about 30 minutes. Serve with green vegetables such as broccoli or spinach and boiled potatoes.

Vegetable Stir-Fry

Ingredients

1 onion (sliced)

1 carrot (in strips)

1 green, yellow, red pepper (in strips)

100 g mushrooms (sliced)

100 g cauliflower/broccoli in florets

2 cloves of finely chopped garlic

50 g peanuts

2 tbsps soy sauce

salt and pepper

olive oil

Method

1. Prepare the vegetables according to kind.

2. Heat the oil to a high temperature in a wok or a large frying pan.

3. Add carrots and stir-fry for 5 minutes.

4. Add onions, garlic, peppers and mushrooms and stir-fry for 3 minutes.

5. Add cauliflower and broccoli.

6. Add seasoning, soy sauce and nuts and heat through for 2–3 minutes.

7. Serve on an oval platter on a bed of rice garnished with fresh parsley and cayenne pepper.

Variation: To improve the protein content of this dish, chicken, meat or fish may be added.

Cheesy Leek and Bacon Risotto

Ingredients
175 g long grain rice
850 ml chicken stock
3 tbsps olive oil
6–8 rashers (chopped)
3 medium leeks, trimmed and sliced
100 g cheddar cheese, grated
salt and pepper
parsley

Method
1. Place the rice in a saucepan with the chicken stock. Bring to the boil. Reduce the heat and simmer, uncovered, for 12–15 minutes until the rice is almost tender.
2. Heat the oil. Add the rashers and leek slices. Cook over a moderately high heat for 5 minutes until lightly golden and softened.
3. Add the rice and cooking liquid to the leeks and rashers, stir well. Continue to cook for a further 5 minutes, stirring occasionally, until the rice is completely cooked.
4. Stir in the grated cheese. Season with salt and freshly ground black pepper.
5. Garnish with parsley. Serve with a green salad and warm crusty bread.

Gelatinisation

Savoury Omelette

Ingredients
2 eggs
2 tbsps water
salt and pepper
knob of butter
$\frac{1}{2}$ tsp herbs (optional)
To fry: butter/oil

Method
1. Beat the eggs lightly in a bowl.
2. Add water, butter and herbs.
3. Heat the omelette pan, add butter/oil and allow it to heat well.
4. Pour in the mixture. As it begins to set, draw it in from sides, allowing the liquid mixture to run under the set edges. Repeat until all the liquid has set.
5. Place under a preheated grill to cook the top.
6. Fold the omelette in two, place on a warm plate.
7. Serve at once, garnished with parsley.

Coagulation

Filled Omelette

Prepare fillings before cooking omelette.
Make basic omelette, as for savoury omelette.
Place fillings in centre of omelette before folding.

Fillings
1. Cheese: Sprinkle on 2 tbsps of grated cheddar.
2. Ham/cooked rasher: Add 1–2 tbsps to the omelette mixture before cooking.
3. Mushroom: Wash and slice mushrooms, sauté in a little oil.
4. Onion and tomato: Sauté 1 small sliced onion in a little butter for 1 minute; add 2 sliced tomatoes, cook for 2 minutes.
5. Smoked haddock: Flake cooked haddock and heat with 2 tbsps cream/milk.

Coagulation

Cheese Soufflé

Ingredients
25 g butter/margarine
25 g flour
125 ml milk
3 eggs separated
75 g grated cheddar cheese
salt and pepper

Method
1. Preheat oven to 185°C (360°F, Gas Mark 4) and grease a 750 ml soufflé dish.
2. Melt the butter, add the flour and cook for 2–3 minutes. Remove from the heat and allow to cool slightly. Add in the milk gradually. Return to the heat, bring to the boil stirring all the time until sauce thickens.
3. Allow the sauce to cool slightly. Mix in the egg yolk and season to taste.
4. Stir in 50 g of the cheese.
5. Whisk the egg whites until stiff and fold into the mixture.
6. Pour the mixture into a prepared dish and sprinkle with remaining cheese.
7. Bake for 40–45 minutes.
8. Serve immediately with a green salad.

Gelatinisation/Aeration/Coagulation

Quiche Lorraine

Ingredients
100 g shortcrust pasty
125 ml milk
2 eggs
100 g cheese
3 rashers
1 small onion, chopped
50 g mushrooms sliced
tomato (to garnish)
cooking oil
salt and pepper

Shortening/Coagulation

Method
1. Roll the pastry out so it fits into a flan case.
2. Cut the bacon into strips and sauté onions, bacon and mushrooms until beginning to brown. Drain on kitchen paper.
3. Beat the eggs, add seasoning, stir in the milk.
4. Grate cheese, sprinkle some over the flan's base. Add the sautéed ingredients. Carefully pour on the egg mixture. Sprinkle on the remaining cheese.
5. Bake in a moderate oven 190°C (375°F, Gas Mark 5) for 30–40 minutes, until the mixture is set.
6. Serve in wedges on a hot plate, with a side salad. Garnish with tomato slices and parsley.

Desserts

Puffed Sweet Omelette

Ingredients per person
2 eggs   2 tbsps water
2 tsps castor sugar   cooking oil

Fillings – choose from:
2 tbsps jam (heated)   2–3 tbsps stewed fruit
sliced banana   chopped pineapple
fresh strawberries or raspberries

Method
1 Separate the eggs.
2. Beat the yolks and sugar until creamy. Add water.
3. Stiffly beat the egg whites, fold in the egg yolk mixture.
4. Heat the oil in an omelette pan.

Aeration/Coagulation

5. Pour on the omelette mixture and cook on a moderate heat until lightly browned beneath. Do not stir.
6. Brown the top of the omelette under a preheated grill or in a hot oven for a few minutes. Slide it onto a hot plate.
7. Slit the centre of the omelette, spread the filling on one half and fold other half over.
8. Serve at once, sprinkled with castor sugar.

Batters

Thin batter

Ingredients
100 g flour
pinch of salt
1 egg
250 ml milk

Use for

Pancakes
Yorkshire pudding

Thick (coating) batter

Ingredients
100 g flour
pinch of salt
1 egg
125 ml milk

Use for

Coating fish
Fritters

Method

1. Sieve flour and salt into a bowl.
2. Make a hole in the centre of the flour and drop in the egg and 1–2 tbsps of the milk.
3. With a wooden spoon, stir the egg mixture in the centre of the bowl, allowing the flour to fall in gradually from the sides.
4. Slowly add about half the milk, beating well to avoid lumps.
5. Beat for about 5 minutes to add air to the batter.
6. Stir in the rest of the milk and use as required.

Aeration/Coagulation

Pancakes

Method

1. Make thin batter and pour into a jug.
2. Brush the pan with melted fat, wait for it to get really hot, then pour on enough batter to barely cover the base of the pan. Tilt the pan to spread it evenly.
3. Fry over a medium heat until golden brown underneath, shaking now and then.
4. Toss the pancake or turn with a fish slice.
5. Fry the second side until golden brown.
6. Slide onto a plate and keep warm.
7. Sprinkle with castor sugar and lemon juice and roll up.
8. Serve warm.

Pancakes may be served with a sweet or savoury filling, e.g. mashed banana, castor sugar and cream, or chopped cooked chicken in a mushroom sauce.

Aeration/Coagulation

Fruit Fritters

Ingredients

Thick batter
Fruit
Apples – peeled, cored, sliced
Bananas – peeled, sliced lengthways in two
Pineapple – drained slices
castor sugar

Method

1. Make the batter and heat the deep-fat fryer.
2. Drop the sliced fruit into the batter, lift out and allow the excess batter to drain off.
3. Lower carefully into hot fat. Fry until golden brown and cooked through.
4. Drain well on kitchen paper.
5. Sprinkle with castor sugar.
6. Serve hot in individual dishes.
7. Custard/cream may be served with fritters.

Aeration/Coagulation

Eve's Pudding

Ingredients

500 g cooking apples   50 g sugar
$\frac{1}{2}$ tsp ground cloves   1 tbsp water
madeira mixture

Madeira mixture

50 g margarine   50 g castor sugar
75 g self-raising flour   1 egg
a little milk

Method

1. Peel, core and slice the apples. Put into a saucepan with water, sugar and cloves, and stew gently until half cooked.

2. Pour into a greased pie dish and leave to cool.

3. Cream margarine and sugar together until white and fluffy. Add some egg and some flour and beat gently. Add remaining egg, flour and beat. Add a little milk if the mixture seems dry.

4. Spread the mixture over cooled apples.

5. Bake in a moderate oven 190°C (375°F, Gas Mark 5) for about 30–40 minutes, until the mixture is fully cooked.

6. Sprinkle with castor sugar and serve on a plate, with a doyley under a pie dish.

Aeration/Coagulation

Bread and Butter Pudding

Ingredients

4 thin slices of brown or white buttered-bread
1 egg
350 ml milk
25 g brown or white sugar
50 g sultanas or raisins
nutmeg

Method

1. Cut the bread into fingers and arrange a layer on the base of the pie dish.

2. Sprinkle fruit on top. Arrange bread and fruit in layers with bread arranged neatly on top.

3. Beat the egg and sugar, heat the milk until steaming.

4. Pour the milk over the beaten egg, stirring well.

5. Strain over the bread and leave to soak for 15–20 minutes (if time allows). Grate nutmeg on top.

6. Place the pie dish on a flat tin containing a little water and bake in a fairly moderate oven 175°C (350°F, Gas Mark 4) for 30–40 minutes, until set and turning brown on top.

7. Decorate with a cherry.

8. Serve on a plate with a doyley under the pie dish.

Coagulation

Lemon Meringue Pie

Ingredients
150 g shortcrust/rich shortcrust pastry

Filling
50 g cornflour
150 ml water
finely grated rind of 2 medium lemons
45 ml (5 tbsps) lemon juice
75 g granulated sugar
2 egg yolks

Meringue
2 egg whites
100 g castor sugar

Method
1. Make the pastry and chill in the refrigerator.
   Roll it out to fit a 20-cm (8-inch) greased pie dish or flan ring. Prick the base with a fork and chill for another 15 minutes, if possible.
2. Bake blind.
3. Put the cornflour and water into a saucepan, mix the lemon rind and juice and bring slowly to the boil, stirring all the time. Simmer gently until the mixture thickens.
4. Remove from the heat and stir in the sugar.
   Cool a little then stir in the egg yolks. Pour the mixture into the cooked flan case.
5. Meringue: whisk the egg whites in a clean bowl until stiff. Add half the sugar (50 g) and whisk again until meringue forms stiff peaks. Fold in the remaining sugar gently.
6. Pile/pipe the meringue onto the lemon mixture.
7. Bake in a cool oven 140°C (Gas Mark 1) for about 30 minutes until the meringue has crisped and the peaks have begun to turn golden brown.

To Serve: Serve hot or cold with cream or ice-cream.

Shortening/Aeration/Coagulation

Lemon Soufflé

Ingredients
3 lemons
3 large eggs, separated
125 g castor sugar
3 tablespoons cold water
15 g gelatine
125 ml double cream

To decorate: Chopped nuts (optional), whipped cream

Method
1. Cut a piece of greaseproof paper long enough to go round the outside of a soufflé dish and about 5 cm deeper than the dish. Tie this around outside of dish to form a 'collar'.
2. Grate and squeeze 3 lemons. Dissolve the gelatine.
3. Put the finely-grated lemon rind, juice, egg yolks and sugar in a bowl over a pan of hot water. Whisk until it just begins to thicken.
4. Stir the dissolved gelatine into the lemon mixture. Leave the mixture in a cold place until it just begins to set.
5. Whisk the cream until it forms soft peaks.
   Fold into the mixture.
6. Whisk the egg whites stiffly and fold into the mixture.
7. Turn the soufflé into the prepared dish and leave in a cold place to set.
8. Just before serving remove the paper carefully. Pipe a little cream round the edge and decorate the side with nuts.

Aeration/Gelling

Baked Custard

Ingredients

2 large eggs   400 ml milk
1–2 tsps sugar   grated nutmeg

Method

1. Beat eggs and sugar in a bowl.
2. Heat the milk until steaming, pour over the eggs, stirring all the time.
3. Strain into a greased pie dish and grate nutmeg over it.
4. Place the pie dish in a bain-marie (tin of cold water).
5. Bake at 175°C (Gas Mark 4) for 30–40 minutes.
6. Decorate by dredging castor sugar on top and serve on a plate with a doyley.

Coagulation

Caramel Custard

Ingredients

3 large eggs   300 ml milk
1 tbsp sugar   vanilla

Caramel:
100 g sugar
150 ml water
1 tbsp hot water

Method

1. Put the sugar and water for the caramel in a small heavy saucepan, and dissolve sugar slowly over a gentle heat, stirring all the time.
2. Boil the syrup until it turns brown, add 1 tbsp hot water, then pour at once into a clean, dry, straight-sided tin or soufflé dish, turning the dish until the base and sides are evenly coated.
3. Make the custard as for baked custard, pour into the caramel.
4. Cover with foil and bake at 175°C (Gas Mark 4) for 40–45 minutes until set.
5. Cool for a few minutes, then turn onto a warmed plate.
6. Serve hot or cold, with cream.

Carmelisation/Coagulation

Lemon Cheesecake

Ingredients

100 g digestive biscuits   220 ml cream
50 g butter or margarine   juice and rind of 1 lemon
225 g cream cheese   15 g gelatine
75 g castor sugar   3 tbsp water
2 eggs (separated)   25 g grated chocolate and piped cream

Method

1. Melt the butter, crush the biscuits and mix together. Spread the mixture on the base of a greased, loose-based tin (20 cm) and chill while making the filling.
2. Dissolve the gelatine in the water and allow it to cool slightly.
3. Soften the cheese and beat in the sugar, lemon rind, juice and egg yolks.
4. Stir the gelatine into the cheese mixture.
5. Whip the cream and fold into cheese mixture.
6. Whisk the egg whites and fold into the mixture.
7. Spoon the mixture onto the base and refrigerate until set.
8. Decorate with lemon twists, grated chocolate and piped cream.

Gelling/Aeration

Coffee Ice-Cream

Ingredients
2 eggs, separated
2 tbsps coffee essence
50 g icing sugar, sieved
125 ml double cream

Method

1. Whisk the egg whites until very stiff, then gradually whisk in icing sugar.

2. Whisk egg yolks and coffee essence together and whisk gradually into egg whites.

3. Lightly whip the cream and fold into the coffee mixture.

4. Pour into a shallow tin/plastic box and freeze. (This ice cream does not need any further beating.)

5. Freeze for about 3 hours or overnight.

Aeration

Sponge Cake

Ingredients
3 eggs
75 g castor sugar
75 g flour

Filling
2 tbsps jam
125 ml cream whipped and sweetened

Method

1. Whisk the eggs and sugar together until thick and creamy.

2. Sieve flour and gently fold into mixture.

3. Divide the mixture between two greased 18-cm sandwich cake tins. Bake in a moderate oven, 190°C (375°F, Gas Mark 5) for about 15 minutes.

4. Cool on a wire tray. Spread with jam and cream, and sandwich together. Sprinkle with icing sugar.

Aeration/Coagulation

Chocolate Chip Cookies

Ingredients
100 g butter
50 g castor sugar
150 g self-raising flour
50 g or 1 bar milk chocolate, chopped

Method

1. Preheat oven to 170°C (325°F, Gas Mark 4).

2. Grease baking tins.

3. Beat the butter and sugar until fluffy. Stir in the flour and chocolate to make a soft dough. Knead by hand if necessary.

4. Divide the mixture into 12–15 even-sized balls. Place apart on baking tins and flatten well with the back of a tablespoon.

5. Cook for 12–15 minutes until evenly browned.

6. Allow to cool in the tin, then lift off and cool on a wire tray.

7. Serve on a plate with a doyley.

Shortening

Shortcrust Pastry

Ingredients

200 g plain flour
100 g fat

$1/4$ tsp salt
cold water

Method

1. Sieve the flour and salt into a bowl.

2. Cut the fat into the flour with a knife, then rub with your fingertips, until the mixture looks like fine breadcrumbs.

3. Add water, a very small amount at a time, and mix with a knife to a smooth, stiff dough.

4. Turn onto a lightly floured board and knead lightly until smooth.

5. Turn upside down and roll lightly to required shape.

Variations

Wholemeal Shortcrust Pastry

Use 125 g plain flour, 75 g wholemeal

Cheese Pastry

Add 50 g of grated cheese to rubbed in mixture.

Rich Shortcrust Pastry/Flan Pastry

Add 1 tsp sugar to rubbed in mixture
Add 1 tsp lemon juice and 1 egg yolk with water

Shortening

Sausage Rolls

Ingredients

200 g shortcrust pastry
200 g sausages
egg (to glaze)

Method

1. Make the pastry and roll into a rectangular shape.

2. Cut the pastry in two lengthways, and place the sausages in the centre of each. Dampen the edges of the pastry.

3. Fold the pastry over the sausages, press lightly to seal. Cut in lengths of 5 cm or 10 cm long.

4. Flake edges, glaze with beaten egg and cut two slits on the top of each sausage roll.

5. Place on a greased tin. Bake in a fairly hot oven, 220°C (425°F, Gas Mark 7) for 10 minutes, reduce the heat to 190°C (375°F, Gas Mark 5) and cook for about 15 minutes more.

6. Serve on a warmed dish garnished with parsley.

Shortening

Almond and Apricot Puffs

Ingredients
225 g puff pastry
a little beaten egg
6 tbsps apricot conserve
25 g castor sugar
50 g flaked almonds
cream or natural yoghurt, to serve

Method

1. Preheat the oven to 220°C (425°F, Gas Mark 7). Roll out the pastry on a lightly floured surface and shape into a 30-cm square. Cut in half to make two rectangles.
2. Place one piece of pastry on a dampened baking sheet and brush all round the edges with beaten egg. Spread over the apricot conserve.
3. Fold the remaining rectangle in half lengthways and cut about 8 diagonal slits from the centre fold to within about 1 cm in from the edge all the way along.
4. Unfold the pastry and lay it on top of the conserve covered pastry on the baking sheet. Press the pastry edges together well to seal, and flake with the back of a knife.
5. Brush the slashed pastry with water and sprinkle over the castor sugar and flaked almonds.
6. Bake in the oven for 25–30 minutes, until well-risen and golden brown. Remove from the oven and leave to cool. Serve sliced with cream or natural yoghurt.

Shortening

Chocolate Éclairs

Ingredients
choux pastry
50 g butter
2 eggs

150 ml water
65 g plain flour
pinch of salt

Filling
125 ml cream
1 tbsp castor sugar
$\frac{1}{4}$ tsp vanilla essence

Topping
100 g chocolate

Method

1. Put the water and butter into a saucepan and bring slowly to the boil. Remove from the heat.
2. Beat in the sieved flour and salt to form a ball that leaves the sides of the pan clean.
3. Allow the mixture to cool slightly, then beat in the eggs one at a time.
4. Put the pastry into a piping bag use a 1 cm nozzle and pipe 8-cm lengths onto dampened baking trays.
5. Bake at 220°C (425°F, Gas Mark 7) in a moderately hot oven for 25–30 minutes or until crisp and golden.
6. Remove carefully from trays and cool on a rack.
7. Lightly whip the cream and add the sugar and vanilla essence. Make a slit down the side of each éclair and fill with cream.
8. Melt chocolate. Spread on top of the éclairs and allow to set.

Aeration/Coagulation

Pizza

Pizza Dough

Ingredients

175 g strong plain white flour
7 g sachet fast–action dried yeast
150 ml warm water

$^1/_4$ level tsp salt
1 tbsp olive oil

Method

1. In a warm bowl, sieve together the flour, salt and stir in the yeast. Make a well in the centre of the dry ingredients and add the 150 ml of warm water and the olive oil.

2. Stir the mixture until it forms a wet dough. Beat for a further 2–3 minutes.

3. Turn out the dough on to a well-floured surface and knead for about 5 minutes, or until the dough becomes very smooth and elastic.

4. Place in a bowl and cover with a clean tea towel. Leave in a warm place until it has doubled in size, about 45 minutes.

5. Turn out the dough on to a floured surface and knead again for 2–3 minutes.

6. Place a lightly oiled flat baking sheet in a hot oven at 220°C (425°F, Gas Mark 7) to heat.

7. Roll out the dough to a circle about 25 cm in diameter. Place on the heated baking sheet and press into a rough circle, making the edges slightly thicker than the centre. Cover with tomato mix and toppings.

Tomato Mix

Ingredients

1 onion
50 g mushrooms, chopped
1 tbsp tomato purée
1 tsp sugar
1 tbsp oil

2 cloves garlic
tin of tomatoes
salt and freshly ground black pepper

$^1/_4$ tsp oregano

Method

1. Slice the onion and garlic and fry in the oil until soft.

2. Add the mushrooms and fry for a few minutes.

3. Add the tinned tomatoes and purée.

4. Season well with salt, pepper, sugar and oregano.

5. Cook gently until the mixture reduces slightly.

Suggested Toppings:
Grated cheese
Chopped ham
Salami, pepperoni
Anchovies, tuna
Peppers, corn, olives

To assemble pizza: Spread the tomato mix over the base and finish with the toppings of your choice. Bake at 220°C (425°F, Gas Mark 7) for 25–30 minutes until the pizza is well-risen and golden brown. Serve hot with a green salad.

Aeration/Coagulation

Yeast Bread

Ingredients
750 g strong flour
2 tsps salt
25 g butter
7 g sachet fast–action yeast
450 ml warm water

Method

1. In a large bowl sieve together the flour and salt, rub in the butter and add the yeast. Stir in the water and mix into a soft dough.

2. Turn onto a floured surface and knead well for 10 minutes by hand or 5 minutes in an electric mixer with a dough hook.

3. Shape the dough as required and place in a greased tin or tray. Cover with greased polythene (a freezer bag or cling film) and leave in a warm place until it has doubled in size.

4. Uncover and bake in an oven, preheated to 230°C (450°F, Gas Mark 8), for 30–35 minutes. The baked loaf should sound hollow when tapped underneath.

5. For a soft, moist crust, remove from the oven and wrap in a clean tea towel to cool.

Note: Dough may be shaped into 8–10 dinner buns and baked for 15 minutes.

Aeration

Preserves

Rhubarb and Ginger Jam

Ingredients
2 kg rhubarb
juice of 4 lemons
2 kg sugar
$\frac{1}{2}$ tsp ground ginger

Method

1. Wipe the rhubarb, top and tail, and slice.
   Place in a bowl with sugar, in layers, and allow to steep overnight.

2. Put the rhubarb into a greased saucepan, add the ginger and heat slowly, stirring all the time, until the sugar has dissolved.

3. Bring to the boil and boil rapidly until the setting point is reached (20–30 minutes).
   Test for setting.

4. Skim, pot, cover and label.

Gel Formation/Preservation

Citrus Marmalade

Ingredients
250 g each of oranges, lemons, grapefruit
2·5 litres water
2 kg sure-set sugar

Method

1. Scrub the fruit and simmer whole in water for at least 2 hours.

2. Remove the fruit, cool and quarter. Remove the pips.

3. Remove the fruit pulp from the skins using a spoon. Cut up and add to the liquid in the saucepan.

4. Slice the peel using a sharp knife. Add to the liquid.

5. Bring to simmering point, stirring well.

6. Add warmed sugar, stir until dissolved and boil rapidly for 4 minutes.

7. Cool slightly before potting.

8. Cover, label and store.

Gel Formation/Preservation

Apple Chutney

Ingredients
1.5 kg cooking apples
1.5 kg onions
500 g sultanas or raisins
$\frac{1}{2}$ tsp mixed spice
1–2 lemons
750 g brown sugar
500 ml malt vinegar

Method
1. Peel, core and chop the apples. Peel and chop the onions.
2. Put the apples, onions, sultanas and spice into a saucepan.
3. Grate the lemon rind, strain the juice and add each to the chutney with sugar and vinegar. Heat gently.
4. Stir until the sugar is dissolved, bring to the boil and simmer gently until the mixture has a thick, jam-like consistency.
5. Pour into warmed jars, cover and label.
6. Store for a few months before using to allow the flavour to develop.

Preservation

Coleslaw

Ingredients
1 small white cabbage
1 large carrot
1 small onion (optional)
1 apple (optional)
lemon juice

Dressing
150 ml French dressing
salt and pepper

Method
1. Wash the cabbage, cut into four, trim away the stalk and shred finely.
2. Wash and grate the carrot. Peel and grate the onion.
3. Wash, core but do not peel the apple. Dice and toss it in lemon juice to prevent browning.
4. Place all ingredients into a bowl and carefully stir in the dressing until vegetables are coated.
5. Transfer to a serving dish, cover and chill in refrigerator until required.

Mixed Pickle

Ingredients
500 g of mixed vegetables – cucumber, onions, cauliflower, French beans
500 ml brine (500 ml water, 50 g salt)
$\frac{1}{2}$ litre of spiced vinegar

Spiced Vinegar
Ingredients (makes 1 litre)

1 litre vinegar	1 tsp cloves
1 tsp allspice	1 tsp peppercorns
$\frac{1}{4}$ tsp cinnamon	1 blade of mace

Method
Infuse all ingredients in a bottle for 1–2 months before use.

Method
1. Wash the vegetables, peel if necessary, and cut into fairly small pieces.
2. Place the vegetables in layers in a tall container, soak in brine. Leave for 24 hours.
3. Rinse the vegetables thoroughly. Place into sterilised jars.
4. Cover with cold spiced vinegar, seal and label.
5. Allow the flavour to develop for 1–3 months before use.

Preservation

Blender Mayonnaise

Ingredients
1 egg
125 ml oil
1 tbsp vinegar
$\frac{1}{4}$ tsp mustard
$\frac{1}{4}$ tsp salt
$\frac{1}{4}$ tsp castor sugar
pepper

Emulsification

Method
1. Break the whole egg into a blender and whisk it with the vinegar and seasonings.
2. Pour oil slowly into the mixture while the machine is still running.

Herbs and Spices

	Uses
Bay leaves	Meat, fish and poultry dishes, soups and stocks.
Chives	Salads, dressings, garnishes for soups and savoury dishes.
Rosemary	Poultry dishes, fish, meat, especially good with lamb.
Fennel	Fish dishes, soups and sauces.
Garlic (not strictly a herb)	Wide variety of savoury dishes.
Mint	Lamb, flavouring for peas, potatoes and other vegetables.
Oregano	Meat, soups, salads, pizza and other Italian dishes.
Parsley	Sauces, garnishing meat, fish, vegetable dishes, stuffings, soups, salads.
Sage	Stuffing, casserole, salads, meat dishes.
Thyme	Beef, lamb, poultry dishes, soups and stuffings.
Caraway	Cakes, biscuit, bread, soups, salads and cheese dishes.
Cayenne pepper	Use sparingly in meat, fish, vegetable, egg and cheese dishes.
Cinnamon	Cakes, biscuits, pickles, chutneys.
Cloves	Apple dishes, Christmas pudding, mince meat pies, ham and pork.
Ginger	Curries, sauces, chutneys, Chinese cooking, cakes and biscuits.
Mustard	Wide variety of savoury dishes, dressings, sauces, cheese dishes, ham and bacon.
Nutmeg	Chicken, vegetable and cheese dishes, cakes, custard and milk puddings.
Paprika	Goulash and garnishing meat, fish, egg and cheese dishes.
Pepper	All savoury dishes.

AREA TWO
RESOURCE MANAGEMENT AND CONSUMER STUDIES

Chapter 11 I Family Resource Management (2.1)

CONTENTS INCLUDE:

▶ Purpose of resource management

▶ Management systems

▶ The family as a managerial unit

▶ Components of management

▶ Attributes affecting management

Family Resource Management (2.1)

<u>Management</u> is the <u>skilful handling</u> or <u>running of something</u>. For example, hotel management involves managing a hotel; personnel management involves managing people.

<u>Resources</u> are anything that is available to help in achieving a goal, e.g. <u>people</u>, <u>time</u>, <u>money</u>, <u>skills</u> and equipment.

<u>Family resource management</u> is a system which assists the family in attaining goals by making efficient use of all possible resources. *having all the resources you need to meet the goals and needs of the family*

The purpose of family resource management

▶ To make <u>wise</u> and <u>efficient</u> use of resources.

▶ To assist individuals and families to achieve goals.

▶ To improve the <u>quality</u> of family life.

Management Systems

Previously, in family resource management systems, all tasks or goals were seen as separate entities. A series of tasks, such as shopping, cooking and childminding, required individual attention.

Today, the most commonly used system is the *overall system*. This type of management system looks at all tasks and all available resources. <u>Priorities</u> are assigned to each task through <u>communication</u> and <u>decision-making</u>. Then after <u>implementation</u>, <u>evaluation</u> allows <u>decisions</u> to be reviewed regularly.

Discussing problems within the family

218

Another method of classifying management systems:

An open system	A closed system
Systems outside the family are utilised to achieve family goals, e.g. education system, health system and social welfare system.	All activities occur within the system's own boundaries, e.g. the self-sufficient Amish community.

The Family as a Managerial Unit

Today's family operates a managerial system so that family members:
- make wise and efficient use of resources,
- have a better quality of life
- and attain their goals more efficiently.

The type of management system used is the ***overall system***. It is an ***open system*** having interaction with other systems outside its boundaries. Although all family members may have their own personal goals, the managerial system requires agreed goals and priorities for effective overall management. *to make it work you must agree on the priorities*

There are many areas within the family which demand management skills. These areas include:

- ▶ Meal planning: Involves nutritional knowledge, decision-making, shopping and cooking skills.
- ▶ Money management: Involves knowledge of budgeting, mortgages, pensions and bill payment.
- ▶ Childcare: Involves safety and hygiene issues and education.
- ▶ Conflict solving: Involves listening, talking and compromising.
- ▶ Problem anticipating: Involves planning for possibilities.

Other areas requiring management skills include: laundry, gardening, maintenance, cleaning and decision-making which relates to all areas of management within the home.

Components of Management (2.1.1)

There are three components or stages of management: ***inputs***, ***throughputs*** and ***outputs***.

Inputs

There are two aspects to inputs: (a) *demands* and (b) *resources*.

(a) Demands are *needs, wants, goals and values*.

1. ***Needs*** are what one must have. Physical needs include food, shelter and clothing. Social needs include love, security and protection.
2. ***Wants*** are what one would like to have, e.g. luxuries such as expensive cars.
3. ***Goals*** are what one strives to achieve. Long-term goals include a pension for a sense of security. Intermediate goals might include getting into college. Short-term goals might include completing an essay before Friday.
4. ***Values*** are beliefs of what is right and wrong. For example, vegetarians may believe that it is wrong to kill animals for food; some people are more concerned about the environment than others.

(b) Resources:

1. *__Human resources:__* People, their time and skills.

2. *__Material resources:__* Money, books and equipment.

3. *__Environmental resources:__* Water, land and temperature.

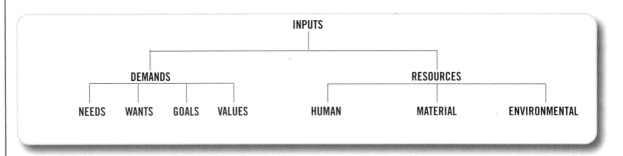

Throughputs

This action section consists of three processes:

1. Planning

- ▷ Identify goal.
- ▷ Gather information.
- ▷ Consider alternatives.
- ▷ Consider the consequences of each alternative.
- ▷ Decide on a course of action.
- ▷ Identify resources.

Managerial activities/skills:
- Communicating
- Planning
- Organising
- Implementing
- Evaluating

2. Organising

- ▷ Allocating tasks and resources to people.
- ▷ Organising the order of work.

3. Implementing

- ▷ Putting the plan into action.
- ▷ Control over this activity or action is necessary to improve effectiveness.
- ▷ Adjustment may be necessary.

Outputs

This is the end product of the inputs and throughputs. It is assessed/evaluated in terms of:

- ▷ Demands met or goals achieved, i.e. has the management system delivered the desired result?
- ▷ Resources used, i.e. were all possible resources used to their full potential?
- ▷ Process followed, i.e. was the procedure followed in the most efficient order?
- ▷ Satisfaction, i.e. is the end result satisfactory?
- ▷ Changes in values, i.e. are there any changes in family values or standards?

The result of this evaluation is **feedback**, which will be used at the input stage in the future. Feedback measures satisfaction levels in relation to inputs, throughputs and outputs. The effective use of feedback contributes to the success of management systems.

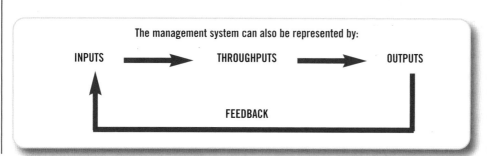

The management system can also be represented by:

INPUTS → THROUGHPUTS → OUTPUTS

FEEDBACK

The Decision-making Process

Decision-making is an essential part of any management system.

The decision-making process involves:
1. Defining the decision or identifying the goal.
2. Gathering information and considering the alternatives or possible solutions.
3. Considering the consequences of each alternative.
4. Deciding on a solution.
5. Drawing up a resources list and a plan of action.
6. Implementing the plan.
7. Evaluating (with feedback).

Decision-making can be influenced by **primary reference groups**, e.g. family and close friends, or **secondary reference groups** such as work colleagues.

Communication

Communication is necessary for any management system to work efficiently. Decision-making involves communication. Each family member may have his/her own individual goals. Communication is therefore necessary so that all goals are first identified.

An understanding of the values of each family member is necessary so that goals can be given priority ranking. Discussion and communication allow for the sharing of values and resolving of conflict.

age appropriate

Discussion and communication are also necessary for the allocation of tasks to individuals, to ensure that all family members are involved and that there is a fair distribution of work in order to avoid conflict.

Communication is particularly important at the evaluation stage, where people can express their satisfaction or dissatisfaction with the output and give suggestions for future improvements at the different stages of the management process.

Attributes Affecting Management (2.1.2)

There are many different factors that can affect the management process, including:

1. **Composition of the family**
   ▶ The number of people in a family can affect management. The more family members, the more people there are to consider.

   ▶ Where families are headed by two adults responsibilities may be shared. In a one-parent family, the parent has sole responsibility when the children are young.

   ▶ Families with disabled members require specific management systems.

2. **Stages in the life-cycle**
   ▶ Families with young children have different priorities to those with teenage children.

   ▶ Elderly people often have limited finance, reduced mobility, and different pastimes all of which affect management.

   ▶ As children grow older, they are usually included in decision-making.

3. **Employment patterns**
   ▶ Couples where both partners work outside the home operate a different management system to couples where one is the earner and the other is often largely engaged in childminding and running the home.

   ▶ Management is affected by patterns of employment such as job sharing, flexitime and working from home. *part-time*

   ▶ Dual earning families often have a larger income than single earning families and therefore have more access to different resources, e.g. money and equipment. *less time*

   ▶ Management in families where people work as shift workers can be affected as sleeping and meal times change. *work one week during night other during the day*

4. **Socio-economic status**
   ▶ People from different socio-economic groups often have different priorities. The lower socio-economic groups place more emphasis on needs, whereas luxuries are often important to those of higher socio-economic status.

   ▶ Education is often viewed as more important to those in the higher socio-economic group – third level education is usually financially attainable.

   ▶ Those from higher socio-economic groups generally have more opportunities in life, e.g. more access to sports clubs, computers and the theatre, all of which result in a different lifestyle.

5. **Management of dual role**
   ▶ In some families, both parents may work outside the home. Therefore, they both play dual roles – that of earner and that of homemaker. Management within this family will differ from that of a family where one is the earner and the other the homemaker. *roles needs to be defined + plans made*

   ▶ In a single-parent family, the parent often has to be both parent and earner without the support of a partner. The demands of both roles greatly affects management within the home.

> ▶ Parents may have to play a dual role – that of a loving caring parent and also the role of disciplinarian – which affects management within the family.

6. Gender roles

> ▶ Management within modern families is not greatly affected by gender roles, as men are now more involved in child-rearing, and many women work outside the home.

> ▶ Gender typing of certain household tasks, e.g. lawn mowing as a male task and meal preparation as a female task, is rapidly decreasing.

> ▶ Management within the family involves all members and tasks are often rotated with little regard to gender and more emphasis on equality and fairness.

7. Culture

> ▶ Culture may affect management within a family, e.g. some countries impose certain rules regarding foods, dress and the status of women.

> ▶ Irish people continue to place emphasis on religion. Christenings, Holy Communion and Confirmation are among the important events in many families' lives.

> ▶ Changes within culture have affected management. For example, it is now acceptable that women work outside the home, which often results in employing childminders.

8. Values and standards

Values and standards affect management as they determine the decision taken.

> ▶ Values within a family can change, e.g. when someone becomes ill priorities change and future management is affected.

> ▶ Decisions can be affected by people's concern for the environment, e.g. type of heating chosen or shopping for products with less packaging.

First Holy Communion

CONTENTS INCLUDE:

▶ The household as a financial unit within the economy
▶ Household income and expenditure
▶ Budget planning
▶ Methods of payment for goods and services
▶ Consumer credit legislation
▶ Methods of saving
▶ Insurance

Management of Household Finances

The household as a financial unit within the economy
The family is an important financial unit within the economy as:

▷ Working adults in a household contribute to the national economy by paying taxes, which are used to maintain state services.

▷ Family income is spent on goods and services generating employment and wealth.

▷ Many families are financially self-sufficient and are not dependent on the state. Some households, however, are not part of the workforce and are financially dependent on the state.

▷ The recent rapid increase in unemployment rates has meant that many families are now experiencing financial difficulties as income levels fall sharply.

▷ Many households have mortgages and loans thereby contributing to the profits of financial institutions.

▷ In households where money is mismanaged, for instance in the use of credit facilities, financial difficulties and debts can arise. Money management skills are therefore vital to running the household as a financial unit.

Household Income

Household income varies greatly and is influenced by a number of social factors.

Age

▷ People's income tends to increase as they get older, more experienced and move up the pay scale.

▷ Unless pensions have been carefully planned, individuals can experience a drop in income on retirement.

▷ Teenagers can earn money in part-time jobs ensuring that they have pocket money and easing the financial strain on the family.

Gender

▷ The number of women in the workforce has increased in the last century for a variety of reasons (See Page 289).

▷ 'Back to Work' schemes help to encourage women back into the workforce having taken time out to rear a young family.

▷ Legislation such as the Employment Equality Act is helping to ensure equal pay and conditions for all regardless of gender.

▷ Managerial positions in Ireland are still male dominated.

Social class

▷ Many individuals from poorer backgrounds tend to leave school early without qualifications. This can lead to unemployment, or only being able to get low-paid jobs, where there are few opportunities for career advancement or for improving income level.

▷ People from middle-class backgrounds on the other hand generally have better educational opportunities and are more likely to get a third-level qualification enabling them to find well-paid work.

Culture

▷ In affluent western societies, disposable income may be spent on luxuries such as foreign holidays.

▷ Different cultures place different emphasis on the value of money.

▷ In poorer societies, such as in parts of Africa, all income is required solely for survival and to meet basic needs.

Sources of Household Income

Sources of household income may include:

▷ Wages and salaries.

▷ Social welfare allowances and benefits.

▷ Pensions

▷ Interest or dividends from savings and investments.

▷ EU farming subsidies.

▷ Income from rented property.

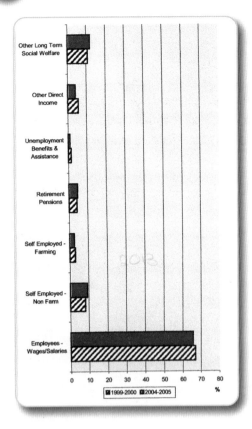

The percentage distribution of average weekly gross household income by source

> The terms wages and salaries refer to fixed regular payments. **Wages** generally refers to weekly payments, **salaries** generally refers to fortnightly or monthly payments.

Gross and Net Income

Gross income is income earned before any deductions are made. **Net income** refers to income after deductions are made, i.e. take home pay.

Deductions		
Compulsory deductions • PAYE (income tax) • PRSI (social insurance) • Health levy • Income levy • Pension levy (public service employees)	**Voluntary deductions** • Private health insurance (VHI/Hibernia Aviva/Quinn Healthcare) • Pension (superannuation) • Union membership • Saving scheme	**Vhi** HEALTHCARE **AVIVA**

Income tax   PAYE

▶ The vast majority of income-tax payers pay their tax through the PAYE (pay as you earn) system.

▶ Under this system employers are legally obliged to deduct tax from employees' wages or salaries before payment and to forward it to the Revenue Commissioners.

▶ The money collected is used by the government to run the country, e.g. by providing and maintaining road networks, health services and education.

Tax liability

Annual income dictates an individual's tax liability. To calculate the tax a person has to pay, total income must be calculated and then taxed at the appropriate rate of tax.

Currently there are two tax rates in Ireland:

- ▶ A low/standard rate of 20%.
- ▶ A high rate of 41%.

Each employee is entitled to pay tax at the low/standard rate on a portion of income up to a certain limit, referred to as 'standard rate cut off point'. This point is calculated by the tax office and it varies from person to person depending on individual circumstances. If a taxpayer has any income above the standard rate cut off point it is taxed at 41%.

The self-employed must calculate their own tax liability and are responsible for payment of any tax due. Individuals on very low incomes are exempt from paying any tax.

Tax liability 2009		
You are	**20%**	**41%**
Single Person	€36,400 *€32,800 2012*	Balance
Married couple One income	€45,400	Balance
Married couple two incomes	€72,800 (€45,400 with increase of €27,400 max)) *2012) €65,600*	Balance
One parent family	€40,400	Balance

Tax credits

Gross tax is calculated on the entire income. Tax credits reduce the amount of tax one has to pay.

An annual tax certificate referred to as 'Notification of determination of tax credits and standard cut off point' gives each individual tax payer details of tax credits and also indicates point at which high rate of tax starts to apply.

PRSI (Pay Related Social Insurance)

- ▶ PRSI is a compulsory deduction made from income.

- ▶ Employees and employers share the cost of the PRSI payment.

- ▶ It is based on a percentage of an individual's income.

- ▶ Employees over 16 years of age must pay PRSI.

- ▶ Payment of PRSI entitles employees to claim benefits such as unemployment, maternity or disability benefit should they need to do so. (Employees must have made a minimum of 39 PRSI contributions in the tax year prior to claim.)

- ▶ PRSI is also used to run employment and training schemes.

- ▶ Certain individuals such as the very low paid are exempt from paying PRSI.

Gross tax – tax credits = tax payable

Examples of current tax credits (annually)	
Personal Credits	**2009**
Single person	€1,830
Married couple	€3,660
PAYE/ Employee credit	€1,830
One-parent family	€1,830

Note: Tax rates and tax credits are subject to change in annual budgets.

Department of Social and Family Affairs

*replaced by universal social charge USC

Health levy

A health levy is currently deducted from income at a rate of 4%–5%. The levy is used to improve health services. Certain individuals are exempt from paying the levy for instance anyone in receipt of one-parent family payment.

Income levy

Due to the recent downturn in the economy the government has introduced a levy of at least 2% on all incomes over €18,304.

Social welfare payments

There are basically three types of payments: contributory, non-contributory and universal.

2013 **Social welfare payments**		
1. **Social Insurance / contributory payments**	2. **Social assistance / non contributory payments**	3. **Universal Payments**
• Paid to individuals who have paid sufficient PRSI.	• Paid to individuals who do not qualify for (1), i.e. have made insufficient PRSI payments/are long term unemployed. • Means tested.	• Payments which do not depend on PRSI contributions. • Not means tested. • E.g. Child Benefit.

Social insurance payments 2010	
Social insurance payments	2013
	2010 (€)
State Pension (Contributory)	
- Under Age 80	€230.30
- Aged 80 and over	€240.30
Widows/Widowers (Contributory) Pension/Deserted Wife's Benefit	
- Under Age 66	€201.50 → 193€
Invalidity Pension	
- Under Age 65	€201.50 → 193€
Jobseeker's/Illness/Health & Safety/Injury Benefit	€196.00 → 188€

Social Assistance Payments 2009/2010

Weekly personal rate	2013
State Pension (Non-Contributory)	
– Age 66 and under Age 80	€219.00
– Aged 80 and over	€229.00
Widow's/Widower's (Non-Contributory) Pension	€196.00 →188€
Carer's Allowance	€212.00 →204€
Pre-Retirement/Disability Allowance	€196.00 →188€
Supplementary Welfare Allowance	€196.00 →188€
Jobseekers Allowance	€196.00 →188€

Pensions

1. State Pensions
Old Age (Contributory) Pension   €230

1. Paid to people over age of 65.

2. Minimum number of PRSI contributions must have been paid over a number of years in order to qualify.

3. Not means tested.

Old Age (Non-contributory) Pension   €219

1. Paid to people over 66 who do not qualify for old age (contributory) pension.
2. Means tested.

2. Occupational Pension
Employees pay a percentage of their wages/salary into a pension fund set up by the employer.
gards, teacher, fireman

3. Private/Personal Pension
Individuals pay a sum of money into a pension fund for a number of years.
self employed people

Additional allowances/benefits which may also be payable
Allowances:
- Living Alone Allowance
- Over 80 allowance
- Fuel Allowance

Benefits:
- Medical card
- Free travel
- Household benefits package (e.g. free electricity, natural gas, TV licence, telephone rental)

Supplementary welfare allowance

The supplementary welfare allowance is a temporary weekly allowance paid by the Health Service Executive (HSE) to people whose means are insufficient to meet their needs and those of their dependants. To qualify for supplementary welfare allowance individuals must:

1. Satisfy a means test.

2. Have applied for any other benefits/allowances to which they are entitled (but have yet to receive payment).

3. Have registered for work with FÁS if they are of working age.

Anyone in receipt of supplementary welfare allowance may also qualify for additional payments such as:

▶ Mortgage allowance (See Page 247).

▶ Back to school clothing and footwear allowance.

Family income supplement (FIS)

Family income supplement is a weekly payment for families including lone-parent families where the earner is in low-paid employment. Income and family size are criteria used to determine the amount paid in family income supplement. To qualify for FIS an individual must:

Family Income Supplement (FIS)	
If you have:	**And your income is less than:**
1 child	€506
2 children	€602
3 children	€703
4 children	€824
	To a maximum of €1,298 for 8 or more children.

1. Be in full-time employment and work at least 19 hours a week.

2. Have at least one dependent child.

3. Have a weekly income which falls below a fixed amount for family size.

> The FIS received is 60% of the difference between the net family income and the income limit that applies to the family.

Family Income Supplement (FIS)	
Example:	
Family of two parents, four dependent children	
Income limit	€824
Net income	€424
Difference	€400
FIS payment	€240 (60% of 400)

Child benefit

Child benefit is a payment made every month to a child's parent (usually the mother) or guardian. To qualify a child must be under 16 years of age or up to age 18 if the child is:

> In full time education.

> Attending a FÁS/Youthreach course.

> Physically/mentally disabled.

Child Benefit Payments (April)

€150 per child per month for the first two children.

€187 per month for third and subsequent children.

Household Expenditure

The average weekly expenditure in 2004–2005 for all households in the state was estimated to be over €787.

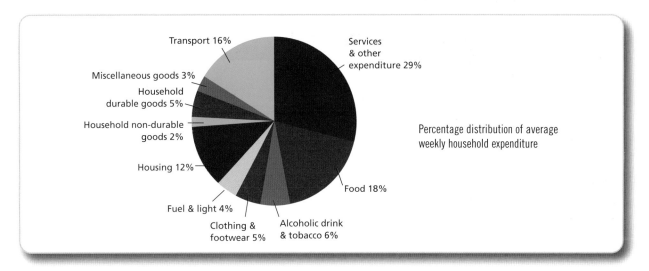

Percentage distribution of average weekly household expenditure

Average weekly household expenditure 1999–2000 and 2004–2005					
Community Groups	1999–2000		2004–2005		change
	€	%	€	%	%
Food	117.67	20.4	142.74	18.1	+ 21.3
Alcoholic drink and tobacco	44.10	7.6	47.18	6	+ 7.0
Clothing and footwear	35.11	6.1	42.67	5.4	+ 21.5
Fuel and light	21.68	3.7	30.65	3.9	+ 41.4
Housing	55.41	9.6	94.51	12	+ 70.6
Household non-durables	14.41	2.5	17.42	2.2	+ 20.9
Household durables	26.86	4.6	35.55	4.5	+ 32.4
Miscellaneous goods	19.08	3.4	23.78	3	+ 24.6
Transport	94.92	16.4	122.74	15.6	+ 29.3
Services and other Expenditure	148.48	25.7	229.83	29.2	+ 54.8
Total	**577.72**	100.0	**787.12**	100.0	**+ 36.2**

* Household budget surveys are conducted every five years.

Pattern of expenditure

▷ The household budget survey shows that the highest increase in expenditure was recorded for *Housing* (70.6%) and *Services and other expenditure* (54.8%).

▷ The lowest increase recorded was for *Alcoholic drink and tobacco* at 7%.

▷ The proportion of income spent on *Food* and on *Transport* fell slightly.

Essential expenditure
Spending on necessities, e.g. food and housing.

Discretionary expenditure
Spending on non-essentials luxuries, e.g. alcohol, cosmetics and entertainment.

Essential expenditure		Discretionary expenditure
Fixed	**Irregular**	**Discretionary**
Rent/mortgage	Food	Furnishings
Electricity	Clothing	Holidays
Fuel/heating	Medical expenses	Savings
Life, medical	Educational needs	Garden
Household, car insurance	Household goods, maintenance	Entertainment, Leisure, Telephone
TV licence	Car maintenance	Personal grooming
Motor tax		
Savings		

Household budgets

A budget is a plan for expected income and expenditure over a fixed period.

Advantages of budgeting:

▷ Helps to develop good money management skills.

▷ Spending and in particular use of credit facilities can be closely monitored.

▷ Areas of overspending/impulse buying become obvious and economies can be made so that serious debt can be avoided.

▷ Provides more financial security as it covers major expenses and allows for some savings.

Planning a household budget
1. Estimate total income. Include all sources of income such as:
    ▷ Wages/salary
    ▷ Child benefit

▷ Social insurance benefits/allowances

▷ Pensions

2. Decide to budget on a weekly/monthly/yearly basis.

3. Identify areas of expenditure.

4. Draw up a budget allocating a percentage of income to each expense and allowing a percentage for saving.

5. Evaluate the budget regularly. Budgets may need to be redrawn as family priorities and circumstances change.

Sample Budget

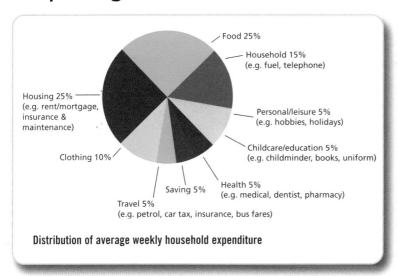

Distribution of average weekly household expenditure

2 adults + 2 teenage children, net weekly income €800		
		€
Food	25%	200
Housing	25%	200
Household	15%	120
Clothing	10%	80
Travel	5%	40
Education/childcare	5%	40
Health	5%	40
Personal/leisure	5%	40
Saving	5%	40
Total	100%	€800

Budgeting guidelines

The suggested division of income in the chart above serves as a guideline for planning household budgets. Because households vary greatly in terms of numbers, income level and other factors, the percentage breakdown must be adapted to suit each individual household.

MABS

The Money Advice and Budgeting Service (MABS) was set up in the early 1990s under the Department of Social and Family Affairs. It operates within the Citizens Information Board assisting families with problems caused by debt.

Functions of MABS see Chapter 28.

3. Methods of Payment for Goods and Services

Method	Advantages	Disadvantages
1. Cash	• Quick transactions. • Convenient for smaller purchases. • Less chance of overspending.	• Risk involved in carrying cash.
2. Cheque • Cheque books and cheque guarantee cards are issued by banks and other financial institutions to current account holders. • Cheques may only be written up to balance in the account.	• Convenient and safe. • Particularly useful for postal transactions. • Overdraft facility can be arranged.	• Expensive way of paying for for goods and services – charge for each cheque. • High rate of interest charged on on overdraft facility.
3. Debit Card (such as Laser) • Issued by banks and building societies to current account holders. • When the card is swiped at the till, money is taken from the customer's bank account and debited to the retailer within five days.	• Convenient, accepted by most retailers. • Cash up to a certain limit may be withdrawn when paying for goods and services ('cashback' option). • Laser card is multipurpose, i.e. laser, cheque guarantee card and ATM card. • Safer than carrying cash.	• Government charge on card. • Charge on each transaction.
4. Credit Card (See Page 236).		
5. 24-hour telephone banking • Service offered by banks to current account holders.	• Bills can be paid over the phone. • Payment can be at the customer's convenience.	• Charge involved for each transaction.
6. Direct debit/standing order • Variable or fixed sums of money are paid directly out of the customers' current account by agreement with bank.	• Convenient and safe for regular bills, e.g. mortgage repayments, car loans. • Important bills/repayments are not forgotten.	• May be a charge for setting up. • Charge may apply for each payment. • Easy to lose complete control if there are numerous direct debits from current account.
7. ATMs (automated teller machines)	• Useful for paying bills such as phone and electricity bills.	• Charge for each transaction.
8. On-line banking	• Bills can be paid over the internet. • Accessible 24 hours a day. • May be accessed from anywhere in the world.	• Charge for each transaction.

Selection criteria:
1. *Ease of use/convenience*
2. *Safety*
3. *Availability*
4. *Charges*

Methods of payment for goods and services		
Method	**Advantages**	**Disadvantages**
9. Credit transfer/giro • A giro slip attached to a bill is signed and brought to a bank/post office. • An amount is debited from the customer's account to pay the bill.	• Convenient because all relevant details of bill are printed on giro slip.	• Charge for each transaction. • Inconvenient when compared to on-line or 24-hour banking because one must go to the bank or post office.
10. Bill pay • Service operated by An Post.	• No handling fee. • Convenient service. • Also available over the internet.	• Inconvenient when compared to on-line or 24-hour banking because sometimes one must go to the post office.

Credit

Many people use credit to pay for goods and services. Credit involves borrowing money, using it to pay for goods and services and paying it back at a later date.

Forms of credit	
• Credit cards • Overdrafts • Term loans • Charge cards	• Mortgages • Store cards • Hire purchase

The advantages of credit

1. The buyer has the use of goods while still paying for them.
2. Credit facilitates the purchase of larger items such as houses and cars – few people could afford to pay cash for such items.
3. It is safer than dealing in large amounts of cash.
4. Some credit facilities, such as credit cards, offer free credit if the balance is paid off in full within a given period of time.
5. Because credit encourages buying, sales, and in turn employment, increase.

The disadvantages of credit

1. High rates of interest apply to many forms of credit such as credit cards.
2. It is easy to take on too many credit agreements which may result in mounting debts.
3. Some credit transactions, such as credit card transactions, are easy and convenient encouraging over-spending and impulse buying.
4. Items bought on credit are usually more expensive due to the interest charged, e.g. in hire purchase agreements.
5. Goods may be repossessed if the consumer cannot make required payments as agreed.

> **Before entering any credit agreement consider:**
> - Whether it is an essential purchase or an impulse buy.
> - Repayments: How much? How often? Over what period of time?
> - Interest rate and other hidden charges – calculate the total cost of the item.
> - Repercussions and penalties involved if the repayment cannot be made.
> - At what point the consumer owns the goods.

Credit cards

Banks and building societies issue credit cards such as Visa and Mastercard.

- ▷ Credit cards are a convenient way of paying for goods and services because they are accepted at most outlets.

- ▷ They are also useful for phone bookings, online shopping and are accepted abroad.

- ▷ They can be used to withdraw money from ATM machines but interest is charged for this facility.

- ▷ The credit card may be used up to an agreed credit limit (which may be extended once a good credit rating has been established).

- ▷ The consumer gets a monthly statement from the credit card company and is usually allowed about 25 days to pay.

- ▷ If the balance is paid in full no interest is charged. If the full amount is not paid a high rate of interest (around 18%) is charged on the balance.

- ▷ Credit cards currently carry a €30 *€40* Government stamp duty. Penalties are charged for exceeding the credit limit and for late payment.

Overdrafts

Overdrafts are available to current account holders in banks and building societies. *not popular in Ireland*

- ▷ This is an agreement which allows consumers to overdraw on their accounts up to a specified sum.

- ▷ Interest is paid on the actual amount overdrawn.

- ▷ If the consumer does not use the overdraft facility no interest is paid.

- ▷ Some lenders charge an arrangement fee.

- ▷ Useful for short-term borrowing.

- ▷ Repayments are not fixed.

- ▷ Penalties apply should the consumer exceed the overdraft limit.

Charge cards
Charge cards, such as American Express, are similar to credit cards but the balance of the account must be paid off in full each month or charges apply.

Term loans

Banks, building societies and credit unions supply term loans.

▶ Unlike overdrafts, the full amount is given to the consumer and interest applies immediately.

▶ The loan is repaid at fixed amounts over a set period of time.

▶ Interest rates vary greatly depending on the lending institution, the borrower and the term of the loan.

▶ Interest rates may be fixed or variable. A variable rate is preferable since it is usually cheaper than fixed rates; if interest rates fall the consumer will benefit and the loan may be repaid earlier than agreed without incurring penalties.

Credit Unions

- Credit unions are co-operative, non-profit making organisations established within a community.
- Term loans from credit unions are generally the cheapest loans.
- Loans are available to members who have shown an ability to save.
- Loan protection insurance provides for repayment of the loan in the event of death or permanent disability.
- The Credit Union Act of 1997 enables credit unions to offer customers larger loans than were previously possible.

Credit union logo

Hire purchase

Retailers and finance companies offer hire purchase.

▶ Hire purchase is an expensive form of credit whereby the purchaser hires goods and pays for them in fixed installments over a set period of time.

▶ Interest rates are high and administrative charges are included in the price of the goods.

▶ The consumer has the use of the goods during repayment, but does not have full ownership until the last installment has been made.

▶ Goods may be repossessed should the consumer default on repayments; a court order is necessary if more than one-third of the price has been repaid.

Hire Purchase Acts, 1946, 1960

By law all hire purchase agreements must be written and must state:

1. Cash and HP price of goods.
2. Description of goods.
3. Amount, number and due date of installments.
4. APR.
5. Details relating to ten day 'cooling off period' which allows the customer to opt out of the agreement.
6. Rights of parties involved, e.g. to terminate agreement/repossess goods.

APR

Annual percentage rate (APR) can be defined as the 'true rate of interest' (includes set up and management costs) charged on credit options. All lending agencies must declare their APR on all advertisements and loan agreements. This allows consumers to compare one source of credit with another. (The lower the APR the cheaper the credit.)

Consumer Credit Act 1995

The Consumer Credit Act 1995 consolidates all consumer credit legislation including the Hire Purchase Acts of 1946 and 1960 into one act. It is enacted by the National Consumer Agency.

1. The Consumer Credit Act regulates most areas of consumer credit including mortgages, loans, overdrafts, hire purchase, credit cards and leasing.

2. It monitors all credit advertising.

3. It stipulates the information which must be written on all credit agreements such as APR, total cost of credit and any extra charges.

Saving

The advantages of saving regularly include:

▶ Savings make it possible to pay cash for goods, avoiding the necessity for loans/credit agreements.

▶ Saving for occasions such as a wedding or a holiday eliminates the need to borrow.

▶ Regular saving builds a sound financial reputation which may be helpful, e.g. when seeking a mortgage.

▶ Savings provide a sense of security, e.g. when saving for retirement. *Rainy day money*

▶ Savings earn interest if invested wisely.

Before choosing a saving scheme consider the following factors:

1. *Ease of access to funds*
   If there is a possibility that the money may be needed in the short term, one should avoid investing in medium or long-term schemes where penalties are generally imposed for early withdrawal or encashment.

2. *Risk/return balance*
   Some schemes such as those offered by An Post are very safe, other equity-based schemes (based on the stock market) may offer greater potential returns but the chance of loss is also increased.

3. *Tax*
   Some schemes are tax-free while others are subject to DIRT (Deposit Interest Retention Tax). *30%*

4. *Rate of interest*
   Interest rates vary between financial institutions and between schemes offered by each institution.

Many financial institutions including An Post, banks, building societies and Credit Unions offer an wide range of saving schemes.

An Post

Savings schemes at An Post include

Scheme	Investment required	Interest	Ease of access
1) Deposit account Various types on offer, e.g. personal account, joint account, child account.	• No fees. • No minimum deposit.	• Interest payable (currently 1%). • Interest subject to Deposit Interest Retention Tax (DIRT) (currently 20%).	• Money can be withdrawn easily at any post office.
2) Installment saving agreement Fixed amount is saved over 12-month period, then left on deposit for 5 years.	• Minimum monthly installment €25; maximum monthly installment €500. • No fees/transaction costs.	• Guaranteed rate of 20% tax-free interest over 5 years from the end of 12-month contribution period. • No interest payable during contribution period.	• 7 days notice necessary for withdrawal. • 30 days notice necessary for withdrawals before the end of the contribution period.
3) Saving certificates	• No fees or transaction costs. • Minimum investment €50, maximum limit €80,000.	*very high* • Interest payable 21% tax free over 5 year + 6 months period (APR 3.53%). • Interest calculated every 6 months. • Early encashment less interest paid.	• 7 working days notice to encash certificates.
4) Saving bonds	• No fees. • Minimum investment €100, maximum investment €80,000.	• 10% tax-free interest over 3 year period (APR 3.23%). • Interest calculated on annual basis. • Lower interest paid if encashed before 3 years are complete.	• 7 working days notice necessary.

Banks and Building Societies

Banks and building societies offer an array of saving and investment options a number of which are outlined below.

✳ 1. Demand deposit accounts

▷ Demand deposit accounts are suitable for short-term saving, e.g. for a holiday.

▷ Savings are secure and earn a variable rate of interest (currently low at about 0.5%).

▷ Money in the account is easily accessed. It may be withdrawn at any time through an ATM machine. Demand accounts, therefore, may not be the best choice for reluctant savers.

2. Notice accounts

▷ Notice accounts are designed for short-term deposits of sums of money between €3,000 and €250,000.

▷ Money placed in account for a period of time earns a higher rate of variable interest than in a demand deposit account.

▷ DIRT is payable on interest earned.

▷ 15 days notice is necessary to withdraw money.

✳ 3. Special term account

stocks + shares

▷ Banks, credit unions and building societies can offer special term accounts where funds are invested for a fixed term of three or five years.

▷ Interest earned each year up to a maximum of €480 (on 3-year option) and €635 (on 5-year option) is not subject to DIRT.

▷ Interest rate is variable.

▷ Minimum lodgement is €6,000, maximum €25,000.

▷ Early withdrawals incur a penalty.

Insurance

short qu.

Insurance is a measure taken to provide against damage and loss to property, health or even life. A large number of people pay a relatively small premium so that the few who actually suffer a loss can benefit. The term insurance applies to something which may happen, e.g. fire or burglary; the term assurance generally applies to something that will happen, i.e. death.

Premium = money paid to insurance company in order to be insured.

Types of insurance include:

1. Life assurance.
2. Health insurance.
3. Salary/income protection insurance.
4. Pay related social insurance (PRSI). ✳
5. Home and contents insurance.
6. All risks insurance.
7. Car insurance.
8. Travel insurance.

Policy = written details of insurance cover and conditions.

Broker = an expert who sells insurance policies.

✳ maternity jobseekers sick

eg. hastings insurance brokers

Before choosing any insurance policy:

- ► Consider needs, priorities and family circumstances which change over the years and influence the amount and type of insurance cover necessary.
- ► Shop around and get some independent advice if possible.
- ► Compare prices and the extent of cover as policies vary greatly.
- ► Take account of cover which family/individuals may already have, e.g. in a private pension scheme.
- ► Finally, when signing up for any policy, do not withhold any relevant facts which might render the policy null and void at a future date.

Life assurance ①

Life assurance provides cover for <u>dependants</u> in the event of premature death. Some policies include an element of saving.

Types of life assurance

1.   Term assurance

- ► Individual's life is insured for a <u>set period</u>. *eg 30 years*
- ► If the insured person dies during the term of the policy dependants receive a lump sum.
- ► If the insured person survives the term, no payment is made.

Example:
— 30 year old
— 10 year policy
— Premium €20–30 a month
— Lump sum payable on death approximately €200,000.

Term assurance	
Advantages	**Disadvantages**
1. Provides peace of mind that dependants will be looked after in the event of death. 2. Cheapest form of insurance. 3. Good idea for individuals not insured through a pension scheme, e.g. unemployed, or full-time housewife. 4. Suitable for young parents on low income.	1. No element of saving. 2. The older the insured the higher the premium. 3. Cost and cover provided vary greatly – shop around carefully.

Convertible term assurance
This is slightly more expensive but includes the option to convert to another type of assurance during the policy term.

Mortgage protection policy
A mortgage protection policy is a type of term assurance which is taken out at the time of the mortgage. Its cover decreases gradually over the term of the mortgage. It is a means of repaying the mortgage in the event of the death of the principle breadwinner or of either spouse, in the case of a joint mortgage. A mortgage protection policy is one condition set down by banks and building societies for the granting of a mortgage.

2. Whole of life assurance

▶ Whole of life assurance is a <u>more expensive</u> form of insurance, which is a means of <u>saving</u> for dependants after one's death.

▶ There is <u>no time limit</u> on the policy. The insured person's life is covered indefinitely and an agreed sum is paid on death.

▶ Option available to pay the premium up until death or to choose to stop paying at a certain age, e.g. 65 years old.

3. Endowment assurance

▶ This type of assurance is primarily a method of saving while also providing a minimum of life cover.

▶ Premium paid each month tends to be higher than for whole of life.

▶ A lump sum may be paid out on death, or when the insured reaches a certain age, e.g. retirement.

▶ The insured individual can also choose to encash the policy at any stage.

Health insurance ⓐ

1. Income protection insurance/Permanent Health Insurance

▶ Many employees are covered by permanent health insurance for income continuance, which covers a limited period when an employee is unable to continue working due to disability or long-term illness.

▶ Individuals who are not covered, such as the self-employed, or people who wish to have extra cover can do so with a salary/income protection policy. A salary protection policy guarantees a percentage of income (about 75 %) on an ongoing basis until retirement.

2. Critical/serious illness cover

▶ A lump sum is paid out if the insured is diagnosed as suffering from one of a stated list of illnesses such as cancer or multiple sclerosis.

▶ Premiums paid may be fixed or may be reviewed periodically.

▶ The lump sum may be used for any purpose such as medical expenses or to supplement income.

3. Private medical insurance

▶ Private health insurance schemes are offered by Hibernian Aviva, VHI Healthcare and by Quinn Healthcare Ireland.) -> LAYA

▶ Companies offer a range of plans to suit individual circumstances. Premiums vary depending on the chosen plan.

The benefits of private health insurance may include:

▶ In-patient treatment in private or semi-private hospital accommodation.

▶ Stays at convalescent homes.

▶ Medical treatment abroad.

▶ Payment of consultants fees.

▶ Treatment in out-patient clinic.

▶ Tax relief (at source) is available.

> **PRSI (Pay Related Social Insurance)** ⓑ
> PRSI is a form of compulsory insurance paid by employees over the age of 16
> (See Page 227).

Property Insurance (4) must have if getting a mortgage

1. House and building insurance

Most policies cover damage to the structure of the house itself, the garage and some out-buildings, walls, gates and fences. Damage may be caused by fire, lightning, burglary, burst pipes and a range of other possibilities. Some eventualities, e.g. flooding may not be covered, so it is important to read the fine print. Public liability is included in most policies. This covers home-owners liability for injury or loss suffered by another person as a result of an accident occurring on the property. Some companies offer discounts for smoke detectors and alarm systems.

2. Contents insurance moveable

Many house insurance policies also cover contents. However, the cost of separate contents' insurance policies vary greatly, depending on a number of factors such as the location of the house and the amount of cover provided. Usually the contents policy covers losses arising from the same causes as the building policy.

3. All risks insurance

Valuable items such as pieces of jewellery, a camera or video equipment may not be covered by the contents policy. A separate all-risks insurance policy may be needed to cover such items, both inside and outside the home.

Motor Insurance

It is compulsory for anyone driving a motor vehicle to have insurance. There are three main types.

Types of motor insurance		
1. Third Party	**2. Third Party Fire and Theft**	**3. Fully Comprehensive**
• Covers third party involved in accident caused by insured. • Insured must pay for any damage/loss to self.	• Covers third party involved in accident caused by insured – also covers damage caused by fire and theft.	• Covers damage to third party fire, theft plus damage, injury or loss to insured or insured person's vehicle.

Travel insurance - protection against medical expenses

Advantages of Insurance

1. Life assurance provides peace of mind ensuring that dependants are looked after financially in the event of death.
2. Some life assurance policies are also a form of saving.
3. Income protection policies provide financial support in the event of illness and loss of income.
4. Tax relief at source is available for some forms of insurance such as medical insurance.
5. Protection is provided against loss/injury through events such as car accidents, house fires and burglary giving a sense of security to the insured.

CONTENTS INCLUDE:

► **Housing finance, including acquiring mortgages and mortgage protection**

► **Factors that determine housing choices**

Housing Finance (2.1.3)

For many people acquiring a house is the single largest financial commitment they will make in a lifetime. Houses are generally purchased with borrowed money. Repayments take a high proportion of the household budget. For this reason, careful consideration must be given to the choice of house and to the choice of lending agency.

There are many different types of homes available from country cottages to loft apartments

Mortgages

A mortgage is a loan acquired from a lending agency to purchase a house. The loan is usually repaid in monthly installments over a fixed period of time such as 20–30 years. The lending agency holds the title deeds until the loan is repaid in full. Mortgages are available from banks, building societies and local authorities.

Banks and Building Societies

Conditions that apply

While there are variations between lending institutions, the following general conditions apply.

(a) Amount which may be borrowed

As a rule, applicants may borrow up to 2–3 times their annual salary. If a joint mortgage is being sought 2–3 times the principle salary and 1.25% of the second salary may be borrowed.

(b) Deposit

As most lending institutions will not lend more than 90% of the house price, the borrower is expected to have saved 10% as a deposit.

(c) Income

All applicants must supply proof of income, e.g. P60 or salary slip. Borrowers are expected to have a steady income.

(d) Good credit record

An applicant for a mortgage should have a good financial reputation, no bad debts, and should have shown an ability to save.

(e) Term of loan

Most house loans are repaid over 20–30 years. An older applicant may have to repay over a shorter term, for instance a 50-year-old may have to repay over a 15-year period.

(f) Insurance

A mortgage borrower is legally obliged to take out life assurance usually in the form of a mortgage protection policy. Home insurance must also be arranged before the mortgage is granted. Some lending agencies require **a mortgage indemnity bond**. An indemnity bond is a form of insurance for a lending agency. It ensures that if the house has to be repossessed the lending agency will not make a loss.

(g) The property

The property must be in a good condition. This applies particularly to older houses. Lending agencies get houses surveyed before granting mortgages to determine if they are good investments.

Interest Rates

Mortgage interest rates may be fixed or variable.

Fixed rate	Variable rate
<ul><li>The interest rate is fixed for a set period of time.</li><li>This is a less risky option but may be more expensive in the long term.</li><li>The borrower knows the exact amount to be repaid each month. Therefore, it is easier to plan the household budget.</li></ul>	<ul><li>Interest rates rise and fall in line with European Central Bank rates. The borrower pays more if interest rate rises.</li><li>The borrower benefits from a fall in interest rates, i.e. pays less.</li></ul>

Types of Mortgage

A range of mortgage options is now available such as annuity mortgages, endowment mortgages and pension-linked mortgages.

Types of mortgage		
Annuity mortgage	**Endowment mortgage**	**Pension-linked mortgage**
<ul><li>Each repayment goes partly to pay off the interest on the loan and partly to repay the principal amount borrowed.</li><li>The amount owed declines over the years, slowly at first then more rapidly.</li><li>A mortgage protection policy is a condition of an annuity mortgage.</li><li>Annuity mortgages are very popular.</li></ul>	<ul><li>Endowment mortgages are a combination of borrowing and investing.</li><li>The borrower pays the interest on the loan, and pays a premium on a savings-type life assurance policy designed to pay off the loan when it matures.</li><li>There is a risk that the yield from the policy may not be enough to pay off the loan.</li><li>A life assurance policy also includes cover for the mortgage repayment in the event of death. Therefore, no extra mortgage protection policy is required.</li><li>Endowment mortgages are a less popular mortgage option.</li></ul>	<ul><li>The borrower pays the interest on the loan and pays a sum into a pension scheme rather than a life assurance policy.</li><li>The loan is repaid from the pension fund on retirement.</li><li>A mortgage protection policy is necessary with this type of mortgage.</li><li>The pension-linked mortgage is favoured by self-employed people because of the better tax relief.</li></ul>

Mortgage Interest Relief/Tax Credit

Mortgage interest relief is allowed for first-time buyers during the first seven years of the mortgage.

Local Authority Housing

Local authorities are the main providers of housing for people who cannot afford it from their own resources. A range of schemes exist which enable people to buy or rent property, or improve their existing living conditions.

To be eligible for assistance or a loan from the local authority a number of conditions apply including:

1. Applicants must be in need of housing and be unable to provide it from their own resources.

2. Applicants must be unable to secure a mortgage from a bank or building society .

3. An income eligibility test must be taken. Single income households must earn less than €40,000 and double income households must earn less than €100,000 gross per year.

4. Under the local authority affordable housing scheme, 97% of the house price may be borrowed and repayments are over 25-35 years.

5. Loan repayments relate to income. Generally, monthly loan repayments do not exceed 35% of the net household income.

Local authority schemes *elective*

Local authorities offer a range of options to people in need of housing but who cannot afford to pay the full market price. These options include:

1. *Tenant purchase scheme*

▶ Anyone who has been a tenant of a local authority house for at least one year has the option of buying the house.

▶ Houses may be bought outright or through the shared ownership scheme (see below).

▶ The house is priced at market value minus discounts.

▶ There is a discount for each year of tenancy up to a maximum of ten years.

2. *Shared ownership scheme*

▶ To be eligible for shared ownership one must be in need of housing and satisfy an income test.

▶ Initially ownership is shared between the shared owner and the local authority.

▶ The applicant must purchase at least 40% of the value of the house and rent the remaining 60% from the local authority.

Housing estate

▶ Applicants may pay for their share by taking out a mortgage loan from the local authority.

▶ Regular outgoings consist of mortgage payments and a rent calculated at 4.5% of the cost of the rented share.

▶ Total outgoings are lower than for a standard mortgage.

▶ Tenants may purchase the remaining 60% share when the initial 40% share is purchased.

3. *Mortgage allowance scheme*

▶ A tenant of a local authority house who wishes to return the existing home to the local authority and to buy or build a private home may qualify for a mortgage allowance.

Local authority housing

▶ The allowance (up to €11,450) is paid on a reducing scale over five years and is paid directly to the mortgage lender, thereby reducing mortgage payments over the initial period.

▶ The scheme is designed to make the transition from rent to mortgage easier.

4. *Affordable housing scheme*

▶ Under this scheme, the local authority provides new houses on land that it owns.

▶ The houses are supplied at discounted prices to eligible purchasers (i.e. in need of housing and satisfy income eligibility test).

▶ Houses are purchased outright through a mortgage provided by the local authority.

▶ Loans of up to 97% price of house are repaid over 25 years.

▶ Generally, loan repayments should not exceed 35% of net household income.

Housing (2.1.4)

There are many different types of housing to choose from, these include:

1. Houses

- Bungalows
- 3- or 4-storey high houses
- Detached houses
- Semi-detached houses

- Terraced houses
- Small town houses
- Duplex houses

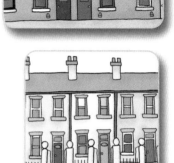

2. Apartments/flats/student accommodation

3. Hostels: Dormitory or a private bedroom with shared kitchen and bathroom facilities.

4. Digs: A private bedroom in a family home where the tenant pays rent to cover all expenses including meals.

5. Sheltered housing: For the elderly or disabled. This type of housing consists of a group of houses or apartments with a caretaker. There are often communal facilities, e.g. a day room.

Factors which Influence Individual and Family Housing Choices

There are different factors which influence the choices people make about housing including:

Socio-economic factors

▶ **Cost** greatly affects one's choice of housing. It firstly determines whether one rents or buys a home. Cost is an influenced by size, condition and location of house. Other costs must also be considered, for example, insurance, furnishing, maintenance, heating, electricity and service charges, e.g. bin charges.

▶ **Location** is an important consideration. It can affect housing prices and can influence the future investment value of the property. Location may also be important in terms of proximity to work, schools, and amenities such as shops and public transport. This can affect expenditure on travel and the amount of time spent travelling daily.

▶ The **size** of the household must be considered when choosing a house. Sufficient sleeping accommodation, bathroom facilities and storage are essential.

▶ The **ages** of children can influence house choice. As they get older, separate bedrooms that can be used as study areas may be appropriate. Young children benefit from garden space.

▶ The **special needs** of a family member may have to be considered when choosing a house, e.g. stairs are

elective

unsuitable for wheelchair users and many elderly people. Sheltered housing may be a more appropriate option.

▶ **Personal preference** will definitely affect housing choice. Whether it is the layout of the house, the size of the garden or the view, there are always reasons why a particular house is chosen.

National housing policy

▶ The national housing policy is formulated and implemented by the Department of the Environment, Heritage and Local Government and delivered through the local authorities.

▶ The central aim of this policy is to enable every household to have an affordable dwelling of good quality and suitable to its needs.

▶ Those who can afford to provide for their own housing needs do so through home ownership or private rented accommodation

▶ Assistance available to lower income purchasers includes:
  – Tenant purchase scheme
  – Shared ownership scheme
  – Mortgage allowance scheme
  – Affordable housing scheme

Modern apartments

▶ Under national housing policy, a renting social-housing sector is also available for those who cannot afford suitable accommodation.

▶ The availability of improvement grants allows people to buy older buildings for restoration.

Building your own home is a popular option

Trends in housing development

▶ Housing estates continue to be popular, offering a range of different houses, e.g. detached, semi-detached and terraced houses.

▶ The development of much smaller, more exclusive housing estates is a current trend. Many of these estates are enclosed behind secure entrances.

Housing development behind gates

▶ Many people buy houses outside towns and cities. Commuting has become very common.

▶ Buying old dilapidated buildings for refurbishment as houses or blocks of apartments is popular.

▶ Mixed developments in town centres including apartments, town houses and larger houses offer plenty of choice in prices and size.

▶ Many people continue to build privately on sites where one can chose one's own house design. Generally, it is better value for money and allows more space for a garden.

Availability of housing

▶ The choice of house is dependent on what is available within one's resources. Current demand for housing exceeds supply in public sectors.

▶ As local authority public housing is allocated in order of priority, it may not be available in the short term.

▶ In private housing, prices often put purchasing a house beyond the reach of many, however currently house prices are dropping.

Chapter 14 I Household Technology (2.1.5)

Household Technology

Technology has greatly changed the way homes are managed today. Technological developments are evident in:

(a) **Food preparation**, e.g. use of liquidisers, food processors and blenders.

(b) **Cooking of food**, e.g. dual rings, halogen rings, contact grills and microwave ovens.

(c) **Laundry**, e.g. programmed washing machines with spin-driers and tumble-driers.

(d) **Cleaning**, e.g. dishwashers, vacuum cleaners and steam cleaners.

(e) **Household surfaces**, e.g. vinyl flooring, ceramic tiles, stainless steel and plastic.

(f) **Security**, e.g. lighting, alarms and gates.

(g) **Automation**, e.g. timers on water heating and central heating.

(h) **Communications**, e.g. email, internet, fax machines, mobile phones.

(i) **Entertainment**, e.g. DVDs and PlayStations.

(j) **Management**, e.g. computer spreadsheet packages for budgeting or word processing packages for typing.

(k) **Maintenance**, e.g. lawn mowers, strimmers, electric drills and saws have greatly assisted in home and garden maintenance.

The Contribution of Technology to Home Management

▶ Workload has been reduced by the use of appliances such as washing machines and dishwashers.

▶ Time is saved by appliances such as food processors, which can, for example, slice or grate large quantities of food in a short time.

▶ Some tasks are performed with increased effectiveness, e.g. steam cleaners to remove stains from carpets, lawn mowers for garden maintenance.

▶ The use of easy-care surfaces such as vinyl floor covering has greatly reduced the amount of time and effort involved in maintenance.

▶ Security technology reduces the risk of burglary and gives peace of mind.

▶ Automation enables heating and cookers (oven-timers) to switch on and off automatically.

▶ Communications technology allows for easier and quicker access to information and to other people.

▶ Home computers and DVD players provide entertainment as well as being functional.

Selection of Household Appliances

When choosing household appliances certain factors should be considered.

1. Cost

Initial cost: Keeping within budget, buy the best quality one can afford.
Running cost: Generally the higher the wattage the more expensive the running cost.
Servicing cost: This is an important consideration for large appliances.
Installation cost: Plumbers/electricians may be required.

2. Brand name

Choose a reliable brand name, buy from a reliable source and check
for quality symbols, e.g. Guaranteed Irish, Quality Approved.

3. Energy efficiency

Choose an energy efficient environmentally friendly product.

4. Safety

Look for safety symbols (See Page 273).

5. Size

Buy a size suitable for family needs, e.g. a six slice toaster would be inappropriate for a family of two.

6. Space available

For example, an upright half-and-half fridge-freezer will not fit under the counter.

7. Design and construction

The appliance should be easy to operate. It should be sturdy, durable and easy to assemble. Colour and shape may also be considered.

8. Ease of cleaning

The appliance should be made of easy-to-clean materials with few crevices.

9. Guarantee

Consider the terms of the guarantee, e.g. length of time, parts and labour (See Page 274).

Electrical Appliances		
Appliances with motor	**Appliances with element**	**Appliances with motor and element**
Food mixer Food processor Blender Liquidiser Carving knife Juicer Vacuum cleaner Refrigerator	Kettle Toaster Grill Cooker Coffee/tea makers Deep fat fryer Iron Steam cleaner Immersion water-heater	Washing machine Tumble-drier Fan heater Bread maker **Electric motors** turn moving parts. **Electric elements** heat up.

Small Appliance with Element

Electric kettle: design and construction

▷ Electric kettles can be made from a variety of materials including stainless steel, chrome and coloured plastic.

▷ Kettles are available in a variety of sizes. The standard capacity of a household kettle is 1.7 litres.

▷ Shape may be the traditional dome-shaped kettle or the more modern jug shape.

▷ Consists of:
  - a lid which is opened or removed for filling;
  - spout often fitted with a filter to remove pieces of scale when pouring;
  - vents allow steam to escape;
  - heat resistant handle;
  - water level indicator;
  - on-off switch;
  - power on light;
  - electric element (sometimes fitted underneath the base to prevent lime scale build up);
  - a thermostat which automatically switches off the kettle when the water has boiled;
  - lead and plug attached to the power base of a cordless kettle, or fits into the kettle itself.

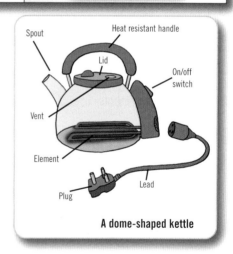

A dome-shaped kettle

Working principle of the kettle

▶ When the kettle is plugged in and turned on electricity flows through the element. The element offers resistance causing it to heat.

▶ The heated element heats the water by conduction and convection currents are set up within the water.

▶ The thermostat automatically switches off the flow of electricity when the water has boiled.

▶ Most kettles are fitted with a boil dry device, which will automatically switch it off if there is insufficient water in the kettle.

Modern jug

Use and care of kettles	
Guidelines for use	**Care and cleaning of kettles**
• Follow manufactures instructions. • Operate with dry hands. • Switch off and unplug before filling. • Ensure that kettle contains at least the minimum quantity of water. • Do not overfill. • Allow to cool before refilling.	• Use only for water. • Unplug before cleaning. • Clean filter regularly. • Descale regularly if necessary. • Never immerse in water. • Clean outside with cloth wrung out in hot soapy water. • Polish off with dry cloth. • Do not use harsh or abrasive cleaners or solvents.

Small Appliance with Motor

Food processor: design and construction

▶ A food processor has:
  – an outer plastic casing enclosing the motor;
  – plastic jug/bowl (average capacity = 2 litres) which rests on a spindle;
  – locking lid with feed tube and food pusher (also measures);
  – on/off/speed controls.

▶ Attachments include:
  – steel blade for chopping meat, vegetables, making breadcrumbs, cakes and mayonnaise;
  – plastic dough blade for yeast mixtures;
  – selection of discs for grating, slicing and making potato chips;
  – shaft which fits on the spindle and onto which the discs are fitted;
  – other possible attachments include juicer, liquidiser and beaters.

Feed tube and pusher

Outer plastic casing

Locking lid

Motor

Attachment fitted on drive spindle

Plastic jug/ bowl

Food processor

Working principle of the food processor

▶ The electric motor turns the spindle which causes the shaft and disc to rotate. Food, e.g. carrots are pushed through the feed tube using the food pusher.

▶ As the food comes into contact with the grating disc it is grated and collected in the plastic bowl.

▶ For chopping and mixing, the correct attachments are fitted into the bowl. The ingredients are then placed in the bowl, the lid is locked in position and the processor is switched on.

> Food processors cannot be switched on if the lid is not locked into position. This is a safety feature.

Use and care of food processors	
Guidelines for use of the food processor	**Care and cleaning of food processors**
• Follow manufacturers instructions. • Never use with wet hands. • Choose appropriate attachment. • Assemble correctly. • Choose correct speed. • Use food pusher not hands when feeding food through tube. • Stop food processor occasionally and scrape food from the sides into the bowl. • Be careful when using sharp blades and discs.	• While using, switch off at intervals to prevent motor overheating or use pulse action. • Do not force switch – check that lid is locked in position. • Switch off and unplug before cleaning. • Dismantle carefully. • All removable parts should be washed in hot soapy water and dried thoroughly. • Wipe over the outer plastic casing with a damp cloth wrung out in hot soapy water. • Polish off with a dry cloth. • Store food processor with the lid off for air circulation.

Refrigerator

A refrigerator is a cooling cabinet designed to keep food clean and fresh. There are three main types of refrigerator:

(a) Standard under the counter fridge.

(b) Larder fridge (taller with no icebox).

(c) Fridge-freezer.

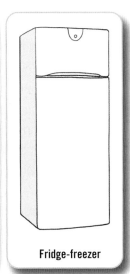

Standard under the counter fridge   **Larder fridge**   **Fridge-freezer**

Refrigerator design and construction (standard fridge, average capacity 150 litres)

- ► A fridge has:
  - – an outer casing of enamelled steel in different colours and finishes
  - – an internal lining of moulded polystyrene
  - – a layer of insulating material between steel and polystyrene
  - – a magnetic door with a rubber gasket which forms a seal
  - – adjustable, plastic-coated shelves inside the cabinet
  - – one or two plastic drawers
  - – a thermostat with a dial control
  - – an interior light which switches on when door is opened;
  - – an icebox at the top of the fridge
  - – the door usually has adjustable bottle racks and moulded
  - – compartments for eggs and dairy products.

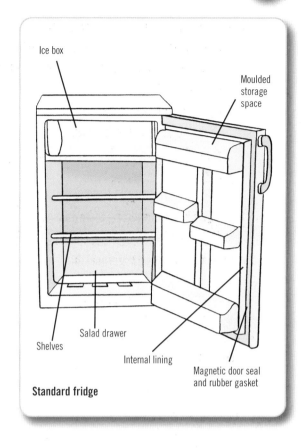

Ice box

Moulded storage space

Salad drawer

Shelves

Internal lining

Magnetic door seal and rubber gasket

Standard fridge

Modern features of refrigerators

- ► Chilled drinks dispenser for fruit juice/water.
- ► Gated shelves for tall containers.
- ► Integrated fridge door to match kitchen cabinet doors.
- ► Digital temperature display.
- ► Different exterior colours and finishes.
- ► Internal or external ice-makers.
- ► Zoned refrigeration with different temperatures in different areas within the cabinet.
- ► Automatic defrosting.
- ► Frost-free fridges do not require defrosting.

Underlying working principle of a compressor refrigerator

Refrigerators work on the principle of a liquid evaporating. During evaporation, heat is drawn from inside the fridge. A special type of liquid called refrigerant (e.g. Freon 12 or liquid ammonia) is used. A refrigerant can easily be evaporated to a gas and condensed back to a liquid again.

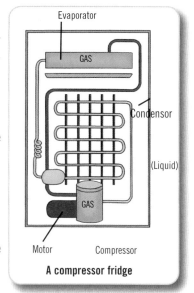

A compressor fridge

- A compressor at the base of the fridge contains gaseous refrigerant.
- A motor attached to the compressor forces the gaseous refrigerant into the condenser.
- The condenser cools the gaseous refrigerant converting it to a liquid.
- The liquid refrigerant then passes into the evaporator where it is changed to a gas drawing heat from inside the fridge.
- The gaseous refrigerant then returns to the compressor and the cycle begins again.
- A thermostat disconnects the motor when the fridge temperature is between 1°C and 4°C and reconnects it when the temperature begins to rise.

Use and care of refrigerators	
Guidelines for use of refrigerators	**Care and cleaning of refrigerators**
• Avoid opening the fridge door unnecessarily as this will raise the temperature. • Cool foods before placing in the fridge to avoid raising the fridge's temperature. • Cover foods to prevent drying out and cross-flavouring. • Store raw meat and fish below cooked food/dairy produce to prevent bacterial contamination. • Use food in rotation and use within the recommended time. • Thaw frozen food in the fridge. • Do not over pack, allow air circulation.	• Position the fridge away from any heat source, e.g. cooker. • Keep clean and defrost regularly. • Wash out the inside with a solution of bicarbonate of soda and water. • Do not use strong smelling cleaning agents or washing up liquid. • Wipe the outside with a cloth wrung out in hot soapy water and polish off with a dry cloth. A silicone polish may be used occasionally. • Keep the back of the fridge dust free. • If not in use leave unplugged, clean and with door open.

Star rating

The star rating on a refrigerator is an indication of the temperature within the icebox, which affects the storage time of frozen foods.

Star rating		
Star Rating	**Temperature**	**Storage**
* one star	−6°C	1 week
** two star	−12°C	1 month
*** three star	−18°C	3 months
**** four star (found on fridge-freezers and deep freezers)	−18 to -25°	Up to 1 year and fresh food can be frozen.

Microwave Oven

Microwave oven: design and construction

▶ A microwave oven is a metal-lined, enamelled steel box.

▶ It has a glass door encasing a perforated metal sheet to redirect waves back into oven.

▶ The door has a safety lock, which turns the microwave oven off when it is opened, and a safety seal to prevent microwaves from escaping.

▶ An internal light lights up when microwave oven is on.

▶ A turntable on a support fits onto a spindle.

▶ Controls are used to select power, e.g. rapid or slow cooking, defrosting or reheating and to set timer.

▶ A transformer increases the voltage. *to a higher frequency for microwaving*

▶ A magnetron converts electrical energy into microwave energy or electromagnetic waves.

▶ A wave guide and stirrer directs the waves into the oven distributes them evenly throughout the oven.

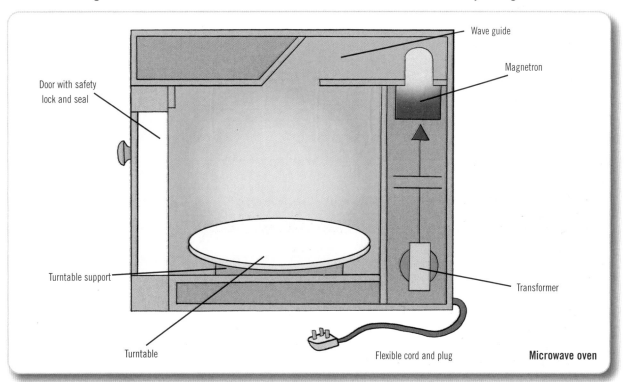

Microwave oven

Underlying working principle of microwave ovens
Microwave ovens work on the principle of electromagnetic waves being absorbed by the food. These waves cause the molecules within the food to vibrate rapidly. The vibrations, or friction, create heat, which cooks the food by conduction.

▶ The microwave oven is plugged in and turned on.
▶ The transformer steps up the standard voltage.
▶ The magnetron converts electrical energy into electro-magnetic energy or waves.
▶ The waves pass into the oven via the wave guide.
▶ The wave stirrer distributes the waves evenly.
▶ The waves are:
  – *reflected* off the metal interior of the oven;
  – *transmitted* through the container holding the food;
  – *absorbed* by the food.
▶ The molecules within the food vibrate rapidly, creating heat.
▶ This heat cooks the food by conduction.

Properties of electro-magnetic waves
Electro-magnetic waves may be:
1. Reflected.
2. Transmitted.
3. Absorbed.

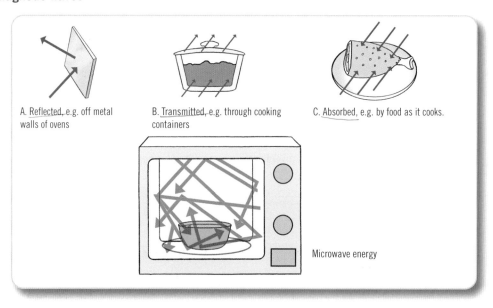

A. Reflected, e.g. off metal walls of ovens

B. Transmitted, e.g. through cooking containers

C. Absorbed, e.g. by food as it cooks.

Microwave energy

Care and cleaning of microwave ovens
1. Follow manufacturers' instructions.
2. Unplug before cleaning.
3. Do not operate when empty, it can cause sparking.
4. Be careful if moving, the magnetron can be damaged.
5. Turn off before opening the door otherwise the fuse may blow.
6. Remove turntable and turntable support for washing.
7. Wipe out with cloth wrung out in hot soapy water and dry.
8. Avoid using harsh abrasives.
9. Ensure that door seal is clean and intact.
10. Have faults dealt with by a qualified person.

Containers for microwave ovens

Suitable containers/materials	Unsuitable containers/materials
Glass	Aluminium plates / foil
Pyrex	Foil containers
China	Gilt trimmed dishes
Porcelain	Very thick dishes
Earthenware	Lightweight plastic
Heat-resistant plastic	
Kitchen paper	
Paper plates	
Microwavable cling film	

Modern features

▶ Combination microwave ovens combine a traditional oven/grill with a microwave. They can be operated independently of each other or in combination. The food browns and crisps from the standard oven elements or the grill element, then cooks quickly by the electromagnetic waves.

▶ Modern microwave ovens have digital/electronic display which allow for accurate timing and power settings.

▶ Defrost setting which can defrost by weight or by time.

See Microwave Cooking (See Page 116).

CONTENTS INCLUDE:

- ► Textiles for household and clothing purposes
- ► Selection criteria for textiles
- ► Care of textiles

- ► Safety considerations in the selection of household textiles
- ► Fire retardant finish
- ► Fire safety (domestic furniture)

Textiles

Textiles are fabrics. They are widely used in the home as a resource for clothing purposes and household purposes.

Functions of Clothing

(a) **Weather protection** – from the rain, wind, sun and cold, e.g. raincoats, gloves, sun hats.

(b) **Safety protection** – from injury, fire and infection, e.g. helmets, firefighters uniforms, plastic gloves.

(c) **Hygiene**, e.g. overalls, aprons, chefs' hats worn by workers in the food industry.

(d) **Modesty** – for decency.

(e) **To impress** – clothing that suits an individual often impresses or attracts others. Designer labels and 'interview clothes' are often used to impress.

(f) **To identify** – uniforms worn by nurses, guards, soldiers and sports teams make them easy to identify.

(g) **To express one's personality** – 'hippy' clothing, biker clothing or sporty clothing often gives information about someone's personality.

Functions of Household Textiles

Household textiles are used in carpets, mats, curtains, cushions, upholstery, wall hangings, bed linen, blankets, duvets, towels, dishcloths and oven gloves.

(a) **Warmth:** Carpets, lined curtains, blankets and duvets provide warmth and insulation.

(b) **Comfort:** Cushions, carpets, duvets and bed linen provide comfort and luxury.

(c) **Protection:**
   - oven gloves protect the user from being burnt;
   - lined curtains prevent the curtain fabric from fading;
   - non-slip mats protect against slipping.

(d) **Absorbency:** Towels and dishcloths absorb moisture; carpets, rugs and upholstered furniture absorb sound.

(e) **Decoration:** One of the main functions of textiles in the home is decoration. A variety of colours, patterns and textures are available to enhance the aesthetics of the home.

A mixture of fabrics adds interest to a room

Selection Criteria for Textiles

1. Suitability

The chosen textile should have properties which make it fit for the purpose intended, e.g. a raincoat must be waterproof. The colour and pattern should also suit the purpose, e.g. curtain fabric in a child's bedroom may differ greatly from that of a sitting room.

Characteristics / Properties of textiles			
Textiles have different properties:			
• Shrinks	• Absorbent	• Drapes well	• Warm
• Colour fast	• Strong	• Fade resistant	• Smooth
• Mothproof	• Textured	• Dry-cleanable	• Stain resistant

Property of a fabric is how it looks and feels and reacts to heat and chemicals.

2. Cost

The amount of money one has to spend greatly influences the type and quality of the fabric that can be bought, e.g. a silk shirt is far more expensive than a polyester shirt; a pure wool carpet is more expensive than a synthetic one.

3. Aesthetic appeal/personal choice

The aesthetic appeal of a textile relates to how attractive you find the fabric. The overall effect will have an influence on one's choice of fabric, e.g. a patterned curtain fabric often looks better with plain walls. The fabric should help to create the desired atmosphere.

Linen blouse

4. Ease of cleaning
Washable fabrics are easier to care for than fabrics that require specialist dry-cleaning.

5. Safety: fire resistance
Safety is an important factor particularly in terms of upholstered furniture and children's clothing.

Textile Care

The method of caring for a fabric is determined by its properties. Properties are influenced by:

(a) The type of fibre used.

(b) The method of fabric construction.

(c) Any finishes that may be applied to the fabric.

Silk

Types of fibres	
Natural	*Animal*, e.g. wool, silk. *Plant*, e.g. cotton, linen.
Man-made	*Synthetic*, e.g. nylon, polyester. *Regenerated* e.g. viscose, acetate.

Woven	e.g. cotton, tweed.
Knitted	e.g. jersey.
Bonded	e.g. felt (fibres bonded together using heat and adhesive).

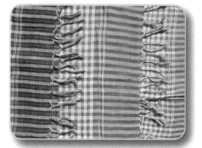

Woven fabric

Knitted fabric

Finishes
Crease resistance
Water proofing
Stain repellence
Fire resistance
Flame retardant
Moth proofing
Shrink resistance

Blended fabric
A blended fabric is one made from a mixture of fibres, e.g. polyester and cotton. This procedure is carried out: (a) to reduce cost and (b) to benefit from the advantageous characteristics of both fabrics.

Cotton shirt

Properties of fibre/fabric relating to care		
Natural		
Fabric	**Properties**	**Care**
Wool	Absorbent Piles and felts Shrinks Stretches when wet Scorches easily	Gentle agitation (minimum wash) Low temperature Dry flat Cool iron
Silk	Absorbent Damaged by careless handling Damaged by chlorine bleach Damaged by high heat	Hand wash or dry-clean Do not bleach Cool iron using a pressing cloth
Cotton	Absorbent Strong when wet Creases easily Shrinks easily Easy to dye Bleaches easily	Hot wash, maximum wash Hot iron Buy pre-shrunk fabric Chlorine bleach may be used
Linen	Absorbent Strong Can withstand high temperatures Shrinks easily Creases easily	Hot wash, maximum wash Iron while damp
Manmade		
Polyester	Strong Resists abrasion Resists creasing Dries quickly	Warm wash Maximum wash
Acrylic	Resists abrasion Does not shrink Does not crease easily	Maximum wash Warm wash Cool iron

Care Labelling

Because of the huge range of fabrics and finishes available, all textile products carry care labels with written instructions and symbols which are internationally recognised. Care labels include washing, drying, ironing, dry-cleaning and bleaching instructions.

Basic scientific principles underlying care of fabrics

1. *Water/dry cleaning solvent* – some fabrics are washable and some must only be dry-cleaned. The temperature of the water and the type of dry-cleaning solvent that is suitable is determined by the fabric.

2. *Washing detergent is used to:*
   (a) Enable the fabric to become wet by reducing the surface tension of the water.
   (b) Dislodge the dirt from the fabric.
   (c) Hold the dirt particles away from the fabric in the water.
   (d) Remove stains from fabrics.
   (e) Soften hard water.

3. **Agitation/friction** – agitation removes dirt. The extent of the friction is determined by the fabric.

4. **Removal of water from fabric** – this is achieved by squeezing/wringing, spinning (centrifugal action) or drip-drying followed by drying – flat or on a clothesline or in a tumble dryer.

5. **Fabric conditioners may be used to:**
   (a) Add scent.
   (b) Soften fabric.
   (c) Prevent static.
   (d) Aid ironing.

> Blends: care as for fibre with the higher percentage.

Care labelling symbols				
Washing	**Drying**	**Ironing**	**Dry cleaning**	**Bleaching**
Hot Maximum wash	Dry flat	Hot iron	The letter is an indication of the solvent which may be used by the dry cleaner	Bleach may be used
Warm Maximum wash	Line dry	Warm iron		
Hand wash only.	Drip dry	Cool iron	(A) (P) (F)	Do not bleach
Do not machine or hand wash	Tumble dry	Do not iron	Do not dry clean	
	Do not tumble dry			

Safety considerations in the selection of household textiles

The safety considerations in the selection of household textiles relate to **fire** and the resulting **toxic fumes** emitted from certain furnishing fillings. Many fabrics catch fire and burn easily, e.g. loosely woven fabrics, fabrics with a pile and blended fabrics which are a mixture of fibres.

Synthetic foam used in upholstered furniture releases toxic fumes when ignited.

In order to reduce the risk of tragedy consumers should choose:

 ▶ Low-risk fabric (see below).

▶ Fabrics that have been treated with a flame retardant finish.

▶ All foam fillings should be CMHR (see overleaf).

Low-risk fabrics	High-risk fabrics
Wool – smoulders and may quench. *go out* Polyester – burns slowly melts and shrinks away from flame.	Cotton – burns quickly. Silk – melts and spatters. *spits* Acrylic – burns quickly, melts and spatters.

a) coated finish - cheaper, comfortable, not very strong protection, non permanent - affected by washing/drying
b) inherent finish - fibres treated before being woven or knitted - more expensive, not as easy to wear, requires careful laundering
- army, garda, fireman, chef

Fire retardant finish

Fire retardant finishes are applied to <u>reduce the flammability of a fabric</u>. The fabrics will continue to burn in the flames, but will <u>self-extinguish when removed from the flames</u>.

> *PROBAN = A fire retardant fabric.

PROBAN	
Treatment	**Effects**
• A <u>phosphorus/chlorine compound</u> is applied to a fabric. • Fabric is then treated with <u>ammonia</u>. • As a result <u>insoluble polymers</u> form and are embedded in the fabric.	• <u>Reduced</u> risk of fabric <u>igniting</u>. burn • <u>Self-extinguishing</u> when removed from flame. • More <u>expensive</u> fabric. • May result in <u>allergic reaction</u>. • <u>Special care</u> may be required <u>during cleaning</u>.

*\
NB

Fire retardant finishes are commonly used in furnishing fabrics and <u>fabrics used for children's clothing</u>.

Fire Safety (Domestic Furniture) Order 1988, 1995

The purpose of this order is to <u>reduce fire-related accidents</u>. The regulations apply to <u>beds, cots, pushchairs, cushions, upholstered furniture, loose covers and pillows</u>. *The order requires that:*

*\
NB

▶ Fabrics used in any of the above must pass <u>a number of fire safety tests</u>.

▶ <u>Permanent safety labels</u> on all items must be <u>securely attached</u>, <u>clearly legible</u> and <u>durable</u>.

▶ A <u>display</u> or <u>swing-safety</u> label must also be attached to all items.

▶ Any foam fillings used must be <u>CMHR</u> (<u>combustion modified high resilience</u>) foam or filling.

Purpose of labelling

1. It <u>informs</u> the consumer about the <u>fabric/fillings used in</u> the production of <u>an article</u>.

2. It <u>warns</u> the consumer of possible dangers.

3. It allows for <u>traceability</u> should an article be found unsafe.

Types of labels	
Display/swing labels	**Permanent labels**

(a) <u>Square</u>
Both fabric cover and filling meet safety requirements.
 	
(b) <u>Triangle</u>
Used when outer fabric is not match resistant, but a fire-resistant interliner is present. 
	• Are usually <u>stitched</u> on.
	• Include a <u>warning</u> 'carelessness causes fire'.
	• Include name, address, date of
	  – <u>manufacturer</u>, importers
	  – <u>batch/identity number</u>
	  – description of fillings and <u>cover material</u>
	  – details of interliner if used. 

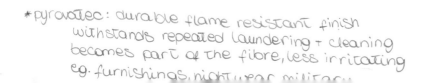

*pyrovatec: durable flame resistant finish
withstands repeated laundering + cleaning
becomes part of the fibre, less irritating
eg. furnishings, nightwear, military

Chapter 16 I Consumer Studies (2.2)

CONTENTS INCLUDE:

- ► **Factors affecting consumer decisions**
- ► **The purchasing process**
- ► **Consumer rights and responsibilities**
- ► **Management of the environment**
- ► **Consumer protection and legislation**

Consumer Studies

> A consumer is someone who buys or uses goods and services.

Consumer Choices (2.2.1)

Consumers are influenced by a range of factors.

1. Personal preferences
Personal likes and dislikes have an immediate impact on choices. A product must appeal to the consumer in terms of colour, style and design.

2. Personal values
Personal values also have an influence on choices. Discerning consumers distinguish between needs and wants and are less inclined to impulse buy. Strongly held beliefs and values on issues such as the environment, animal rights or civil liberties will influence choices of goods and services. For example, some consumers will only buy cosmetics from companies which do not use animals when testing their products.

3. Other people
Family, friends, peer groups and sales people influence consumer choices. Many people tend to conform to standards set down by members of their social group, for example in terms of current fashions, clothing, cars and interior decor. Celebrities in the world of sport and entertainment also have an impact on consumer choices when they endorse products or services.

4. Income
Income has a bearing on consumer choices. A limited income means there is less to spend on luxuries and all purchases have to be carefully considered. Access to borrowed money and social pressures, for example, to live in a particular area or drive a new car, may result in people getting into debt and living beyond their means.

5. Marketing
Marketing is an industry which specialises in making products sell. Techniques used include advertising, packaging and presentation, sales promotions such as '2 for the price of 1'.

6. Advertising
Consumers are bombarded with a range of different forms of advertising on radio and TV and in the press. Other forms of advertising include sponsorship, billboards and posters, all of which have an impact on consumer choices.

7. Packaging and labelling
There is growing competition between different brands of products, particularly in the food industry. Goods must have instant appeal. Consumers are also becoming more discerning about labelling – demanding clearer, more accurate information. (See Page 153).

8. Selling/merchandising
Many techniques and shopping systems are used to increase the sale of goods and services. Techniques include easy pay systems, loyalty schemes, mail order and shopping online.

The Purchasing Process

Classification of retail outlets		
Outlet	**Features**	**Examples**
Independent shops	• Small • Often family run • May specialise in one range of goods	• Jewellers • Shoe shops
Multiple chain stores	• One company, many branches • All similar in design and layout • Competitive prices (due to bulk buying and shared advertising)	• Dunnes Stores • Penneys • Lidl
Supermarkets	• Large, self service stores • Broad range of groceries and household goods. • Own brand goods generally cheaper	• Chain Stores, e.g. Tesco • Voluntary chain stores, e.g. Mace, SuperValu
Department stores	• Wide range of goods, e.g. clothing, furniture, electrical goods	• Debenhams • Arnotts
Discount stores	• Chain stores/independently run • Goods usually less expensive • Range of goods, e.g. food, toys, furniture, household equipment. • If goods are ordered from catalogue they are collected, prepacked and unsatisfactory goods may be returned.	• Argos • Lidl • Aldi

Argos

Tesco

Other retail outlets or shopping systems include:
- Street markets
- Auctions
- Shopping centres
- Party selling
- Television buying
- Vending machines
- Mail order
- Door-to-door selling
- Online/internet shopping

Persuading consumers to spend involves engaging all of their five senses.

Retail psychology

▷ Retail psychology involves the study of consumers and the factors which influence their spending.

▷ Information on consumer attitudes and behaviour is collected through market research. This is used by retailers in advertising and marketing strategies, which aim to encourage consumers to spend.

▷ Many techniques are employed to increase spending and impulse buying. Some of these techniques are subliminal (i.e. you are unaware of them as they effect your subconscious), other techniques are more obvious.

▷ Many shops are self-service. They are designed and laid out with much attention to detail. Soft background music, comfortable heating, ventilation and lighting, pleasant smells and attractively packaged and displayed goods create a soothing atmosphere.

▷ Essentials such as milk and bread are often placed towards the rear of the store so that customers must walk past an attractive range of products. Store layout may also be changed occasionally so that consumers are forced to search shelves for the required products.

▷ Fruit and vegetables are placed near the entrance. The colourful display of fresh produce looks attractive. It also encourages the use of a trolley rather than a basket.

▷ Luxuries and high-profit items tend to be displayed at eye level.

▷ Foods are often positioned by association, e.g. cones and wafers are placed beside the ice-cream fridge; nuts and crisps beside soft drinks.

▷ Magazines and health and beauty products are placed at the checkout to encourage impulse buying, as are sweets to tempt children.

▷ Special offers such as '3 for the price of 2' and free samples give the impression of extra bargains and the loss leader technique (selling one product at cost) is used to attract customers.

▷ Club card schemes such as those run by Dunnes Stores and Tesco encourage store loyalty. Customers can build up points which accumulate in money back vouchers.

Shelf position is so important that manufacturers sometimes send merchandising staff to visit retailers to check that their particular products are prominently and effectively displayed.

Shopping patterns

Shopping patterns have undergone some radical changes in recent times.

▷ Large shopping centres offer 'one stop shopping', reducing the stress of traffic and parking. Restaurant and crèche facilities are available so that consumers spend more time on the premises.

▷ Shops accommodate consumers in terms of opening hours, such as late night shopping and Sunday opening. On-line and TV shopping are becoming increasingly popular. Goods can be purchased at any time, regardless of opening hours, and then delivered to the consumer's home.

▷ Consumers are more price conscious and want value for money. They are better educated and informed of their rights as consumers and feel free to complain if goods are not up to the expected standard.

▷ There is increased competition brought about by the entry of more foreign-owned companies into the Irish market. This has led to 'price wars' particularly among the multiple chain stores such as Tesco, Dunnes Stores, Aldi and Lidl.

▷ The consumer base is changing and retail outlets are adjusting to take multicultural influences into account.

▷ Consumers are more environmentally aware, e.g. choosing energy efficient appliances and products with less wasteful packaging.

▷ High standards of hygiene are also expected. Food shops in particular must be well maintained: well-stocked shelves, no bad odours, goods prepared, packaged and displayed safely and hygienically.

▷ Cash transactions are generally being replaced by debit and credit cards.

Debit and credit cards

Consumer Research

Consumer research involves collecting and processing information regarding consumer needs. Information may be collected via a variety of techniques.

Desk Research	Field Research
• Involves collection of data from sources such as state agencies, trade associations and the internet.	• Involves the study of consumer behaviour in the marketplace. • Information is collected through observation, interviews and surveys.
Advantages • Information collected quickly. • Relatively inexpensive.	**Advantages** • Accurate and detailed information is collected.
Disadvantages • Collected information is general and not very detailed.	**Disadvantages** • More expensive and time consuming.

Value of consumer research

▷ Reduces the financial risk involved in launching a new product or business.

▷ Provides an insight into consumer attitudes, behaviour and factors which affect decision-making. This information is valuable for developing new products and services or improving existing ones.

▷ Enables manufacturers, producers and retailers to compile consumer profiles for their products and services in terms of age, gender, disposable income and any other relevant factors.

▷ Provides information on current market trends and market size so that over-production is avoided.

▷ Identifies competitors. Analysis of their strengths and weaknesses can be a useful source of information, enabling companies to protect their position in the market.

Research Methods
- Questionnaires
- Interviews
- Surveys
- Observation

Consumer Rights and Responsibilities

Consumers have certain rights, many of which are protected by law. Consumers also have responsibilities. They should be aware of their rights and should make informed decisions when choosing goods and services with due regard to the impact their choices may have on the economy and on the environment.

Consumer Rights

1. The right to honest and truthful information

Consumers need clear and accurate information if they are to make wise choices when selecting goods and services. Consumer protection legislation makes it an offence for a manufacturer or a retailer to give false or misleading information about a product or service.

2. The right to choice

Consumers have the right to choose from a range of available goods and services. Manufacturers and suppliers compete with one another to provide products and services. By exercising their right to choose, consumers can compel producers to raise the standard of their goods and services. The competition also helps to keep prices down.

3. The right to value for money

Consumers are entitled to feel that they are getting value for the money they spend on goods and services. All products on sale, regardless of price, must be of *merchantable quality*. This means that they must be of a certain standard and must be fit for the purpose for which they are intended. All services on offer must also be of an acceptable standard.

4. The right to safety

All consumers have a right to know that a product will not be harmful to their health or put their lives at risk. Safety legislation and testing protect consumers. Products such as cleaning agents carry instructions and safety warnings and symbols. Items such are electrical goods and children's toys are subject to rigorous testing before they are placed on the market.

5. The right to redress

Consumers have a right to complain if goods prove to be faulty or services are unsatisfactory. Compensation for faulty goods may take the form of a repair, replacement, or refund depending on the fault and other circumstances, such as the time elapsed since purchase.

Consumers have a right to:
- Honest information
- Choice
- Value for money
- Safety
- Redress

Consumer Responsibilities (2.2.2)

Consumers have the following responsibilities:

▶ To know their rights as consumers and to educate themselves about consumer laws.

▶ To be well informed about goods and services, thereby enabling them to choose services and products wisely.

▶ To be conscious of the balance between price and quality.

▶ To complain and seek redress when consumer rights have been infringed or a consumer law has been broken.

▶ To read labels and follow manufacturers' instructions when using goods, paying particular attention to any safety warnings on the packaging.

▶ To use resources carefully, avoiding waste, and minimising any damaging effect the product may have on the environment. (See Page 278).

Consumer information

Consumer information is knowledge that allows a consumer to shop wisely. Various sources of information are available to consumers including:

Source	Information available
Magazines/newspapers	• Features on products/services. • Compare and evaluate a range of goods and services.
TV/Radio programmes	• Evaluate various goods and services.
Sales people	• Knowledgeable about the product for sale, but can pressurise the consumer in order to sell.
Showrooms, exhibitions, e.g. 'Ideal Home and Garden' exhibitions	• Provide information on a range of products on display.
Advertising	• Limited information about products which tends to be biased in favour of products being marketed.
Manufacturers leaflets and labelling	• Often supply detailed information about products.
Other consumers	• The experience of other consumers tends to be one of the best sources of consumer information.
Organisations concerned with consumers' rights and protection	• (See Page 275).

Approval and quality marks

Sometimes manufacturers have their product tested by an independent body. If the product attains certain standards in terms of quality and safety it is awarded a recognised seal of approval or quality mark. Such quality marks may be withdrawn if the high standard is not maintained.

Approval and quality marks

Symbol		Testing body	Awarded to
Q mark		Excellence Ireland Quality Association	Products and services which are of high quality as set down in ISO 9000.
Guaranteed Irish		Guaranteed Irish Ltd.	Goods which are Irish made and are of high standard.
ISO Symbol		National Standards Authority of Ireland (NSAI)	Goods of high quality.
Kitemark		British Standards Institution	Goods of a high standard of quality and safety.

Hazard symbols

Highly flammable	Irritant	Toxic	Corrosive

Safety symbols

	Goods comply with British Standards of safety	Electrical or gas appliances
	Goods comply with European standards of safety	Toys, electrical goods
	Doubly insulated	Smaller electrical appliances, e.g. hair driers
	Irish mark of electrical conformity	Found on electrical goods.

Consumer Protection (2.2.3)

Consumer rights are protected by legislation. Such laws are necessary:

> To prevent unscrupulous manufacturers and suppliers taking advantage of consumers, e.g. by misleading consumers about goods, services or price.

> To ensure that if rights are infringed consumers have a means of redress.

> Many laws protect consumer rights, in particular:
> 1. The Sale of Goods and Supply of Services Act 1980.
> 2. The Consumer Information Act 1978.

1. Sale of Goods and Supply of Services Act 1980

Under this act legal responsibility lies with the retailer or supplier as follows. *The retailer must ensure that all goods on sale are*:

> Of merchantable quality, i.e. must be of reasonably good standard and fit to be sold.

> As described, e.g. in a written description as on a label or in a verbal description as given by a salesperson.

> Fit for the purpose intended: goods must be suitable for use, e.g. food must be edible, electrical goods must function safely and efficiently.

> Conform to sample: goods sold by sample such as wallpaper or floor covering must correspond to the sample.

> Services must be supplied with due skill and any materials used or goods supplied must be of merchantable quality.

> Signs which limit the liability of the retailer/supplier are illegal. Examples of such signs include:
> - 'No Cash Refunds'
> - 'Credit Notes Only for Returned Goods'
> - 'No Liability Accepted for Faulty Goods'

Redress for consumer

Under the *Sale of Goods and Supply of Services Act* the consumer may be entitled to compensation if goods prove faulty or services are unsatisfactory. Compensation may take the form of:

> A replacement.

> A repair.

> A refund/partial refund.

> Or in the case of a service, service repeated without charge.

Type and amount of compensation depends on:

> The seriousness of the fault.

> How soon after purchase the fault developed or became evident.

> How quickly the fault was reported to the retailer/supplier.

If goods are clearly marked as 'seconds' or have defects which are pointed out to the consumer at time of purchase, the consumer does not have a claim under this Act.

Guarantees

Guarantees are also covered by the Sale of Goods and Supply of Services Act. A guarantee is a contract between the manufacturer and the consumer. It is an undertaking that the goods purchased will be satisfactory for a stated length of time. A guarantee does not affect consumer rights and manufacturers are not legally obliged to give a guarantee. However, a guarantee offers extra protection against faulty goods. Under the Sale of Goods and Supply of Services Act all guarantees must:

► Be clearly legible.

► Refer to specific goods.

► State the name and address of the individual or company offering the guarantee and against whom claims should be made.

► Clearly state the period of the guarantee (from the date of purchase).

► Detail the procedure for making claims.

► State what the manufacturer intends to do in relation to unsatisfactory goods.

► State what charges (e.g. cost of carriage) the buyer must meet if goods become faulty under the guarantee.

> **Electronic Commerce Act 2000**
> Contracts that are conducted electronically are valid and enforceable

2. Consumer Information Act 1978

► The Consumer Information Act 1978 protects the consumer against false or misleading claims about goods or services, such as in advertising and descriptions in a catalogue.

► It also forbids false or misleading information regarding price, previous price (as in a sale) or recommended retail price of goods or services.

Consumer protection bodies	
Statutory bodies	**Voluntary bodies**
• National Consumer Agency • The Office of the Ombudsman • The National Standards Authority of Ireland (NSAI)	• The Consumer Association of Ireland • The Advertising Standards Authority of Ireland

Statutory Consumer Protection Bodies

> Consumer Credit Act 1995 (See Page 238).
> Food legislation see (See Page 186).

The National Consumer Agency (NCA)
The National Consumer Agency was set up in 2007 under the Consumer Protection Act 2007.

Functions:

► To promote and protect the interests of the consumer.

► To enforce consumer law and to investigate any breaches.

► To inform the public of their consumer rights.

► To increase awareness of consumer issues through publications, e.g. Shoppers' Rights card, a helpline and website (ConsumerConnect.ie).

► To advise the government on consumer legislation.

Electronic Commerce act 2000 protects you when you shop online

The Office of the Ombudsman

The Ombudsman is an independent body which investigates complaints made by the public against government departments, local authorities, the HSE and An Post. Any complaints should first be pursued as far as possible with the agency concerned. The Ombudsman may then be contacted if a valid complaint is not dealt with to the consumer's satisfaction. While the Ombudsman has no legal power to enforce its recommendations, most public bodies comply to avoid negative publicity.

Financial Services Ombudsman: investigates consumer complaints against banks and other credit institutions.

Citizens Information Board

Citizens Information Board is a statutory body which supplies the public with information and advice relating to all aspects of social services such as social welfare benefits and entitlements, health services and consumer rights. This information is distributed through a website and Citizen Information Centres located throughout the country.

Citizens **Information** Board
information · advice · advocacy

The National Standards Authority of Ireland (NSAI)

The NSAI is a statutory body which sets and monitors quality and safety standards in Irish industry. It runs the ISO 9000 scheme. ISO 9000 is an internationally recognised award given to firms who attain very high quality standards.

NSAI
Standards

Voluntary Consumer Protection Bodies

The Consumers' Association of Ireland

The Consumers' Association of Ireland is an independent non-statutory body which works on behalf of Irish consumers. Its functions include:

- ► Carrying out surveys and producing reports on consumer products and services.
- ► Providing the public with advice and information regarding consumer issues through the publication of various leaflets and *Consumer Choice* magazine.
- ► Lobbying the government for improvements in consumer legislation and small claims procedures.
- ► Representing the public on various bodies such as the Food Safety Authority.
- ► Encouraging high standards of quality in Irish goods and services while highlighting problem areas which affect consumer rights.

The Advertising Standards Authority of Ireland (ASAI)

The ASAI is an independent self-regulatory body set up by the advertising industry in Ireland.

Functions:

> ▶ To ensure that all advertisements are legal, decent and truthful.
>
> ▶ Investigate complaints made by the public.
>
> ▶ It may recommend that an advertisement be altered or removed.

Consumer complaints procedure

1. Return to the retailer with the goods and proof of purchase as soon as the fault becomes evident. In the case of unsatisfactory service complain promptly to the supplier.

2. Speak to the manager outlining the complaint and stating what the retailer or supplier should do about the faulty goods or service. Consumer must be realistic in terms of compensation.

3. If the response is not satisfactory, the complaint should be put in writing to the retailer or head office. Letter should include:
   - description of goods – model, brand, price;
   - where and when purchased;
   - compensation sought;
   - copies of receipts and guarantee should be enclosed.

4. If the response is still unsatisfactory, help may be sought from consumer bodies such as the Consumer Association of Ireland or the NCA.

5. If the retailer or supplier refuses to accept responsibility for faulty goods or unsatisfactory service the consumer may take legal action through the Small Claims Court.

Small claims procedure

Function

The Small Claims court was set up to deal quickly and inexpensively with consumer disputes. Claims up to the value of €2,000 may be resolved by the Registrar or Court and the services of a solicitor are not required.

Operation

1. The claimant (person making the claim) fills in an application form and lodges it with a small fee with the District Court Registrar.

2. The complaint is registered and a copy is sent to the respondent (individual against whom the claim is made).

3. If the respondent does not refute the claim within 15 days the claim is settled in the claimant's favour by the Registrar.

4. If the complaint is disputed the Registrar will attempt to settle the dispute. If this is not possible, the case will be resolved by a court hearing.

Managing the Environment (2.2.2)

Laws that monitor, maintain and protect the environment are enforced by local authorities and by the Environmental Protection Agency under the Department of the Environment, Heritage and Local Government. Ultimately, however, consumers must play a responsible role in managing the environment.

Consequences of not managing the environment responsibly include:

1. A depletion in non-renewable resources such as coal and oil.
2. Global warming from greenhouse gases such as chlorofluorocarbons (CFCs) and subsequent damaging climatic changes such as flooding and drought.
3. An increase in litter, and air, water and soil pollution.
4. Depletion of the protective ozone layer.
5. Destruction of tropical rain forests.
6. The growing problems of waste disposal such as concerns about incineration and about gas emissions from landfill sites.

Managing resources	
Renewable resources	**Non-renewable resources**
Renewable resources are resources which can be used without permanently reducing the amount available, for example:	Non-renewable resources are resources which once used up are gone forever and cannot be replaced, for example:

Renewable resources

Renewable resources are resources which can be used without permanently reducing the amount available, for example:

- **Wind power:** Harnessing the power of the wind to produce energy.
- **Solar power:** Using the sun's rays as a source of energy.
- **Biomass energy:** Combustion of organic matter, e.g. wood, to produce energy.
- **Hydropower:** Using flowing water to create energy.
- **Geothermal power:** Using the internal heat of the earth to generate energy.

Use of renewable resources

- Renewable resources can be used to generate electricity and for space and water heating.
- Renewable resources are clean and efficient and have little effect on the environment.
- There are some problems in consistency of supply, e.g. in wind and solar energy.
- The costs involved in setting up plants tend to be prohibitively high.

> Due to global warming and depleting supplies of fossil fuels many countries are now committed to seeking alternative sources of energy from renewable resources (Kyoto Agreement).

Non-renewable resources

Non-renewable resources are resources which once used up are gone forever and cannot be replaced, for example:

- **Fossil fuel:** Natural fuels formed in the geological past from the remains of living organisms such as coal, oil, gas and peat.
- **Uranium:** Used as source of nuclear energy chiefly used to generate electricity.

Use of non-renewable resources

- **Fossil fuels** are used to generate electricity and for space and water heating.
- Scientists believe that oil and gas supplies could run out in a few decades if the use continues at the current rate.
- Fossil fuels, with the exception of gas, are a major source of air pollution.
- Uranium is not in any immediate danger of depletion as presently there are unlimited supplies available.
- While becoming safer due to improving technology, nuclear power plants produce hazardous waste.

Wind power   Solar power

Plastic bag levy - introduced in 2002 to combat problem of plastic bag polluting the environment

waste prevention act 1996 - aimed to reduce the amount of waste in Ireland & to encourage **better** waste dumping practices such as recycling, reducing, reusing, refusing, repairing & composting

Waste management

Each local authority has a waste management plan. The plan covers the treatment of all non-hazardous wastes in accordance with national and EU waste legislation and policy. Such plans are based on the EU Waste Hierarchy.

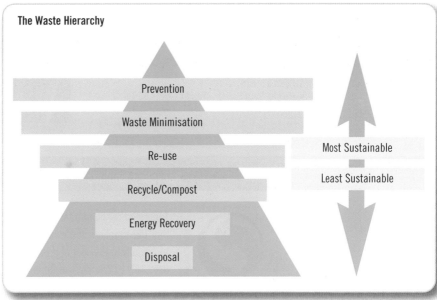

The Waste Hierarchy

Prevention
Waste Minimisation
Re-use
Recycle/Compost
Energy Recovery
Disposal

Most Sustainable
Least Sustainable

1. ***Prevention:*** Consumers should consider whether they actually need the goods.

2. ***Minimisation:*** Goods may be maintained or repaired rather than replaced; journeys could be minimised by car-pooling.

3. ***Reuse:*** Many items such as plastic bottles, cardboard and metal boxes can be reused.

4. ***Recycling:*** Some materials such as plastic and glass can be re-used, conserving resources.

5. ***Energy recovery:*** Energy can be recovered. For example, gases produced by landfill sites can be harnessed to produce heat energy; energy produced by combustion of waste in an incinerator can also be recovered.

6. ***Disposal:*** This is the least favoured option since it is wasteful of resources and causes disposal problems.

Consumers can play an active role in waste management by refusing, reusing and recycling.

ENFO
ENFO is a free public service which supplies information on environmental matters such as waste management and energy conservation.

Refusing	Reusing	Recycling
• Products which are not environmentally friendly. • Excess packaging. • Disposable products such as napkins and paper plates. • Goods wrapped in individual sachets and wrappings. • Pre-packed fresh fruit or vegetables.	• Plastic, cardboard and metal containers. • Rechargeable batteries. • Shopping bags. • Goods such as furniture, clothes and appliances may be reused by charities. • Ink cartridges • Mobile phones	• Buying products made from recycled material such as kitchen rolls and greeting cards. • Buying goods packaged in recyclable materials, e.g. aluminium cans, glass bottles. • Composting organic matter. • Recycling paper, plastic, metal, glass, batteries, oil and textiles.

WEEE Directive (Waste Electrical and Electronic Equipment)

Under this EU directive producers must organise for the collection and treatment of waste electrical and electronic equipment. Since August 2005 - retailers have to take back WEEE from the public, free of charge, on a one-to-one basis, when purchasing a similar type new item.
→ reduces amt. of items in landfill
→ 15 days to return the item
→ prices quoted must display cost e.g.
     fridge / freezer €20   (EMC)

Advantages of recycling
1. Reduces waste disposal costs.
2. Reduces litter and water, soil and air pollution.
3. Lowers production costs.
4. Conserves non-renewable sources of energy such as oil.
5. Creates employment.

Recycling symbols

The *green dot*		The *green dot* is an internationally recognised symbol, which indicates that the suppliers of packaging bearing the green dot have contributed financially to the cost of recycling. (In Ireland the green dot symbol is used only by members of Repak.)
PET symbol		*PETE* (commonly referred to as PET) stands for polyethylene terephthalate. PET bottles are the most commonly recycled household plastic. The recycled PET bottles are used for carpets, sleeping bags, upholstery and a variety of other uses.
The *recycling symbol*		The *recycling symbol* is used by manufacturers to indicate that goods and packaging contain recyclable material or are recyclable.

Air Pollution

Causes	Effects	Preventative measures
• Gases such as nitrogen, carbon dioxide and sulphur dioxide produced by burning fossil fuels. • Chlorofluorocarbons (CFCs) used in fridges and aerosols. • Traffic emissions, e.g. carbon monoxide. • Overuse of chemical sprays and cleaning agents. • Smoke from domestic and industrial combustion of fossil fuels.	• Acid rain lowers the pH of soil and water, harming animal and plant life. • Acid rain also corrodes metal and stone – a threat to historical buildings which require expensive maintenance to counteract effect. • Global warming alters the earth's climate over time. • Depletion of ozone layer and increased risk of skin cancer and eye cataracts. • Increase in respiratory conditions such as asthma and bronchitis.	• Using cleaner, less polluting sources of energy such as gas, smokeless fuels, wind and solar energy. • Buying energy efficient appliances. • Choosing pump action and ozone friendly aerosols. • Servicing and maintaining car engines and walking and cycling rather than using the car. • Using unleaded petrol.

Acid rain harms trees

Acid rain corrodes buildings and statues

Emissions from car exhausts cause pollution

Water pollution

Causes	Effects	Preventative measures
• Seepage from sewage and slurry. • Illegal dumping. • Overuse of detergents containing phosphate. • Leeching of artificial fertilisers, pesticides and chemical waste. • Oil spillages.	• Alga bloom uses up available oxygen and destroys aquatic life. • Kills fish. • Unsightly – destroys beauty spots. • Kills marine animals and birds so that species become depleted. • Harms fishing and tourism industry.	• Ensuring that all agricultural practices comply with law. • Choosing phosphate free detergents. • Limiting the use of artificial fertilisers and pesticides. • Safe disposal of all garden chemicals, e.g. weed killers. • Heavy penalties for companies and individuals involved in the illegal disposal of rubbish.

Algal bloom

Noise pollution

Causes	Effects	Preventative measures
• Car and burglar alarms. • Transport systems. • Barking dogs. • Night clubs and discos. • Lawn mowers. • Construction work.	• Headaches. • Irritation. • Insomnia. • Tension between neighbours.	• Turn down TVs, radios and music systems. • Insulation, e.g. double-glazing, carpets. • Housing should not be located too near night-clubs or transport systems, e.g. airports.

Energy

Ireland is committed to a policy of sustainable energy. This policy ensures that there is enough energy to sustain development while protecting the environment.

SEI (Sustainable Energy Ireland)

SEI is a national authority whose role is to:

- Improve energy efficiency.
- Promote the move towards renewable energy resources.
- Reduce the impact on the environment of energy production and use.
- Advise government on policies and measures on sustainable energy.

Eco label

The eco label (flower) is a voluntary scheme designed to encourage businesses to market products and services which are environmentally friendly. Products are assessed on such principles as:

- Use of energy and other resources during manufacture.
- Potential to pollute (air, soil and water pollution).
- Whether the product is reusable or recyclable.

Energy labelling

Energy labelling of household appliances enables consumers to choose appliances based on their energy efficiency. Household appliances which carry energy labels include refrigerators, freezers, washing machines, tumble-driers, dishwashers and ovens. Appliances are rated on an A–G scale, A and B rated appliances are the most energy efficient.

Consumers can be more energy efficient and reduce their consumption by:

▷ Choosing energy efficient appliances.

▷ Not leaving appliances such as TVs, radios and computers on stand-by.

▷ Using some appliances rather than others can be a more energy efficient option, e.g. using a toaster instead of a grill.

▷ Microwave ovens use less energy than conventional methods of reheating and cooking food.

▷ Line dry clothes rather than using a tumble-drier.

▷ Lagging the hot water cylinder and hot water pipes.

▷ Using the shower instead of the bath.

▷ Avoiding washing items under running water and mending leaking taps.

▷ Using the half load or economy cycle on washing machines.

▷ Filling dishwasher completely before running it.

▷ Fitting a timer to the immersion heater.

▷ Using thermostats and timers efficiently.

▷ Insulating the house well.

▷ Keeping heating appliances and systems serviced and in good repair.

▷ Turning off unused lights.

▷ Using cfls (compact fluorescent lamps).

Energy — Washing Machine

Manufacturer
Model

More efficient

A
B
C
D
E
F
G

Less efficient

B

Energy Consumption
kWh/year
(Based on standard test results
for 60° C cotton cycle)
Actual consumption will depend
on how the appliance is used

Washing Performance
A: higher   G: lower

Spin Drying Performance
A: higher   G: lower
Spin speed (rpm)

Capacity (cotton) kg

Water Consumption   1

Noise   Spining
(dB(A) re 1 pW)   Washing

Further information is contained
in product brochures

Norm EN 60456
Washing Machine Label Directive 95/12/EC

[Handwritten note:] Sustainable development: managing development so that resources (eg. wood, plastic, concrete) are used in a way that has a minimum impact on the environment, and, without depleting/destroying them for future generations

AREA THREE
SOCIAL STUDIES

CONTENTS INCLUDE:
- ▶ **An introduction to sociology and sociological concepts**
- ▶ **Defining the family**
- ▶ **Family structures**
- ▶ **Functions of the family**

Social Studies

Sociology is the science of society. It involves the study of the family, relationships, behaviour patterns, customs and social problems. In order to study sociology some sociological concepts or terms must first be understood.

Sociological Concepts and Terms (3.1.1)

Society
Society is how we describe a group of people sharing a common purpose or way of life, e.g. the Society of St Vincent de Paul, Irish society.

Culture
Culture is the way of life of a society, including language, music and behavioural patterns. Culture is passed on from one generation to the next.

Irish dancing

Kinship

Kinship is a family relationship based on blood relations.

Norms

Norms are expected patterns of behaviour that are regarded as normal, e.g. children going to school.

Values

Values are beliefs and attitudes regarding what is right and what is wrong.

Mores

Mores are the established norms and values of a society considered to be most important, e.g. loyalty and honesty.

Role

The pattern of behaviour considered appropriate for an individual according to his or her position in society is called a role, e.g. priest or student.

Status

Status is the position held by a person in society, often defined by the amount of respect given by other members of society.

Social groups: sub-groups within society

(a) Primary social group – small intimate groups, including family and close friends.
(b) Secondary social groups – larger more impersonal groups, including colleagues and acquaintances.

Socio-economic group

Socio-economic groups are the classification of people within society according to their wealth or income. In Ireland, three main groupings exist: upper, middle and lower socio-economic groups. This division is known as *social stratification* or *layering.*

Social mobility

Social mobility is the movement of people from one socio-economic group to another. Education enables people to climb the 'social ladder'.

Socialisation

Socialisation is the passing on of types of behaviour that enable a person to fit into society. Primary socialisation happens within the family. Secondary socialisation is learned through school, work and through the media. Socialisation is a life-long process.

Social institutions

Organised social arrangements that are common to many societies, e.g. the family, marriage and religion.

Social change

Social changes are changes which occur within society due to, for example, wars, new laws and technology.

Defining the Family (3.1.2)

The family may be defined as 'a group of people related through blood, marriage or adoption'.

The United Nations defined the family as 'the basic unit of society, which acts as a support for its members and which transmits values from one generation to the next' (1994).

According to the Irish Constitution (Article 41), the family is the 'natural, primary and fundamental unit group of society'.

A nuclear family

The Universality of the Family

The family is among the oldest and most fundamental of social institutions and is present in virtually all known societies. Individuals are born into a family, which is known as the 'family of orientation'. The family formed with a partner is known as 'the family of procreation'. Although the form the family takes may differ from one society to another, the concept of 'the family' is universal.

Family Structures (3.1.3)

The main types of modern family structures are:

- ▶ Nuclear families
- ▶ Extended families
- ▶ Lone-parent families
- ▶ Blended families.

Lone-parent family

The characteristics of nuclear families

- ▶ Nuclear families consist of parent(s) and children.
- ▶ They are usually small families, their relatives are widely dispersed.
- ▶ They are economically self-sufficient.
- ▶ They are mobile; they may move for career or other reasons.
- ▶ Nuclear families have integrated conjugal roles, i.e. the role of mother and father overlap.
- ▶ They are democratic in decision-making.
- ▶ Nuclear families are isolated in times of crises.

The characteristics of extended families

▶ Extended families consist of parents, children, grandparents, aunts, uncles and cousins.

▶ They are usually large families living together in one home or living nearby.

▶ They are often economically inter-dependent. Many members working on the family farm or in the family business and therefore immobile.

▶ Extended families have more segregated roles for men and women.

▶ They are authoritarian, usually patriarchal (controlled by the father) rather than democratic.

▶ They are strong and supportive during times of crises.

▶ Extended families are generally long lasting.

Characteristics of lone-parent families

▶ Lone-parent families may occur for a number of reasons. Causes include divorce, separation, death, imprisonment, unplanned pregnancy outside marriage and no desire to marry.

▶ More women head single-parent families than men.

▶ Lone-parent families may suffer difficulties such as poverty, isolation, stress, increased workload and childcare problems.

▶ They are often dependent on state benefits.

Characteristics of blended families

▶ Blended families consist of partners with children from previous relationships and often their own children.

▶ Blended families are increasingly more common because of divorce and separation.

▶ They have a large extended family.

▶ Blending families may lead to conflict within the family.

▶ Relationships with the absent biological parent may be difficult in blended families.

▶ There may be extra financial pressure (if two families have to be supported).

Extended family

Historical Development of the Family in Ireland

Early twentieth century

- ▶ During the early twentieth century the extended family was the most common form of family.

- ▶ The majority of people lived in the country (rural) on farms.

- ▶ Many marriages were arranged, and greatly influenced by landownership and dowries.

- ▶ The number of children was usually large as they were considered an economic asset, each of whom would work on the family farm or in the family business.

- ▶ There were segregated conjugal roles, the women caring for the family and the home, as well as doing some light farm work. The men worked solely on the farm or in the business.

- ▶ The family was authoritarian (discipline was very important) and usually patriarchal (ruled by the father). Warmth and closeness did not feature highly.

- ▶ Inheritance was generally along the male line, i.e. from father to son (patrilineal) and usually on death.

- ▶ Child mortality was high due to poor nutrition and sanitation, and a lack of medical knowledge.

Large families were common in the early twentieth century

Late twentieth century

- ▶ During the late twentieth century there was a move from rural to urban life, which also meant a move away from farming.

- ▶ The nuclear family became more common.

- ▶ The number of children decreased.

- ▶ Male and female children were treated equally.

- ▶ Generally, people chose their own partners and the family focused more on the nurturing of children and the emotional fulfilment of their partners.

- ▶ In earlier times – up to 1970 – men were the breadwinners and women the homemakers.

- ▶ Education became more important with fewer children leaving school at primary level.

- ▶ The family became more democratic with everyone involved in decision-making.

- ▶ Improved standards of living, health services and education reduced infant mortality and extended the life span of the family.

- ▶ A decrease in the influence of religion occurred during the late twentieth century.

- ▶ The status of older family members lessened.

Contemporary Irish family

▶ In the contemporary Irish family there is an increase in the number of separations and divorces, and the introduction of new family structures, i.e. single-parent families and blended families.

▶ The availability of contraception allows people to plan their families. This has lead to a decrease in the number of children.

▶ Some families are dual income, i.e. both partners working outside the home thereby involving others, such as childminders, in child-rearing.

▶ Some men are now the homemakers while many women are the breadwinners.

▶ The number of inter-racial partnerships has increased because of the rise in the number of immigrants.

▶ There have been fewer marriages as cohabiting has increased. This reflects a decrease in the influence of religion.

▶ The state is now more involved in financial, educational and nurturing functions of the family (See Page 290).

▶ There has been an increase in social problems affecting the family, e.g. alcohol and drug abuse.

Changes Affecting Modern Family Structure

Social changes

▶ Due to the increase in marital break-up, divorce, and children born outside marriages, there are now more one-parent families and blended families than in past generations.

▶ It is now more common to have fewer children in families. This social change is attributed to:
  – the high costs involved in child-rearing
  – the increased stresses in child-rearing
  – the desire of parents to follow careers leaving less time for family life
  – the availability of contraception – allowing people to plan the number and the spacing of children.

▶ As more mothers now work outside the home, the tradition of the father as breadwinner and mother as homemaker has changed. Fathers are now far more involved in child-rearing and homemaking and women may be the sole earner in families. This has led to more equality of roles within the family.

▶ Education is far more highly regarded today than in the past. Then, usually only male children availed of third-level education and often only those from the more wealthy families. Today, however, only a small minority of students leave school before finishing second level and many avail of third-level education.

▶ Modern society has brought with it many social problems such as violence, drug and alcohol abuse, all of which directly or indirectly affect the modern family.

Economic changes

- Increased incomes in recent times have improved the standard of living and the quality of life for many families.

- The economic boom of the late 20th century greatly reduced unemployment. Both parents of many families worked outside the home. However the economic downturn of recent years has lead to a rapid increase in unemployment and many families are affected by job losses.

- Easier access to borrowed money during the economic boom means that many families are now experiencing financial difficulties in an effort to repay loans.

- The family is no longer the 'unit of production' of the traditional extended family. The smaller, nuclear family is an independent economic unit that is mobile and may move locality or emigrate to find employment.

- Couples are choosing to have smaller families due to the cost of childcare.

- Property prices had increased dramatically. This made it extremely difficlut for people to buy homes, often necessitating large mortgages which have to be repaid over many years.

Technological changes

- The development of time and energy-saving equipment such as dishwashers and food processors has made housework faster and easier.

- Nowadays, farming is more mechanised and is less labour intensive, offering employment to fewer people.

- Technology has greatly improved worldwide communications. Internet, telephone and fax allow people to make contact more easily and cheaply than ever before.

- Entertainment technology in the home has changed pastimes from the people-based pastimes of old, e.g. card games, to the more modern ones such as DVDs and computer games.

- Security technology is a feature of modern day life. Alarm systems, security lighting and security gates are becoming more commonplace.

- Rapid technological development has resulted in increased employment in this area. Third-level colleges offer a variety of technology courses.

- Technology has brought with it the ability to mass-produce, which reduced the cost of many products, making them more readily available.

Family Functions (3.1.4)

Family functions may be classified as:

1. Physical function ⎫
2. Emotional function ⎬ (nurturing function)
3. Social function ⎭
4. Economic function
5. Educational/intellectual function

Physical function

Description	State support or intervention
• The family <u>protects the vulnerable</u>, which includes the <u>young</u>, the <u>old</u> and the <u>disabled</u>. • The family <u>provides for the basic physical needs</u> of its members. Such needs include <u>food, warmth, shelter and clothing</u>. • The family unit serves to <u>regulate sexual behaviour</u> and it plays an essential role in <u>procreation</u> (reproduction), ensuring the <u>survival of the human race</u>.	• The state supports the family in its physical function by <u>allowances</u> such as <u>child benefit</u>, and by providing <u>support services</u> such as Community Mothers Programmes and <u>Family Support Projects</u>. • If parents are <u>unable to provide for children's physical needs</u>, the children may be <u>removed from the home either temporarily or permanently and placed in foster care</u>.

Emotional function

Description	State support or intervention
• The family should nurture children, <u>providing a safe and secure place to discuss feelings and express emotions</u>. A <u>loving, caring home will help children to develop self-esteem</u>, which in turn will enable them to <u>become well-adjusted personalities</u> capable of forming healthy relationships <u>outside the home environment</u>. • <u>Parents</u> should also support each other emotionally, providing <u>positive role models</u> for <u>children in future relationships</u>.	• State-funded or state-subscribed <u>parenting courses</u> offer <u>parents guidance</u> and support in all aspects of <u>child-rearing</u> including dealing effectively with <u>childhood feelings</u> and <u>emotions</u> and <u>developing high self-esteem in children</u>.

Caring for an elderly person

Social function		
Description	**State support or intervention**	
• Children learn much through observation and imitation. They absorb mores and norms in the home and learn to conform in a way that is acceptable in society. This process is referred to as socialisation and is a long-term process that begins in the family. • Children need consistent discipline, which will help them to develop a set of values and behaviour patterns which will enable them to mix comfortably in wider society.	• Pre-schools and later primary and post-primary schools continue the process of socialisation. • Where the family unit fails in the social function, the state has to deal with non-conforming individuals through the judicial system. *court system*	

Economic function		
Description	**State support or intervention**	
• In more primitive societies, large families co-operate as an economic unit, each member contributing to the group. In modern society, usually one or both parents have opportunities to work and children must be economically supported until the age of 18 (23 years old if in full-time education). • Working family members pay taxes and spend money on goods and services, thereby contributing to the country's economy.	• The state social welfare system supports some families through payments such as unemployment benefit, disability allowance and carers' allowance. Old age pensions and child benefit also supplement the family income. *(SFI) income supplementary family* • Many state-supported services, such as medical card schemes and homes for the elderly, also help to ease the economic burden on the family.	

Educational/intellectual function

Description	State support or intervention
• The family is seen as the primary educator. It passes on valued beliefs and customs to its children. Much learning and intellectual development takes place in early life. • Praise, encouragement and a stimulating environment are important aids to this period of informal education. • The home plays a vital role in supporting the work of the school and in helping children to develop to their full potential.	• When formal schooling begins at around five years of age, the state takes over much of this function. • The state also supports families with children who are experiencing learning difficulties, for instance psychological assessments to identify learning problems and resource teaching to assist the child. SNA - special need assistant

Children with special needs require extra help

CONTENTS INCLUDE:

▶ **Definition of marriage**
▶ **Legal obligations, rights and responsibilities within marriage**
▶ **Preparation for marriage: the facilities and services available**
▶ **Marital stability and marital breakdown**

Marriage

Definition

Marriage can be defined as a socially and legally acceptable union between a man and a woman who will live together and remain faithful to each other to the exclusion of all others.

> In Article 41 of the Irish Constitution: In the state 'pledges itself to guard with special care the institution of marriage on which the family is founded and to protect it against attack'.

Some form of marriage exists in most societies throughout the world. However, there are many cultural variations.

Cultural Variations

1. Minimum age

The minimum legal age for marriage in Ireland is 18 years. A minimum age for marriage is not a restriction in all societies.

A valid marriage creates a new relationship between two individuals and changes their legal status.

2. Choice of partners

All societies place some form of restriction on the choice of marriage partner. These restrictions may be based on religion, class or close family relationship between the couple. In Ireland certain relationships prohibit marriage. Prohibitions are based on either consanguinity (blood relationship) or affinity (relationship by marriage).

Examples of prohibited relationships	
A man may not marry his:	**A woman may not marry her:**
1. Father's sister *aunty*	1. Husband's grandfather
2. Wife's mother *mother in law*	2. Mother's sister's husband
3. Son's daughter	3. Husband's mother's brother
4. Sister's daughter	4. Brother's daughter's husband
5. Sister's son's wife	5. Husband's brother's son

3. Number of spouses

Monogamy

A monogamous marriage consists of one male and one female. This is the most common form of marriage. In Ireland, all marriages are based on monogamy. Serial monogamy is a term used to describe a situation where an individual marries and divorces a number of times. Bigamy is a crime committed when an individual marries again, while still legally married to someone else.

Polygamy

Polygamy is a form of marriage where more than one partner is allowed. A marriage between one male and several females is known as ***polygyny***. Polygyny is commonly practiced in many parts of Africa and in most Islamic societies. Where polygyny is prevalent control within the family unit is generally patriarchal with the male making all major household decisions. Polygyny is seen as a symbol of a man's wealth and success, enabling him to support several wives and children.

A marriage between one female and several men is known as ***polyandry***. The practice of polyandry is rare and is limited to Tibet – where one woman could marry several brothers – and small areas within India. Polyandry occurs in very poor cultures where a number of working males are considered necessary to support one wife and children.

Polygyny

Laws Relating to Marriage

For an Irish marriage to be valid and legal, the following conditions must apply.

1. The marriage must be entered into voluntarily by both partners.
2. The partners must be over 18 years of age.
3. While in some societies, such as Denmark, marriage between same sex partners is legal, in Ireland partners must be of the opposite sex.
4. Neither spouse may be in an existing marriage.
5. The couple are restricted by consanguinity (blood relationships) and affinity (relationships by marriage).
6. Three months notice is required. This notice must be given to the Registrar of the district in which the marriage will take place. If the wedding is to be a religious ceremony, the church also requires three months notice.
7. All marriage ceremonies must take place in a registered building or other approved location – religious ceremonies take place in a church; civil ceremonies may take place in a registry office.
8. All marriages must be registered after the ceremony.

Rights and Responsibilities Within the Marriage Relationship

1. The couple are obliged to cohabit and to share each other's company.

2. The marriage must be consummated and sexual intercourse should be a feature of the marriage.

3. A dependent spouse has a legal right to maintenance.

4. Spouses are the joint guardians of children born within the marriage. They are obligated to provide for their children's needs and to raise them with due regard for their moral, physical, social, emotional and intellectual welfare.

5. Spouses have a legal right to inherit from each other.

Civil marriage at a registry office

Preparation for Marriage

Considering that marriage is possibly the biggest commitment that most people make in a lifetime, there is very little formal preparation. Some preparation takes place on an informal level: at home, at school and through pre-marriage courses.

At home

A child reared in a home where there is a good family atmosphere and a stable loving relationship between the parents will grow up with a positive image of marriage. A child who grows up in an atmosphere of tension and physical or emotional violence is more likely to develop a negative image of married life. It is in the home too that one first forms role expectations. In some homes, there are distinct male and female roles, while in other homes roles are less defined.

At school

Social Personal and Health Education (SPHE) allows students to study topics such as relationship-building skills and self-esteem, and to research and discuss social factors such as alcohol and drug abuse, which often lead to problems in Irish marriages.

The study of relationships is also included in *Home Economics* and *Religious* courses.

Pre-marriage courses

While many couples go through long relationships and many even cohabit before marriage, they may never have discussed important marital issues in any depth. A pre-marriage course is designed to force couples to consider these issues and to discuss problems that may have already arisen during their relationship. Most pre-marriage courses are run by:

1. 'Accord' Catholic Marriage Counselling Service, and

2. Marriage and Relationships Counselling Services.

Topics covered at pre-marriage courses

Areas discussed at pre-marriage courses include relationships, sexuality, family planning, parenthood, role expectations, finance, and potential problem issues such as alcohol. The courses are run by marriage counsellors. Professionals such as doctors and lawyers are also involved, offering advice and guidance in their specific areas of expertise.

5C's: CHURCH, CHILDREN, Commitment, communication & conflic resolution

Advantages of pre-marriage courses

1. The couple are encouraged to communicate and to share their feelings on all aspects of marriage, such as family planning, children and role expectations.

2. Couples are forced to face reality on issues such as finance and housing.

3. The couple become more aware of potential problem areas that they may have been ignoring, e.g. a drink problem or violence.

4. The couple discuss each other's personal qualities with emphasis on the positive areas, e.g. kindness, trustworthiness, honesty and thoughtfulness. Negative qualities such as poor communication, selfishness and jealousy, which may have a destabilising effect on a marriage, are also discussed.

Marital Stability

Marital stability relates to the strength of the relationship between the couple. It is influenced by many factors.

1. Expectations of marriage	Many people enter marriage with very unrealistic expectations and when the marriage fails to live up to the ideal they become disillusioned with the whole concept of marriage. *infedelity-lack of trust roles-women working*
2. Family background	One's family background influences role expectations within a marriage and will often determine whether one has a positive or negative view of marriage. *social cultural religious*
3. Age	Research has shown that couples who marry while one/both partners are still in their teens are more likely to separate. The individuals involved need to be mature enough to withstand the responsibilities of marriage.
4. Similar culture and interests	A marriage between partners who come from a similar socio-economic background and who share the same race and religion has a greater chance of survival since there is less likelihood of disharmony occurring.
5. Social factors	A growing number of social factors influence the stability of modern marriage. Financial commitments may mean that many couples have to work long hours, endure exhausting commutes to and from work, and find themselves spending less time together as a couple. Alcoholism, drug abuse, gambling, child abuse and marital violence are all social problems which put a tremendous strain on marriage.

Marriage counselling

The purpose of marriage counselling is to assist couples to resolve marriage problems before they become grounds for separation or divorce. Marriage counselling is a confidential service provided by:

1. Accord
2. Marriage and Relationships Counselling Services.

Qualified counsellors work with the couple and may refer them to experts on issues such as sex, law or alcohol. Marriage counselling may not be successful if:

- Only one partner is willing to seek counselling and attend sessions.
- The couple's problems are so far advanced that their relationship is irretrievable.
- The problem is so serious that the best solution is separation, such as in the case of child abuse.

Family mediation

- Family mediation is a means by which a separating couple can negotiate a separation agreement.
- During mediation, the couple meet in the presence of an impartial mediator.
- They discuss issues and make decisions relating to all aspects of their future as separated partners, such as children and property.
- Mediation is provided on a free and confidential basis by the Family Mediation Service under the Department of Social and Family Affairs.

The advantages of mediation

- Mediation helps to reduce conflict between partners.
- It enables the couple to make their own decisions – often easier to adhere to than decisions which are forced upon them.
- It helps the people involved to come to terms with the reality of separation.
- It encourages a spirit of co-operation and responsibility between partners, particularly in relation to children.

Deed of separation

An agreement made through mediation may then be formally drawn up in a *Deed of Separation* by a solicitor.

Legal separation

Couples may separate legally by:

Entering into a separation agreement/Deed of Separation

1. Separation Agreement/Deed of Separation

The Deed of Separation is a legally binding contract between spouses, which sets out their future rights and responsibilities. The Deed includes:

- An agreement to live apart and not to interfere with each other.
- Arrangements regarding the responsibility for the care of dependent children.
- Amount of maintenance to be paid for the support of a dependent spouse and children.
- Arrangements regarding ownership and occupation of the family home such as mortgage repayments.
- Arrangements regarding rights of spouses to inherit from each other.

Legal Aid Board

Getting a decree of judicial separation in court

2. Judicial separation/decree of separation
- If a couple cannot reach a separation agreement, or if only one spouse wishes to separate, an application can be made to the court for a decree of judicial separation under the Judicial Separation Act 1989.
- A solicitor advising an individual on judicial separation is required to advise him/her about counselling and mediation services available.
- Grounds for a judicial separation include:
    - Adultery.
    - Desertion. (leaving)
    - Unreasonable behaviour.
    - No normal marriage relationship for a least one year.
    - Spouses living apart for one year before application (where both consent to separation), or living apart for three years where one spouse does not give consent.
- In making a decree of separation the court may also make additional orders in relation to matters such a child custody and access, maintenance, barring and safety orders and property.

Separation does not give spouses a legal right to remarry.

Nullity of Marriage
Civil/legal annulment
A decree of nullity of marriage means that in the eyes of the state the marriage never existed. Grounds for nullity include:

▶ ***Lack of capacity:*** Parties were not capable of marrying each other. For example, parties were of the same sex, one party was already married to someone else, one or both parties were under 18 years of age.

▶ ***Non-observance of certain formalities:*** For example not giving three months notice to the Registrar of Marriages.

▶ ***Absence of consent:*** One of the parties did not give full, free and informed consent due to insanity, drunkenness or being under duress. For example, parental pressure at the time of the ceremony, or perhaps one party did not intend to fulfil a fundamental part of the marriage contract, e.g. to have sexual relations with the other.

▶ ***Impotence:*** One of the parties for physical or psychological reasons is unable to engage in complete sexual relations with the other. not consumated

▶ ***Inability to form and sustain a normal marital relationship:*** This may be due to extreme immaturity or to homosexuality. Manic depression or extreme schizophrenia may also be grounds for civil annulment.

Effects of a decree of nullity

When the court grants a decree of nullity:

► Partners are <u>free to marry.</u>

► <u>Neither party can claim for maintenance or</u> has a legal <u>right</u> to share <u>in the estate</u> of the other party.

► The decree <u>does not affect the rights of dependent children.</u>

Church Annulments

Church annulments <u>may be granted on similar grounds to those for civil annulments.</u> A church annulment has <u>no</u> <u>legal standing.</u> When a person <u>remarries within a church,</u> the <u>state will not recognise the marriage</u> unless a <u>decree</u> <u>of divorce</u> or a <u>decree of nullity was</u> granted in respect of the first marriage.

Marriage never existed in the eyes of the church;
needed if a person wishes to remarry in church;
Divorce *very long process.*

► Under the <u>Family Law (Divorce) Act 1996,</u> a <u>spouse</u> who wishes to end an existing legal marriage <u>can make</u> an application to court for a decree of divorce.

► An advising <u>solicitor</u> must inform the applicant about available <u>counselling</u> and <u>mediation services.</u>

Grounds for divorce

A court will grant a divorce if:

Family Support Agency

► Spouses have lived apart for at least <u>four of the previous five years.</u>

► There is <u>no prospect of reconciliation.</u>

► It is satisfied that <u>adequate provision</u> has been <u>made for spouses</u> and <u>dependent children.</u>

The <u>court</u> may make <u>additional orders</u> to cover such issues as <u>child custody</u> and <u>access,</u> property, <u>maintenance</u> and if <u>deemed necessary,</u> <u>safety</u> or <u>barring orders</u> (See Page 311). A decree of divorce gives spouses <u>a right to remarry.</u>

Marital Breakdown

Marital breakdown is on the <u>increase in Irish society</u> due to a number of factors including:

1. <u>Separation</u> and <u>divorce</u> are more <u>socially acceptable</u> than in the past.

2. Acquiring a divorce has become <u>easier</u> and <u>less expensive.</u>

3. <u>Women</u> are more likely to be <u>financially independent.</u>

4. <u>State assistance</u> is available for <u>lone parents.</u>

5. There is a marked <u>increase</u> in the <u>social problems,</u> which <u>place a strain</u> on modern <u>marriage,</u> such as <u>alcohol</u> and <u>drug abuse.</u>

The effects of marital breakdown on spouses

1. Spouses may experience a <u>sense of failure, rejection</u> or <u>guilt.</u>

2. Spouses may become <u>lonely, isolated</u> and depressed and <u>may resort to drink or drugs.</u>

3. Spouses may <u>suffer financial loss</u> and a <u>fall in living standards.</u>

4. One spouse (usually the <u>mother</u>) gains <u>custody of the children</u> and <u>assumes full responsibility</u> for their <u>upbringing,</u> leaving the <u>other</u> feeling lonely and rejected.

5. <u>Future</u> relationships are difficult because often they do not have <u>legal recognition.</u>

The effects of marital breakdown on children

1. Children may experience <u>emotional</u> or <u>physical violence</u> during the breakdown period.
2. Children of broken marriages may <u>feel responsible</u> for the <u>break-up</u> and <u>feel a sense of guilt</u> and <u>insecurity.</u>
3. Children can be <u>used for emotional blackmail</u> during the breakdown of a marriage, when their <u>loyalties are torn.</u>
4. The loss of a parent results in the <u>lack of a mother</u> or <u>father figure.</u>
5. If the <u>break-up</u> is traumatic, children may be left with <u>negative views of marriage</u> and <u>parenthood</u> and tend to have <u>difficulties themselves in forming stable relationships in later life.</u>
6. A <u>drop in living standards</u> or a <u>change of home</u> can be emotionally <u>upsetting</u> and <u>stressful for children.</u>

The effects of marital breakdown on society

1. Marital breakdown affects society because it <u>undermines the family,</u> which is the basic unit of Irish society, leading to more <u>one-parent families,</u> <u>blended families</u> and <u>serial monogamy.</u>
2. In many cases of break-up (e.g. desertion), the <u>family is dependent on the state for financial support.</u>
3. Marital breakdown results in a <u>greater need for accommodation.</u>
4. <u>Disturbed children</u> of a <u>broken marriage</u> may resort to <u>aggression,</u> <u>vandalism</u> and <u>violence.</u>
5. <u>Future relationships involving children</u> can be <u>legally complicated.</u>

Marriage and marital breakdown in Ireland	
Year	Marital breakdown as a percentage of first marriages
1986	3.1
1996	7.0
2002	10.9
2006	13.0

Recent trends:
marriage rates Rave
declined

couples are choosing
to cohabit

Separation, divorce
& one-parent family
→ increase

CONTENTS INCLUDE:

- ▶ **Roles and responsibilities of family members**
- ▶ **Gender issues in relation to family roles**
- ▶ **Social and economic factors that have affected the changing roles of family members**
- ▶ **Family law**

The Family as a Caring Unit

The family is a caring unit within society. One of the functions of the family is its protective function where the family cares for the more vulnerable members such as children and the elderly. Partners and children within a family also care for each other.

Roles and Responsibilities of Family Members Through the Life-cycle

Role has already been defined as 'the pattern of behaviour considered appropriate for an individual'. Roles of family members include mother, father, son, daughter, grandparent, grandchild, sibling and partner roles. Within the family, people play different roles towards different individuals, e.g. mother to children, partner to spouse. The role a person plays brings its own responsibilities.

In life, people play many other roles. For example, a woman may be a spouse, a mother, a daughter, a sister, an aunt, a professional, a colleague, a union member, a member of a club and may have many more roles.

Role conflict

Role conflict may arise because of the many roles a person plays. Role conflict occurs when the expectations of a person in one role clash with what is expected in another role. For example, a parent's role when a child is ill versus their role as a worker outside the home. Role conflict can be a major cause of stress in everyday life.

Role overload occurs when one attempts to play many roles at the same time.

Children's Roles in the Family

A child's role includes being a son or daughter, possibly a brother or sister and a grandchild. The responsibilities of children are influenced by their age but include:

- ▶ Showing respect to parents/adults.
- ▶ Learning to behave in a socially acceptable manner.
- ▶ Acquiring knowledge informally and formally.
- ▶ Achieving gradual independence.

Older Children – Adolescents

- ▶ Usually accept extra responsibilities, such as babysitting younger siblings or helping them with homework.
- ▶ They generally become more involved in decision-making and the running of the home.
- ▶ Are expected to attend school and do their best and act as role models for younger siblings.

Parents' Roles

In general responsibility for fulfilling the functions of family lies with the parents. Their roles and responsibilities are therefore extensive. They include:

- ▶ Reproduction.
- ▶ Nurturing – caring for young children.
- ▶ Socialisation – preparing children so that they will be accepted into society.
- ▶ Providing financially for all family members so that their needs are met.
- ▶ Parents are the primary educators of their children.
- ▶ Parents also have a role to play in caring for each other.
- ▶ Sometimes parents roles extend to caring for their own elderly parents.

Grandparents' Roles

As people tend to live longer nowadays and are generally in good health, grandparents play a more prominent role in family life.

- ▶ Grandparents are usually retired and so have more time to spend with their children and grandchildren.
- ▶ The stresses and strains involved in child-rearing are now with the parents, so the relationship between grandparents and grand-children is generally more relaxed and easygoing with fewer rules and regulations.

Grandparents can help with childcare

- ▶ Grandparents can play a valuable role in childcare.
- ▶ Because of the high cost of housing many grandparents help their children financially with deposits for houses.
- ▶ Grandparents often indirectly teach young people to have respect for older people.
- ▶ Grandparents can be a great source of emotional support for their children and grandchildren.

Gender Issues in Relation to Family Roles

Gender issues do not feature as strongly in the modern family as they did in the traditional family of the past.

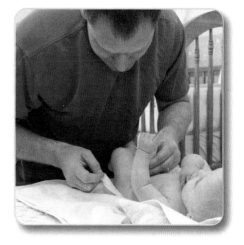

▶ There is now <u>increased equality</u> between men and women in the home.

▶ Nowadays, <u>men</u> are involved in <u>childminding</u> and <u>running the home</u>.

▶ Earning an income is no longer a role confined to males. Many <u>women now work outside the home</u> and in some cases are the sole breadwinners.

▶ Because of the <u>increased</u> number of <u>one-parent families</u>, <u>male and female roles have become less defined.</u>

▶ <u>Education</u> is now considered <u>equally important</u> for both <u>male and female children.</u>

▶ <u>Gender issues</u> are probably most obvious in <u>children</u> where certain colours and <u>toys</u> are regarded as <u>feminine</u> or <u>masculine.</u> Allocating household tasks to children is often <u>gender based</u>, for example, girls set the table for meals whereas boys wash the car. As children progress into adolescence this <u>segregation becomes</u> less obvious.

Social factors affecting the changing roles of family members

▶ In the <u>past</u> many <u>women</u> were full time housewives <u>financially dependent on their husbands.</u> *now more women are in the workplace*

▶ Because of the <u>move from the extended to the nuclear family</u>, men are now more active in <u>child-rearing and home management.</u>

▶ <u>Education</u> is now seen as more <u>important for both males and females</u>. This has resulted in many women having well-paid jobs whereby they may be the <u>sole breadwinner</u> and the male may be the 'house husband'.

▶ With <u>improved healthcare</u> and <u>knowledge of nutrition lifespan has extended</u>. This means that grandparents have a greater involvement in family life.

▶ The <u>number of children in families has decreased</u> and the family has become <u>more child-centred.</u> *more time to spend with family → shorter working week*

• relaxation of roles less clearly defined
• legislation on equal pay & greater opportunities
• acceptance of divorce & separation / single parent & blended families
• reduction on influence of religion

Families have become
more child-centred *2 parents
working - higher standard
of living*

*because women are
earning are financially
independent - increase
separation / divorce*

Elderly people enjoy good health for longer

Economic factors affecting the changing roles of family members

► In many families both parents work outside the home. This generally changes the role of parents within the home as both are involved in childcare and home management.

► When both parents work outside the home it is often necessary to employ a childminder, which can be an expensive monthly outlay.

► In many cases, high living costs necessitate both partners working outside the home.

► Well-educated women have the ability to acquire high-paying employment. Therefore, sometimes it is the men who play the major role in child-minding and home management.

► The state has increased welfare entitlements for the elderly, e.g. increased old age pensions and free travel. Many elderly people are financially independent and physically healthier for longer.

► As many young people now attend third-level colleges, some well into their 20s, they continue to be financially dependent on their parents.

The Rights of the Child Within the Family *NB*

Children under 18 years of age have the following rights:

► The right to life.

► The right to have a name and be granted a nationality.

► The right to live with parents unless considered to be against the best interests of the child.

► The right to basic physical needs: food, clothing and shelter, considered to be an adequate standard of living.

► The right to develop physically, mentally, socially, morally and spiritually.

► The right to access medical care so as to ensure the highest attainable standard of health.

► The right to protection from all forms of abuse and neglect.

► The right to education, leisure, recreation and cultural activities.

► Children with a disability have the right to special care, education and training.

Child-Parent Relationships

▶ The first relationship in a child's life is with parents. Children are completely <u>dependent</u> on their <u>parents</u> for all of their <u>physical</u> and <u>psychological needs.</u>

▶ As toddlers, children need <u>mental</u> and <u>physical stimulation</u>. Parents provide books and toys. They read to and play with their children and the relationship gradually becomes more two-way.

▶ <u>Parents and older children</u> act as <u>role models</u> for young children in the <u>process of socialisation.</u> Through <u>encouragement</u> and <u>consistent discipline</u> children <u>learn to behave in an acceptable way.</u>

▶ <u>Informal education begins in the home.</u> Many children have a basic understanding of numbers, letters and colours before formal education begins. <u>Children need praise and encouragement as they learn so that they will develop good self esteem.</u>

▶ A <u>close and open child-parent relationship</u> provides a <u>safe environment</u> for children to <u>express their feelings</u> and get involved in <u>discussions</u> on a range of topics.

▶ During <u>adolescence</u> the need for <u>privacy</u> and <u>space</u> is usually respected by parents. <u>Adolescents</u> are usually given <u>more freedom</u> and <u>responsibility,</u> helping to prepare them for future life.

Physical needs
- Food
- Clothing
- Shelter

Psychological needs
- Love
- Protection
- Security
- Understanding
- Encouragement
- Praise

Playing with your child helps it to develop skills

Adolescent–Adult Conflict

Adolescence is a time of rapid development. It is the <u>stage when a young person is no longer regarded as a child and yet not old enough to be considered an adult.</u> This transition period may lead to role conflict for the adolescent.

Causes of conflict

▶ Conflict may arise between the adolescent and the parents as many young people <u>question rules and authority that were accepted up to this stage.</u>

▶ <u>Peer groups</u> become very <u>important</u> during adolescence, <u>reducing the influence of parents.</u>

▶ The <u>need for more freedom,</u> which comes with adolescence, is often a <u>source of conflict with parents.</u>

▶ <u>Boy/girl relationships</u> during adolescence may be a cause of conflict as <u>study</u> and <u>school work may begin to suffer as a result.</u>

▶ Many adolescents take <u>part-time jobs</u> so that they have their <u>own money. Parents have difficulty controlling what the money is spent on.</u> Study and <u>school work may suffer</u> because of the job.

▶ Decisions about <u>future careers</u> can often be a cause of <u>conflict,</u> e.g. when <u>idealistic adolescents' aspirations differ from those of more practical parents.</u>

Dealing with conflict

▶ Rules and methods of disciplining must change as children become teenagers but it is necessary that both teenagers and parents have a clear understanding of what is expected and how any deviation from these new rules will be treated.

▶ The ability to empathise often helps to reduce conflict as each party understands how the other one feels.

▶ Compromise is often the best way to solve conflicts, but it involves give and take on both sides.

▶ Avoid confrontation by taking time out and giving people time to calm down and become less emotional or angry.

▶ Communication between adolescents and parents is most important in dealing with any conflicts that may arise. It is necessary that both parties talk and listen to each other, so that each is aware of the other's position.

Importance of Good Communication within the Family

▶ Communication involves listening and talking, and non-verbal forms of communication such as expressions and gestures.

▶ Good communication is necessary so that family members are aware of how others feel about certain issues.

▶ Conflicts within families cannot be resolved without communication as there is no possibility for compromise.

▶ Effective communication allows people to express their feelings and can help to prevent stress. Discussions involving communication give people a broader view of issues.

▶ Praise and encouragement, which are very important in the development of positive self-esteem, involve communication.

Role of older people within the family (See Page 303).

Importance of Independence for Elderly within the Family

► As life-expectancy increases it is important that older people maintain independence as much as possible. Their roles change when they retire from work. They are often living as a couple or alone. Their children are reared and educated and now financially independent.

► Sometimes elderly people's health begins to deteriorate and they are less physically able. As a result, the elderly sometimes have low feelings of self-worth and many feel they are a burden on others.

► Social welfare payments allow retired people to continue to be financially independent within the family. Medical cards for some over 70 years olds has also eased a possible financial burden.

► Free travel for those over 66 years of age allows people to take long journeys, when they might no longer feel able to drive a long distance.

► Community care focuses on keeping the elderly in their homes rather than taking them into hospitals.

► Good family and neighbours can help greatly by calling regularly and being available for the elderly should they be required.

► Different housing options can help the elderly to maintain independence, e.g. if they are no longer able to live alone a sheltered housing scheme is a possible option, where they will still have a certain level of independence.

Sheltered housing

Generation Conflict

Just as conflict may arise between parents and adolescents so too can it arise between parents and their parents. Generational conflict occurs when the views and attitudes of one generation clash with those of another generation.

Causes of conflict

► Elderly people may still regard their children as 'children' often telling them what to do and how to do it. This can cause inter-generational conflict.

► Elderly people may interfere in the upbringing of their grandchildren.

► Behaviour that is accepted as the 'norm' changes from generation to generation.

► Sometimes younger generations lose respect for the elderly as they physically and mentally slow down.

► People are often torn between their responsibilities to their partner and children and trying to care for elderly parents.

► Lack of privacy may cause conflict when three generations live together.

Dealing with this conflict

▶ Communication among all generations will help in dealing with conflict. If everyone knows what is expected of them and where boundaries lie there is less chance of conflict.

▶ Understanding for others, consideration and patience will all help to prevent conflict.

▶ Many elderly people keep themselves physically fit and their minds active. They keep up with the changes in today's world, which keep them in touch with younger generations.

Many older people enjoy using the internet

▶ Younger generations should appreciate the experiences of older generations.

▶ If elderly people live independently there is far less chance of conflict arising, and less likelihood of interference or lack of privacy.

The Family Caring for those with Special Needs

Special needs are the extra physical, intellectual (mental) and emotional needs of family members with disabilities.

▶ Those with special physical needs include: the deaf, the blind, those with speech disorders and wheelchair users.

▶ Mental disabilities include a wide range of mental illnesses and disorders, e.g. addiction, depression, Down's syndrome and schizophrenia.

▶ Emotionally disturbed people may have feelings of low self-esteem and have an inability to express emotions. They may suffer from conditions such as autism.

Problems experienced by family members with special needs include:		
Problems	**Family response to special needs**	
• Lack of independence. • Lack of mobility and difficulties accessing public transport systems and facilities. • Fewer educational and employment opportunities. • Lack of state financial support. • Medical and educational facilities are often inadequate.	• Being there to provide emotional support and assistance to those with special needs. • Modification of the family home to assist those with physical disabilities. • Encouraging independence and helping them to integrate into society. • Applying for all social assistance and grants available.	

A guide dog allows a blind person independence

Statutory services available

▶ **Special schools** for those with special needs, e.g. schools for the deaf.

▶ **National Disability Authority (NDA):**
  – advises the government on policy and practices,
  – promotes and helps secure the rights of people with disabilities.

▶ **The Equality Authority** – works to prevent discrimination in employment, training and advertising.

▶ **Citizen Information Board** – a national support agency providing information on social services. (See Page 276)

▶ **Psychiatric hospitals** and HSE provide assistance for those with mental disabilities.

The kitchen has been adapted for a wheelchair user

Voluntary services available

▶ **Rehab:**
  – offers training and education for people with physical and intellectual disabilities
  – provides health and social care services
  – lobbies the government to bring about positive changes in the lives of people with disabilities.

> Accessibility and facilities in public buildings, disability allowances, free travel, sheltered workshops, reserved places in employment and community care services, all assist those with special needs.

▶ **Irish Wheelchair Association** – provides quality services to people with limited mobility.

▶ **DeafHear** – promotes the welfare of deaf people and their families in all aspects of life.

▶ **National council for the Blind in Ireland** – works to enable people who are blind or vision impaired to have the same opportunities, rights and choices as others to fully participate in society.

▶ **Enable Ireland** works with the disabled to achieve maximum independence, choice and inclusion in their communities.

The Irish Wheelchair Association helps wheelchair users to learn to drive

▶ **AHEAD (Association for Higher Education Access and Disability)** – works to promote full access to and participation in further and higher education for students with disabilities and to enhance their employment prospects on graduation.

Family Law (3.1.7)

A number of laws protect the family unit.

The Family Law (Maintenance of Spouse and Children) Act 1976

▶ Maintenance is financial support paid by a person for the benefit of a dependent spouse and dependent children.

▶ A dependent child is any child under 18 years old, a child under 23 years old who is in full-time education or a child who is dependent due to a disability.

▶ A dependant may apply for maintenance even if living with their spouse.

▶ A parent may apply for <u>maintenance</u> for a <u>dependent child</u> from the other parent regardless of <u>whether or not the parents are married to each other.</u>

▶ Maintenance <u>may be agreed between the parties.</u> If they cannot agree, an application may be made to the <u>District or Circuit Court</u> depending on the amount being sought. A <u>court order</u> will be <u>issued detailing amount and method of payment.</u>

The Family Home Protection Act 1976

The <u>family home</u> – the dwelling where a married couple ordinarily live – <u>may not be sold or mortgaged without the consent of both spouses.</u> This applies regardless of which spouse owns the family home.

Domestic Violence Act 1996

Spouses can <u>apply to the court</u> for a <u>safety, barring</u> or <u>protection order</u> if they or <u>dependent children</u> are under <u>threat of physical, sexual</u> or <u>psychological violence from any family member.</u> Protection available under Domestic Violence legislation includes the following Orders:

▶ A *Safety Order* prohibits a person from using or threatening violence against the person applying for the <u>order</u> and/or dependent children. It may apply for a period of up to <u>five years.</u>

▶ A *Barring Order* <u>obligates the person against whom the order has been made to leave the place</u> where the spouse and dependent children live and <u>not to return</u> until a time specified by the court. It may apply for a period of up to <u>three years.</u>

▶ A *Protection Order* is a <u>temporary</u> safety order which lasts until the full court hearing of the application for a <u>barring or safety order.</u>

Judicial Separation Act 1989

The Judicial Separation Act enables the <u>court to grant</u> a decree of <u>Judicial Separation</u> where a marriage 'has broken down to the extent that the court is <u>satisfied</u> that a normal marital relationship has not existed between the spouses for a period of at least one year immediately preceding the date of the application'.

Family Law (Divorce) Act 1996, (See Page 300).

Child Care Act 1991

▶ The Child Care Act makes <u>provision for the care and protection of children.</u>

▶ <u>Health Boards</u> have the power to <u>intervene</u> in family situations <u>if a child</u> is deemed to be at risk, for instance, <u>if the child has been assaulted, neglected or sexually abused.</u>

▶ The <u>Health Board may apply to the courts</u> for a <u>care order</u> allowing the <u>child to be removed</u> from the family <u>home and placed in care for a long or short term.</u>

▶ Alternatively, the Health Board <u>may apply for a supervision order</u> enabling <u>Health Board</u> officials to visit <u>the child in the home periodically to monitor the child's</u> health and welfare.

Children's Act 1997

The Children's Act enables unmarried fathers to become joint legal guardians of a child (with mother's consent) without having to go to court. An agreement must be signed by both parents in the presence of a Peace Commissioner.

Making a Will

Making a will ensures:

▶ Peace of mind knowing that your wishes will be carried out and major problems which could arise, particularly for a spouse, are avoided.

▶ Your property passes to the people you choose.

▶ You appoint your own executor thereby making the administration of your estate much easier.

▶ The amount dependants have to pay in inheritance tax can be reduced.

In order for a will to be valid:

▶ An individual making a will must be over 18 and of sound mind.

▶ The will itself must be written.

▶ It must be signed and dated in the presence of two witnesses.

▶ A will may be drawn up independently by an individual or a solicitor may be employed to oversee the task.

Procedure for making a will

1. It is probably best to employ a solicitor who will be familiar with legal and taxation issues pertaining to succession and inheritance.
2. Draw up a list of assets such as property, deposit accounts and shares.
3. Details concerning beneficiaries such as names, addresses, dates of birth may need to be supplied.
4. Appoint an executor who will carry out provisions made in the will.
5. Allocate estate/assets, with due regard to limitations imposed by the Succession Act.
6. Provision may be made in a will for funeral and burial arrangements.
7. The will is formally drawn up and signed in the presence of two witnesses.
8. Lodge the will in a safe place such as a bank, ensuring that the executor and some trusted others know where it is kept.
9. The will may need to be reviewed periodically if the life situation changes. For example, a marriage renders an existing will void and a new one must be drawn up to take account of the change in circumstances. (It is recommended that both spouses draw up the will.)

> **Will** – a legal document directing the disposal of ones property (estate) after death.

> **Succession Act of 1965**
> If there is no will and no children each spouse is the sole inheritor of the estate on the death of his/her partner (two-thirds of the estate if there are children).
>
> If there is a will the spouse is legally entitled to half of the estate (if there are no children). If there are children, the spouse is entitled to one-third of the estate.

ELECTIVE ONE
HOME DESIGN AND MANAGEMENT

This elective aims to provide students with an understanding of the design, building and management of the home to meet individual and family needs, with consideration for environmental and social responsibility.

The elective is an extension of the Resource Management and Consumer Studies section of the core. Links may also be made between this elective and the Social Studies section of the core.

CONTENTS INCLUDE:

▶ Historical development of housing styles ▶ Regulation of house-building standards
▶ Factors influencing choice of housing styles ▶ House building and design
▶ An evaluation of housing provision in Ireland

Housing Styles in Ireland (4.1.1)

Early Nineteenth Century

▶ The most common house in rural areas in the early 1800s was the single-storey thatched cottage. It generally consisted of two rooms, a kitchen and a bedroom. The walls were constructed from solid stone, the windows were small and the door – usually a half-door, opened into the kitchen. An open turf fire was used for cooking and to provide heat. The thatch was of reeds, straw or hay and some cottages had a room, or loft, directly under the thatch, which was accessed by a ladder, where children slept.

Thatched cottage

▶ Better-off farmers lived in large two-storey stone houses with slated roofs. Wealthy landowners lived in big estate houses.

▶ In urban areas, Georgian style houses were popular at this time. Some were detached but many were two, three or even four-storey terraced houses. The Georgian house, which is still popular today, is a simple classical design based on the architecture of the Greeks and the Romans. The main features include columns and decorative doorways with a range of fanlights. The houses often had basements. The rooms had high ceilings with deep cornicing (decorative mouldings), architraves around doorways and distinctive fireplaces. Walls were made of stone covered with a layer of lime plaster and roofs were slated.

▶ The suburbs of the larger towns and cities housed the middle classes who lived in small terraced houses. Many shopkeepers lived over their shops and ordinary workers lived in single-storey cottages.

Late Nineteenth Century

▶ Although building slowed during the 1800s there was a move away from the simple classical Georgian style of house to more ornate styles including Gothic and Tudor styles. The Gothic style, although more often seen in cathedrals and churches, did feature in the houses built during this period. The main features of Gothic architecture include pointed windows, arches and doorways and high pitched roofs. Stone continued to be an important building material.

Late nineteenth-century style house

▶ Tudor style houses also included high pitched roofs, plaster panels with timber framing and projecting (bay) windows.

▶ Two-storey houses with slated roofs became more common in rural areas. Improved transportation resulted in the availability of a greater variety of building materials and brick became popular. As many of the wealthier families moved from city centre Georgian terraced houses to newly built houses in the suburbs the Georgian houses were divided and rented to poorer families. These families often lived in overcrowded and unsanitary conditions.

Early Twentieth Century

▶ The early twentieth century saw a move away from the terraced house to the detached or semi-detached house. Council and housing estates were built on the outskirts of towns and cities. These houses were built of brick with plaster walls. As land became more expensive, the houses were usually two-storeys high. A common design was used which was less ornate than the Gothic or Tudor styles of the previous century. Tiles were introduced to replace roof slating.

Early twentieth-century style housing

▶ During this period 70% of the population still lived in rural Ireland. The end of the Second World War (1945), rural electrification (1946) and government housing grants brought changes to housing in rural Ireland. The slate roofed bungalow gradually replaced the thatched cottage of the past.

Late Twentieth Century

Private housing estates using a common design became very popular during the late twentieth century. There was huge variety in design in private houses including classical and modern designs. Building regulations greatly improved housing standards. High-rise apartment blocks were built because of the high cost of land. Local authorities continued to build housing schemes throughout towns and cities. New materials and methods, e.g. PVC, fibreglass and double glazing were commonly used.

Popular Housing Styles in Ireland Today

▶ Many of the housing styles of the last two centuries can still be seen throughout Ireland.

▶ More people are now classified as urban dwellers, living in terraced, semi-detached, detached houses and apartments.

▶ Complexes, which include a variety of town houses and apartments, can be found in many towns and cities throughout Ireland. These complexes are often enclosed behind security gates.

Semi-detached houses

▶ Housing estates continue to be built. Although each housing estate usually consists of one style of house, there are many different styles including single-storey detached, dormer style and two-storey semi-detached.

▶ The old style thatched cottage can be found in tourist areas throughout the country.

▶ Custom-designed houses, where plans are drawn to the customer's specifications, are popular when building on a private site.

▶ A popular method of extending space within houses is to convert attic space and install velux windows. Conservatory extensions can be seen on many houses throughout the country.

▶ Sheltered housing is commonly used for the elderly or disabled.

Factors that Influence Choice of Housing Styles

Social and cultural factors

▶ **The location of the house:** It may be in a rural or an urban area. Proximity to work, schools and amenities such as shops and public transport is important for many.

▶ **The size of the house:** There must be sufficient space for all family members to live in relative comfort.

▶ **Family members with special needs:** Houses with a 'granny flat' may suit some families with elderly members. Wheelchair users require single-storey houses, wide doorways and as few steps as possible.

New housing developments

▶ **Personal choice:** Some people prefer privacy and seclusion and therefore would probably choose a detached house with space around it. Old houses in need of refurbishment appeal to some, whereas others would choose newly built houses.

▶ **Availability:** New trends develop and become fashionable, e.g. complexes of living accommodation.

Economic factors

▶ **Income** determines if one can afford to buy a house. Sometimes renting privately or local authority housing are more appropriate options.

▶ **The cost of sites** adds considerably to house building costs, often making the choice of ready-built houses the only option.

▶ **Extra costs**, e.g. legal fees, stamp duty, repairs, furnishing, decorating and services can all affect choice of housing.

▶ **Household bills**, e.g. heating, lighting, insurance and maintenance influence choice.

▶ **Resale value** is an important consideration in choice of housing. While most properties are a good investment, it may be worth doing some research into the plans for the area.

Environmental factors

▶ **Building regulations:** It is necessary to comply with local regulations, e.g. in terms of the height of the house.

▶ **Climate:** The temperate climate of Ireland produces a variety of conditions including wind, rain, cold and sunshine. Houses must protect from these conditions or avail of their benefits.

▶ **Surrounding area:** The gradient of some sites may be best suited to split-level houses. The aspect of the house is often chosen to benefit from the best view.

▶ **Energy efficiency:** An energy efficient home with good insulation using sustainable materials and making use of alternative energy will have a less detrimental effect on the environment for future generations.

▶ **Local materials:** local stone may be used in the house's facade.

Local stone is used

Housing Requirements

Different people have different housing requirements. For example, housing that would appeal to a family might not be suitable for a single person or an elderly couple.

Families
The ages of family members and the size of the family will determine housing requirements.

1. A well-equipped, ventilated, adequately lit and spacious kitchen is a requirement for most families.

2. Sufficient bedrooms to accommodate all members are necessary including adequate storage for clothing. Teenagers may require study facilities.

3. Extra bathrooms may be required for larger families.

4. A living room used by family members for relaxing, e.g. TV viewing, is a requirement.

5. A large hot-press is particularly important for families with young children, as large amounts of laundry require airing.

6. A safe, enclosed back garden is a requirement for a family with young children.

7. A garage or garden shed may be required for the storage of garden equipment. A garage may be necessary for a family owning a car.

8. Proximity to work, schools, shops, parks and public transport may be important to some families.

Single people
1. The housing requirements of single people vary only slightly from those of families – a smaller space will be required.

2. Small town houses or apartments may be suitable options.

3. House sharing is common among young singles where the rent and all expenses are shared among the occupants.

4. Proximity to work or college is usually important to young single people who may not own cars or wish to travel long distances.

The elderly

The basic housing requirements remain the same for elderly people as for other people. However, there are some alterations to consider due to age and possibly special needs.

1. Because many elderly people are less mobile single-storey compact accommodation is more appropriate. Chairlifts may be fitted on stairways.

2. A downstairs bathroom fitted with handrails, non-slip flooring, raised toilet level and shower seat can assist elderly people.

3. There are many household and kitchen gadgets on the market to help elderly people who may have less dexterity because of arthritis, e.g. tap-turners, pull-plugs and electric can-openers.

4. Because elderly people feel the cold more, an easy, safe and effective method of home heating is very important.

5. To reduce the risk of falls good lighting is essential.

6. Proximity to local shops, libraries and church is often important to elderly people who are on their own and may not drive.

7. A telephone is essential for ease of communication with family and friends.

8. Security is particularly important to elderly people living on their own. Secure windows and door locks are essential. Doors can be fitted with door-chains and a peep-hole for extra security.

9. An alarm communication system can be fitted. This is activated in emergencies giving peace of mind to many elderly people.

10. In some situations, sheltered housing or institutional care may be more appropriate than continuing to live alone.

Specially adapted tap turner

Plug-pull

People with disabilities

Certain adjustments are necessary to the basic housing requirements in order to cater for people with disabilities. The specific requirements will depend on the type of disability, for example, people with mobility problems using a walking aid or wheelchair will require:

Specially adapted knife

- ▶ Ramp access to the house.
- ▶ Wider doorways for ease of entry.
- ▶ Kitchen worktops at a lower more accessible level.
- ▶ Light switches, sockets and door handles positioned appropriately.
- ▶ Raised toilet level with rails beside the toilet, bath or shower.
- ▶ Alarm bells are important for the visually impaired.
- ▶ People with hearing disability require flashing lights to alert them to doorbells.
- ▶ Alarm communication systems are helpful in case of emergencies.

The homeless

The local authorities liaise with voluntary organisations in an effort to provide ongoing accommodation for the homeless. The requirements of homeless people are the basic requirements of all people.

▶ They require shelter – in the form of hostel accommodation, emergency bed and breakfast, rent assisted private accommodation or local authority housing.

▶ This shelter should be regular and not on a queuing-nightly system.

▶ Privacy is an important requirement for the homeless to allow them to regain some dignity.

▶ A safe place to store their possessions is often a priority.

▶ Communal facilities, e.g. kitchen, bathroom and day-room are features of many hostels which may reduce the feelings of isolation.

▶ In relation to Travellers, serviced halting sites for mobile homes and caravans are a necessity.

Housing Provision (4.1.2)

Distribution of housing

▶ Ireland has a very high level of home ownership which is a reflection of government policy. Since the 1970s, governments have subsidised owner occupation with schemes such as the tenant purchase scheme, and the shared ownership scheme. (See Page 247)

▶ Many homes are in the process of being purchased, i.e. mortgages are being paid to the local authority or other lending institutions.

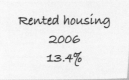

▶ Some houses are rented by the occupiers. Rented housing is subdivided into houses which are privately rented, i.e. paying rent to a landlord, and social housing which is paying rent to (a) the local authority, or (b) a voluntary housing body (See Page 324).

▶ Less than one-third of the population lived in urban areas in 1926. By 2007, 61.1% of the population were living in urban areas.

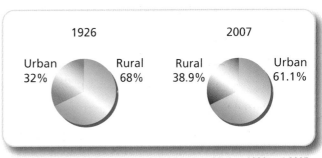

Urban/rural population, 1926 and 2007

Quality of accommodation

▶ The quality of housing in Ireland has greatly improved in recent years. Any new houses or extensions constructed or alterations carried out since 1991 must comply with the Building Regulations Act of 1991 (**See Page** 330).

▶ The National House building guarantee scheme 'HomeBond' also ensures a high standard quality in Irish housing.

▶ In relation to rented accommodation the Housing (Standards for Rented Houses) Regulations, 1993 sets down minimum standards with which proprietors are obliged to comply.

▶ The Housing (Registration of Rented Housing) Regulations 1996* require that all rented accommodation is registered with local authorities. They have the power to investigate any breaches in relation to quality and to prosecute offenders.

▶ There is a higher incidence of poor quality housing in older houses because of the lack of standards in terms of insulation, damp proofing and ventilation at the time of building. Many of these older dwellings are occupied by elderly people, often living alone on fixed incomes, unable to afford repairs and upgrades.

*Regulations oblige owners to ensure that:

- The house is structurally sound, i.e. the roof, floor, walls, doors, windows and stairs are in a good state of repair.
- Plumbing, heating, lighting and ventilation are safe and up to standard.
- There is adequate washing, storing and cooking facilities.

All houses for sale or rent must have a BER Certificate.

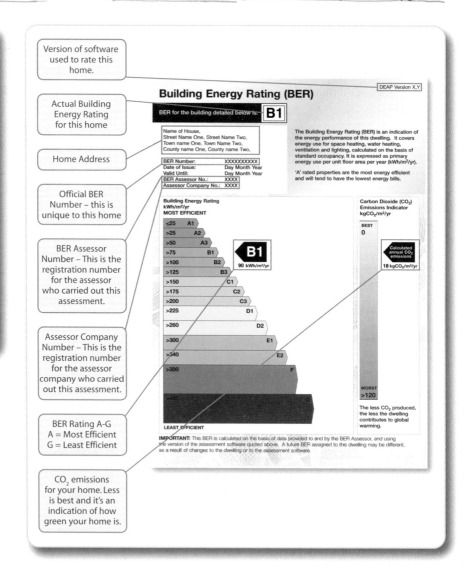

Version of software used to rate this home.

Actual Building Energy Rating for this home

Home Address

Official BER Number – this is unique to this home.

BER Assessor Number – This is the registration number for the assessor who carried out this assessment.

Assessor Company Number – This is the registration number for the assessor company who carried out this assessment.

BER Rating A-G
A = Most Efficient
G = Least Efficient

CO_2 emissions for your home. Less is best and it's an indication of how green your home is.

Comparative costs of buying and renting

Buying	Renting
Initial costs	**Initial costs**
• **Deposit** Usually 10% of purchase price In the case of local authority mortgages 5% of purchase price	• **Deposit** Usually one month's rent in advance. • **Agency fee** Applies if an agency secures the accommodation for renting.
• **Lending agency fees** – an application fee – lenders survey cost – searches – indemnity bond (**See Page** 245).	
• **Legal fees** May be a fixed or a percentage of the purchase price in addition to: – legal searches – and registry fees which are part of the legal process.	Although expenses relating to renting appear to be far less than for buying, actual rent is often more expensive than the repayments on a mortgage for the average house. Buying a house is an investment as property prices usually increase in value whereas renting does not offer a long-term return.
• **Buyer's survey fee** Particularly important when purchasing second-hand housing.	
• **Stamp duty** Government tax payable at different rates.	
Ongoing costs of buying	**Ongoing costs of renting**
• **Mortgage repayments:** a monthly expenditure based on the amount borrowed.	• **Rent.**
• **Mortgage protection/life assurance policy:** may be a monthly or once yearly premium.	• **Insurance of contents.**
• **Home insurance:** for building and contents.	• **Minor repairs.**
• **Furnishing costs.**	
• **Maintenance/repairs costs.**	
• **Service charges:**, e.g. refuse collection.	

Adequacy of Housing Provision

▶ The population of Ireland has been gradually increasing since the 1960s. This increase has resulted in high demand for housing in both the social/public and the private sectors.

▶ In the late twentieth and early twenty-first century high demand had increased property prices to such an extent that many young people did not earn enough to qualify for mortgages. Some who secured mortgages have difficulty in meeting the repayments, a problem which would escalate greatly with an increase in interest rates.

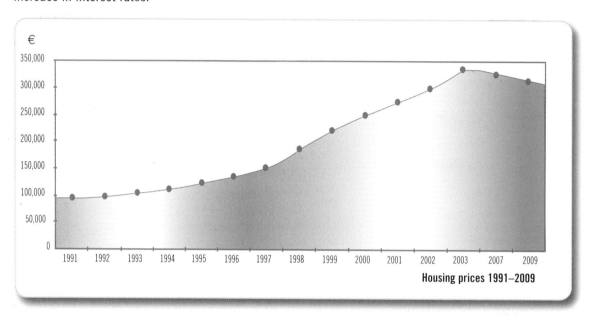

Housing prices 1991–2009

▶ The private rental sector is an option available to those not ready to enter owner-occupation, e.g. young single workers or students. Legislation demands registration and minimum standards, but low compliance means that much of this housing sector is of poor quality. Purpose-built housing for students provides rental accommodation, but availability may be limited.

▶ The government has responded to the high cost of housing with schemes such as 'Affordable Housing'. The Voluntary Housing Sector also provides housing for elderly, disabled and single people, families and the homeless.

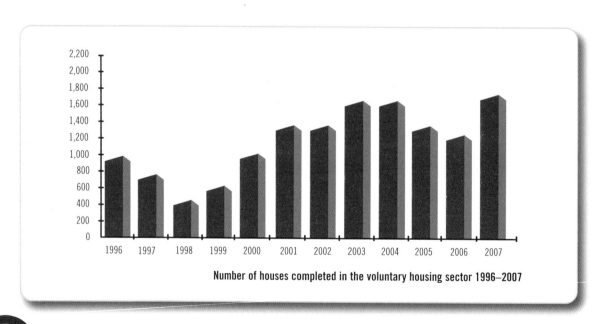

Number of houses completed in the voluntary housing sector 1996–2007

▶ There are over 56,000 households on local authority housing lists at present (2009).

▶ In terms of the disabled – local authorities pay for the provision of additional accommodation or adaptation of houses to meet their needs (90% of the costs involved for private houses and the full cost for local authority houses).

Breakdown of local authority housing waiting lists 2002, 2005 and 2008				
Category of need	2002	2005	2008	Change
Homeless	2,468	2,399	1,394	–41.9%
Travellers	1,583	1,012	1,317	30.1%
Unfit accommodation	4,065	1,725	1,757	1.9%
Overcrowded accommodation	8,513	4,112	4,805	16.9%
Involuntary sharing	4,421	3,375	4,965	47.1%
Leaving institutional care	82	262	715	172.9%
Medical or compassionate reasons	3,400	3,547	8,059	127.2%
Elderly	2,006	1,727	2,499	44.7%
Disabled	423	480	1,155	140.6%
Not reasonably able to meet the cost of accommodation	21,452	25,045	29,583	18.1%
TOTAL	**48,413**	**43,684**	**56,249**	

Social Housing Provision

There are three main areas within the social housing sector:

1. Local authority housing is dealt with in detail in Chapter 13 (See Page 244).

2. Voluntary housing.

3. Co-operative housing.

Voluntary housing
association complex

Voluntary Housing

Voluntary housing associations play an important role in providing rental housing for people who could not otherwise afford to pay for suitable accommodation. These associations are non-profit organisations formed to meet housing needs.

Voluntary housing associations include:

▶ Respond and The Iveagh Trust

▶ The range of accommodation includes houses and flats, sheltered housing with on-site communal welfare facilities, group homes and hostels.

▶ Voluntary housing organisations must be approved by the Department of Environment, Heritage and Local Government to qualify for financial aid. Such aid is available under two schemes:

> The National Association of Building Co-operatives (NABCo) is the central representative body of housing co-operatives in Ireland.

The Capital Assistance Scheme	Rental Subsidy Scheme/Capital Loan and Subsidy Scheme
This scheme provides funding through the local authorities, towards the capital costs for accommodation (generally for one or two-bedroomed units), to meet the needs of small families and those with special housing needs such as the elderly, disabled or homeless.	This scheme is financed by the Housing Finance Agency. It supplies funding, through the local authorities, to provide rental accommodation for low-income families.

Co-operative Housing

▶ Housing co-operatives are a form of non-profit housing association working to relieve the housing needs of a community.

▶ A group of people form the co-operative to build houses at an affordable price, sharing the costs of the site, builder, materials and legal fees.

▶ Co-operative housing schemes benefit from low-cost housing sites provided by the local authority if 75% of the members are either tenants of the local authority or on the local authority waiting list.

▶ Some housing co-operatives supply housing for rent. They provide and manage dwellings, for members who are the tenants. Other co-operatives supply housing for ownership.

Co-operative housing policy

Provision of Local Amenities and Services

The local amenities and services available in housing developments contribute to the appeal of an area and often affect the value of the houses. Such amenities and services include:

Play area

- ▶ *Schools* – provided by the Department of Education and Science depending on the number of children in an area.

- ▶ *Shops* – proximity to shops is important to most people. Supply usually follows demand.

- ▶ *Community centres* – partly funded by the local authority and partly by the community. These centres offer many facilities including sport and education, and are important in the development of community spirit.

- ▶ *Transport* – planning will only be granted for housing developments when the local authority is satisfied with the planned road infrastructure. Proximity to public transport is often a selling factor for housing developments. Local authorities erect signage and introduce traffic calming within housing developments as a safety measure.

- ▶ *Play areas* – play and green areas are now included in the plans of all housing developments. They increase appeal and give a sense of space.

- ▶ *Street lighting* – the provision of adequate street lighting is the responsibility of the local authority and the ESB. These lights generally operate by sensor rather than timer.

- ▶ *Refuse collection* – this service is provided by private companies in many towns in Ireland.

- ▶ All of the services and amenities provided by the local authority including water, sewage, street cleaning, libraries and swimming pools contribute to the quality of life in an area.

House Building and Design (4.2)

There are various factors that influence the choice of location and the choice of housing style.

Location

1. The area where the site is located is an important consideration which will have a bearing on cost. The setting, whether it is urban or rural, the surrounding neighbourhood and the proximity to family, friends, work and schools may all be influencing factors.

2. The size and orientation of the site required will influence the location. The site must be large enough for the chosen design and provide adequate room for the safe disposal of sewage. Orientation will influence the view from the site and the amount of natural shelter and light available.

3. Ideally, the site should be slightly raised or sloping with good drainage, stable soil structure and no danger of flooding. It should be easily accessible from a road. Accessibility in terms of the water supply and electricity is also important.

4. Any proposed development plans for the area should be checked. It might not be desirable to be located near a nightclub or factory in future years.

5. Building and planning permission regulations which apply to the proposed location will have a major impact on the size and type of house which may be built. Different counties have different planning requirements which must be adhered to by all home builders.

House style

1. Costs involved will influence the size and design of the house. Most people are restricted by budget limitations.
2. The size, age group and lifestyle of the family will influence house size and style. The special needs of some family members, e.g. wheelchair users, must be carefully considered in relation to the design and layout of the home.
3. The personal taste of the homeowner will influence the chosen style and layout. House styles are subject to fashion trends, e.g. styles and materials used in doors, windows and wall finishes change over the years.
4. The chosen style should suit the landscape and blend in with existing buildings. Planning regulations will dictate the design to a certain extent, ensuring that it does not detract from the surroundings particularly in scenic rural areas.
5. The aspect of the house is important to take advantage of views and to gain maximum sunlight to brighten and heat the house while respecting the privacy of neighbouring houses.

Planning requirements

Planning permission is necessary for the construction of a new building or for large extensions onto existing buildings. When planning permission is not necessary by-law approval (See Page 327) may be required.

Planning permission

After choosing the site, planning permission must be sought from the local planning authority, e.g. County Council or Urban District Council. Outline or full planning permission may be sought.

Outline planning permission

An application for outline planning permission is used to ascertain whether or not planning permission would be granted for a particular site. No house plans are necessary for outline permission, just a site map showing the location and layout of proposed site. If granted, it means that the planning authority will consider development of the proposed site, but full planning permission must be obtained before any building work commences.

Full planning permission

An application for full planning permission is a detailed submission containing:

▶ Site layout maps detailing site boundaries, the entrance, water supply and drainage.

▶ House plans and specifications including elevations, sections, finishes and details of all materials to be used in construction.

▶ Copies of notice of application to the planning authority, which must have been published in a local newspaper.

▶ Copies of the erected site notice.

▶ Completed application form and planning fee.

Application for planning permission

General procedure

1. Notice of application for planning permission must be placed in a local newspaper and a site notice (legible from the main thoroughfare) must be erected on the proposed site.

2. An application is lodged with the relevant planning authority.

3. The application is placed on the planning register and any member of the public may inspect the plans and is free to object in writing to the proposed development.

4. Planning officials inspect the site.

5. The planning authority must notify the applicant of their decision within two months. If permission is granted, full planning permission will be approved after four weeks provided no objections have been lodged. If permission is refused, the applicant must be given reasons for the refusal. Appeals against the planning authority's decision can be made to An Bord Pleanála (The Planning Appeals Commission).

> Note: Planning permission may be granted with conditions. These conditions vary among different planning authorities and may apply to such issues as height of building, wall and roof finishes, landscaping and road clearance at the entrance.

By-law approval

Planning permission is not necessary for all construction work. Bylaw approval is needed for some extensions, out-buildings and for major internal renovations. Bylaw approval assesses the safety of the structure in question and ensures that it will not endanger health or welfare.

Professional services available to assist in the design and building of a house
Architects

▶ Advise on the choice of site and on the house design that is suitable for the site.

▶ Design and draw up plans for the house to suit individual specifications and requirements.

▶ Advise on contractors and may oversee construction of the house.

Engineers

▶ Will oversee a building project.

▶ Advise on any building problems that may arise and on ways of rectifying problems.

Surveyors

▶ Carry out comprehensive site survey.

▶ Identify potential problem areas.

▶ Advise on how to deal with these problems before they affect building.

Solicitors

▶ Deal with the legal aspect involved in acquiring a site and building a house.

▶ Check issues like title deeds and rights of way.

▶ Advise on building regulations and planning permission.

- mortage

Builders

► Draw up a building contract covering issues such as starting and completion dates, price and details of work to be carried out.

► Are responsible for site preparation, construction and finishing of the house in compliance with building regulations.

► May sub-contract work to specialists, e.g. tilers, cabinet makers.

► Rectify any building flaws that arise within a specified period of the completion date.

Books of house plans

A number of books of house plans are available. They are a useful resource for anyone considering building a house. Some of these books contain very high quality computer generated colour images of the exteriors of houses as well as interior layouts. Issues such as planning permission, siting, landscaping, and interior design are often included. House designs may be ordered as they appear in the book or may be modified to suit personal requirements.

House Design

There are various factors that influence the design of a house.

Aesthetics

1. The chosen design should be well-balanced and proportioned. It should be visually attractive. It should blend well with the landscape and existing buildings.

2. Considerations should be given to the orientation of the site and to the aspect of the house to take full advantage of any views from the site.

3. Thought should be given to landscaping the site and to any materials used, e.g. use of local stone in boundary walls.

4. The internal layout should be aesthetically pleasing. The arrangement and layout of the rooms need to be carefully planned to make maximum use of space and natural lighting.

Environmental factors

1. Ecological principles such as sustainability should be borne in mind when choosing building materials for the house, e.g. using wood in the construction and recycled materials in insulation.

2. A radon barrier must be installed to eliminate the risk of radon seepage into the house. Radon is a naturally occurring radioactive gas. Overexposure to radon has been linked with increased incidence of lung cancer.

3. Waste/sewerage disposal systems must be laid in strict compliance with the law to minimise risk to the surrounding environment, such as contamination of a fresh water supply.

4. The heating system should be clean and environmentally friendly. Use of a sustainable source of energy such as wood or solar energy is desirable.

5. Trees and hedging which would benefit the environment could be used to provide a shelter belt from prevailing winds.

Family requirements

1. The house needs to be an adequate size to cater for the present needs of the family and adaptable to cater for future needs. If finance is limited, an extension or attic conversion could be considered at a later stage.

2. Rooms should have sufficient living and storage space and may need to be multipurpose, e.g. a bedroom may be used for sleeping, relaxing and studying.

3. The house must be safe and comfortable and, where possible, children should have a safe outdoor play area.

4. Disabled and older family members may require specific design features to be incorporated at the planning stage and all new houses must have wheelchair access.

5. Family members who are old, ill or bedridden may need a bedroom at ground level and access to toilet and shower facilities.

Energy efficiency

1. The house should be well insulated to conserve heat. The use of a timer and lagging on the water cylinder and lagging of hot water pipes conserves energy on water heating.

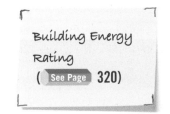
Building Energy Rating
(See Page 320)

2. Large windows on south facing walls are a source of passive solar energy used to heat living space and to maximise natural light. All windows should be double-glazed to prevent heat loss.

3. The heating system should be as energy efficient as possible. The system should be zoned allowing heating to be switched off in parts of the house, e.g. upstairs, if desired. Thermostats and timers also contribute to an energy saving system.

4. Energy efficient appliances should be chosen when designing fitted kitchens and utility rooms. Installing night-saver electricity may also be an energy efficient option.

Ergonomics

▶ Ergonomics is the study of the efficiency of people in their working environment. Houses should be designed to be energy efficient including the conservation of human energy.

▶ A house should be designed to be low maintenance and surfaces should be stain resistant and easy to clean.

▶ The layout should allow ease of assess and movement.

▶ Adequate storage space, well-positioned power point switches, surfaces and appliances placed at a comfortable height are all desirable features in an ergonomically designed work space.

▶ The food preparation sequence and the work triangle in kitchen planning are good examples of where ergonomics may be used to increase efficiency and minimise the walking, labour and time involved in food preparation.

Technological developments

1. Computer aided design (CAD) and the high quality graphics used in house plan books afford individuals a realistic image of what the finished house will look like, minimising the need for costly changes at building stage.
2. Technology in terms of timers, thermostats and zoned heating allows for more energy efficient heating systems.
3. Developments in lighting have led to the availability of compact fluorescent lamps (CFLS), sensor lights and solar-powered garden lighting.
4. Easy-to-clean, stain-resistant flooring, e.g. laminated flooring and work surfaces such as stainless steel reduce maintenance.
5. Remote controls for electronic gates, garage doors, alarm systems and a range of other uses.

Cost

► The chosen site and design will have an influence on initial costs.

► Where budget is limited, a smaller house with less elaborate design features may have to be chosen.

► Money spent in the initial designing and planning stages may help to reduce long-term maintenance costs, e.g. opting for a cut stone exterior finish is expensive but maintenance free.

Initial costs	Maintenance costs
• Site cost	• Mortgage
• Architect	• Insurance – life assurance, home and contents, all risks insurance
• Engineer	
• Planning fee	• Mortgage protection policy
• Survey costs	• Services – electricity, gas/oil, waste disposal, telephone
• Legal costs	• Redecorating/repairs
• Builder – construction	• Replacing furniture/furnishings
• Heating, plumbing, electricity	• Garden maintenance
• Painting/decorating	
• Fixtures/fitting, e.g. fitted kitchen, tiling	
• Furniture and furnishings	
• Landscaping	

Regulation of House Building

The Building Regulations Act 1991 and more recent legislation set out standards which must be complied with when designing and building houses. They ensure that houses are safe, comfortable living spaces for occupants. Regulations apply to such areas as building materials, construction standards, insulation, waste disposal, heating, lighting and ventilation. Local authorities are responsible for enforcing this legislation.

National House Building Guarantee Scheme (HomeBond)

This scheme is operated by the National House Building Guarantee
Company and the Department of the Environment, Heritage and Local Government.

▶ Builders pay a fee to register any house they build.

▶ The house is inspected three times during construction by department inspectors.

▶ If the house meets the required standards the builder is issued with a HomeBond Certificate which is a guarantee that:

1. Should any major structural fault develop within a ten-year period it will be rectified free of charge by the builder.

2. The customer will not lose the deposit should the builder go out of business.

▶ Many lending agencies now require that new houses are protected by a Homebond Certificate.

Certificates of Compliance

▶ Certificates of compliance are issued by the Department of the Environment, Heritage and Local Government.

▶ They confirm that any alteration or extention to a property has been constructed in compliance with planning permission and building regulations.

▶ A certificate of compliance is required by the solicitor when selling, purchasing or refinancing a house.

Floor area compliance certificate

▶ This certificate states that the floor area of a house does not exceed 125 square metres and complies with construction standards.

▶ Houses with a floor area of less than 125 square metres are exempt from stamp duty.

Grant provision

▶ Home improvement grant: Local authorities will improve or extended privately owned houses as an alternative to the provision of local authority housing.

▶ S.E.I. grants (See Page 378).

CONTENTS INCLUDE:

▶ **Elements and principles of design and their application in the home**

▶ **Flooring, wall finishes, furniture and soft furnishings**

▶ **Selection, properties and uses of materials in the home**

Elements of Design

> The elements of design include **colour**, **pattern** and **texture**.

Colour

> Colour is a powerful design device which has a considerable impact on the mood of a room.

The human eye can distinguish millions of colours, all of which are based on the colours of the colourwheel plus black and white. The colourwheel is a useful device for understanding how colours relate to one another and how they may be combined in colour schemes.

▶ ***Primary colours:*** Red, yellow and blue are referred to as primary colours because they cannot be mixed from other colours.

▶ ***Secondary colours:*** Green, orange and purple are referred to as secondary colours because they are mixed from equal amounts of the primary colours.

> yellow + blue = green
> red + yellow = orange
> red + blue = purple

▶ ***Tertiary colours:*** They are created by mixing a primary with a secondary colour, e.g. blue + green = turquoise.

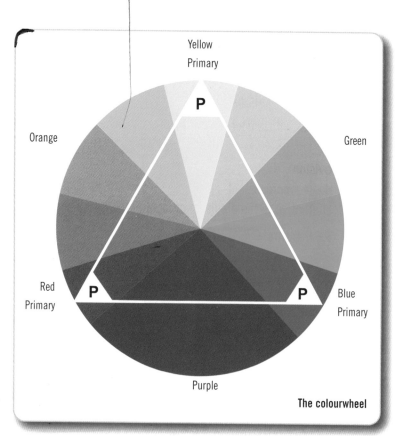

The colourwheel

► **Warm colours:** Reds, pinks, oranges and yellows, colours associated with sunshine and firelight, are referred to as warm colours.

► **Cool colours:** Greens, blue-greens and blues, the colours of shady forests and the ocean, are referred to as cool colours.

► **Pastel colours:** Pastels are soft delicate shades of colours such as pink, blue, green and yellow.

► **Neutral colours:** In interior design neutrals refer to a range of colours which include white, cream, beige, tans and pale greys.

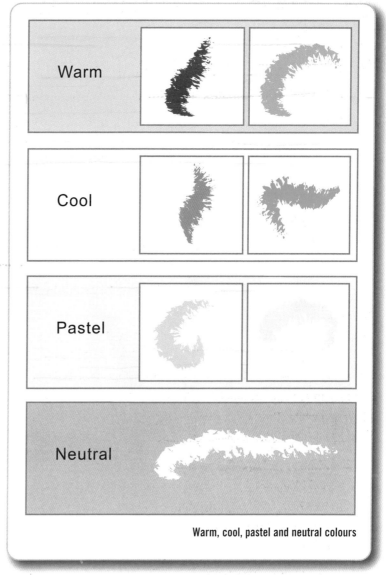

Warm, cool, pastel and neutral colours

Colour schemes

▶ An **_harmonious colour_** *scheme* is based on colours that lie next to each other on the colourwheel and go well together, e.g. green and yellow.

▶ A **_contrasting/complementary_** *colour scheme* is based on colours that lie opposite each other on the colour wheel, e.g. red and green.

▶ A **_neutral colour_** *scheme* is based on neutral colours which are easy to live with and create a good background for interesting and attractive furniture, ornaments, pictures and plants.

▶ A **_monochromatic colour scheme_** is based on various tones of the same colour.

Harmonious colour scheme

Contrasting colour scheme

Neutral colour scheme

Monochrome colour scheme

Shade: Darkening a colour by the addition of black creates a shade of that colour.

Tint: Lightening a colour by the addition of white creates a tint of that colour.

Tone: Describes the lightness or darkness of a colour.

Planning a colour scheme/use of colour in the home

1. The house should be considered as a whole unit when planning colour schemes. Colour can be used effectively to link various rooms and to give the house a feeling of harmony.

2. Colour can be used to visually alter the proportions of rooms.
    (a) Light colours reflect light and make a room appear larger and more spacious.
    (b) Warm colours can be used to make a large room feel smaller and cosier.
    (c) Dark and warm colours advance, they make objects seem nearer. A single wall painted in a dark colour will be drawn into the room.
    (d) Cool colours recede, they make objects seem further away. A wall painted in a light colour will appear further away than it really is.
    (e) A dark colour used on a ceiling and the upper part of the wall makes the ceiling appear lower.
    (f) A light colour used on the ceiling makes the ceiling level appear higher.

3. Colour can be used to highlight good features, e.g. an attractive ceiling, and to disguise less attractive features, e.g. radiators.

4. The mood and function of the room need to be considered when choosing a colour scheme. For example, pastels can be used to create a restful and relaxing atmosphere suitable for nurseries and bedrooms.

5. The amount and quality of natural and artificial light in rooms will influence colour choices. Warm colours should be used in a north-facing room where daylight is limited, whereas a south-facing room with a more favourable aspect can be decorated in cooler colours.

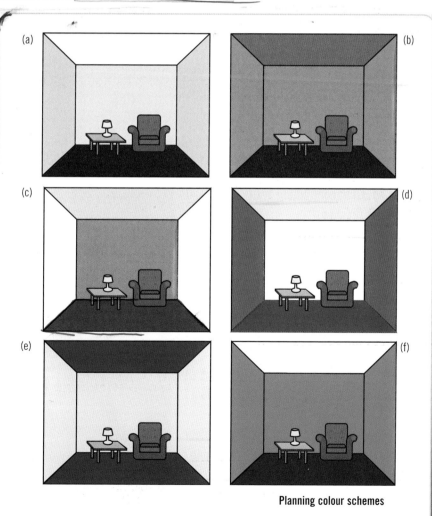

Planning colour schemes

Pattern

Patterns are decorative designs which add variety and contrast to a room. An endless range of patterns can be skilfully used to suggest a particular period or style, such as a country kitchen style, and to create the desired atmosphere.

Use of pattern in the home

1. Pattern should be used carefully. Overuse can make a room appear crowded and fussy, under use can render a room bland and uninteresting.
2. When using several patterns in a room they work best if they are linked, i.e. have colour, texture or a motif in common.
3. Use patterns of various scales. Generally large-scale patterns are used on the largest areas such as on floor or walls. Smaller patterns are used on smaller areas such as on cushions.
4. Patterns, like colour, can be used to alter the proportions of a room. For example, bold patterns advance, vertical lines give the impression of height.

Texture

Texture refers to the feel or touch of an object or surface. The colours and patterns in a scheme will work more effectively if thought is given to the textural quality of materials and fabrics used, e.g. smooth or rough, cold or warm.

Use of texture in the home

1. Avoid 'flat' schemes by using contrasting textures instead of materials with similar finishes.
2. Textures affect the atmosphere of a room. Smooth textures such as tiling, glass, mirrors and granite are cold and hygienic and are therefore best suited to bathrooms and kitchens. Many are light reflective increasing a sense of space. Rough surfaces such as carpeting and upholstery are warm and comfortable creating a welcoming atmosphere in a sitting room.
3. Texture affects how colours are perceived. Matt surfaces such as emulsion paint absorb light and make colours appear darker.
4. Texture is of particular importance in neutral colour schemes where colour and pattern are kept to a minimum.
5. Effective lighting is essential to make the most of textured finishes.

*Principles of Design

The principles of design include: *balance, emphasis, proportion* and *rhythm*.

Balance

Balance occurs when all aspects of a design or room plan work well together. The colours, patterns and textures are in harmony with one another. A well-balanced room is visually attractive.

A well-balanced room

Emphasis

Emphasis involves drawing attention to a particular feature in a room, e.g. an attractive fireplace or a picture. It can be achieved using colour, lighting, pattern or shape. Emphasis adds interest and variety to a room giving it a focal point.

Emphasis

Proportion

Proportion is achieved when the pieces of furniture in a room relate to one another in size. The furniture must also relate to the size of the room. Small delicate pieces of furniture would look lost in a very large room. Similarly, large heavy pieces of furniture would crowd a small room. The principle of proportion must also be applied to the colours, textures and patterns used in the room.

A well-proportioned room

Rhythm

Rhythm involves the repeated use of a colour pattern or texture in a room. The object is to connect different areas within a room so that the plan works as a whole. Rhythm gives harmony and unity to a room.

Rhythm

Interior Design

When planning interior design, the size, shape and aspect of a room are important considerations. The position of fixtures such as doors, windows and fireplaces need to be considered. The function of the room is a factor which will have an impact on choices in terms of colour scheme, materials used and the layout of the room.

A number of other factors influence the interior design of the home including aesthetics, comfort, ergonomics, cost, environmental awareness and the family's needs.

Aesthetics

▶ The factors which make a room plan aesthetically pleasing depend largely on the personal taste of the occupants.

▶ Trends in colour schemes, patterns and textures change over time. Care should be taken to choose a design which will not date too quickly and which will be easy to live with in the long term.

▶ Use design principles to create a visually attractive room.

Comfort

▶ Room design and layout must suit the designated function of the room so that occupants are comfortable whether working or relaxing.

▶ Heating, ventilation and lighting must all be at a comfortable level, relating to the room's function.

▶ All heights, e.g. work surfaces, desks and seats must be at a suitable level to avoid any physical discomfort.

Ergonomics

▶ Rooms should be designed and laid out to allow ease of movement and to accommodate the natural traffic flow.

▶ Spaces should be easy to clean with free access to all areas including windows and sockets.

▶ Room design should facilitate maximum efficiency. (The work triangle in kitchen design is an example of how ergonomics can improve efficiency and work rate.)

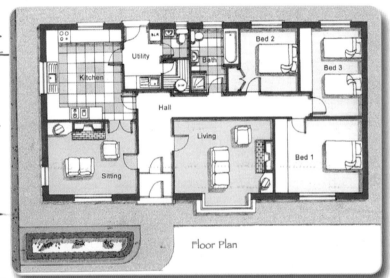

Floor Plan

A floor plan is a sketch of a room drawn to scale, showing the position of fixtures such as doors, windows and sometimes the layout and arrangement of the furniture.

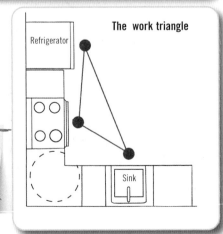

The work triangle

Cost

▶ For many, cost is a limiting factor in terms of interior design.

▶ Interior design does not have to cost a lot of money. Attractive room plans can be achieved on a tight budget using cheaper furniture and furnishings.

▶ Where possible, essential furniture such as beds or suites of furniture which affect comfort levels should be of good quality.

Environmental awareness

▶ Interior decor should be considered at the planning stage so that natural materials can be incorporated into the design, e.g. wooden floors or a stone fire-place.

▶ Features such as a wood-burning stove form an attractive focal point, while also being environmentally friendly (See Page 278).

▶ Tiling is an energy efficient and attractive flooring option in conservatories and south-facing kitchens as it absorbs solar energy and releases the heat gradually within the house.

Family size and circumstances

▶ It is important, particularly when a family is large, to use space efficiently and practically and to avoid unnecessary clutter.

▶ Where there are young children surfaces need to be stain resistant, durable and easy to clean.

▶ The interior design must be flexible enough to adapt to the changing needs of the occupants, e.g. teenagers or elderly people.

Special needs (See Page 318).

Features of a well-designed room
A well-planned room is visually attractive, comfortable and safe when it has:

- Sufficient living and storage space for the purpose of the room.
- Good natural lighting and an effective and attractive system of artificial lighting.
- Sufficient, well-positioned power points.
- An efficient system of heating and ventilation.
- A layout which allows ease of access and movement and accommodates the natural traffic flow.
- Sufficient furniture for the function of the room, but not so much that it appears cluttered.

Floors and Flooring

Flooring is often the first consideration when planning a room since a large portion of the budget is likely to be spent on the final choice. The selected flooring should be safe, comfortable, attractive and easy to live with in the long-term.

Floors may be solid or suspended.

Solid floors	Suspended floors
• Solid floors are usually used on the ground floors of houses. • They consist of a layer of concrete laid over hard core. • A damp-proof course and insulation are then inserted followed by another layer of fine concrete which forms the sub-floor.	• Suspended floors are usually used on upper floors, but may also be used on ground floors. • They consist of joists of wood onto which tongue-and-grooved floorboards are laid at right angles to the joists. • Insulation may be inserted in the air space between the joists to conserve heat and to absorb sound.

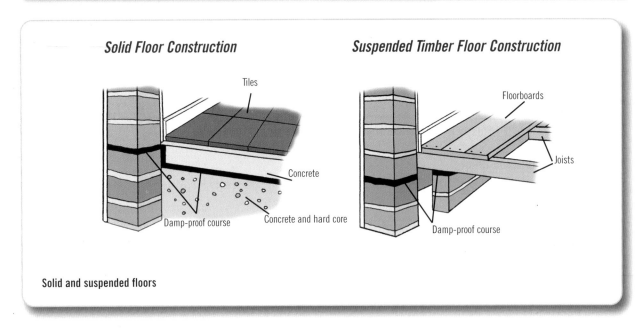

Solid and suspended floors

Selection of flooring

When choosing flooring for a particular room or area the following factors should be considered:

▶ **Cost:** Choices may need to be made between what is desired and what is achievable within the budget.

▶ **Function of the room:** Flooring must be comfortable and safe (non-slip) and must suit the purpose of the room.

▶ **Ease of maintenance:** Flooring must be durable and easy to clean.

▶ **Aesthetic appeal:** Colour pattern and texture of flooring must be carefully chosen to create a visually attractive room.

▶ **Adjoining rooms:** An aesthetically pleasing flow from room to room will give unity and will add to the appearance of the house as a whole.

Flooring

Flooring may be loosely classified as hard, semi-hard and soft.

Types of flooring		
Hard	**Semi-hard**	**Soft**
Ceramic tiles Slate Terracotta Mosaics Stone	Wood Vinyl Linoleum Cork Coir* Sisal* * plant fibre	Carpet

Hard flooring		
Type	**Properties**	**Uses**
• **Ceramic tiles**	• Durable and hard-wearing. • Non absorbent and stain resistant. • Low maintenance and easy to clean. • Available in a wide range of colours, designs, sizes and finishes. • Relatively expensive. • Cool and hard to stand on for long periods. • Can crack or chip if something heavy is dropped on them. • Are not easily repaired or replaced.	1. Ideal for kitchens, utilities, bathrooms and conservatories. 2. Require a solid underfloor.
• **Slate**	• Long lasting and hard wearing. • Warmer underfoot than ceramic tiles. • Uneven texture. • Limited range of darker colours. • Slightly absorbent so needs to be sealed at regular intervals to ensure that it does not stain. • Can be expensive to lay, due to uneven texture they need to be carefully positioned.	3. Because of low maintenance required suitable for busy households where there are children and pets. 4. Absorb solar energy and give out heat gradually within the house so are an environmentally friendly choice of flooring.

Semi-hard Flooring

Wooden flooring

Wooden flooring is available in a wide variety of qualities, finishes and price ranges.

Options in wooden flooring include:

1. Soft wood planks — i.e. sanding and sealing the existing floorboards of a suspended floor is a cheap and practical option.

2. Strip flooring — this consists of strips of hardwood such as oak, beech or maple, or soft wood such as pine or spruce, which are tongue and grooved to form a smooth finish. Strips used vary in thickness and may be solid wood or may be laminated, with a plastic veneer.

3. Block flooring — parquet or mosaic flooring consists of blocks of hard wood laid in a pattern such as herringbone and basketweave.

Wooden flooring is low maintenance

Properties of wood flooring	Uses of wooden flooring
• Attractive, durable and low maintenance. • Some such as oak strip floor are available ready sealed. • Some are expensive, e.g. wood block. • Some such as parquet, are hard, cold and noisy. • Solid wood may be marked and scratched.	• Wooden flooring is a popular option for living rooms, halls, playrooms, studies and bedrooms. • Wood is not a suitable flooring option for areas with a high moisture content such as a bathroom.

The type and quality of a wooden floor should depend on the function of the room and the amount of wear and tear the flooring will have to endure.

Vinyl

Vinyl is a plastic floor covering.

Properties of vinyl	Uses of vinyl
• Available in sheet or tile form. • Unlimited variety in colour, design and texture. • Durability depends on quality and thickness. • Warm and soft underfoot, relatively non-slip. • Easy to clean and maintain, stain resistant. • Scorches and melts when subjected to heat, marked by furniture, heels.	• Very suitable for kitchens, utility rooms and bathrooms as it can withstand moisture. • Also suitable for playrooms and children's bedrooms as it is hygienic, easy to clean and can be kept relatively dust free (suitable for asthmatics).

Vinyl flooring

Soft Flooring

Carpets

Carpets vary in quality and price from the more luxurious woven carpets to the practical and more basic tufted carpets and carpet tiles. Options in carpeting include:

1. **Woven carpets**

    Pile is woven into a backing. The two main types of woven carpets are Axminster and Wilton.

Axminster	Wilton
<ul><li>Cut pile is woven into backing.</li><li>Pile may be of various lengths.</li><li>Unlimited range of colours and designs.</li></ul>	<ul><li>Thread is woven into backing in a continuous strand so only a limited number of colours can be used and a thicker carpet is produced.</li><li>Pile may be cut or uncut.</li></ul>

2. **Tufted carpets**

    Tufts of pile are inserted into a woven backing and are held in place by adhesive and backed with foam. Pile may be cut or uncut. Tufted carpets are generally a cheaper alternative to woven carpets as synthetic fibres are often used in the pile.

> *A carpet pile which is composed of a mixture of natural and synthetic fibres (e.g. 80% wool and 20% nylon) incorporates the virtues of both types of fibre.*

Properties of fibres used in carpets

Materials used in carpet pile will have an impact on carpet quality and characteristics.

Fibres	Properties
Natural fibres • Wool	• Warm, durable, resilient, insulating, soft, expensive.
Synthetic fibres • Acrylic • Nylon • Polypropylene	• Wool-like appearance, very durable. • Warm, hard-wearing tends to attract static, tends to compact over time. • Cheap, hard-wearing, highly flammable, water resistant.

Different types of carpet

General properties of carpet

- ► Available in a wide variety of colours, patterns, and textures, e.g. pile may be short, long, looped or twisted.
- ► Wide choice in terms of quality and price range.
- ► Warm, soft and comfortable underfoot.
- ► Good insulator and noise absorber.
- ► Variety in thickness, materials used and construction techniques.
- ► Carpet tiles may be easily lifted and replaced if stained or worn.

> *A good quality underlay will increase the life of the carpet and make it feel more luxurious and provides additional warmth and insulation.*

Classification of carpets

Carpets are graded according to the traffic flow they will withstand into the following classes:

Classification of carpets		
Class	**Use**	**When choosing a carpet consider:**
Light domestic:	Bedrooms	• Cost.
Medium domestic:	Study, playroom, dining room	• Colour, patterned or plain. • Pile: cut, uncut, long, short, textured, closeness of pile (the closer the pile the more hard-wearing the carpet).
General domestic:	Living rooms	
Heavy domestic:	Hall, stairs, landing	• Backing: good quality, closely woven.

Wall Finishes

Walls may be finished using paint, wallpaper or ceramic tiles. Other finishes include fabric, wood panelling, metal, glass and mirrors. Stone and brick are also used as interior wall finishes.

Selection of wall finishes

When choosing a wall finish consider the following factors:

1. **The function of the room:** Areas with a high moisture level such as a kitchen or a bathroom need a finish that will withstand steam and moisture. The function of the area also affects the durability required. A hallway or child's bedroom would need a durable, cleanable finish.

2. **The size and shape of the room:** The aspect and amount of available natural light should have an impact on the choice. A small room should be decorated in a light colour and using small patterns.

3. **The type of room and the desired effect:** Some finishes are reminiscent of certain periods, e.g. flock wallpaper is associated with Victorian-style rooms. Care must be taken to choose a style which does not date too quickly.

4. **The condition of the walls:** Most modern homes have smooth walls which can be finished as desired. In older houses walls may be less than perfect and may need more careful finishing to mask blemishes.

5. **Cost:** If a chosen finish needs to be applied by an expert this will add to the cost.

6. **Ease of maintenance:** This is a particularly important factor in family homes where surfaces should preferably be washable, durable and easily 'freshened' up as and when necessary.

Paint

Paints are either water based or oil/solvent based.

Wall finish

Water-based paints

1. Emulsion paints

▶ Emulsion paint is available in a wide range of colours and a variety of finishes such as vinyl matt, silk matt and soft sheen. Some finishes, e.g. soft sheen, are more durable than others.

▶ *Uses:* Walls and ceilings of light wear areas such as bedrooms and sitting rooms.

2. Non-drip/thixotropic emulsion

► Non-drip emulsion has a thick, jelly-like consistency. It should not be stirred and colours cannot be mixed. Easy to apply and only one coat is usually necessary.

► *Use:* Ceilings.

3. Kitchen and bathroom paint

► A durable emulsion paint with a satin or soft sheen finish, which can withstand high levels of moisture. It also resists grease and general wear and tear. It may contain an antifungicide which prevents mould growth.

► *Uses:* Kitchens, bathrooms, utility rooms.

Water-based paint

Properties of emulsion paints

► Easy to apply, quick drying and without a strong odour.

► Inexpensive.

► Readily available in an unlimited range of colours.

► Variety of finishes, e.g. matt, satin, soft sheen.

► Durable and easy to clean.

► Matt finishes help to mask minor imperfections.

Oil-based paint

Oil/solvent-based paints

1. Gloss paint

► Very hard-wearing, water-resistant paint which dries to a shiny finish.

► *Uses:* Doors, window frames/sills, skirting-boards.

2. Radiator paint

► Paint devised for use on radiators. Will not discolour over time when subjected to high temperatures.

► *Uses:* Radiators. *extremely durable.*

3. Polyurethane/strengthened paint

► Tough, hard-wearing paint that is difficult to apply and dries quickly.

► *Uses:* Areas such as skirting-boards, doors and furniture.

Properties of oil/solvent-based paints

► More difficult to apply than water-based paints.

► Slow to dry and strong odour.

► Durable and easy to clean.

► Wide range of colours.

► Very water resistant.

► Suitable for a range of surfaces such as wood or metal.

► Most need an undercoat, but one-coat paints are also available.

► Shiny finish may highlight surface blemishes.

Specialised paints

Specialised paints

1. *Flame retardant paint*
   ▶ *Uses:* Walls and ceilings of high risk areas such as kitchens and interiors of caravans and boats.

2. *Floor and step paint*
   ▶ *Uses:* Durable, water-resistant finish for floors and steps.

3. *Textured paint*
   ▶ *Uses:* Plastic fibres give the paint a textured finish which can be used to hide minor wall blemishes.

Decorative Paint Effects

Some techniques may be used to achieve various effects on a painted surface. Paint effects are a means of introducing pattern and colour to a wall finish while still achieving an easy-to-clean surface. These effects include:

1. *Colour washing:* A mixture of emulsion paint and an acrylic glaze is used to create a soft cloudy effect.

2. *Sponging:* This involves dabbing paint onto a base coat using a sponge to produce a texture.

3. *Rag rolling:* A watery flowing finish is created by rolling a piece of fabric through the wet paint.

4. *Stencilling:* Paint is applied through a cut out shape to produce a decorative motif/pattern.

Colour washing

Sponging

Wallpaper

Types of wallpaper	
Types	**Uses**
• **General purpose paper** The design is printed onto paper which varies in thickness.	Light wear areas such as sitting rooms, dining rooms and adults bedrooms.
• **Embossed paper** The design is stamped onto paper producing textured effect. 'Relief' paper is a type of thick embossed paper which is usually painted over after hanging.	As above. Used to hide an uneven or imperfect wall surface.
• **Washable paper** Wallpaper is coated with a thin plastic base layer which enables the paper to withstand light sponging.	As above and living rooms.
• **Vinyl paper** Paper is covered with a layer of vinyl. Some are ready-pasted. 'Blown' vinyls are heavy papers and are designed to look like tiles.	Kitchens, bathrooms.

Rag rolling

Stencilling

Different types of wallpaper

Other wall coverings include: woodchip (chips of wood embedded in paper), flock (pattern created using short velvety fibres) and fabric (e.g. hessian and silk).

Ceramic tiles

Properties of wallpaper
1. Wallpapers are available in a wide range of colours and designs.
2. Rolls are of standard width and length but thickness varies.
3. Vinyl papers are strong, durable and washable and can withstand condensation.
4. Variety in pattern and texture adds interest to interior design.
5. Embossed papers can be used to mask minor wall blemishes.

See ceramic tiles

(See Page 341)

Furniture

Styles in furniture undergo constant change, but they may be broadly categorised as antique, traditional and modern.

Antique furniture
Antique furniture refers to furniture which is over 150 years old. Georgian and Regency style furniture would be described as antique. Pieces were hand-crafted from high quality materials and are usually very expensive. Cheaper imitations called reproduction furniture are also available.

Traditional furniture
Furniture dating from the last 100 years is referred to as traditional. Cottage style furniture such as dressers, which are simpler in design than antique pieces, are also popular.

Modern furniture
Modern furniture is made from materials such as textiles, glass and metal as well as wood. Lines tend to be clean and simple.

Antique furniture

347

Selecting furniture

When choosing furniture, consider:

1. *Cost:* This may be a limiting factor but for larger pieces of furniture, likely to be in use for many years, good quality furniture should be chosen where possible.

2. *Space available:* The size and shape of the room will dictate furniture choices. Furniture should be in proportion to the size of the room. The amount of furniture should also be considered.

3. *Style of room:* Furniture should suit the decor and style of the room. Colours, patterns and textures should be carefully combined to achieve the desired look.

4. *Function of room:* The function of the room must be considered. A family living room requires furniture which is practical, comfortable, stain resistant and durable.

5. *Construction and materials used:* Furniture whether cheap or expensive should be well made, e.g. secure handles and hinges.

Traditional furniture

A contemporary look

Upholstered furniture

Upholstered furniture generally consists of a wooden frame, springs and/or webbing, padding/filling and outer covering fabric (e.g. cotton, wool, velvet).

When selecting upholstered furniture check for:

▶ A solidly constructed frame. Castors should be well fitted and secure.

▶ Firm supportive springs, webbing and padding.

▶ The outer furnishing fabric should be strong, closely woven, durable and resilient. Some are treated with a finish which makes them less moisture absorbent and more stain resistant.

▶ Labels detailing the composition of the materials used, care and cleaning.

▶ Fire safety labels which indicate that the outer fabric and inner filling/padding meet criteria set out in the fire safety legislation (See Page 265).

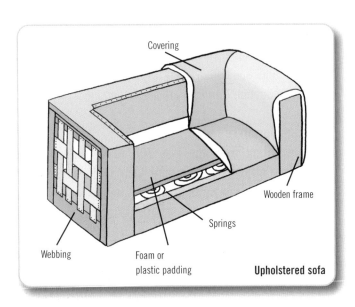

Upholstered sofa

Furniture for storage

Furniture for storage takes the form of built-in and free-standing storage units and open shelving. Modular units popular for bedrooms and studies consist of ready-made units that piece together to form a wall of furniture. Quality varies from solid hardwood pieces to cheaper laminates, which are available in flat-packs for home assembly.

When selecting furniture for storage:

1. Ensure that there is sufficient storage space for the purpose of the room.
2. Ensure storage areas such as wardrobes and chest of drawers are the correct size and shape to accommodate the items to be stored.
3. Choose strong durable materials which will withstand wear and tear.
4. Ensure good workmanship, e.g. doors and drawers should open and close smoothly, handles and hinges should be securely fitted.

Dining chairs and tables

Dining chairs and tables are available in a wide variety of styles. The quality depends on the workmanship and the materials used, e.g. wood (hard and soft woods), laminates, plastic, metal, glass.

When selecting dining tables and chairs ensure that:

1. Tables and chairs are strong and sturdy. The chairs should offer good back support.
2. Tables and chairs are at a comfortable height.
3. The table is large enough to accommodate all diners comfortably.
4. The table surface is moisture and stain resistant and easy to clean.
5. Any textiles used on chair seats are easy to clean and durable.

Beds

▶ Beds vary in size:
Single bed: 100 x 200 cm
Double bed: 150 x 200 cm
Kingsize bed: 180 x 200 cm
Convertible sofa beds, bunk beds and foldaway beds are also available.
Divan beds consist of a solid base on castors. Sometimes there are drawers in the base for extra storage.

▶ Bed bases may be:
1. Spring-edged which are more comfortable but more expensive.
2. Box-edged which are more hard wearing.
3. Stretch wire/wooden slats and rubber webbing are used on bunk beds.

▶ Mattresses consist of springs padded on both sides by synthetic wadding, foam or horsehair and covered by a layer of ticking which in turn is covered by a layer of outer fabric. The springs may be arranged as open individual springs or continuous springing (a network of interlocking springs).

▶ Also available are foam mattresses which consist of latex or polyether foam. They are made in different thicknesses.

▶ Headboards made from a variety of materials such as wood, metal or upholstery protect the wall behind the bed and may also be a decorative feature.

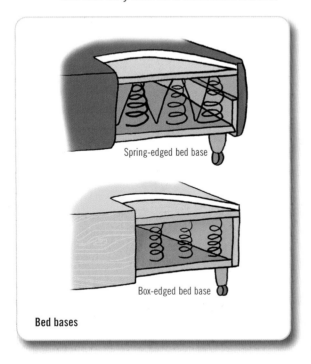

Spring-edged bed base

Box-edged bed base

Bed bases

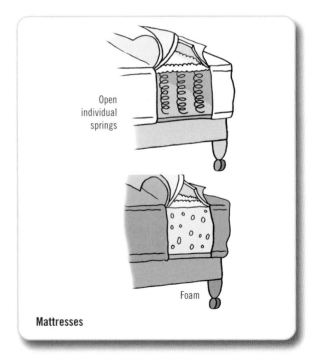

Open individual springs

Foam

Mattresses

Soft Furnishings

Soft furnishings are textile-based, practical and decorative items that add to the overall appearance of a room. Examples include curtains, blinds, cushions and bed linen.

Curtains	
Choice of curtain depends on:	**Curtains vary in:**
1. Style of room. 2. Colour scheme. 3. Aspect of windows. 4. Size and shape of windows. 5. Cost.	• Colour, pattern, texture and weight of fabric. • Style of heading, e.g. pencil pleat, French pleat, gathered. • Curtain length, e.g. to reach the windowsill or the floor. • Lining or no lining. • Lining: standard, heavy, insulating. • Type of curtain rail, e.g. wood, plastic, wrought iron. • Presence or absence of a pelmet.
Functions of curtains:	**Desirable properties of curtains:**
• Curtains give privacy. • They darken a room. • Insulate and help prevent draughts. • Are a decorative feature.	• Good draping quality. • Pre-shrunk and fade resistant. • Flame resistant. • Durable, cleanable and stain resistant. • Insulating.
Fabric used for curtains includes:	
• Cotton (chintz) • Linen • Wool • Polyester • Dralon (velvet)	

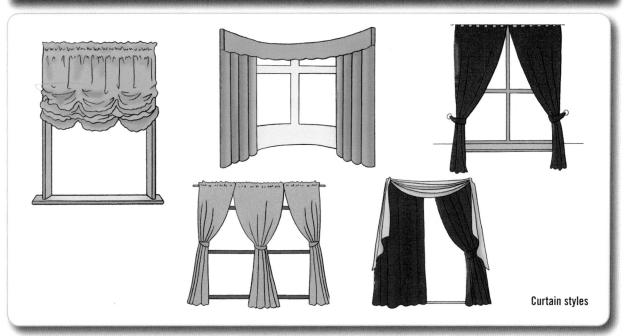

Curtain styles

Blinds

Blinds which may be used with curtains or on their own are a practical and decorative window dressing. They are available in a wide range of styles and colours and some are suited for use on windows where curtains are not an option such as on velux windows. Choices include:

1. Roller blinds, made from Holland (stiffened linen), cotton or vinyl, and available in a wide range of colours. Some 'black out' blinds used in bedrooms do not allow any light to pass through.

2. Roman blinds, generally made from cotton, and available in a variety of colours and patterns. There are wooden slats at the back of the blind. When pulled up they fall in folds at the top of the window.

3. Austrian blinds which consist of generous amounts of fabric which are gathered to produce decorative window dressings. Any light fabric with good draping qualities is suitable.

Cushion covers
Any closely woven upholstery fabric which is durable and easy to clean is suitable.

Cushions	
Functions	**Fillings**
• Add comfort to seats.	• Down
• Add to decor of room.	• Feathers
• Available in an array of shapes and sizes.	• Polyester wadding
	• Foam

Bed Linen

Bed linen consists of sheets, pillowcases and duvet covers.

▶ Sheets may be fitted, valanced or flat. Quality and price vary depending on the fabrics used. Fabrics used include cotton (brushed/smooth), linen and polyester-cotton in a range of colours and patterns.

Desirable properties of bed linen

- Smooth
- Easy to launder
- Closely woven
- Shrink resistant
- Absorbent

Pillows

The quality of pillows varies but a good pillow should support the head and neck. Fillings used in pillows may be natural or synthetic. Synthetic fillings are best for asthma sufferers.

Natural	Synthetic
• Down • Down and feather	• Polyester • Latex

It is recommended that a pillow be replaced approximately every three years.

Duvets

Duvets consist of two layers of closely woven cotton or polyester cotton fabric. A filling is sandwiched between the layers and held in place by lines of stitching. The filling consists of natural substances such as goose and duck down (which is expensive), a mixture of down and feathers, or cotton wadding. Synthetic fillings such as polyester are also used. The air trapped in the duvet filling acts as an insulating layer. The warmth of a duvet is measured in togs and varies from 4.5 togs (lightest and coolest) to 15 togs (warmest).

Advantages of duvets

► Light and cool in summer, warm in winter depending on tog rating.

► Save time on bed-making.

► Non-allergic fillings are useful for asthma sufferers.

► Not as expensive as several blankets.

10.5 TOG DUVET

Outer Fabric: 70% Polyester 30% Cotton
Filling: 100% Hollow Polyester
Weight (approx) 700g/m³
La Tela exterior: 70% Poliester 30% Algodón
El relleno: 100% Poliester de Fibra Hueca
El peso (approx) 700 g/m³

ANDALUCIA S.A.   C.I.F. A-29139037
SUP.LAS RAMPAS S.A.   C.I.F. A-29058328

MACHINE WASH	LAVAR EN PROGRAMMA DE LANA
DO NOT DRY CLEAN	NO EN SECO
DO NOT TWIST OR WRING	NO ESTRUJAR NI RETORCER
WARM TUMBLE DRY	POSIBLE SECADO EN SECADORA

40 wool cycle

Double 200cm x 200cm
STYLE NO 7551331
MADE IN THE EU

Tog rating

Materials Used in the Home

Wood used in the home		
Types of wood	**Properties**	**Uses**
Hardwood Produced from slow-growing, deciduous trees. Examples: Mahogany, teak, ash, maple, beech, oak and cherry.	• Attractively grained. • Strong and durable. • Expensive. • Variety of colours and shades. • Can warp and swell when subjected to moist conditions. • May be stained and varnished for a long-lasting finish.	• Good quality furniture. • Fitted kitchens. • Flooring.
Softwood Produced from fast growing coniferous trees. Examples: Spruce, pine, fir (collectively known as deal).	• Cheaper than hardwoods. • Easier to work with than hardwoods. • Not as strong – more easily marked and scratched. • Can warp and swell.	• Doors and windows. • House construction. • Fitted kitchens, furniture.
Man-made boards • **Plywood** consists of thin sheets of softwood glued together with the grain of each sheet lying at right angles to the next.	• Relatively strong. • May be laminated/veneered with layer of hardwood or plastic. • Cheap.	• Cheaper furniture. • Flooring, e.g. under hardwood floor or tiles.
• **Chipboard** is made from chips of wood glued together under pressure and heat.	• Available in various thicknesses and strengths. • May be laminated. • Warps when wet.	• Laminated furniture. • Kitchen cupboards. • Flooring (as above).
• **Hardboard** is made from compressed wood pulp.	• Cheap. • Lightweight. • Smooth sheets are easy to work with.	• Notice boards. • Bases and backs of cheaper pieces of furniture. • Flooring (as above).
• **Medium-density fibreboard** (MDF) consists of wood fibres glued together under heat and pressure.	• Dense, flat and inflexible. • No grain, easy to work with. • May be painted, veneered or laminated. Caution must be taken when working with MDF because it releases formaldehyde, an irritant to lungs and eyes.	• Furniture. • Storage units. • Display cabinets.

Metals used in the home		
Types of metals	**Properties**	**Uses**
Stainless steel	• Strong and durable. • Non-toxic. • Resistant to rust. • Saucepans may have a copper or aluminium base to aid heat transfer.	• Cutlery. • Kitchen utensils. • Appliance casings. • Countertops. • Furniture.
Iron **Wrought iron**	• Attractive matt finish. • Heavy. • Strong and durable.	• Ornaments, e.g. candle sticks. • Curtain poles. • Garden furniture, light fittings. • Headboards. • Stairs.
Cast iron	• Usually enamelled or finished with non-stick coating. • Heavy and durable – retains heat well.	• Casseroles. • Saucepans.
Tin	• Cheap. • Lightweight. • Rusts easily. • May be treated with a non-stick coating.	• Baking tins and trays.
Aluminium	• Conducts and holds heat well. • Strong and durable. • Can react with acidic foods (lining with enamel/non stick finish prevents this). • May darken and discolour with use.	• Cooking utensils, saucepans. • Internal parts of electrical appliances.

Glass used in the home

Types of glass	Properties	Uses
Soda lime glass	• Jars, bottles, drinking glasses, light bulbs.	• Varies in quality and price.
Toughened safety glass	• Patio doors, glass-panelled doors.	• Rigid and reasonably strong.
		• Translucent.
		• Stain resistant.
Heat-resistant glass (Pyrex)	• Oven-to-table ware.	• Available in various weights and designs.
		• Recyclable.
		• Crystal and stained glass are attractive.
Stained glass	• Ornamental fanlights and inserts in doors and windows.	• Easily chipped, cracked or broken.
		• May be scratched by abrasives.
		• Will not withstand sudden changes in temperature.
Crystal glass	• Good quality glasses, bowls, vases and ornaments.	

Plastics

There are basically two types of plastic: *thermoplastics* and *thermosetting resins*. The distinction is based on their molecular structure and on their response to heating during manufacture.

Plastics used in the home

Thermoplastics	Properties	General properties of plastics
These are soft plastics which can be moulded, melted and remoulded several times. **Examples:** Polytetrafluoroethylene (PTFE): used as non-stick coating on cookware. Polyvinyl chloride (PVC): used in vinyl flooring.	*Thermoplastics* • Fairly soft and flexible. • Soften further on heating, harden on cooling. • Damaged by solvents but not by acids and alkalis. 	• Strong, resilient and lightweight. • Available in a range of colours. • Versatile – many uses. • Cheap. • Hygienic. • Scratched by knives or harsh abrasives. • May discolour. 
Thermosetting resins These are hard plastics which once moulded cannot be reshaped (moulding is irreversible): **Examples:** Melamine – used to laminate counter, table and desktops. Bakelite – used for control knobs on appliances such as cookers. 	*Thermosetting resins* • Hard rigid plastics. • Can withstand very high temperatures. • Blister and crack when overheated. • Damaged by strong acids and alkalis but not by solvents.	**Uses of plastics** • Kitchen utensils. • Casing for electrical appliances: plugs, sockets, switches. • Vinyl paint, wallpaper and flooring. • Packaging. • Insulation. • Toys.

Fabrics

A vast array of natural and synthetic fabrics which vary in colour, pattern and texture are available for use in interior decor. Many of these textiles have been treated with finishes which increase their suitability as household fabrics, for example, water or stain resistance.

Fibres	
Natural fibres	**Synthetic fibres**
Cotton	Polyester
Linen	Viscose
Silk	Acrylic
Wool	

Fabrics used in the home		
Types of fabric	**Properties**	**Uses**
Cotton		
	• Strong and smooth. • Wide range of colours and designs. • Cool and absorbent. • Easy to launder. • Range of price and quality.	• Curtains. • Upholstery. • Bed linen. • Towels. • Tablecloths.
Polyester		
	• Often blended with cotton. • Strong. • Crease resistant. • Cheap.	• Bed linen. • Curtains. • Cushions. • Tablecloths. • Sleeping bags.
Wool		
	• Warm. • Good insulator. • Used in blends, e.g. with acrylic. • Strong. • Absorbent.	• Upholstery. • Curtains. • Cushion covers. • Rugs. • Blankets.

CONTENTS INCLUDE:
- ▶ Sources and sustainability of energy supplies to the home
- ▶ Emissions produced by burning fossil fuels and their effects on the environment
- ▶ Energy inefficiencies in the home

Energy Suppliers to the Home

Energy is supplied to the home through different sources: electricity, gas, oil, solid fuel and renewable energy.

Electricity

Electricity is a form of energy generated in power stations. It is a clean and efficient energy source used in the home for space and water heating, lighting and to power appliances.

Source of electricity

Energy, released chiefly by burning fossil fuels, which powers a generator to produce electricity. The electricity then passes through transformers which alter the strength of the current. The strength (voltage) is reduced to one which is suitable for use in the home.

Moneypoint Power Station, Co. Clare

Sustainability of electricity

Most of the world's electricity is generated by burning fossil fuels. In Ireland, coal, gas, oil and peat are used to produce electricity. A small percentage is supplied by hydropower and wind power. Supplies of fossil fuels are limited and non-renewable. Therefore, renewable sources of energy such as wind, solar power and hydropower need to be used more to ensure the supply of electricity into the future.

> The Irish government aim to produce 40% of electricity from renewable sources by 2020.

Oil

Oil is the principle source of the world's total energy supply. Oil is an efficient and relatively clean fuel producing little waste or pollution when burned. In Irish homes, it is used for cooking and heating space and water.

Source of oil

Oil is a fossil fuel created millions of years ago by decayed plant and animal remains buried between layers of earth and rock, and subjected to heat and pressure. Oil rigs drill for oil on land and at sea. The crude oil must be refined before use.

Oil rig

Sustainability of oil

The world's remaining oil reserves are limited. If consumption was to remain constant, experts predict that supplies would run out around 2040. Although oil exploration is expensive new reserves need to be sourced quickly.

Gas

Natural gas and bottled gas (LPG/liquefied petroleum gas) are increasingly used as sources of energy in Ireland. Natural gas burns completely and does not release any polluting particles into the atmosphere. It requires no refining and little processing before use. Therefore, it is considered the most environmentally friendly of the fossil fuels.

Oil tank

Source of gas

Gas is a fossil fuel which occurs naturally under the sea-bed. Ireland has an indigenous supply of natural gas located off the coast. The gas is piped ashore and is supplied to urban areas through a network of pipes. Rural areas not supplied by this network are reliant on bottled gas. Despite domestic supplies, however, Ireland continues to be dependent on imported natural gas to meet growing demand.

> Gas consumption is measured in cubic metres.

Sustainability of gas

Gas is a non-renewable source of energy therefore gas reserves are finite (limited). Annual consumption worldwide is increasing. If consumption continues to rise, natural gas reserves will be depleted by 2050.

Solid Fuels

Coal, peat/turf and wood are described as solid fuels. The higher the carbon content, the more energy the fuel produces when burned.

Carbon content
Wood 50%
Turf 60%
Coal 88%
Anthracite 94%

Coal

Coal is a relatively cheap fuel producing more heat when burned than turf or wood. However, burning coal produces ash, soot and smoke. It also creates more CO_2 than gas or oil, and more sulphur dioxide and nitrogen oxides. It is therefore a major source of pollution. Smokeless coal such as anthracite burns slowly producing more heat and less smoke, but is more expensive than standard (bituminous) coal.

Source of coal

Coal is a non-renewable fossil fuel which was formed over millions of years in beds and seams under the earth's surface. It must be mined (extracted) from beneath the ground.

Sustainability of coal

Millions of tons of coal are burned each year. While coal supplies are finite, the reserves are large and more evenly distributed throughout the world than either gas or oil. Ireland imports most of its coal, which is used to generate electricity and for heating space and water.

Coal mining

Peat/Turf

Turf is used in Ireland as a fuel for domestic heating and for the generation of electricity. Turf is a relatively cheap fuel, but produces waste in the form of ash, soot and smoke. Briquettes made from dried compressed peat produce more heat than turf and are classified as smokeless fuel.

Peat bog

Source of peat/turf

Peat consists of partially decomposed remains of plants which have accumulated in water-logged areas where climate is relatively cool. Ireland has its own source of peat. Approximately one million tons of turf is cut annually in Ireland. It is machine cut by private individuals and chiefly by Bord na Móna. Bord na Móna supply briquettes and machine turf for residential and industrial use.

Sustainability of peat/turf

While not in any immediate danger of depletion, turf is a non-renewable fossil fuel and supplies will run out in time. It is also a source of pollution. For these reasons Bord na Mona are now researching wind as a renewable and environmentally friendly source of energy.

Wood

Wood has been used as a source of energy for thousands of years. Its use declined with the increased availability of fossil fuels. However, it is still a major source of energy worldwide. Wood burns quickly and does not produce as much heat as fossil fuels. Wood has one major advantage. It is CO_2 neutral. The CO_2 it releases on burning is only the carbon that was absorbed from the atmosphere by the growing tree.

Source of wood

Ireland's terrain and climate make it an ideal location for growing trees. State forests grown by Coillte are an underdeveloped resource at present, but the environmental benefits of wood as a fuel are now being recognised. If wood was developed as an indigenous energy source dependence on fuel imports would decrease.

Sustainability of wood

Wood is a renewable source of energy but the renewing period takes years. Coniferous trees such as fir, spruce and pine are considered to be fast growing but still require years to mature. Wood currently supplies 3% of EU energy. It is envisaged that biomass, including wood, will supply an increasing portion of energy in the future.

Renewable Energy

Sources of renewable energy include solar power, wind, biomass, water and geothermal energy. (See Page 278).

Solar energy

Solar power involves using the sun's rays as a source of energy. A number of systems are used in buildings to get the maximum benefit of solar energy including:

1. *Passive solar architecture:* Involves designing a house in terms of orientation, layout, glazing and insulation to maximise solar gains. Comfort is ensured by controlling ventilation and daylight. Passive solar architecture can reduce heating requirements by up to 80%.

2. *Active solar heating:* Solar collectors covert sunlight into heat. This system is used for heating space but is more commonly used for heating water.

3. *Solar photovoltaic systems:* Involve converting solar energy into electricity. This technology is widely used in consumer goods such as watches, calculators and garden lights. Solar photovoltaic systems are one of the fastest growing sources of renewable energy worldwide.

Solar panels

Sustainability of solar energy
The sun will burn for billions of years and will remain sustainable into the future (its intensity varies). Materials used to make photovoltaic cells are non-renewable but are recyclable, therefore solar energy is sustainable.

Wind Energy

Wind energy involves capturing the energy in the wind and converting it to electricity. Wind power is the fastest growing electricity technology available. Ireland is ideally located to capitalise on wind energy. Ireland's first wind farm was established in 1992 in Co. Mayo. Since then several other wind farms have been set up.

Initial set-up costs are expensive but running costs are low. Care is taken to ensure that wind farms are appropriately situated in an environmentally sensitive manner since they produce noise and some may find their appearance unsightly.

Hydropower

Hydropower involves using the power of flowing water to produce electricity. The sea (tidal power) and fast-flowing rivers supply the energy to hydroelectric power stations.

Hydropower supplies almost 20% of the world's electricity. About 6% of Ireland's electrical needs are supplied by hydroelectric power plants. These plants are mainly large scale ESB power stations such as Ardnacrusha. However, a growing number of smaller independently owned plants are also producing electricity.

While initial outlay is high, hydroelectric power stations are clean and efficient with no polluting emissions. Running costs, once the plant is set up, are relatively low.

Ardnacrusha Hydropower Station

Bioenergy

Bioenergy is energy derived from biomass. Biomass is any organic matter. The types of biomass used to produce bioenergy include wood, organic household waste and animal manure. Bioenergy is used to produce a range of products including electricity, heat and fuels such as ethanol and methane. The use of biomass as an energy source is promoted in EU policy. Development of this industry in Ireland would reduce the dependence on imported fuel and would significantly decrease greenhouse gas emissions.

Emissions from Burning Fuels (4.4)

Emissions produced as a result of burning fossil fuels in the home include:

► Carbon dioxide, water vapour, methane and other gases such as chlorofluorocarbons which cause global warming and climate change.

► Nitrogen oxide and sulphur dioxide which cause acid rain.

► Smoke and smog which cause air pollution.

Effects of Emissions on the Environment

Effects on the environment include:

► Global warming.

► Acid rain.

► Smog and smoke.

Natural gas	
LPG	
Kerosene	
Gas oil	
Peat briquette	
Anthracite	
Smokeless fuel	
Bituminous coal	

0   100   200   300   400

Emissions of CO_2 per unit

Global warming

Global warming occurs when greenhouse gases such as carbon dioxide, nitrous oxide and methane trap heat from the sun in the earth's atmosphere. This heat causes a gradual rise in the earth's surface temperature.

Effects of global warming

1. **The sea levels rise as the polar cap melts.** It is estimated that levels will rise by 1.5 metres in the next 40 years.

2. **Climate change occurs.** Rainfall is increasing in some areas and decreasing in others leading to flooding and droughts. More extreme weather conditions are developing and the climate is less predictable.

3. **Agriculture is affected.** Carbon dioxide, a natural fertiliser, causes crops but also weeds to grow more vigorously making pest control more difficult.

4. **Infectious diseases could spread.** Diseases, such as malaria, could spread to new areas through insects that thrive in warmer weather conditions.

5. **Many species could be endangered.** Animals such as pandas and polar bears are already under threat.

A map of the 'ozone hole' over the Antarctic (white area) caused by global warming

Acid Rain

Sulphur dioxide and nitrogen oxide created by burning fossil fuels combine with rain, forming a weak acid referred to as acid rain.

Effects of acid rain

1. **Damage to crops and plant life:** Acid rain can severely deter the growth of forests because it reduces the soil's pH to a level which is unsuitable for trees.
2. **The erosion of buildings:** Stone, stained glass and paint work may be damaged or destroyed and metal may be corroded.
3. **The depletion of aquatic life in lakes:** Many aquatic organisms cannot tolerate acidic conditions so species become endangered and ecosystems destroyed.

Smog and Smoke (air pollution)

Smog forms when smoke produced by the incomplete combustion of fossil fuels combines in the atmosphere with fog.

Effects of smog and smoke

1. The increased risk of respiratory problems such as bronchitis, asthma, and eye, nose and throat irritation.
2. Reduced levels of sunshine affecting plant growth and crop yields.
3. Increased level of air pollution.

Smog

Reducing emissions from the burning of fuels

▶ Choose gas and smokeless fuels over other fossil fuels.

▶ Make use of renewable sources of energy.

▶ Be an energy efficient consumer. (See Page 282).

▶ Do not waste heat.

▶ Insulate housing well.

▶ Avoid burning rubbish.

Energy Inefficiencies in the Home

Energy inefficiencies can occur in many areas in the home.

Space heating

▶ Boilers and heating systems which are not regularly serviced.

▶ Setting thermostats too high.

▶ Not making use of individual room thermostats and timers.

▶ Heating unused rooms more than required.

Water heating

- ▶ Unlagged pipes and cylinder.
- ▶ Taking baths instead of showers.
- ▶ Turning on the heating system rather than the immersion to heat small amounts of water.
- ▶ Not having the correct setting on the immersion thermostat.
- ▶ Not having a timer on the immersion.
- ▶ Leaking hot taps.
- ▶ Washing items under running water.
- ▶ Choosing unnecessarily high temperature cycles for the dishwasher and washing machine.

Insulation

- ▶ Draughty, ill-fitted doors and windows.
- ▶ Insufficient roof, attic and wall insulation.
- ▶ Not drawing heavy, lined curtains at night.

Lighting

- ▶ Using higher wattage bulbs than necessary.
- ▶ Not using compact fluorescent lamps (CFLs).
- ▶ Leaving on unnecessary lights.

Appliances

- ▶ Not choosing A or B rated energy efficient appliances.
- ▶ Choosing less energy efficient option when using appliances, e.g. using a grill instead of a toaster.
- ▶ Over-running appliances such as food mixers.
- ▶ Using conventional cooking methods instead of microwaving, e.g. to reheat food.
- ▶ Not making full use of economy/half load cycles in dishwashers and washing machines.
- ▶ Using tumble-driers to dry clothes.

Strategies to improve energy efficiency
(See Page 282)

Carbon Footprint
A carbon footprint is a measure of the impact our activities have on the environment, and in particular climate change.

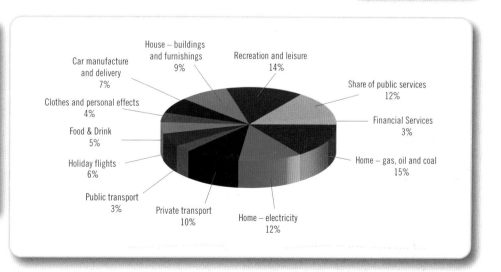

- House – buildings and furnishings 9%
- Recreation and leisure 14%
- Car manufacture and delivery 7%
- Share of public services 12%
- Clothes and personal effects 4%
- Financial Services 3%
- Food & Drink 5%
- Home – gas, oil and coal 15%
- Holiday flights 6%
- Public transport 3%
- Private transport 10%
- Home – electricity 12%

CONTENTS INCLUDE:

▶ **Household electricity supply**

▶ **Cold-water supply and storage**

▶ **Domestic central heating system**

▶ **Insulation methods**

▶ **Ventilation methods**

▶ **Household lighting**

Electricity (4.5.1)
Household Electricity Supply

Electricity enters the house through the service cable. It passes through a sealed fuse box and a meter records consumption. There may also be a second meter to record consumption of night rate/off peak electricity.

The electricity then flows to the main fuse box/consumer unit which contains the main switch and circuit breakers for a number of different circuits within the home. The main switch may be used to turn off all electricity if a fault develops, or if electrical work is being carried out. Each circuit has its own fuse. The amperage of the fuse depends on the type of circuit. A lighting circuit may have a 6-amp fuse, whereas a circuit for an immersion heater requires a 20-amp fuse.

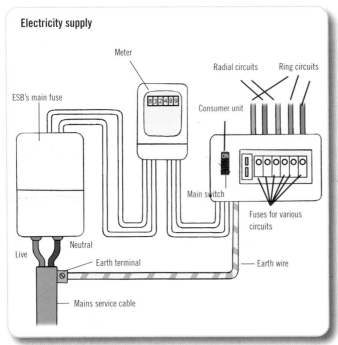

Electricity supply

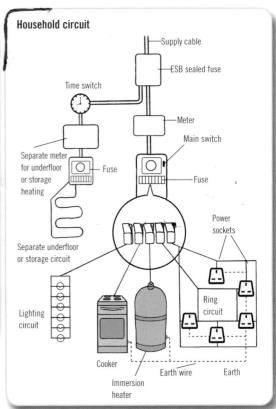

Household circuit

Ring circuits

▶ Socket ring circuits consist of an electrical wire leading from the consumer unit to a number of sockets and back again to the consumer unit. Each circuit has its own fuse, usually 35 amp.

▶ Lighting ring circuits require a 6-amp fuse and serve several light switches.

▶ Some household appliances require a separate individual circuit referred to as a **radial circuit**. These are used for more powerful appliances, such as a cooker or immersion heater, which require stronger fuses.

Electrical terms

▶ *Electricity:* A form of energy resulting from the <u>flow of charged particles of atoms</u>.

▶ *Current:* The flow of electricity. It is measured in units called amps/amperes.

▶ *Amperage:* A measure of the rate at which electricity flows to an appliance. It is determined by the amount of energy used by an appliance, e.g. electricity will flow to a vacuum cleaner at 1 amp.

$$\text{Amperage} = \frac{\text{wattage}}{\text{voltage}}$$

▶ *Voltage:* A measure of the electrical force driving the current and is expressed in volts. Standard Irish voltage is 230 volts. – (120 America)

▶ *Wattage:* The amount of electrical power used by an appliance and is measured in watts, e.g. a 100 watt bulb uses 100 watts of electricity.
1,000 watts = 1 kilowatt.

$$\text{Wattage} = \text{amperage} \times \text{voltage}$$

▶ *Kilowatt per hour (kWh):* A unit of electrical consumption/unit of electricity.

▶ *Conductor:* Material which <u>offers little resistance to the flow of electricity</u>. A conductor allows electricity to flow through it easily. Metals and water are good conductors.

▶ *Insulator:* Material which offers resistance to the flow of electricity (<u>bad conductors</u>). Good insulators include plastic, rubber and air.

Costing

Bills, issued every <u>two months</u>, are calculated on the basis of a <u>meter reading</u>. There are three elements involved in costing:

1. *Standing charge:* This covers the <u>maintenance of the electricity network</u> and costs such as <u>meter reading</u> and <u>the issuing of bills.</u> The standing charge is <u>higher in rural areas than in urban areas.</u>

2. *Unit charge:* The amount of electricity the household uses is recorded in units. <u>One unit</u> is equivalent to <u>1,000 watts</u> of electricity used for <u>1 kilowatt-hour (kWh).</u>

3. *Public service obligations (PSO) levy:* This is a levy used to cover the cost of purchase by the ESB of some sources of electricity, e.g. from generating stations that use renewable sources of energy.

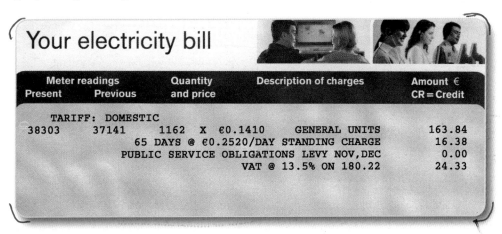

Your electricity bill

Meter readings Present	Previous	Quantity and price	Description of charges	Amount € CR = Credit
TARIFF: DOMESTIC				
38303	37141	1162 X €0.1410	GENERAL UNITS	163.84
		65 DAYS @ €0.2520/DAY	STANDING CHARGE	16.38
		PUBLIC SERVICE OBLIGATIONS LEVY NOV,DEC		0.00
			VAT @ 13.5% ON 180.22	24.33

Electrical Safety Devices

Fuses

A fuse is a <u>deliberate weak link in</u> an electrical circuit. It is a safety device. A fuse contains a thin <u>piece of wire which forms part of an</u> <u>electrical circuit.</u> If a fault develops the wire will melt or break cutting off the current. Different strength fuses are used for different circuits:

Fuses		
Disc colour	**Strength**	**Circuit**
Green	6 amp	Lights
Red	10 amp	Lights
Blue	20 amp	Water heater, storage heater
Black	35 amp	Socket outlets – ring
		Cooker
		Electric shower

 A blown fuse may be caused by:

▶ A <u>faulty appliance</u> such as a toaster or kettle with a faulty thermostat.

▶ Overloading an electrical circuit – using too many appliances.

▶ Faulty or incorrect wiring.

A blown fuse must be replaced with a fuse of the same strength.

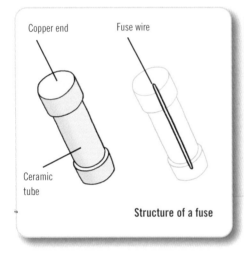

Structure of a fuse

13-amp fuse

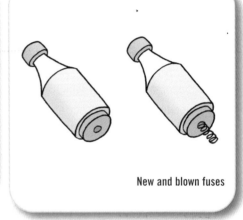

New and blown fuses

Miniature circuit breakers (MCBs)

Most modern household installations have <u>miniature circuit breakers</u> instead of fuses. An MCB also acts as a <u>safety device</u>, 'tripping' and cutting off the current, if a fault develops. An MCB can be reset when the fault is identified and repaired.

Residual current device (RCD)

A residual current device is an <u>additional safety feature found in modern</u> <u>household installations.</u> It can detect a fault in an electrical circuit, such as in an electrical shower, and immediately cuts off the current from the faulty circuit.

Earthing

Normally, electricity flows through the live wire to all electrical appliances as required and returns to its source through the neutral/return wire. If a fault developed, allowing the live wire to come into contact with metal such as the outer casing of a dishwasher or washing machine, anyone who touched the appliance would be in danger of electrocution. <u>Earthing</u> prevents such accidents by carrying electricity from the faulty appliance safely to earth.

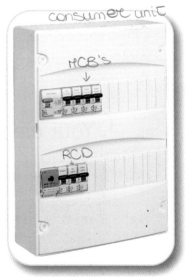

Miniature circuit breakers

Electrical Safety

Although the number of fatal accidents involving electricity in Ireland is small, care must be taken in the home to ensure electrical safety.

Appliance safety

1. Buy appliances which carry a safety or approval mark (See Page 273).
2. Before using a new appliance read the instructions carefully and follow the manufacturers directions for use.
3. Ensure that plugs are correctly wired and replace immediately if defective in any way, e.g. if casing is cracked.
4. Treat flexes with care – do not pull the flex while working with appliances, examine for signs of wear and tear and replace (do not repair) if necessary.
5. Extra care must be taken when using electrical appliances outdoors such as an electric lawn mower.

Kitchen safety

Electricity, water, hot surfaces and trailing flexes combine to make the kitchen an area of potential danger.

1. Never handle sockets, plugs or electrical appliances with wet hands.
2. Do not allow flexes to trail across the cooker hob or sink.
3. Do not use adapters or extension leads to overload sockets.
4. Do not use or attempt to repair a faulty appliance.
5. Switch off or unplug all appliances before cleaning.

Bathroom safety

Special precautions apply to wiring in bathrooms because of the high moisture content.

1. No socket outlets other than shaver outlets are allowed in a bathroom.
2. Portable electric appliances such as heaters or hairdriers should not be used in a bathroom even if plugged in outside the room.
3. Only pull cord switches are suitable for wall heaters or strip lights.
4. Electric showers require their own radial circuit and a residual current device.

Bedroom safety

1. Read and follow manufacturers instructions for electric blankets.
2. Check electric blanket regularly for signs of wear and do not use or attempt to repair a defective blanket.
3. Keep portable heaters away from bedding and clothing.
4. Keep heaters free from dust and fluff.

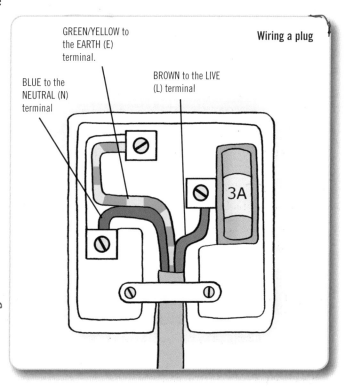

GREEN/YELLOW to the EARTH (E) terminal.

BROWN to the LIVE (L) terminal

BLUE to the NEUTRAL (N) terminal

Wiring a plug

3A

Water (4.5.2)

Cold-water Supply

A supply of pure uncontaminated water to the home is essential. Local authorities are responsible for the water supply in towns and cities.

Source of water

Water source

The water supply for the home begins as rain. Sunshine causes moisture to evaporate from the oceans. This water vapour forms clouds and returns to the earth as rain, sleet or hail. Rain that falls on high ground forms streams and rivers which flow into lakes. Many lakes situated on high ground are natural reservoirs storing water for local authority distribution. Man-made reservoirs are also constructed.

Some rural areas depend on wells or springs for their water supply. Rain water seeps through the ground until it reaches non-porous rock. The water then accumulates and forms a spring or, if drilled, a well.

Water treatment

Water must be treated to remove impurities and make it fit for human consumption. During storage in the reservoir the water is purified by fresh air, sunlight and plants which produce oxygen (algae). As the water flows from the reservoir to houses it passes through the treatment plant. At the treatment plant the following processes are carried out:

► *Screening:* Water is screened to remove any floating debris.

► *Sedimentation:* Chemicals are added which collect any dirt, which then sinks to the bottom.

► *Filtration:* The water then passes through filter-beds of sand and stones to remove any suspended matter.

► *Chlorination:* Chlorine is added to kill micro-organisms.

► *Fluoridation:* Fluoride is added to strengthen teeth.

► *Softening:* Chloride of lime is added to soften the water.

► *Testing:* The treated water is tested for purity and quality and then stored in the 'high storage' reservoir.

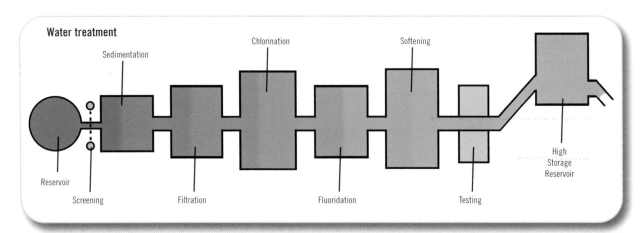

Household Water Supply

Local authority supply

Water flows from the storage reservoir to towns and cities in large pipes called mains. A service pipe supplies each building. A valve known as a stopcock, situated outside each building, allows water to be turned off during repairs. The service pipe usually enters the house under the kitchen sink where there is another stopcock. This pipe supplies the kitchen sink with fresh drinking water while another branch fills the storage tank or cistern in the attic. This storage tank supplies all the other cold taps, toilets, the hot press tank and the back boiler. Sinks in utility rooms are usually connected directly to the mains.

Wells

In rural areas, water for household supply can sometimes be sourced from deep wells. Any water for human consumption is tested and treated for harmful impurities. The wells are lined with steel or concrete to prevent contamination from the soil. The water is pumped into the building through a pipe by an electric pump. Water purifiers are usually fitted to remove suspended impurities.

The local authority ensures safe water supply by:

- Treating water at water treatment plants.
- Quality checks carried out by local authorities.
- Strict building and planning regulations to prevent contamination of the fresh water supply.
- Safe waste-water and sewage disposal systems.
- Investigation of reported effluent discharge into waterways.

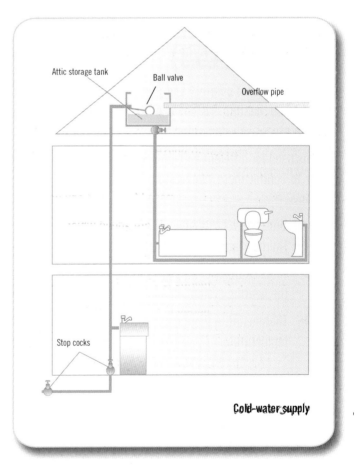

Cold-water supply

Water storage

Water is stored in the storage tank in the attic. The high level gives pressure to supply the system. The tank is made of heavy duty plastic and holds approximately 230 litres of water. A ball valve controls the level of water in the tank.

Attic storage tanks are fitted with an overflow pipe leading to the outside in case the ball valve fails to work. Insulating the tank and water pipes in the attic prevents the water from freezing and a cover keeps out the dirt and dust. Water from the storage tank is not recommended for drinking.

Hard water

As water seeps through soil and stones it absorbs minerals which cause hardness. There are two types of hardness:

▶ *Temporary hardness* caused by calcium and magnesium bicarbonates is easily removed by boiling.

▶ *Permanent hardness* is caused by calcium and magnesium sulphates. It requires the addition of washing soda, bath salts or a commercial water softener, e.g. limescale tablets.

A water softening unit can be fitted to the kitchen sink, which removes both temporary and permanent hardness.

The effects of hard water

▶ Build up of limescale in water pipes, boilers, kettles and washing machines.

▶ Difficult to produce a lather with soap and shampoo.

▶ Results in dry skin and dull hair.

▶ Scum formation on baths and sinks.

Heating (4.5.3)

Levels of thermal comfort and their control

An efficient heating system can contribute greatly to the comfort of a home without excessively damaging the environment or wasting financial resources.

Rooms used for different activities within a home require varying temperatures. In order to control these temperatures two devices are commonly used in heating systems:

Living rooms:	17–21°C
Kitchens :	15–19°C
Bedrooms:	12–16°C
Bathrooms:	16–19°C
Corridors:	13–15°C

(i) Timers/programmers.

(ii) Thermostats.

▶ Timer: A timer is an electrically operated device used to switch the heating system on and off at pre-determined times.

▶ Thermostat: A thermostat is a device used to control temperature.

Underlying principle of a thermostat

The working principle of a thermostat is based on the scientific principle of thermal expansion, i.e. solids expand when heated and contract on cooling.

Electric thermostats consist of a bimetal strip made of brass and invar. These two metals expand at different rates on heating. This causes the metal strip to bend, breaking the electrical circuit and switching off the appliance. On cooling the bimetal strip returns to its original shape switching the appliance on again.

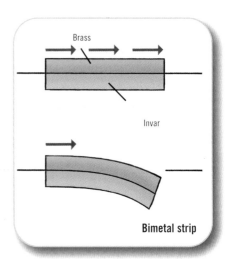

Bimetal strip

Brass expands easily on heating. Invar expands only slightly on heating.

Gas thermostats

Gas thermostats consist of an invar rod fixed within a brass tube. As the temperature rises the brass tube expands pulling the invar rod with it. A valve at the end of the invar rod restricts the gas flow. On cooling the brass contracts and the valve opens again, allowing more gas to flow.

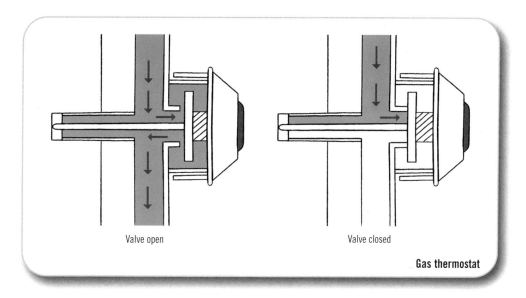

Valve open   Valve closed

Gas thermostat

Thermostatic devices

The following thermostatic devices are used to control thermal levels:

▶ A ***room thermostat*** is mounted on the wall of a room and set to the desired temperature. Room thermostats detect the surrounding temperature and respond by turning the heating on when the temperature falls below the desired level, and off when the required temperature is reached.

▶ A ***boiler thermostat*** is connected to the central heating boiler. It controls the temperature of the water in the boiler. When the desired temperature is reached the thermostat switches off the boiler. When the water temperature falls the boiler restarts.

▶ A ***thermostatic radiator valve (TRV)*** is fitted to an individual radiator. It opens and closes a valve allowing or preventing the flow of water into the radiator. It has a number of different temperature settings that can be adjusted to suit the room in which it is used.

Use of thermostats

- Ovens
- Kettles
- Deep fat fryers
- Immersion water heaters
- Electric blankets
- Washing machines
- Tumble-driers
- Toasters
- Irons
- Room thermostats
- Thermostatic radiator valves
- Boiler or central heating systems

Room thermostat

Thermostatic radiator valve

Zoned heating

Zoned heating systems allow separate parts of the house to be heated independently, e.g. the downstairs living area can be heated without heating the upstairs sleeping area.

Heating options

Homes can be heated by one or a combination of the following systems:

Storage heater and oil-filled radiator

▶ **Full central heating:** The whole house is heated from a central source, e.g. a boiler with radiators. The boiler may be fuelled by oil, gas or solid fuel. Solar energy may also be used.

▶ **Partial central heating:** This system is used to heat part of the house, usually the most frequently used rooms, e.g. living room and kitchen. Other spaces, e.g. bedrooms rely on residual heat and local heaters.

▶ **Background heating:** This method heats the whole house to approximately 13°C. Local heating, e.g. an open fire in the living room is required to increase the heat to a more comfortable level. Electric storage heaters are often used to provide background heating.

Gas fire

▶ **Local heating:** Individual heaters are used, e.g. an open fire in the living room, a stove in the kitchen and electric or gas heaters in other rooms when required.

▶ **Passive solar heating:** South-facing rooms with large windows heat up during the day, but an additional form of heating is usually also necessary.

Choosing a heating system

There are different factors to consider when choosing a heating system.

1. **Costs involved:** The installation cost, running and maintenance costs. Electric storage heaters are easier and therefore cheaper to install than a wet central heating system; solid fuel is cheaper than gas and boilers require servicing regularly.

2. **Convenience:** Most central heating systems operate automatically using timers and thermostats, solid fuel involves manual labour.

3. **Comfort level and control:** The heating system should provide sufficient thermal comfort and the temperature should be controllable, e.g. background heating requires supplementary heating and it is difficult to control the heating output of an open fire.

Portable electric heaters

4. **The size of house:** Larger houses often require more elaborate heating systems.

5. **Water heating:** Some heating systems heat the household water supply, e.g. wet central heating system. Whereas electric storage heating requires a separate water heating system.

6. **Impact on the environment:** Gas and smokeless fuels produce less pollution, wood is a renewable source of energy. Energy efficient systems are less damaging to the environment. (Sufficient insulation greatly reduces energy costs.)

7. **Safety:** is a priority in housing for the elderly, people with disabilities and families with young children.

> **S.E.I. grant** is available to home owners who intend to update to a renewable energy heating system.

Home Heating Systems

A wet central heating system

This type of system usually incorporates a boiler fuelled by oil, gas or solid fuel, small bore pipes (narrow diameter) and radiators. It uses water as the heat transfer medium and is fitted with an electric pump to assist the circulation of water.

▶ Water is heated in the boiler.

▶ The hot water leaves the top of the boiler and travels in a narrow pipe known as the heat exchanger through the cylinder indirectly heating the domestic hot-water supply. Then it returns to the boiler.

▶ Another pipe leaves the top of the boiler and goes to the radiators giving out the heat from the flowing water.

▶ This pipe then returns to the boiler bringing the water back for re-heating and the cycle begins again.

▶ An expansion pipe carries overheated water to the expansion tank in the attic.

▶ A pipe leading from the expansion tank back down to the boiler replaces any evaporated water.

Central heating systems	
Wet central heating systems	**Source of energy**
Water circulating through pipes, e.g. radiators or underfloor heating.	Oil, gas, solid fuel, geothermal energy, solar energy.
Dry central heating systems	**Source of energy**
Storage heaters Underfloor heating Warm air central heating Air conditioning	Oil, gas, electricity, geothermal energy

> The central heating system is an enclosed system with the same water travelling from the boiler to the radiators and back to the boiler.

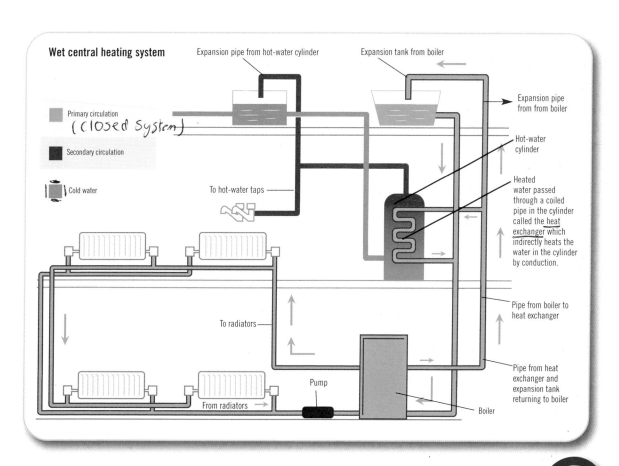

Wet central heating system

Heat transfer

- **Conduction:** Heat travels from molecule to molecule along a solid object.
- **Convection:** Hot air/water rises, cool air/water falls setting up convection currents.
- **Radiation:** Direct rays of heat from the source to the nearest solid object.
- **Thermal expansion:** The expansion of materials when heated.

Scientific principles underlying wet system

▶ The water in the boiler is heated as **convection** currents are set up.

▶ **Thermal expansion** allows the heated water to flow upwards to the hot-water cylinder and overheated water to flow up into the expansion tank in the attic.

▶ Space heating occurs because **convection** currents are set up in rooms by the heat from the radiators.

▶ Radiators give off a little **radiant** heat.

Advantages of wet central heating system

- Heats domestic hot water supply
- Easy to operate and control
- May be zoned
- May be operated using renewable energy

Conduction is not a factor in space heating, but is the main reason why insulation is required as glass and concrete blocks are good conductors of heat.

A dry central heating system

Electric storage heaters are compact, slimline heaters in a fixed position. They have an outer casing of enamelled steel with a metal grille for heat output. Inside these heaters are fireclay or concrete blocks with heating elements running through them. A layer of insulation surrounds the blocks. The heaters are connected to a night-rate electricity meter. Electricity heats the elements at night time. The blocks hold the heat and gradually release it during the following day. They have an output or boost control which adjusts the daily heat output, and an on/off button.

Scientific principles underlying the dry system

▶ The blocks heat up by **conduction** as the elements are embedded in them.

▶ The heat output sets up **convection** currents creating space heating (thermal expansion).

▶ A small amount of heat is **radiated** from the storage heater.

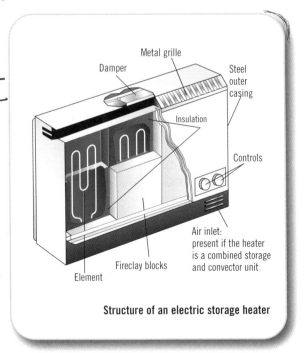

Structure of an electric storage heater

Insulation (4.5.4)

The purpose of insulating a house is to reduce heat loss. Insulation will not eliminate all heat loss but can reduce it considerably, by as much as two-thirds.

Underlying principles of insulation

Insulating materials which are poor conductors of heat are used throughout the house to prevent heat loss. Insulating materials include air, polystyrene, fibreglass and fabric.

Advantages of insulation

1. Reduces heat loss.
2. Saves energy, reducing heating costs.
3. Results in less damage to the environment.
4. Acts as a noise insulator.
5. Creates a more comfortable living space.

Methods of insulation
Attic and roof insulation

Attic and roof insulation is very important because as heat rises a considerable amount can escape if the attic is not insulated. Building regulations now require that all new houses have a minimum amount of attic insulation. Extra layers can easily be inserted.

Types of attic insulation

▶ *Fibre blanket insulation:* Strips of insulation blanket made from glass fibre or mineral fibre are laid between the joists in the attic.

▶ *Loose fill insulation:* Pellets of polystyrene or vermiculite are poured between the joists in the attic.

▶ *Foam insulation:* Foam is sprayed between the roof rafters and solidifies. This method of insulation is often used in attic conversions.

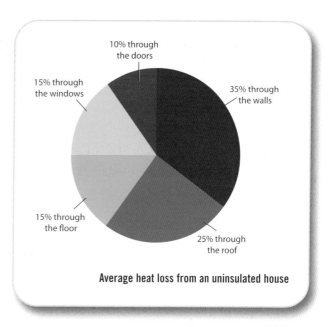

10% through the doors
15% through the windows
35% through the walls
15% through the floor
25% through the roof

Average heat loss from an uninsulated house

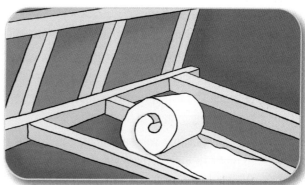

Fibre blanket insulation

Loose fill insulation

The cold-water storage tank should be insulated to prevent it from freezing. The space directly underneath the tank should be left free of insulation. The cold-water pipes in the attic also require insulation, e.g. split foam insulation.

Wall insulation

As wall space is usually the largest surface area of a house wall insulation is very important. Building regulations now demand that all new houses have a minimum requirement of wall insulation.

Types of wall insulation

▶ Cavity walls: These walls are built with two layers of blocks, 5–10 cm apart. The air in the space acts as an insulator. Polystyrene sheets are also inserted at the building stage for extra insulation. In older houses polystyrene foam can be pumped into the cavity which then solidifies.

▶ Solid walls: This insulation is usually internal.

　1.　Blanket insulation, e.g. fibreglass or rockwool is inserted into a wooden frame on the wall. A layer of plasterboard covers the insulation.

　2.　Insulation sheets are attached to the walls and then covered with a plasterboard layer.

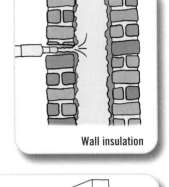

Wall insulation

Floor insulation

▶ Any gaps between floorboards or around skirting-boards should be filled.

▶ Fitted carpets with thick underlay help to prevent heat loss through the floor.

Outside　　Inside

Air/Argon gas

Double glazing

Window and door insulation

▶ Well-fitting doors and windows help to prevent draughts.

▶ The use of double-glazing greatly reduces heat loss through windows. Double-glazed windows are made up of two sheets of glass with a space between them. The space can be filled with air, which is an insulator, or argon gas which further reduces heat loss. The use of low emissivity glass (Low-e) ensures even less conductivity of heat to the outside.

▶ Draught-proofing will save energy and keep the home warmer. Doors and windows can be fitted with draught excluders. There are a variety available on the market including flap excluders, brush excluders, flexible strips, adhesive strips and letterbox draught excluders.

▶ Heavy, lined curtains protect against draughts and may have an extra insulation interlining attached.

▶ Unused fireplaces should be blocked off to prevent heat loss up the chimney.

Hot-water cylinder

Modern, hot-water cylinders are permanently insulated with a spray-on coating of insulation. Older, copper cylinders can be insulated by using a lagging jacket. This is a relatively inexpensive yet efficient method of conserving energy and finances. The hot-water pipes should also be lagged with split foam sleeving.

S.E.I. grants are available to those who wish to improve the energy efficiency of their home.

Split foam insulation

Ventilation (4.5.5)

Ventilation is the removal of stale air and the introduction of fresh air without causing
a draught or significantly lowering the temperature.

Composition of air		
	Fresh	**Stale**
Nitrogen	79%	79%
Oxygen	20.96%	16.96%
Carbon Dioxide	0.04%	4.04%
Water vapour	Varies	Saturated
Impurities	Varies	Microbes, odours, dust, smoke
Temperature	Varies	Varies, but usually warmer than fresh air

All rooms in
new houses
must have a
permanent
vent.

Principle of ventilation

Ventilation is based on the principle of hot air rising (thermal expansion). Outlets are
placed high up on walls, which allows the exit of stale air. Fresh air is drawn in lower
down, e.g. under doors or down chimneys. This sets up convection currents with
gentle continuous movements of air.

**Recommended air
changes per hour:**
Kitchen/bathroom	3
Living room	2
Bedroom	1

Importance of good ventilation

► Provides fresh air for respiration.

► Removes stale air laden with impurities,, e.g. odours.

► Assists combustion, e.g. open fires.

► Controls the humidity levels of the air. *moisture*

► Prevents or reduces condensation.

► Assists in controlling air temperature.

Effects of poor ventilation

► Poor concentration, drowsiness, headache and even fainting.

► Increased risk of illness and infection due to the presence of microbes.

► Long-term exposure can result in respiratory diseases, e.g. bronchitis.

► Condensation builds up which will eventually cause structural damage.

Humidity

The level of humidity is a measure of the amount of moisture in the air. As warm air
holds more moisture, kitchens and bathrooms often have high levels of humidity.
Activities that increase humidity are:

All bathrooms without a
window must be fitted
with an extractor fan.

► Cooking

► Showering/bathing

► Washing clothes

► Tumble-drying clothes

► Breathing

► Use of some heaters, e.g. free-standing gas heaters

Problems associated with high humidity levels
- ▶ Increased condensation.
- ▶ Aggravation of bronchial conditions.
- ▶ Drowsiness.

A good system of ventilation in the home will usually control the level of humidity in the air. However, an electrical appliance known as a dehumidifier is available. This appliance draws in moist air, condenses it, collecting the water in a bottle enclosed in the dehumidifier. It then releases drier air into the room. The water bottle must be emptied occasionally.

Dehumidifier

Some heating systems, e.g. electrical and central heating may dry out the air. Low humidity levels may irritate the nose and throat and cause sinus aggravation. The use of a simple humidifier, e.g. a container of water attached to or close by heaters or radiators can alleviate this problem.

Condensation

Condensation occurs when warm humid air meets cold air or cold surfaces, e.g. single-glazed window panes. The water vapour condenses into water droplets.

Double-glazed windows

Effects of condensation
- ▶ Mould growth on walls and ceilings.
- ▶ Damage to wall-coverings and paint work.
- ▶ Rusting of metals.
- ▶ Musty, damp smell.
- ▶ Bronchial problems.

Preventing condensation
- ▶ Adequate ventilation.
- ▶ Increase ventilation when necessary, e.g. in kitchen and bathrooms.
- ▶ Good insulation.
- ▶ Efficient heating system.
- ▶ Avoid over use of cold glassy surfaces.
- ▶ Make use of hydroscopic (water absorbing) materials in soft furnishings.
- ▶ Vent tumble-driers to the outside or use condenser driers.

Sash window

Methods of ventilation	
Natural	**Artificial**
Windows	Extractor fans
Doors	Cooker hoods
Room vents	Air conditioning
Open fireplaces	

Air vent

Natural ventilation

Natural ventilation involves openings to the outside whereby stale air leaves the room and is replaced by fresh air. Examples of natural ventilation include:

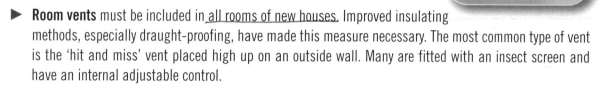

▶ **Windows** which can be opened to varying degrees in order to provide ventilation.

▶ **Doors** may be left open to provide ventilation but often result in draughts and dramatic heat loss.

▶ **Room vents** must be included in all rooms of new houses. Improved insulating methods, especially draught-proofing, have made this measure necessary. The most common type of vent is the 'hit and miss' vent placed high up on an outside wall. Many are fitted with an insect screen and have an internal adjustable control.

▶ **Trickle vents** are commonly used in window frames.

▶ **Air bricks** were often used in older houses to provide ventilation, and are still used below ground-floor level, to prevent dry and wet rot.

▶ **Open fireplaces** are a natural form of ventilation as stale air leaves the room up the chimney and fresh air is drawn in to replace it.

Artificial ventilation

Artificial ventilation involves using mechanical means to bring about the air change. This type of ventilation is usually used where more frequent and rapid changes are necessary, for example in bathrooms and kitchens. Methods of artificial ventilation include extractor fans and cooker hoods.

Extractor fans

Extractor fans are positioned high up on an outside wall, in the ceiling or in the window of a bathroom. They operate by electricity and are activated by the light switch or a pull cord.

Construction

Extractor fans are made up of an outer casing of strong plastic or aluminium. Inside is an electric motor and rotating blades. The blades are enclosed behind louvre shutters which close when the fan is not in use. Some extractor fans have a pull cord switch.

Working principle

When the fan is turned on the shutters open and the electric motor rotates the blades. The high speed of the rotation creates suction drawing stale air out of the room. This is naturally replaced by fresh air.

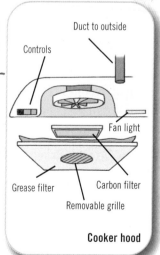

Duct to outside

Controls

Fan light

Grease filter

Carbon filter

Removable grille

Cooker hood

Cooker hoods

A cooker hood is a canopy-shaped fan fitted over the hob of a cooker to expel cooking odours and water vapour. Cooker hoods may be ducted to the outside or may be ductless.

Ducted cooker hoods

Ducted cooker hoods are fitted onto an outside wall to ensure the shortest and most direct route to the outside. This type of cooker hood is made up of a metal canopy with a removable grille at the bottom. Inside the canopy are filters to remove odours and grease and an electrically operated fan. A hole cut in the external wall allows odours and vapour to exit.

Cooker hood filters should be replaced periodically.

Ductless cooker hoods

Ductless cooker hoods are used when there is no access to the outside. They are similar in construction to the ducted cooker hood, but do not have a duct leading to the outside.

Both hoods are fitted with a light to illuminate the hob and have a variable speed switch.

Working principle

Cooker hoods operate by electricity. When turned on an electric motor rotates a fan. The high-speed fan creates suction, drawing in the odour-laden, warm, greasy air. The filters purify the air. In the ducted hood the air is expelled to the outside. The ductless hood recirculates the air back into the kitchen.

Lighting (4.5.6)

Importance of good lighting

An efficient lighting system is essential in the home for the following reasons:

- ▶ To give light, allowing the performance of many activities.
- ▶ To prevent eyestrain.
- ▶ To prevent accidents.
- ▶ To create atmosphere and mood.
- ▶ To enhance design features, objects and interior decoration.

Classification of Lighting

Lighting can be classified into two categories: (i) *natural lighting* and (ii) *artificial lighting*.

Natural lighting

Natural light/daylight enters the home through windows, glass doors and glass blocks. Certain factors influence the amount of natural light in a room:

Velux windows

- ▶ **Aspect:** Rooms facing south get more natural light than north-facing rooms.
- ▶ **Colour scheme:** Dark colours absorb light, whereas pale, light colours reflect light.
- ▶ **Windows:** Number and size in a room affects the amount of natural light present.
- ▶ **Materials used:** Mirrors, glossy ceramic tiles and stainless steel increase the amount of natural light as they reflect light, whereas textured fabrics such as carpets and upholstery absorb light.

Artificial lighting

Classification of artificial lighting	
Tungsten bulbs	**Fluorescent bulbs**
Tungsten filament bulb	Fluorescent tube
Tungsten halogen bulb	Compact fluorescent lights (CFLs)

Tungsten bulbs

The light produced by tungsten bulbs is called incandescent light and is closer to natural light than fluorescent light.

Tungsten filament bulb

▶ The tungsten filament bulb is made of pearl, clear or coloured glass filled with a mixture of nitrogen and argon gases. A coiled filament of tungsten wire runs through the bulb. When switched on electricity flows through the filament causing it to glow white hot. This is because of the resistance of the thin wire.

▶ These bulbs are available in a range of shapes and strengths (determined by wattage – 25w to 200w). They give approximately 1,000 hours of light.

▶ Both bayonet cap and screw-in bulbs are available.

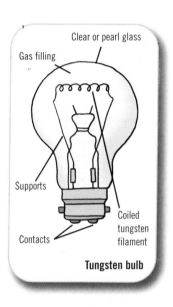

Clear or pearl glass
Gas filling
Supports
Contacts
Coiled tungsten filament

Tungsten bulb

Tungsten halogen bulb

▶ A halogen bulb is usually smaller and is made of quartz glass. The gas inside includes halogen elements.

▶ These bulbs give a greater light output and they last three times longer than the tungsten filament bulb.

▶ They produce an attractive light, which resembles sunlight, but are more expensive to run.

▶ Energy saving halogen bulbs are now available.

Fluorescent bulbs

The light produced by fluorescent bulbs is called fluorescent light.

Fluorescent tube

Fluorescent bulbs are tubular in shape and available in various lengths (30 cm–2.5 m), of different wattage. They may be straight, circular or looped.

A fluorescent bulb consists of a glass tube. The inside of the glass tube is coated with phosphor and contains argon gas and mercury. When electricity flows electrodes at each end of the glass tube heat up. This heat causes the mercury to vaporise in the argon gas. These gases then react with the phosphor coating on the inside of the tube causing it to glow.

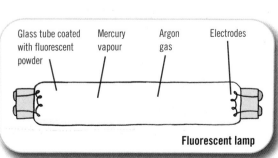

Glass tube coated with fluorescent powder
Mercury vapour
Argon gas
Electrodes

Fluorescent lamp

Compact fluorescent lights (CFLs)

Compact fluorescent lights were designed to replace the fluorescent tubes which were not suitable replacements for tungsten filament bulbs or for decorative lighting. They are made more compact by looping the tube a number of times.

They work in the same way as the traditional fluorescent tube and are available in different strengths, sizes and shapes and may be fitted with an outer cover which improves their appearance.

Compact fluorescent bulbs

Energy efficient lighting

► Replacing tungsten filament bulbs with CFLs has a significant effect in reducing lighting costs.

► Although more expensive than filament bulbs compact fluorescent lights last eight to ten times longer therefore the extra initial cost is eliminated.

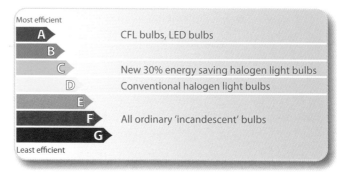

► They use only one-fifth of the electricity for an equivalent amount of light.

► They are ideally suited for use in locations where plenty of light is required for long periods.

► CFLs are generally unsuitable for use with dimmer switches and are slow to light fully.

Properties of light and their application

Light travels in a straight line until it meets an obstacle. The light is then either reflected, absorbed, diffused, refracted or dispersed.

► *Reflected light*: When light falls on a shiny or pale coloured surface it is reflected. This is evident with glazed ceramic tiling, mirrors and pale colours used in decorating.

► *Absorbed light:* Dark colours absorb light. A darkly-painted room will appear smaller because of the absorption of light. Matt surfaces also absorb far more light than shiny surfaces.

► *Diffused light:* When light shines on a dull surface or passes through a translucent substance it is diffused or scattered in many directions. This property is utilised with opaque lamp shades and indirect lighting, i.e. shining a light on a wall which is then reflected and diffused back into the room.

► *Refracted light:* When rays of light pass through very thick glass they bend, e.g. light shining through a glass block.

► *Dispersed light:* When light passes through a prism or crystal it is broken down into its component colours, e.g. using crystal lampshades.

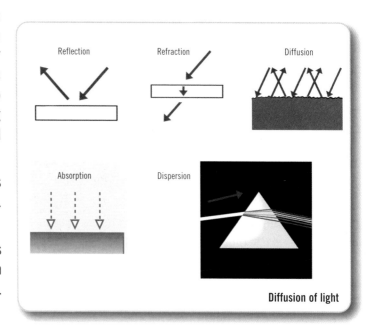

Diffusion of light

Principles for planning a lighting system

As lighting is the presentation of space there are many principles to consider when planning a lighting system.

1. The key to a successful lighting system is to plan or design it at the earliest possible stage preferably during construction to allow for the installation of light fittings and sockets.

2. Always include:
   – general lighting, i.e. central ceiling light;
   – task lighting, e.g. desk lamp or spotlights on kitchen counters;
   – accent lighting to create interest and focus, e.g. to enhance a fireplace, or picture.

3. Ensure sufficient lighting for the size and function of the room. Kitchens will have more task lighting whereas accent lighting will feature more in living rooms.

4. Avoid glare which causes discomfort and can lead to eyestrain. Make use of shades, indirect lighting and pearl bulbs.

5. Include a number of sources of light. Natural lighting may be an important source during daytime but a combination of natural and artificial sources make both a practical and an aesthetic contribution.

6. Allow for flexibility so that the lighting system within a room can be changed, e.g. moving table lamps, making use of dimmer switches, rotating spotlights.

7. Maintenance is an important consideration. All lights and light fittings should be easy to clean and replacement parts should be easily obtained.

8. Safety should always be considered when planning a lighting system.

Contemporary lighting

Central lights	Wall brackets	Table/desk lamps	Ceiling lights	Floor lamps	Outdoor/garden
Central pendant Semiflush pendant Flush central light Chandelier Rise and fall lights	Wall washers Picture lights Swivel lights Wall spots	Huge variety of stands/shades available Pivot action lamps Flexible stem lamps Touch lights	Eyeball spots Recessed lights Track and flexi-track lighting	Standard lamps Floor pivots Two light standard lamps Uplighter/downlighter	Wall brackets Column lighting Sensor lighting Solar powered lights Fountain lights

Lighting Safety

▶ All light fittings should be properly installed.

▶ Use fuses of the correct strength and recommended bulb wattage.

▶ Allow space between lamp shades and bulbs.

▶ Switches should be easily accessible.

▶ Bathroom light switches should be outside the door.

▶ Danger areas (i.e. staircases, exterior paths and steps) should be well lit to prevent accidents.

Contemporary Lighting Developments

▶ Compact fluorescent lights

▶ Low energy halogen bulbs

▶ Dimmer switches – vary the amount of light produced.

▶ Changing the colour of the lighting of a room at the push of a button – aided by computer technology.

▶ Furniture lighting such as light sensitive LED (Light Emitting Diode) cluster tables.

▶ Lights accenting curtains or special wall finishes.

▶ The use of fibre optics in water features.

Blue light setting – the lighting in this room changes colour

Furniture lighting

Fluorescent light emphasises the wall finish

Energy saving light

ELECTIVE TWO
SOCIAL STUDIES

This elective is an extension of the Social Studies section of the core with particular links to the following areas:

Chapter 17
- Changes affecting modern family structures.
- Family functions.

Chapter 19
- The family as a caring unit.
- Social factors affecting changing roles of family members.
- Economic factors affecting changing roles.

Links may also be made between this elective and the Resource Management and Consumer Studies sections of the core.

CONTENTS INCLUDE:

The impact of social and economic change on the family in areas such as:

▶ Settlement patterns
▶ Work/leisure
▶ Education

▶ Social welfare
▶ Marriage
▶ Roles within the family

▶ Parenting

Social and economic changes occur for a variety of reasons. These changes are reflected by changes in traditional family roles and behaviour patterns and have had a significant impact on family life over the years. Some of the more influential changes follow.

Change in Settlement Patterns from Rural to Urban

In the early part of the twentieth century the majority of the population lived in rural areas. During the course of the century there was a gradual movement towards urban areas, so that at the beginning of the twenty-first century most people reside in urban areas.

Factors that brought about the migration from rural to urban

- Technology has made farming a less labour intensive activity. Fewer workers are needed on the land so they must earn their living elsewhere.
- Industry and the services sector were concentrated in urban areas so people moved to towns and cities to have more access to employment.
- Urban life can be seen as an attractive way of life with many services, educational opportunities and amenities within easy access.

Impact on family life in rural areas	Impact on family life in urban areas
• Urbanisation leads to population imbalance, rural depopulation and a sense of isolation for the chiefly elderly population who remain behind.	• Services and amenities become concentrated in urban areas.
• Services such as post offices and banks, schools and transport services are cut back.	• Entertainment and leisure facilities are more accessible.
• Fewer amenities are available so that social life declines.	• Increase in air and noise pollution and traffic congestion.
• Younger people leave an area to seek employment. This leads to a fall in marriage and birth rates so that the population continues to decline.	• Educational and health services become inadequate due to rapid population growth.
• Less government funding is put into developing and maintaining rural infrastructure and transport systems, making it a less attractive option for investors so the cycle of unemployment continues.	• Employment opportunities eventually decline due to overpopulation leading to unemployment black spots and subsequent social problems such as drug and alcohol abuse, vandalism and street violence.

Efforts have been made to reverse this trend and to halt population decline in rural areas. These efforts included:

- A policy of redeployment of government departments and state agencies to rural locations.
- Rural resettlement schemes which aimed to move families from urban to more isolated rural areas in the West.

Reduced Working Hours and More Leisure Time

The change to shorter working hours and increased leisure time occurred due to:

1. EU legislation which governs maximum working hours for various occupations and for young people (under 18s). Any extra work is viewed as overtime and must be paid accordingly.

2. Legislation governs minimum holidays and paid leave such as maternity and sick leave. Parental leave (unpaid leave) is also a legal entitlement for parents.

3. The development of the trade union movement which seeks to improve working conditions including reduced working hours.

4. Due to the recent economic decline many people have become unemployed or have had their working hours reduced.

5. The growth in the leisure industry indicates a greater appreciation of the benefits of leisure in reducing work-related stress.

Impact on family life

▶ Reduced working hours/unemployment has resulted in a drop in income for many families and a subsequent change in lifestyle.

▶ Parents have more time to spend with children, leaving them more free to attend sport days, matches, concerts and other events which are important in their children's lives.

▶ Leisure pursuits, such as cycling or hill-walking, can be pursued as a family.

▶ Participation in active leisure pursuits improves health and the fitness level of the whole family and helps to reduce the incidence of obesity.

▶ Mental health benefits as sport and hobbies help to alleviate stress and depression.

Improvement in the Provision of Education

A number of measures greatly improved the education system and made it more accessible to all. These measures included:

- ▶ Free education – introduced in the late 1960s.

- ▶ Government investment in school building, equipment, staffing and running costs.

- ▶ School transport systems particularly in rural areas.

- ▶ The introduction of a range of courses at second level to accommodate a variety of ability levels.

- ▶ State financial assistance such as means-tested grants for university students.

- ▶ Adult and second chance education encouraged in government policy.

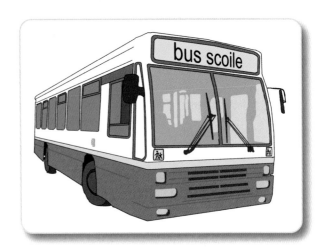

Impact on family life

- ▶ Education is more accessible to all. State assistance such as the back to school allowance and grants for third level help to ease financial pressure for the less well off.

- ▶ Improvements in resources and special needs education help the families of children with learning difficulties or disabilities.

- ▶ The present educational system provides courses for a range of abilities. This enables the less academic to remain in school and to realise their potential.

- ▶ Parents can avail of second chance education if they so wish, allowing them to improve their skills, develop self esteem and help children with home work. (See Page 401)

Improvements in the Provision of Social Welfare

Before the introduction of a social welfare system members of the immediate and extended family cared for each other and protected vulnerable members. Today, the state has taken over much of this protective role by the provision of pensions, allowances and benefits (**see Chapter 12**).

Impact on family life

► The family unit feels less responsibility for the retired, disabled, unemployed or widowed since the introduction of social welfare.

► The family would appear to be adapting a less caring attitude towards vulnerable members such as the elderly, a great number of whom live alone.

► Old age pensions, living alone allowances and a range of benefits such as free electricity have helped to alleviate hardship among the elderly.

► Child benefit has helped to reduce the incidence of child poverty.

► Families dependent on one parent, as in the case of widowed people or lone parents, can receive state assistance.

► Families on low incomes can avail of social welfare in the form of family income supplement.

Changing Attitudes to Marriage

Traditionally people married young and remained committed to each other for life. In recent times attitudes to marriage have changed radically due to:

► The decreasing influence of the Church which in the past exerted great control over Irish Catholics.

► Women are more educated, capable of pursuing their own careers and less financially dependent on partners.

► Marital breakdown is more socially acceptable than in the past.

► Single parents and blended families are becoming more commonplace.

► Marriage is often postponed. Young couples tend to cohabit and advance their careers rather than marrying and having children.

More than one in four births occur outside marriage.
(CSO 2006)

Single-parent family

Impact on family life

► There is a breakdown in the traditional family unit the effects of which may not become obvious for some time.

► There is an increase in the number of single-parent families generally headed by women. In many cases, children do not have a male role model.

► Fewer marriages are taking place as many people choose to cohabit.

► There is more marital breakdown and divorce.

► There is no longer a stigma attached to children born out of marriage and many children must adapt to being a member of a blended family.

Changing gender roles

Changing Attitudes to Traditional Roles within the Family

In the past roles were segregated. Women stayed at home to look after housework and children. Men were breadwinners. Over time these roles changed, affected by the social and economic factors outlined in **Chapter 17**.

Impact on Family Life see Chapter 17)

Changing Attitudes to Parenting

Formerly, while childcare was chiefly the domain of the mother, the father was seen as disciplinarian and control within the home was patriarchal. Nowadays, parenting is a more egalitarian (equal) process with mother and father sharing parental responsibilities. Younger children can also spend a lot of time with child carers who play a role in disciplining children.

Impact on family life

- ► The provision of day-care facilities in the workplace, paid maternity leave and options of flexitime or job sharing encourages a woman to remain at work while acknowledging her role as a parent.

- ► There is more democracy in family life. Children have a greater say in family matters.

- ► Discipline is less likely to take the form of corporal punishment.

- ► Sometimes parents of teenagers tend to be lenient, allowing their children more freedom than is advisable. Lack of parental supervision is often seen as a factor in the increasing social problems of alcohol, drug abuse and street violence.

- ► The introduction of paternity and parental leave acknowledge the role of the father as well as the mother in parenting and childcare.

Improved Pay and Work Conditions

Pay and work conditions have improved for all employees due to a number of factors.

Impact on family life

- ► Most families have sufficient income to meet basic needs.

- ► Some families enjoy a high standard of living.

- ► Parents tend to be happier and more fulfilled when work is satisfying and well paid. This has a positive effect on family life.

- ► Research has shown that when people are happy at work they are healthier and less prone to physical and mental illness, which have a negative impact on family life.

Increased Participation of Women in the Workforce

The increased participation of women in the workforce has occurred for a variety of reasons outlined in **Chapter 26**.

Impact on family life

► Families tend to be smaller as women return to work after childbirth and pursue careers.

► Dual income contributes to a higher standard of living.

► Children spend more time in childcare.

► Women in full-time, paid employment may experience stress as they attempt to balance roles.

► Children, particularly teenagers, may become more responsible and mature and do their share in the home.

Legislation on Equal Pay and Employment Opportunities

Nowadays, legislation governs all aspects of work including working hours, minimum age, working conditions and minimum wage. The Employment Equality Act was introduced to help eliminate inequality in the workplace.

Impact on family life

► Jobs are less gender specific and women workers receive equal pay for equal work.

► Some people such as the disabled and travellers still may not experience equal employment opportunities.

► Average pay for women is lower than that of men since women workers are concentrated in low paid jobs in the service sector and are less likely to hold positions in the management and administration.

► Back to education and retraining schemes such as VTOS increase employment opportunities among unskilled workers.

Unemployment/Impact on family (See Page 421).

CONTENTS INCLUDE:
- ▶ **The purpose of education**
- ▶ **The provision of education in Ireland**
- ▶ **The accessibility of education**
- ▶ **Factors that influence educational achievement**

The Purpose of Education
Education and Socialisation

- ▶ While socialisation begins in the family, it is a process which continues during schooling. Socialisation during education may be *informal* through the 'hidden curriculum', e.g. interacting with others or it may be *formal*, e.g. transmitting culture by learning the language or music of a society.

- ▶ Schools are also important agents of social control. They encourage acceptance and compliance with basic school rules and ways of behaviour, e.g. punctuality and respect for authority. Rewards and sanctions are used to encourage compliance.

- ▶ Although socialisation continues throughout life it is extremely important during the formative years as it enables a person to fit into and be accepted by society.

> Education is considered a fundamental right under the Irish Constitution.

> The Department of Education and Science has overall responsibility for education in Ireland.

> Areas of socialisation fostered by education:
> - Communication skills
> - Ability to mix with others
> - Consideration of others
> - Punctuality
> - Responsibility
> - Leadership qualities
> - Sharing
> - Generosity
> - Respect
> - Patience

Education and the Development of the Individual

Physical development

▶ Dexterity (skill) is achieved by taking part in activities such as playing with building blocks and jigsaws. Physical skills are developed in subjects such as Home Economics and Art. Sport and Physical Education also contribute to physical development.

Emotional development

▶ The education process contributes to the emotional development of an individual as young children gradually gain emotional independence from parents. They also learn to be sensitive to the needs of others and to be supportive of others. Certain subjects allow for discussion relating to emotions such as RSE (Relationship and Sexuality Education).

▶ Co-educational schools allow for the development of healthy, friendly relationships between the sexes.

Intellectual development

▶ Education can contribute greatly to the intellectual development of an individual. Resources such as games, books and computers, and comfortable physical surroundings with appropriate lighting, heating and ventilation all assist in attaining intellectual potential.

Female students doing woodwork

▶ The broad range of subjects and the variety of extracurricular activities provide many opportunities for intellectual development. Classmates and exams provide intellectual challenges and competition which can encourage intellectual development.

Moral development

▶ Moral development of an individual is encouraged in education through the ethos of the school, which sets down the values and the moral thinking of the school and defines what is expected of students.

▶ Certain subjects within the curriculum such as SPHE (Social, Personal and Health Education) and Religious Education cover topics dealing with morality.

Education and Work

Education plays an important part in preparation for work.

▶ At school certain qualities are encouraged such as responsibility, trustworthiness, punctuality and self-discipline, all of which are valuable in the workplace.

▶ Basic education, i.e. numeracy and literacy are essential for any type of employment.

▶ Certain skills taught at school are required for specific jobs, e.g. typing and woodwork.

▶ Programs within the schooling system, e.g. Transition Year and Leaving Certificate Applied incorporate work experience which gives students practical experience of certain careers.

▶ Qualifications obtained through the education system are used to determine career choices.

Factors That Influence Educational Achievement

1. **Intellectual ability:** Everyone inherits a certain degree of intellectual ability. In order to reach full intellectual potential the following factors come into play.

2. **Parental attitude to education:** Positive parental attitudes towards education encourage and assist learning. Parents who value education instil these values in their children, resulting in self-motivated determined students. The educational level of parents may also influence achievement. Educated parents have an understanding of the system and can help students in terms of subjects, exams and career options.

3. **Family size:** Parents with large families often have less time to spend assisting young children with homework. Economic restraints may result in fewer educational aids, e.g. computers and books in the home. The possibility of availing of third-level education may not be an option for children of larger families as the cost may be prohibitive.

4. **Home environment:** Poor housing conditions, i.e. over-crowding, poor heating and lack of educational aids can hinder study. The health of children can be affected by poor housing conditions and a bad diet, which can in turn affect school attendance.

5. **Locality and school environment:** Children from socially deprived areas with high levels of unemployment and social problems are often less motivated. Schools often have large class numbers and few resources. Problems such as bullying, negative peer pressure and discipline issues have a negative effect on educational achievement.

6. **Peers:** Peers are particularly important during adolescence and can have a positive or negative affect on educational achievement. When one's friends are interested in achieving, this will encourage positive behaviour and intellectual challenge.

Provision of Education in Ireland

Education in Ireland may be categorised into the following areas:

- Pre-school education
- Primary education
- Second-level education
- Third-level education
- Adult/second chance education
- Special needs education

Pre-school Care and Education

Many young children in Ireland avail of some form of pre-school care. County Childcare Committees have been set up nationally under the Department of Justice, Equality and Law Reform to address the childcare needs of each specific county. Funding is available under the government Early Childhood Care and Education Scheme (ECCE). Although not regarded as part of the formal educational system pre-schools generally offer a stimulating and creative environment which encourages learning and development. The options available follow.

Crèches, day-care centres and nurseries

- ▶ Crèches, day-care centres and nurseries are community based or privately run.

- ▶ Cater for children up to 5 years of age.

- ▶ Provide eating, sleeping, changing, washing and playing facilities.

- ▶ Are run by qualified persons with the ratio of carers to children sufficient to ensure due care and attention.

- ▶ Hygiene and safety standards must be maintained in order to receive these grants.

- ▶ Community-based centres give preference to children most in need.

Playgroups and playschools

- ▶ Playgroups and playschools are community based or privately run.

- ▶ They operate 3–4 hours daily (often mornings only).

- ▶ They cater for children between 2–5 years of age.

- ▶ They provide planned pre-school programmes.

- ▶ Playgroups and playschools offer a stimulating environment where children learn by doing.

Montessori schools

- ▶ Montessori schools are generally privately run.

- ▶ They provide education for pre-school children up to 7 years old.

- ▶ They are run by Montessori-trained teachers.

- ▶ Learning is encouraged through play and at one's own pace.

- ▶ Special teaching materials, e.g. counting devices and flash cards are used.

Early Start pre-school project (See Page **405).**

> **The Childcare (pre-school) Regulations 1996** govern standards of crèches, playgroups and nursery schools in Ireland. These regulations are enforced by HSE.

Childminders

Many parents pay private childminders for childcare.

Primary Education

Although many children begin primary school at 4 or 5 years of age it is not compulsory until the age of 6 and runs for 8 years. The majority of Irish children receive primary education in state-supported National Schools.

> **Educate Together** schools cater for children of different religions and ethnic backgrounds.

Private, fee-paying primary schools, Educate Together schools and Gaelscoileanna also offer primary education.

Primary education is child-centred and activity-based and follows a very broad set curriculum in the following areas: language, maths, social, environmental and scientific education, arts education, physical education, social, personal health education and religious education.

Learning support and resource teachers are available in most schools to offer specialised help to pupils with specific needs.

There are also special schools which offer primary education to children with special needs, e.g. children with mental disabilities or children with hearing impairments.

Primary schools, which may be mixed or single sex, are usually denominational and are run by Boards of Management.

Mixed primary school

Second-level Education

Second-level education is offered in post-primary schools including secondary schools (some of which are private fee-paying schools) vocational schools, community schools/colleges and comprehensive schools. Although these schools differ in management structure and ownership the education provided is basically the same.

> Attendance in full-time education is compulsory in Ireland from 6 to 15 years of age.

All schools offer a three-year, junior cycle culminating with the Junior Certificate examination. The curriculum is a broad set curriculum. Subjects examined in the Junior Certificate examination include compulsory and optional subject areas. Level differentiation, i.e. higher, ordinary and foundation levels, in some subjects caters for students of varying abilities.

The senior cycle offered in post-primary schools may differ slightly from school to school. In some schools there is a Transition year before beginning a two year Leaving Certificate programme in one of the following areas:

1. The (established) Leaving Certificate programme
2. Leaving Certificate Vocational Programme (LCVP)
3. Leaving Certificate Applied (LCA)

Transition year programme

The Transition year programme is a student-centred non exam-based programme which encourages self-development. Mini-companies, work experience and drama feature in the programme, together with mainstream subjects.

Leaving Certificate programme

Students study at least five subjects including Irish, English and Maths. Level differentiation caters for students of varying abilities. A written examination completes the Leaving Certificate programme. Some subject areas are awarded marks for practical work carried out during the two-year programme, e.g. Home Economics and Construction Studies.

Leaving Certificate Vocational programme

This programme involves studying at least five subjects, two of which are vocational subjects. A foreign language is also taken together with two compulsory link modules: (i) Enterprise Education (ii) Preparation for work.

The emphasis on work is designed to introduce the student to the world of business and employment.

The link modules are assessed by a written exam (40%) and by a portfolio of coursework (60%). 'Pass', 'merit' or 'distinction' may be attained. This result may be used instead of one of the traditional Leaving Certificate results for points to qualify for entry to higher education.

Vocational subjects include	
• Business	• Home Economics
• Accounting	• Construction Studies
• Technical Drawing	• Agricultural Science
• Art	• Music

Leaving Certificate Applied

Leaving Certificate Applied is designed to cater for those who do not intend to avail of third-level education. It is to prepare students for work. The course is divided into four half-year modules. Subject areas are grouped into three areas:

1. General Education – English, languages, communication.

2. Vocational Education – which includes work experience, maths, information technology.

3. Vocational Preparation – development of practical skills in such areas as leisure, technology and business.

Students are assessed over the two-year period with written exams, orals, interviews and assessments of student tasks which are done during each module. Certification is awarded on a 'pass', 'merit' or 'distinction' basis. Successful Leaving Certificate Applied students are eligible for many Post Leaving Certificate Courses (PLCs).

Post Leaving Certificate Courses

A variety of PLCs is available as full-time one or two-year courses in many second level schools throughout the country. Courses include Childcare, Community Care, Sport and Leisure, Hotel and Catering, Business and Secretarial Skills, and Computer Studies. The aim of PLCs is to provide young people with the technological and vocational skills necessary for employment or further education. Certificates are awarded by the Further Education and Training Awards Council (FETAC).

> Ireland has one of the highest educational participation rates in the world. Second-level education is completed by over 80% of Irish students.

Third-level Education

The number of young people availing of third-level education is continually increasing. Almost six times as many now attend third level compared to the 1960s. Over 50% of all students go on to higher education. Entry is gained by application to the Central Application Office (CAO). Points are calculated on Leaving Certificate results.

The three main sectors involved in the delivery of third-level education are:

   (i) Universities
   (ii) Colleges of Education
   (iii) Institutes of Technology

Universities

There are seven universities in Ireland:

▶ University College Dublin (UCD)

▶ University College Galway (UCG)

▶ University College Cork (UCC)

▶ National University of Ireland Maynooth (NUI)

▶ University of Dublin (Trinity College)

▶ University of Limerick (UL)

▶ Dublin City University (DCU)

Trinity College Dublin

They offer diploma and degree courses in many areas including Arts, Law, Sciences, Medicine and Business Studies. Universities award their own certification.

Colleges of Education

Colleges of Education are specifically involved in teacher training. They are affiliated to universities and offer Bachelor of Education degrees (B.Ed). The colleges include:

▶ Mary Immaculate College of Education, Limerick – Primary School teacher training

▶ St Patrick's College of Education, Drumcondra – Primary School teacher training

▶ St Angela's College, Sligo – Home Economics teacher training

▶ National College of Art and Design (NCAD) – Art teacher training

Institutes of Technology

There are 13 ITs situated in cities and large towns throughout Ireland. They provide education and training in a wide variety of areas including business, journalism, engineering and music. HETAC awards non-university higher education qualifications, i.e. certificates, diplomas and degrees.

HETAC
Higher Education and Training Awards Council.

Adult and Second Chance Education

It is government policy to develop a culture of lifelong learning. This means creating opportunities for people of all ages and educational levels to gain new skills within a flexible learning system and qualifications structure. Adult education is a vital part of lifelong learning and each year more and more adults participate in education and training opportunities. There are many reasons why adults choose to return to education.

▶ To improve qualifications in order to enhance the chances of promotion or for self-fulfilment.

▶ To keep up with technological changes, e.g. computer courses.

▶ To follow a particular area of interest, e.g. photography.

Aontas
The Irish National Association of Adult Education promotes the development of learning. It develops, supports and co-ordinates all aspects of adult education.

▶ To meet other people.

▶ To increase the chances of gaining employment.

▶ As second chance education – many people leave school early possibly with poor literacy skills and no qualifications. Some choose to avail of second chance education by taking literacy classes or studying for Junior or Leaving Certificate examinations (Youthreach, See Page 405).

Availability of adult education

Adult education is available in part-time and full-time courses. These courses may be held during the day or in the evening. Sources of adult education include:

Adult literacy class

▶ Third-level colleges/universities throughout the country and run Adult Literacy and Community Education schemes providing basic literacy courses.

▶ Distance Learning (offered by Dublin City University and Open University courses).

▶ Vocational Education Committees (VECs) who run evening courses.

▶ PLC courses are run in many second level schools throughout the country.

▶ FÁS – 'Ireland's national training and employment authority' provides a range of training and employment programmes in community training workshops.

▶ VTOS (Vocational Training Opportunities Scheme) offers a range of courses designed to meet the educational needs of unemployed people (See Page 436).

▶ Statutory agencies, e.g. Teagasc, Coillte also provide training in specific areas.

Special Needs Education

Special needs include physical, intellectual or emotional needs. Various measures and programmes have been put in place in an attempt to address the educational requirements of those with special needs.

Teaching a child with a hearing disability

▶ Mainstream classes in standard schools with support services such as learning support, resource teachers and special needs assistants.

▶ There are special classes for students with disabilities attached to a number of schools in Ireland. These classes usually cater for the learning needs of students with a mild or moderate level of learning disability. Pupil to teacher ratios are smaller than in mainstream classes.

▶ The Department of Education and Science recognises that children with autism have distinct educational needs. There are now many special classes for children with autism. Each class has a pupil teacher ratio of 6:1 and has a childcare assistant.

▶ **Special schools**

Special schools provide education for students from 5–18 years of age with learning disabilities at a mild or moderate level. In addition there are schools for the visually and hearing impaired. There are a small number of schools for students with physical disabilities and some for students who are emotionally disturbed. These schools provide education to Leaving Certificate level but make provision for students whose level of disability would make it difficult for them to benefit from Junior and Leaving Certificate programmes.

> Third-level institutions generally provide services for those with special needs, e.g. special equipment, learning aids, interpreters, assistants and exam procedures.

▶ **Children's detention centres**

Children's detention centres for young offenders cater for children under 16 who have been convicted or placed on remand by a court. These schools aims to provide care, education and training for the young people, e.g. Trinity House School, Lusk, Co. Dublin.

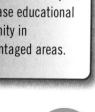

Equality of Opportunity in Education

Certain factors influence equality of opportunity in education.

Gender inequity

▶ Gender inequity is no longer as strong a factor as it was in the past when it was mainy males who were educated to third level. Equal numbers of males and females now avail of third-level education.

▶ Textbooks are becoming less gender stereotypical.

▶ Inequity may lie in the lack of availability of certain subjects in single-sex schools, e.g. Construction Studies may not be available in an all girls' schools.

Socio-economic status

▶ Costs for uniforms, books, and extra-curricular activities such as school tours, can be prohibitive for children from lower income families.

▶ People from the higher socio-economic groups usually have an appreciation of education and encourage their children to have positive educational experiences.

▶ Some parents of lower socio-economic families lack education and may not be able to assist young children with homework, which may put the children at an educational disadvantage.

▶ Children from less well-off, large families may not receive the same attention as their better-off counterparts. As a result, they may not be able to read and write as well as other pupils when they begin school.

▶ Research shows that children are far more likely to progress to Leaving Certificate and third level if they come from upper socio-economic families.

> **DEIS**
> Delivering equality of opportunity in schools. A government funded plan to increase educational opportunity in disadvantaged areas.

Disadvantaged students

▶ Certain schools in the country are in designated areas of disadvantage. This status was based on factors such as:
  – unemployment levels;
  – quality of housing;
  – basic literacy and numeracy information.

The students from these areas because of their lower socio-economic background are at an educational disadvantage. To counteract this certain programmes have been put in place (see below).

▶ People with special needs may also be regarded as disadvantaged because of their specific needs, e.g. visual impairment. Although education is available to people with special needs, they are often restricted by location.

▶ Travellers may be regarded as disadvantaged. Their movement renders equality of opportunity in education very difficult. There are Traveller training centres throughout the country offering education and training in an effort to compensate for this inequality.

▶ Young offenders may be regarded as disadvantaged, see Children's Detention Centres.

▶ Children of immigrant families may be disadvantaged because of their cultural differences and of their language difficulties.

Early school leavers

A variety of home, community and school-based factors can contribute to early school leaving. Statistically, early school leavers are more likely to experience social exclusion and unemployment. Young people without a Leaving Certificate are at high risk of marginalisation and social exclusion. Certain programmes are now available to assist early school leavers' re-entry into education. A 'School Completion Programme' is in operation in selected primary and second-level schools with high levels of early school leavers. These schools must develop a plan to retain pupils in schools and to increase numbers who successfully complete the senior cycle. Tracking of attendance of pupils is in operation in all schools.

Improving Access to Education

Contemporary government-funded initiatives aimed at the disadvantaged, designed to improve access to accessibility of education include:

Financial support

▶ The 'Back to School Clothing and Footwear Allowance' – this scheme is run by the HSE as part of the Supplementary Welfare Scheme. It is designed to meet the cost of uniforms and footwear for children of low-income families.

▶ A 'Back to Education Allowance' (BTEA) is available to the unemployed, to single parents and to those with a disability for approved second or third-level courses. The allowance is paid weekly for the duration of the course and is not means tested. In addition, an annual 'Cost of Education Allowance' is paid at the start of each academic year.

▶ Grants for third level and further education colleges are available subject to means testing.

Examination systems

Changes in examination systems have improved the accessibility of education.

▶ Level differentiation allows for higher, ordinary and foundation examination papers which cater for the varying abilities of students.

▶ Awarding of marks for practical exams, project work, orals, and report books allows for credit to be gained from other aspects of study rather than solely from a final written examination.

▶ Availability of readers/scribes during state exams for students with reading/writing difficulties has also made education more accessible to many students.

The Early Start project

The Early Start project is a one year programme offered under DEIS targeted at 3–4 year olds who are most at risk of not succeeding in education. Its objective is to expose these young children to an educational programme which will enhance their overall development and lay a foundation for successful educational attainment in future years. Research shows that high quality pre-school education can play an important part in offsetting the affects of social inequality and in preventing educational disadvantage.

Vocational Training Opportunities Scheme

The Vocational Training Opportunities Scheme (VTOS) which operates through Vocational Educational Committees, offers a wide selection of courses to the long-term unemployed. The scheme, which offers a training allowance, makes education accessible to the unemployed. (See Page 436).

The Home School Community Liaison Scheme

The Home School Community Liaison Scheme operates, with the assistance of a home school liaison teacher, in many schools throughout the country at primary and second levels.

The scheme is targeted at students who are at risk of not reaching their potential in the educational system because of economic or social disadvantage. This scheme aims to retain them in the educational system past compulsory education. The scheme also aims to raise awareness among parents of their own capacity to enhance their children's educational progress and to assist them in developing relevant skills. Co-operation between home, school and the community is also promoted.

Youthreach

Youthreach is part of a national programme of second chance education and training in Ireland. It is designed specifically for 15 to 20-year-old school leavers without qualifications. There are many Youthreach centres, including Traveller training centres and community training workshops, based in local communities throughout the country. They offer a two-year integrated training and education programme and participants can receive an allowance for attending.

The National Educational Welfare Board

The National Educational Welfare Board, set up under the Education Welfare Act 2000, is an agency designed to support regular school attendance and the education of children and young people.

Educational Welfare Officers provide support and advice to parents and schools and follow up on absences from school. Schools must notify the National Educational Welfare Board if a child has missed a total of 20 days in the school year.

The Board also assesses education conducted outside a recognised school, e.g. in the home. Early school leavers of 16 and 17 years of age must register with the Board so that they can be helped with further education and training.

LCA (See Page **400).**

Community-based crèches and playschools (See Page **397).**

HEAR scheme

The **H**igher **E**ducation **A**ccess **R**oute (HEAR) is an admissions scheme aimed at improving access to third level education for students from socially disadvantaged backgrounds. A number of third level places allocated on a reduced points basis are reserved for school leavers who qualify under the scheme ie. meet certain financial and social criteria. Application for the scheme is through the CAO system.

CONTENTS INCLUDE:

- ▶ Defining work
- ▶ Attitudes to work and to work attainment
- ▶ Changing patterns of work

- ▶ The role of voluntary work in the community
- ▶ Reconciling employment with family responsibilities
- ▶ Causes and effects of unemployment

Concepts of Work (6.3.1)

Defining Work

Work has been defined as 'the application of mental and physical effort to a purpose'. The term however means different things to different people and is influenced by factors such as culture and age group. For many people work is an economic necessity, vital for their survival. Other people work to maintain or increase wealth. Work may be categorised as:

- ▶ Paid work
- ▶ Unpaid work
- ▶ Voluntary work.

Paid work

For many people work takes the form of employment or an occupation which is a means of earning an income. It can involve working for an employer or being self-employed. It may be full-time, part-time or temporary work. The skills required and the level of responsibility depend on the nature of the work, varying from basic operative positions through to different managerial levels.

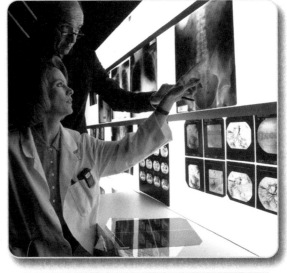

It is advantageous if one derives a sense of satisfaction from work, but for many it is solely a means of making a living providing little in terms of self-esteem or status.

Unpaid work

Many women and a growing number of men are engaged in unpaid employment in the home. Household tasks include cooking, cleaning and laundry work. Childcare too is often an unpaid occupation.

Carers look after elderly or disabled relatives in the home. Such unpaid workers are often an undervalued resource and many suffer feelings of low self-esteem, boredom and stress from the sheer monotony of tasks.

Voluntary work

Voluntary work can involve working for charities or pressure groups which seek to bring about social change. Voluntary work is not financially rewarded but can be intrinsically rewarding.

Voluntary worker

Why people work

▶ For job satisfaction, a sense of achievement.

▶ To earn money – for resources to meet basic needs.

▶ To make use of educational qualifications.

▶ For status and a sense of personal identity.

▶ To increase affluence and raise their standard of living.

▶ For social contact with colleagues and a chance to establish friendships which extend beyond the workplace.

▶ Individuals have a right to work.

Attitude to Work and to Work Attainment

For many people work occupies a larger part of life than any other single activity. Attitudes to work and to work attainment are influenced by a number of elements.

1. Home background

Attitudes to work are formed during childhood. They are greatly influenced by the work ethic shown by parents and by the positive or negative attitudes parents hold regarding their own jobs or occupations.

2. Social class and educational level

Children from middle and upper-class backgrounds tend to have high educational aspirations and long-term goals in relation to careers. They are encouraged to pursue these ambitions and are therefore more likely to attain work in their preferred field. Children from less privileged backgrounds, whose parents are long-term unemployed or in low-paid employment, tend to have fewer educational opportunities and are often less qualified when seeking work. Consequently, they may find employment in low-status positions with no job satisfaction and little chance of advancement.

3. Intrinsic satisfaction

Intrinsic satisfaction or intrinsic motivation occurs when work is pleasant and satisfying in itself. The worker is interested and derives a sense of achievement from simply carrying out a task. Intrinsic satisfaction involves pleasurable internal feelings and thoughts. It confers confidence and a sense of pride, which contributes greatly to a high level of job satisfaction. Research has shown that people are at their most creative when they feel motivated mainly by the interest, satisfaction and challenge of the work itself rather than by external pressures or incentives.

Jamie Oliver

4. Extrinsic satisfaction

Many jobs are not intrinsically satisfying enough in themselves so extrinsic motivation is necessary. Extrinsic satisfaction is not derived directly from the work itself, but from the other benefits the work may supply. This usually takes the form of financial rewards such as a high salary, bonuses or benefits such as a company car. Status conferred by occupation is also a factor. Income can be spent on luxuries such as expensive cars and foreign holidays, which may invoke an extrinsic sense of satisfaction. Many people stay in boring unfulfilling jobs for extrinsic reasons and not for any sense of satisfaction they get from their occupations.

> The balance between intrinsic and extrinsic sources of satisfaction varies from one individual to another and between different occupations. The majority of workers are motivated by both intrinsic and extrinsic rewards and both affect performance, job satisfaction and long-term commitment to a particular job.

5. Personal identity and self-esteem

In modern society having a job is an important element in maintaining self-esteem. For men in particular self-esteem is often linked with the economic contribution they make to maintaining the household. Some occupations such as highly-paid professions in the medical or legal fields confer status which also contributes to one's sense of personal identity.

6. Social contact

For many, work provides opportunities for developing friendships and to participate in shared activities with others. This accounts to a large extent for the loneliness and isolation experienced by people when they retire or are made redundant.

7. Work ethic

A work ethic is a set of morals or principles relating to one's work. It is a code of conduct which influences attitudes to work and to work attainment. Work ethic is an inherent quality developed in the home and influenced by peer groups and social class.

A good work ethic is a desirable quality in an employee as it generally means the individual is honest, loyal, motivated and will endeavour to do the job to the best of his/her ability. It also impacts on other work-related issues, such as time wasting, punctuality and absenteeism, which can affect the success or otherwise of a company or business.

8. Working conditions

Working conditions have an influence on attitudes to work and on the choice of workplace in the first instance. They also have an effect on job satisfaction levels.

Variations in Working Conditions

Working hours

While generally the working day and week have decreased many people do not work a conventional 9–5 day but do shift work or can avail of flexitime (i.e. working within a time range rather than at a set time). Some avail of part-time work, seasonal work, or job sharing. An increasing number of people work from home due to advances in technology.

New technology means that some people can work from home

Manual work

In many areas, such as farming, manual work and physical labour have become safer and less strenuous due to technology and automation, so chances of physical injury are reduced.

Entitlements

All workers are entitled to fair treatment and not to be exploited by unscrupulous employers. Legal entitlements include paid holidays, insurance rights and being able to avail of benefits such as maternity leave or disability benefit. Some employees, such as young people or foreign nationals employed in the hospitality industry, could find themselves exploited if they were unaware of their entitlements.

Manual worker

Stress levels

Many jobs particularly in the medical profession and at managerial level in business can be stressful, which may manifest itself in physical symptoms such as cancer or coronary heart disease. While such occupations confer status and are well paid, the long hours and pressure involved can impact negatively on health and on family life.

Worker participation

Companies encourage worker participation by providing opportunities for promotion within the organisation, profit-sharing schemes and democratic decision-making. Workers feel empowered when given the freedom to demonstrate their skills and creativity. Worker participation creates a sense of company loyalty and pride.

Work affects:

- Health (physical and mental)
- Family life
- Social standing

- Personal identity/self-esteem
- Lifestyle
- Social life and leisure pursuits

Changes in Patterns of Work and Work Availability

The effect of developing technology on industry

The use of technology and automation in industry has increased significantly in recent times.

Automation involves the use of machinery to perform tasks formerly done by people. The machines are computer controlled requiring only a minimum amount of human supervision. Increased use of automation has the following effects on work and work availability in industry:

> Technology refers to the application of science to machinery to achieve greater production efficiency.

- ▶ Automation has made industrial work cleaner, easier and safer. Work is less physical, reducing the risk to workers' health.

- ▶ The increased output, over shorter periods of time, has lead to a reduction in working hours and an increase in leisure time for workers.

Primary industry

Secondary industry

Tertiary industry

▶ Mass production by machines is consistent in quality and design. Complex machines can carry out highly-skilled tasks with greater accuracy than people.

▶ While start up costs are high an automated plant has lower labour costs.

▶ Tedious repetitive work has been taken over by machines. This has led to an increase in unemployment among unskilled workers.

▶ Fewer workers and the use of electronic communication mean less social interaction takes place at work.

▶ Workers who are involved in the supervision of machinery need the skills required to keep the machinery operating smoothly. However, there is little craftsmanship involved and many more artisan skills such as welding are being lost through the increased use of technology in industry.

The decline in primary and secondary industries and the increase in service industries

▶ Changes in the global economy and advances in technology have radically changed the type of work available. In modern society fewer people are involved in primary industry than in the past.

▶ At the beginning of the twentieth century more people were involved in the manufacturing industry. Over time the balance has shifted away from secondary industry towards positions in the service industry.

- Primary industries are natural resource-based industries. They are directly dependent on the resources provided by nature. Primary industries include agriculture, fishing, mining and forestry.

- Secondary industries are involved in manufacturing or processing the raw materials supplied by the primary sector into finished goods e.g. cheese-making.

- Tertiary industries are service industries which do not produce goods but supply services. This sector includes areas such as tourism, television and radio, music, banking, insurance, education, catering, leisure and transport.

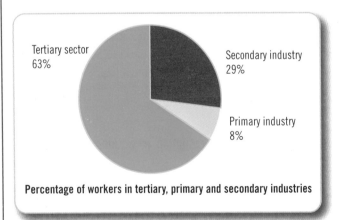

Tertiary sector 63%

Secondary industry 29%

Primary industry 8%

Percentage of workers in tertiary, primary and secondary industries

There are several reasons why such changes have occurred, including:

1. Continuous development of labour saving machinery in both primary and secondary sectors which has brought about a decline in labour force in these areas.

2. Wide use of information technology in industry which has changed the nature of the work that is available.

3. Increase in the manufacturing industry in areas such as the Far East, where labour costs are lower and production methods more efficient, has led to a decline in similar industries in the West.

4. There has been an increase in the demand for services in recent times.

Increased educational requirements to acquire employment

▶ The move from primary and secondary to tertiary industries has increased the demand for education. An increasing number of people are availing of third level education with growing numbers qualifying in areas such as business, science, and computer and software engineering.

> In a recent survey the Irish educational system was ranked fourth out of 55 countries for meeting the needs of a competitive economy.
>
> (Source: IMD Word Competitive Yearbook 2003)

▶ Early school leavers and unskilled workers have more difficulty acquiring long term and well paid employment.

▶ Leaving certificate is now considered a minimum requirement for employment.

▶ In the past a primary degree was a highly regarded qualification whereas nowadays many young people obtain a masters or doctorate degree before entering the workforce.

▶ The young well educated labour force is one of the key factors in attracting multinational investment into Ireland. The Irish educational system is highly regarded and is seen as very effective in meeting the needs of a competitive economy.

Increased participation of women in the workforce

Over the past 50 years an increasing number of women have moved into the workforce. This increase has been attributed to a number of factors including:

▶ The average age for childbirth has increased. Women tend to establish themselves in their careers while young and return to work after having children.

▶ Birthrate has declined in recent years. Smaller families mean that the time many women previously spent at home rearing children has now been reduced.

▶ Economic pressure brought about by a rise in male unemployment has led women to seek paid employment.

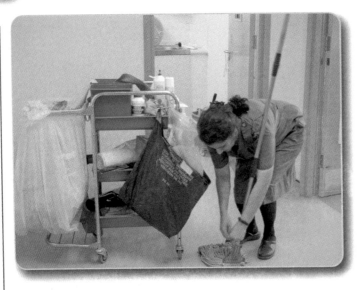

▶ Two incomes are required in some households in order to sustain a particular lifestyle.

▶ Women are nowadays more likely to be educated to third-level standard and wish to pursue their careers and make use of the qualifications attained.

▶ Support structures have been put in place by the state in recent years to encourage lone mothers and married women into the workforce, e.g. crèches in the workplace and community-based playschools.

▶ Employment structures have become more flexible with the increased availability of part-time work and job-sharing arrangements. This option may suit women who are trying to balance work with family obligations.

Despite advances in recent times women still experience a number of inequalities in the workforce:

▶ Women workers tend to be concentrated in poorly paid routine jobs in the clerical and services sectors although many well qualified younger women are moving into higher paying professional occupations.

▶ More women than men tend to hold jobs with no control or authority and no opportunities for promotion, while men hold more powerful managerial positions, e.g. in banking, government and on boards of state agencies.

> Male managers outnumber women by almost three to one, while the opposite is the case for clerks and secretaries (CSO).

▶ For working mothers, childcare is still a major problem. Childcare facilities can be prohibitively expensive especially for women with few qualifications in low-paid employment.

Improved working conditions
Conditions of work have improved for all regardless of occupation. Issues which impact on health such as heating, lighting, ventilation and hygiene are set down in labour legislation and are monitored by the Health and Safety Authority.

HEALTH AND SAFETY AUTHORITY

▶ Employers must take precautions to minimise risks and to safeguard the health and wellbeing of employees.

▶ Workers also must behave in a responsible way while in the workplace so that they do not endanger themselves or their colleagues in any way.

- ▶ Adult workers are legally entitled to a minimum wage (**See Page** 437).

- ▶ There is also increasing flexibility in working hours.

- ▶ Technology enables a growing number of people to work from home.

Increasing flexibility in working hours

- ▶ Parental leave to care for a child is available to any employee who is parent to a child under 8 years of age. The 14-week unpaid leave may be taken as a whole or broken up over an agreed period of time.

- ▶ Career breaks are an option in some jobs. Workers may take unpaid leave and can return to work at a later stage.

Protection of Young Person (Employment) Act 1996

Protection of Young Person (Employment) Act applies to all employees under the age of 18. It stipulates working conditions in terms of minimum age limits, working hours and rest periods. Employers found to be in breach of this legislation are liable to be prosecuted and fined. Under the Act:

- ▶ The employment of under 16s in full-time positions is prohibited.

- ▶ 14 and 15 year olds may be employed for 'light' work during school holidays, or during term time, if the work is part of an educational programme or work experience.

- ▶ 14 and 15 year olds may work a maximum of 35 hours per week, 16–18 year olds may work up to a maximum of 40 hours per week.

- ▶ Under 18's cannot be required to work after 10pm.

- ▶ Employers must obtain a copy of the birth certificate if the employee is under 18 and need written permission from a parent/guardian if the employee is under 16.

The Role of Unpaid and Voluntary Work in the Community

Voluntary work for charities and other organisations and institutions has a valuable social role.

- ▶ Voluntary workers are involved in supplying a wide range of services to disadvantaged and underprivileged groups such as the elderly, the disabled or the homeless.

- Voluntary organisations complement work carried out by statutory bodies but offer a more local and personal service.

- When state funding is lacking or inadequate, voluntary organisations organise and run services which should otherwise have been provided by the state.

- Much voluntary work is preventative in nature, i.e. issues can be dealt with quickly before these issues become major social problems.

- Voluntary organisations can assert influence by highlighting social problems, attracting media attention and can therefore initiate change and social reform.

- Some voluntary workers become expert in their field and their advice is sought in the development of government policies and legislation, e.g. 'Combat Poverty'.

Benefits of voluntary work
The volunteer

- Voluntary work benefits the volunteer as it tends to be rewarding in itself. It aids the personal development of volunteers in terms of organisational and communication skills.

- Voluntary work affords workers an opportunity to see life from other perspectives thereby cultivating altruistic traits.

- Voluntary workers build relationships with co-workers and with those they seek to help.

The community

- The community benefits from voluntary work as services are provided quickly and at low or no cost.

- Attention is focused on social issues affecting a community.

- A sense of community or neighbourliness is cultivated since volunteers tend to be local and not unfamiliar representatives of state organisations. (For more about voluntary organisations See Page 438).

Reconciling Employment with Family Responsibilities (6.3.2)

Changing patterns in gender roles within the family

- Traditional segregated roles are changing due to the growing number of women entering the paid workforce.

- There appears to be a move towards more egalitarian (equal) relationships in many households although women still tend to do most of the housework and bear most of the responsibility for childcare.

- There is a more egalitarian division of labour among younger couples than among older couples.

- Middle-class couples where the woman is in full-time employment tend to share responsibility for household tasks.

- The control of family finances is more fairly divided between genders than in the past.

See Page **304** for gender issues in relation to family roles.

The impact of dual-earner families on family life

Dual-earner families – where both parents are in paid employment – impacts on family life in a number of ways including:

1. The increased disposable income can be used to meet the needs of all family members and to sustain a good standard of living.

2. Children of working parents who hold healthy attitudes towards work have positive role models and tend to develop a good work ethic and a sense of gender equality.

3. Fathers have become increasingly involved in family life taking a more active role in areas such as meal preparation and childcare. As a result they form closer bonds with their children and there is a more equal distribution of parental and home care responsibilities.

4. Dual career families tend to have fewer children. The cost of childcare and the lack of suitable childcare facilities are still considerable problems for working parents.

5. Women, particularly those in full-time employment in responsible positions, may experience **role overload** and **role conflict** as they strive for balance between paid employment, childcare and running a home. Working lone parents in particular are subject to **role overload**.

Role overload occurs when an individual attempts to play several roles at one time.

Role conflict occurs when the expectations of a person in one role clash with what is expected in another role (**See Page** 302).

Family requirements for childcare

Childcare needs vary and depend on a number of factors including:

▶ *Safe/hygienic environment:* A safe hygienic environment is a priority when seeking childcare.

▶ *Reliable childcarers/minders:* Parents need to feel that the childcarer is capable of looking after their child. In situations where they have no personal knowledge of the individual involved they should seek references, and investigate qualifications and experience level.

▶ *Affordable/cost:* Sometimes parents, when they weigh up the economic impact of childcare, decide that the best solution is for one of them to give up work to look after the children.

▶ *Suitability to age and needs of child:* The age and needs of the child influences choice of childcare. A baby's needs differ from those of an 3–4 year old pre-schooler. If a child has special needs extra care is required when choosing suitable facilities and a minder who will cater for those needs.

▶ *Convenience:* Ideally childcare arrangements need to be convenient in terms of working hours and proximity to home or work.

Childcare options available

▶ Childminder: For this option a relative, trusted friend or childminder looks after children in their own home or in the childminders home.

▶ Nurseries/crèches, day-care centres (See Page 397).

▶ Playgroups and playschools (See Page 397).

▶ Montessori/Froebel schools (See Page 398).

LILLIPUT MONTESSORI

CRECHE & PLAYSCHOOL

Monday to Friday

ENROLMENT BY APPT ONLY
PHONE: 0401 2854907

▶ Naoínraí: These schools provide playgroup facilities where children learn through the medium of Irish. Naoínraí may be used as pre-school preparation for Gael Scoil.

▶ After school groups: These are community-based or privately-run facilities which look after primary school children after school hours until parents finish work. Children are sometimes collected from the school, a meal provided and the children may play, socialise or do homework under the supervision of child carers.

Evaluation of Two Types of Childcare Options

Childminder

Childminders look after children in their own or in the children's homes. While no specific qualifications are necessary, a minder caring for four or more children (maximum for insurance purposes is six) must inform the HSE. The characteristics desirable in childminders include:

► A genuine liking for children whereby a loving, secure environment is created.

► The ability to cater for the physical, emotional, social, recreational and intellectual needs of children.

► Good health and freedom from any physical or mental impairment that might interfere with their capacity to look after a child responsibly.

► The ability to provide an environment which is comfortable, safe and hygienic and fully supervised. (The HSE sets out guidelines on such standards.)

► Maintaining good communication with parents so that children's health, happiness and development can be closely monitored. In addition, mis-understandings regarding issues such as unhealthy eating habits or discipline are less likely to occur.

Advantages of childminders	Disadvantages of childminders
1. Childminders look after children in a home setting where children are familiar with the surroundings and feel safe and secure.	1. Some childminders do not have adequate training or experience to provide for the physical, emotional, social and intellectual needs of the child.
2. Because childminders generally care for fewer children than playschools or crèches, children benefit from more time and attention. This type of childcare therefore often suits children with special needs.	2. If a childminder is unreliable, unpunctual or frequently ill, it can greatly upset family routines and work schedules.
3. Childminders tend to be a less expensive option than many other childcare facilities.	3. The child-rearing methods of the minder may differ considerably from those of the parents on issues such as nutrition, discipline and intellectual stimulation leading to tension between the parties involved.

Childminding Ireland
Childminding Ireland is the national association for childminding funded by the Department of Health and Children which aims to promote high standards in home-based childcare.

Day-care centres

Criteria for choosing a day-care centre

Day-care centres, nurseries, crèches (See Page 397).

- ▶ Premises should be sufficiently spacious with efficient systems of heating, lighting and ventilation.

- ▶ It should be a self-contained unit which includes indoor and outdoor play areas, sleeping and nappy changing facilities, a bathroom and a separate area for food preparation.

- ▶ While it should be easily accessible for parents and children it should also be safe and secure so that children are not at risk.

- ▶ It should be run by qualified personnel who like children, are warm and caring and are capable of creating an environment which promotes the physical, social and emotional development of children.

- ▶ A good selection of toys and a variety of activities encourages creativity and the development of intellectual and motor skills.

Advantages of day-care centres

1. Day-care centres provide a stimulating environment and an organised routine, which suit many children and help to develop imagination and creativity.

2. Premises are regulated in terms of hygiene and safety by the HSE, run by qualified staff and usually adhere strictly to the staff child ratio commended by the Department of health and Children.

3. Well-run centres, where emphasis is placed on trust and relationship-building, help children to develop into well-rounded social beings who are independent, self-disciplined and capable of positive interaction with others.

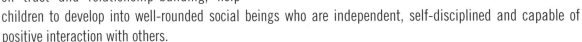

Age	Ratio
Under 1 year	3:1
1–3 years	6:1
3–6 years	8:1

Disadvantages of day-care centres

1. Some children may have difficulty settling in and adapting to a set routine.

2. Because of numbers, there may be little opportunity for one-to-one interaction between carer and child so a child could feel isolated and vulnerable if unable to cope.

3. Day-care centres, unless community run, can be an expensive form of childcare.

The National Children's Nurseries Association (NCNA)
The National Children's Nurseries Association (NCNA) is a support group for day-care centres which aims to improve and maintain the high quality of day-care in Ireland.

Unemployment (6.5)

Defining Unemployment

Unemployment results when people who are available for and willing to work do not have paid employment. The term does not include people who willingly exclude themselves from the paid labour force such as full-time housewives. Children under 15 years, retired people and others not on 'the live register' are also excluded from unemployment figures.

Unemployment in Ireland

► Unemployment rates reflect cycles in the economy. When the economy is strong unemployment rates fall, when the economy weakens unemployment levels increase.

► In Ireland during the 1980s an economic slump brought record unemployment figures (18% in the late 1980s).

► As the economy gradually improved through the late 1990s and the early years of the twenty-first century unemployment levels fell (3.1% in 2001) as Ireland enjoyed an economic boom referred to as the 'Celtic Tiger'.

► The current economic decline has led to a rapid rise in unemployment levels.

Unemployment figures are measured by the Quarterly National Household Survey.

Persons under 25 yers on Live Register, Jan 2008 - Jan 2009		
2008	January	36,900
	February	39,500
	March	40,800
	April	41,000
	May	42,700
	June	48,200
	July	52,300
	August	55,000
	September	53,700
	October	54,500
	November	57,900
	December	62,300
2009	January	70,600

January 2010
436,900
on live register.

Unemployment rates					
	2005	**2006**	**2007**	**2008**	**2009**
Annual Average	4.4%	4.4%	4.6%	6.4%	12.5%
Total labour force	2,040,400	2,132,800	2,217,000	2,239,600	2,203,100
Total unemployed	95,800	97,900	103,100	126,700	264,600

Causes of unemployment

The causes of unemployment vary depending on a number of circumstances. They include:

1. **Seasonal variation:** Some employment by its nature is seasonal. Areas of employment subject to seasonal variation include tourism, fishing and farming. Off-season, workers are laid off and become unemployed or in the case of students return to full-time education.

2. **Geographical variation:** There are variations in employment in different regions throughout Ireland. At present unemployment is highest in the Border Region (5.4%) and in the South East (5.3% and lowest in the Mid-East (3.1%) and West (3.7%).

3. **Automation/technical advances:** When manufacturing and production companies update to include the latest developments in technology fewer workers are needed to run the plant. Redundancies occur, particularly among unskilled workers.

4. **World economy:** A downturn in the global economy has caused a rapid rise in unemployment rates in Ireland. Some multi-national companies have chosen to move their business out of Ireland because production costs are lower elsewhere.

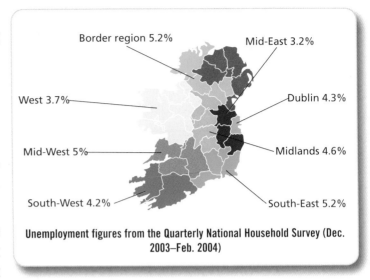

Unemployment figures from the Quarterly National Household Survey (Dec. 2003–Feb. 2004)

The live register is not a measure of unemployment since it includes part-time seasonal and casual workers who are entitled to unemployment assistance or benefits.

Number of persons on Live Register 1999–2009

5. **Globalisation:** Jobs especially those in the agri-food sector and in manufacturing are currently at risk due to cheaper imports and greater economies of scale abroad.

6. **Incentive:** When the wages offered are low there is little incentive for the long-term unemployed to return to the workforce. A return to work could mean a loss of certain benefits such as rent supplement and subsequently a drop in income.

7. **Levels of demand for products and services:** The increased availability of cheaper imported products has led to a fall off in demand for Irish goods. The services industry also suffers when demand falls. For example, employment levels in Irish tourism are affected by the increased availability of less expensive foreign holidays.

8. **Residual unemployment:** This term refers to the unemployed remaining during times of full employment. It is made up of people unable to work because of poor physical or mental health.

Effects of unemployment
Unemployment does not just affect the individual but also the family unit and society.

On the individual
1. The most immediate effect is loss of income and the stress related to financial insecurity and fear of poverty.

2. Unemployment brings loss of status and erodes self-esteem and confidence.

3. Loss of purpose can lead to feelings of inadequacy and hopelessness. Individuals can suffer from ill health and depression. Alcohol abuse may develop as people strive to forget their problems.

4. The individual may feel a sense of guilt and may feel that they have failed themselves or their families.

5. Work is important for the social contact involved. Unemployment can mean social isolation particularly when social life and leisure activities are restricted by limited finance.

On the family unit

1. A drop in income leads to a decline in living standards which affects all family members. Repossession of cars or even homes is a possibility in some severe circumstances.

2. Poverty is prevalent among the families of the unemployed. Poverty has an impact on issues such as nutrition and schooling, setting children at a disadvantage.

3. Unemployment places a strain on family relationships. A bored and frustrated former breadwinner might create tension in the home. A man may resent being forced into the role of house-husband while his spouse goes out to work.

4. Lack of financial security and worry about the future creates stress and can result in ill health for family members.

On society
1. In areas where long-term unemployment is accepted as the norm children lack role models in terms of employment and a positive work ethic. A pattern of unemployment develops over generations.

2. Lack of employment and the subsequent boredom can lead to anti-social behaviour such as drug or alcohol abuse, vandalism and crime so that areas develop bad reputations and become unemployment black spots.

3. People may be forced to leave an area to seek employment elsewhere. This is particularly true in rural areas. The decrease in population has a negative impact on other business and services in the area sometimes leading to further unemployment.

4. The more people who are unemployed the higher the cost to the state since they are financially dependent on social welfare for their income.

Chapter 27 | Leisure (6.4)

CONTENTS INCLUDE:

▶ Defining leisure

▶ Function and value of leisure in today's society

▶ Influences on leisure patterns

▶ The role of leisure in development

▶ Evaluation of leisure facilities available in the community

Defining Leisure

Leisure may be defined as 'time not spent working or meeting the necessities of life', 'time available for ease and relaxation' or 'freedom from occupation or business'. Leisure time is time not spent on anything that has to be done such as education, employment or household chores.

There is a wide range of leisure activities available and people avail of them for a number of reasons.

▶ Shorter working hours and guaranteed holidays allow more time for leisure activities.

▶ Labour-saving equipment in the homes frees up much time that used to be spent on household chores.

▶ More disposable income to spend on leisure activities.

▶ The availability of career breaks and job sharing in many occupations allows more time for leisure activities.

▶ Health awareness – as people appreciate more and more the benefits of physical fitness many take part in energetic leisure activities.

Sometimes the distinction between work and leisure activities can be blurred. What is work for one person may be leisure for others, e.g. gardeners and professional sports people and people involved in voluntary work.

Function and value of leisure

In today's society leisure can contribute to physical, emotional, intellectual and social development. Leisure activities:

- ► Allow people to relax and unwind from the stresses of everyday life.
- ► Improve physical wellbeing when active leisure pursuits are enjoyed.
- ► Allow for the development of new skills which contribute to personal development.
- ► Introduce challenges (physical and intellectual) which result in a sense of satisfaction and wellbeing.
- ► Gratify the senses, such as sight and hearing, from following the arts.
- ► Enable family bonding when leisure is enjoyed as a family unit.
- ► Encourage social interaction with other people, e.g. peer group development.
- ► Set good examples for young children with regards to making use of their free time.

Influences on Leisure Patterns

Social influence

- ► Socio-economic grouping may affect one's choice of leisure activities as membership and other costs involved in clubs, such as sports centres and golf clubs, can be prohibitive to those of lower socio-economic groups.
- ► Where one lives can often influence the choice of leisure activity. People are usually interested in what is available locally, e.g. a rugby club or swimming pool.
- ► Leisure activities can follow trends and what is fashionable is usually dictated by society. Trends come and go, e.g. line-dancing and skateboarding.
- ► There is less social division nowadays in terms of leisure pursuits. Horseracing, hunting and foreign travel were mainly undertaken by the upper classes, whereas today these sports and travel are enjoyed across the social divide.

Cultural influence

- ► Certain games are associated with particular countries, e.g. basketball with the USA and Gaelic football with Ireland.
- ► Within Ireland, different GAA games are culturally associated with different counties, e.g. football with Kerry and hurling with Kilkenny.
- ► Different styles of dance may be chosen as a form of leisure activity, e.g. Irish dancing would be very common in Ireland, whereas flamenco would be a more common style in Spain.
- ► Family culture may also influence leisure choices. For example, when one is a member of a family which plays traditional Irish music this form of leisure may be common to many family members.

Hurling

Occupational influence

▶ How much one earns may affect the choice of leisure activities, as some are expensive and outside the reach of low-paid workers.

▶ Many people choose a leisure activity which contrasts with their occupation. For example, a sedentary worker may choose a physical leisure activity for energy release. Workers in strenuous occupations may prefer physically relaxing or mentally stimulating activities.

▶ In some professions, leisure may be an extension of work, for example, dinner with clients or business golf outings.

▶ Some professions choose particular leisure activities as a means of networking, i.e. to meet a wide range of people with the possibility of extending their client base.

Age

▶ As people become older their participation in extreme physical activity usually decreases. For example, squash might be replaced by the less demanding sport of golf.

▶ Some sports are regarded as too dangerous for children, e.g. scuba diving or shooting.

▶ Interests can vary depending on age. Children and teenagers tend to like computer-based games, whereas adults may choose hill-walking, gardening or card playing as leisure activities.

▶ Age can determine the amount of time available to partake in leisure. Young, single people usually have more leisure time, whereas couples with young families choose leisure activities to suit the time available.

▶ Age may also affect the amount of disposable income available to spend on leisure. Young families with mortgages quickly use up finances so less expensive leisure activities are the only option.

Gender

► Although both males and females now partake in most sports, some continue to be dominated by one gender, e.g. men play rugby and women play camogie.

► Certain crafts are associated with men, e.g. woodwork and building model planes and ships, whereas other crafts, e.g. embroidery, crochet and knitting are dominated by women.

► The amount of time available to engage in leisure activities is often influenced by gender. Career women often have less leisure time than their partners.

The Role of Leisure Activities in Physical, Social and Emotional Development

► Physical leisure activities whether enjoyed as an individual or as a family contribute to physical development. They help with physical fitness, weight control, muscle development and possibly learning a new skill such as swimming.

► Many sports are played outdoors allowing people to avail of fresh air which is important for general good health.

► Leisure activities play a part in social development as many leisure pursuits are regarded as social outlets and allow for meeting new friends. They can also be a social outing for a family, e.g. community sports days which can help with relationship building between family members as they spend time together.

► Team sports involve co-operation which is a major part of social development.

► Winning and losing in sporting situations help people to cope with the successes and failures of everyday life.

► Many leisure activities are run by committees. Committee membership can enhance social development as people learn to listen, and to form and express opinions.

► Self-esteem and confidence can be boosted by achievement in leisure activities.

► Many leisure activities bring with them a sense of belonging, which is part of emotional development, particularly those activities involving team games, e.g. quiz teams or sports teams.

► Some people choose personal development courses as their leisure activities – these courses often enhance both social and emotional development.

► Some leisure activities enhance appreciation of art, literature and music.

► Inner peace can be achieved by activities such as meditation.

► Relaxation and stress reduction are among the emotional benefits of engaging in leisure activities.

Leisure options		
Sporting activities	**Entertainment activities**	
Leisure centres with swimming pools and gymnasiums	Cinemas	
Athletics	Theatre	
Basketball, volleyball	Musical societies/ choirs	
Football, soccer, rugby	Drama groups	
Hurling, camogie	Card games	
Squash, tennis, badminton	Bingo	
Golf	Toastmasters (public speaking)	
Water Sports:	Classes, e.g. art, photography	
Sailing, canoeing, rowing, scuba-diving	Pottery	
Mountain climbing, hill walking	Restaurants	
Horse-riding	Discos	
Ice-skating	Youth clubs	
Skateboarding, rollerblading	Music, e.g. piano, guitar	
Boxing, wrestling		
Judo, karate		
Snooker, billiards		
Bowling		
Yoga		

Leisure Facilities Available in the Community

The leisure facilities in different communities vary greatly. Cities and larger towns offer options like theatre and ice-skating which might not be available in rural areas where fishing, horse-riding and hill-walking can be enjoyed.

Evaluation of leisure facilities

Using the following example evaluate two leisure facilities available in the community.

Leisure centre	
Facilities available	• 3 swimming pools – 20 x 9 metre pool, heated children's pool, luxury leisure pool • Jacuzzi • Sauna • Turkish steamroom • Plunge pool • Gymnasium equipped with cardiovascular and strength-training stations • Personal trainer • Beauty salon • Sunbed • Childcare facilities • Aerobics classes
Membership fee (annually) **Ongoing costs**	€450 – single €750 – family Swimming and gym attire = €200
Personal benefits	**Physical** Promotes fitness Controls weight Strengthens muscles **Emotional** Relaxation Stress relief Sense of achievement **Social** Meeting people Developing new friendships
Value in the community	Provides employment within the community. Only of personal value to those who can afford to avail of it. Valuable to young mothers as childminding facilities are available. (Benefits depend on regular usage.)
Time involved	To benefit from a leisure centre between 90 minutes and 2 hours per session is required.

CONTENTS INCLUDE:
► Concepts of poverty
► The extent and distribution of poverty in Ireland today
► Statutory and community responses to creating employment and eliminating poverty

Concepts of Poverty (6.6.1)

Defining Poverty

Poverty refers to being poor. A person who does not have sufficient income or resources to have a reasonable standard of living is said to be living in poverty. The Irish Government's definition of poverty in its National Action Plan for Social Inclusion is as follows:

> "People are living in poverty if their income and resources (material, cultural and social) are so inadequate as to preclude them from having a standard of living that is regarded as acceptable by Irish Society generally. As a result of inadequate income and resources people may be excluded and marginalised from participating in activities that are considered the norm for other people in society."

Absolute poverty

► People who are starving, living without proper housing, clothing or medical care and who struggle to stay alive, live in *absolute poverty*. Some people in Ireland, including homeless people, may experience this type of poverty, but it is far more common in Third World and developing countries.

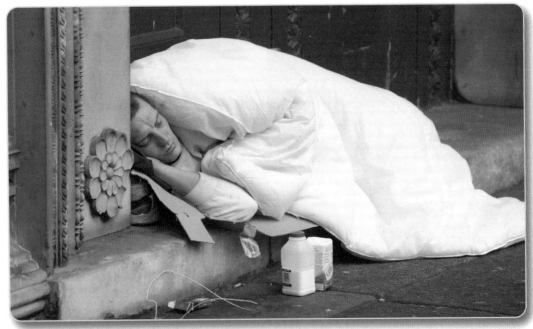

Homeless person

Relative poverty

▶ People are considered to be living in relative poverty or "at risk of poverty" if their standard of living is substantially less than the general standard of living in society.

▶ In Ireland and other developed countries, poverty is usually described as *relative poverty* where people endure income poverty and deprivation.

Income poverty

Income poverty is assessed by identifying a **poverty line** below which people are considered poor.

The poverty line may be described as the estimated minimum income considered necessary to maintain a basic standard of living.

Minimum disposable income required to avoid poverty in 2009		
Household containing	Weekly poverty line	Annual poverty line
1 adult	229.47	11,965
1 adult + 1 child	305.20	15,914
1 adult + 2 children	380.92	19,862
1 adult + 3 children	456.65	23,811
2 adults	380.92	19,862
2 adults + 1 child	456.65	23,811
2 adults + 2 children	532.37	27,759
2 adults + 3 children	608.10	31,708
3 adults	532.37	27,759

Deprivation

Deprivation is assessed by using non-monetary indicators, e.g. owning a winter coat or not able to afford to keep one's home adequately warm. The combination of income poverty (falling below the poverty line) and enforced deprivation is called ***consistent poverty***.

The Extent and Distribution of Poverty in Ireland Today

▶ The rate of consistent poverty (combining income poverty and deprivation) has increased slightly in recent times.

▶ Lone-parent households and those headed by a person who is ill or disabled are at greatest risk of consistent poverty.

▶ Unemployed people have the highest incidence of consistent poverty.

▶ Children and the elderly are the age groups at greatest risk of poverty.

▶ Women have a greater risk of income poverty than men. The gap has widened significantly in recent years and is age related Women over 65 years have higher poverty risk than their male counterparts.

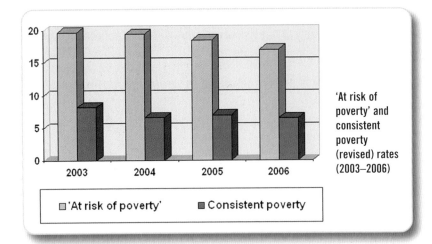

'At risk of poverty' and consistent poverty (revised) rates (2003–2006)

☐ 'At risk of poverty'   ▪ Consistent poverty

Groups most at risk from poverty

- Ill/disabled
- Unemployed
- Large families
- Elderly
- Lone-parent families
- Women
- Children
- Poorly educated
- Ethnic minorities

Composition of adults in poverty, by principle economic status, 2003-07			
	2003	**2006**	**2007**
At work	21.4	21.9	22.7
Unemployed	10.2	11.3	12.4
Students and school attendees	11.5	20.4	19.0
On home duties	30.1	25.1	25.2
Retired	12.0	7.9	9.6
Ill/ disabled	12.2	10.9	10.0
Other	2.5	2.5	1.1
Total	**100.0**	**100.0**	**100.0**

Causes and Effects of Poverty (6.6.2)

There are many reasons why poverty continues to be a feature of modern western society.

1. Economic recession and unemployment
Unemployment increases during times of economic recession resulting in dependence on social welfare.

2. Lack of education and low wages
Poorly educated or unskilled people often depend on the minimum wage or may be unemployed.

3. Housing costs and shortages
The high cost of housing prevents many people from buying homes. Many of these people do not qualify for social housing, and therefore privately rent homes, which further reduces their chances of buying.

A shortage of social housing means that some people continue to live in poor and overcrowded conditions.

4. Increase in one-parent families

One-parent families are in the high-risk group for poverty in Ireland. Single parents who cannot avail of employment depend on social welfare.

5. Large families

Because of the high cost of living and the expenses involved in child-rearing, families with a large number of children are more likely to suffer poverty.

6. Drugs and gambling

Addiction to drugs or gambling causes people to spend any available finances on their addiction which may result in poverty.

7. The cycle of poverty

The children of the poor will more than likely be poor when they grow up. This is known as the *poverty cycle*. Children from lower socio-economic families generally do not get the same opportunities, and place less importance on education, than the children of the better off in society. They end up unemployed or in low-paid jobs and have their own children who are born into the perpetual cycle of poverty.

Another interpretation of the cycle of poverty is that many of the causes of poverty are also the effects of poverty, e.g. poverty results from lack of education and lack of education is also a result of poverty. This is also referred to as the *cycle of deprivation*.

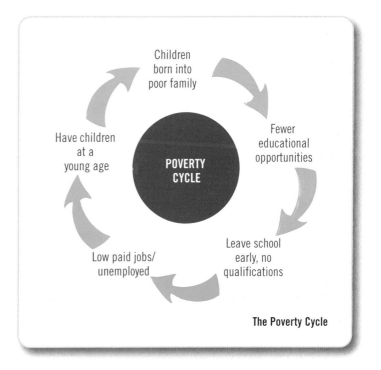

The Poverty Cycle

The cycle of deprivation is often a feature of geographical location:

 (i) Inner cities and urban areas of economic decline.

 (ii) Isolated and undeveloped rural areas.

 (iii) Large social housing estates.

8. The poverty trap
The poverty trap is a situation in which an increase in income results in a loss of benefits so that a person or family is no better off.

9. Social policy
► Poverty is an outcome of the way society allocates resources such as money, jobs, education, housing and healthcare.

► Social policy can perpetuate poverty as some believe that the benefits of social welfare are generous and therefore there is little incentive to seek employment.

► The poverty trap is activated when any increase in income is cancelled out by a loss of benefits.

The effects of poverty
Poverty has many negative effects on quality of life:

► *Debt:* When people are unable to pay bills they may resort to borrowing from moneylenders who charge very high interest rates.

► *Unemployment:* As many of the poor are unskilled, they have difficulty finding employment.

► *Poor housing conditions:* Many poor people live in overcrowded inferior housing.

► *Educational disadvantage:* Because of parental lack of education, disinterest in education and poor facilities in the home, the children of the poor are regarded as educationally disadvantaged.

► *Poor health:* The poor may suffer ill health due to lack of nutritional knowledge and poor housing conditions.

► *Stress/psychological problems:* The continuous pressure of managing the household budget on a small income may result in stress and tension in individuals and among family members. Depression, poor self-image and feelings of hopelessness may result from poverty.

► *Social isolation/exclusion:* Poverty can prevent people from participating as equals in society.

Impact of poverty on children

Inequality may result because of three potential risks of exclusion:

- Exclusion from everyday social activities and experiences of other children.
- Early school leaving and unfulfilled educational potential.
- Exposure to drug and alcohol abuse, anti-social behaviour and early lone motherhood

Creating Employment (6.7)
Statutory and Community Responses

FÁS

FAS is Ireland's national training and employment authority.

Role:

► FÁS provides community based employment and training programmes aimed primarily at the long term unemployed.

► Community employment gives participants an opportunity to help develop their own locality in areas such as heritage, tourism or sport.

► Training programmes in areas such as childcare and horticulture help people to gain experience and progress to further training or into employment.

► FÁS offers advice to job seekers and gives practical assistance, e.g. CV profiling and access to job vacancies.

► FÁS offers training programmes for minority groups such as travellers and people with disabilities and promotes social equality and inclusion.

► FÁS encourages education in the workplace and the improvement of skills/'up skilling' Specially designed training programmes allow apprentices to qualify as craftspeople.

Enterprise Ireland

► Enterprise Ireland is the state agency responsible for developing and promoting Irish business at home and abroad.

► Its aim is to help Irish companies to compete and grow on an international level.

► Companies are helped to build markets, increasing sales and exports and employ more people.

County Enterprise Boards

► There are 35 CEBs throughout Ireland whose aim is to support small businesses (10 employees or less) at a local level.

► They encourage job creation and the maintenance of sustainable jobs.

► CEBs offer advice, mentoring, and financial assistance in the form of grants.

Employment Support

The Employment Subsidy Scheme is a government grant aid introduced in 2009 to assist companies in meeting wage bills.

Reserved Third Level places

Unemployed workers will have access to 2500 reserved places on part-time undergraduate and postgraduate courses from September 2009.

This government initiative is aimed at retraining and upskilling the Irish labour force to help counteract unemployment.

Industrial Development Authority (IDA)

IDA Ireland is a government agency with responsibility for securing new investment from overseas. It also encourages existing investors to expand and develop their business thereby creating even more employment. IDA Ireland markets Ireland as an attractive location for overseas investment.

Almost 1,000 overseas companies have chosen Ireland as their European base and are involved in a wide range of activities in sectors as diverse as IT services, computer software and engineering, pharmaceuticals and financial services.

Initiatives Encouraging Foreign Investment

Ireland offers a unique investment environment because it has:

- a skilled and flexible workforce;
- the youngest and one of the best-educated populations in Europe;
- a positive political and economic environment;
- one of the lowest corporate tax rates in the world; (12.5% in 2009) and grant assistance;
- excellent telecommunication infrastructure;
- logistical advantages – Ireland has easy access to EU market.

European corporate tax rates	
Ireland	12.5%
Poland	19.0%
UK	28.0%
Spain	30.0%
France	34.43%

The Emergence of Co-operatives and Cottage Industries

Co-operatives

▶ A co-operative is a group of people who come together to pool their resources, skills and knowledge to provide goods and services to meet their members' needs.

▶ The contribution of co-operatives to the Irish economy and particularly development of rural areas is very substantial.

▶ Co-operatives have been particularly successful in the agricultural sector. e.g. milk collection and processing and animal breeding.

▶ Co-operatives are also substantially involved in areas such as fishing, horticulture, credit unions and housing.

> Credit unions are co-operatives which provide employment and low-interest loans to members (See Page **237**).

Cottage industries

▶ Cottage industries are defined as small scale industries where the creation of good is home based.

▶ Speciality foods are emerging as the contemporary cottage industry. This sector is supplied by small-scale producers usually employing less than 10 people. Speciality food products include cheese (See Page **86**), breads, yoghurts, preserves and chocolate.

▶ The growth in this sector is attributed to the superior quality of speciality foods over their mass-produced equivalents, and the perception that speciality foods are safer and more nutritious than standard foods.

> Housing co-operatives provide housing at an affordable price (See Page **324**).

▶ Examples of traditional Irish cottage industry products include:

- Hand-spun tweed
- Knitting
- Lace
- Hand embroidery
- Crochet

While a number of these goods continue to be produced on a small scale most are now commercially produced.

Knitting

Cheese-making

Community-based Educational Training and Employment Initiatives

Many of the community-based educational training and employment initiatives have already been covered:

FÁS Community Employment and Community Training programmes

County Enterprise Board

Co-operatives

Cottage Industries

LCA, LCVP, PLCs

Adult and Second Chance Education.

See chapter 25
Education

Vocational Training Opportunities Scheme (VTOS)

▶ VTOS is a scheme operated through the VECs, which offers a range of courses to the long-term unemployed.

▶ The aim is to give unemployed people education and training which will increase their chances of finding work.

▶ Courses on offer include Junior and Leaving Certificates, art and design, computer skills and business administration.

▶ Participants must be over 21 and in receipt of unemployment payments for at least 6 months.

▶ Courses are free of charge and participants receive a training allowance instead of their social welfare payment.

Eliminating Poverty

Eliminating Poverty Statutory and Community Responses

Social welfare assistance and benefits

The government attempts to eliminate poverty by providing those most at risk with a number of social assistance payments and benefits including:

Unemployment Assistance

Old Age Pension

One-Parent Family

Supplementary Welfare Allowance

Family Income Supplement

Child Benefit

Local Authority Housing

See chapters 11
and 12

National Action Plan for Social Inclusion 2007–2016

▶ This government plan aims to 'reduce the number of those experiencing consistent poverty to between 2% and 4% by 2012, when the aim of eliminating consistent poverty by 2016'.

► **The Office for Social Inclusion** under the department of Social and Family Affairs has overall responsibility for developing and co-ordinating the plan with the support of **Combat Poverty**.

► The aim is to work towards eliminating all aspects of social exclusion and inequality including poor housing, high crime environments, unemployment and deprivation.

National minimum wage

A national minimum wage was introduced in April 2000. The minimum wage for an experienced adult employee is €8.65 per hour with effect from May 2009. An experienced adult employee is an employee who has had employment in any two years over the age of 18.

Money Advice and Budgeting Service (MABS)

► MABS is a national, free and confidential service within the Citizens Information Board which identifies people who are in debt or are in danger of getting into debt.

► It offers practical advice on budgeting and money management to enable people to avoid further debt.

► MABS discourages dependence on money lenders and helps families to access cheaper sources of credit, e.g. Credit Unions. Credit Unions also operate a 'special accounts' system to enable MABS clients to repay debts.

► It highlights changes in government policy that need to be made to eliminate poverty and over borrowing.

Combat Poverty Agency works to eliminate poverty and social exclusion by:
• Examining the causes and extent of poverty in Ireland
• Advising the government and helping to develop anti-poverty initiatives
• Raising public awareness of poverty and social exclusion

Schemes to Reduce Expenditure for Low-income Families

There are many schemes in Ireland to reduce expenditure of low-income families.

1. Back to School Clothing and Footwear Allowance (See Page 404).
2. Mortgage Allowance Scheme (See Page 247).

The National Fuel Scheme

The National Fuel Scheme is a scheme that is intended to help households in Ireland who are dependent on long-term social welfare or HSE payments and who are unable to provide for their own heating needs.

The scheme operates for 32 weeks from the end of September to May. The fuel allowance is €20 per week and is paid in addition to Unemployment Assistance or directly from the HSE.

School books grant scheme

A grant scheme is available in Ireland for students in some state primary and post-primary schools to help with the cost of school books. The scheme is mainly aimed at pupils from low-income families and families experiencing financial hardship.

Funding for this scheme comes from the Department of Education and Science and the scheme is administered in each school by the school principal.

Parents/guardians should apply for assistance directly to the school principal. The principal has total discretion in deciding which students are most in need.

Book loan/rental schemes

Many schools throughout the country operate book loan/rental schemes where a fee is charged for renting the books, which remain the property of the school. This scheme is often funded by the school books grant scheme.

Medical cards

Medical cards are issued by the HSE and enable the bearer and dependants to receive certain health services free of charge. Services covered include:

- ▶ GP services
- ▶ Prescribed drugs and medicines
- ▶ In-patient public hospital services
- ▶ Out-patient services
- ▶ Dental, optical and aural services

The Work of Voluntary Organisations

Voluntary organisations in the local community can help in the alleviation of poverty. Such organisations include:

- ▶ Society of St Vincent de Paul
- ▶ Focus Ireland

Society of St Vincent de Paul (SVP)

The SVP is the largest voluntary, charitable organisation in Ireland with over 9,500 volunteers.

Role:

- ▶ To promote social justice and a more caring society.
- ▶ To give practical support to those experiencing poverty and social exclusion.
- ▶ To provide a wide range of services for people in need.

Activities/services provided include:

- ▶ Visitation – homes, hospitals, prison.
- ▶ Hostels for the homeless and social housing projects.
- ▶ Pre-school/crèches, homework and breakfast clubs.
- ▶ Holiday breaks.
- ▶ St Vincent de Paul shops.
- ▶ Personal development/self help education.

Funding:

- ▶ Corporate and public donations.
- ▶ Government support for various projects.
- ▶ Internal collections and members make a contribution at weekly meetings.

Focus Ireland

Focus Ireland was founded as a result of research into the needs of homeless women in Dublin in the early 1980s.

Role:

▶ To respond to the needs of people out-of-home and those at risk of becoming homeless, through a range of services.

▶ To provide emergency short and long-term accommodation for people out-of-home.

▶ To campaign for the rights of homeless people and the prevention of homelessness.

Activities/services include:

▶ Streetwork services to young people, e.g. advice, information, helping finding a home.

▶ Providing a warm and welcoming place to meet.

▶ Low-cost meals.

▶ Low rent short and long-term housing developments.

Funding:

▶ Corporate and public donations.

▶ Government grants.

▶ Sale of Christmas cards.

▶ Events, e.g. golf tournaments.

▶ Challenges, e.g. bungee jump.

 Lifelines

Sample Food Studies Assignment
Home Economics – Practical Food Studies Assignment 2008
Eacnamaíocht Bhaile - Tasc Praiticiúil i Staidéar Bia

Area of Practice:
Réimse Cleachtais: | B: Food Preparation and Cooking Processes

Assignment No.
Uimhir an Taisc | 3

PPSN
USPP

Assignment
Tasc
Many consumers have now added a wok or a steamer to their range of kitchen equipment.
Select either a wok or a steamer and research
• The different types available
• Uses i.e. dishes/foods, including main course dishes that can be cooked using this item of equipment.
• The reasons for its popularity
• Key points necessary for successful use of the equipment.
Prepare, cook and serve one of the main courses you have investigated using the selected item
of equipment to maximum advantage.
Evaluate the assignment in terms of (a) implementation and (b) the advantages and/or the
disadvantages of using this item of equipment.

Assessment Weighting for Assignment
Ualú Measúnachta don Tasc

		Assessment Weighting *Ualú Measúnachta*
Assessment Weighting *Fiosrúchán: Anailís/Taighde*		30
Practical Application: *Feidhmiú Praiticiúil:*	**Planning and Preparation** *Ulmhúchán agus Pleanáil*	6
	Implementation *Feidhmiú*	28
	Evaluation *Measúnúchán*	16

Investigation: Analysis/Research *(30 marks)*
Fiosrúchán: Anailís/Taighde (30 marc)

Wok = popular all purpose Asian pan distinguished by high sloping sides resembling a bowl, originated in China.

The different types available

• **Conventional wok** – made from carbon steel (best for conducting heat), cast iron, aluminium, stainless steel.

• **Sizes vary from 25cm to 60cm** – standard household wok generally 30–32 cm.

• **Electrical wok** – considered expensive and not as effective as conventional wok.

• **Non stick, Teflon coated** – common in West – easily scratched and damaged by extreme heat (in excess of 230°C).

• **Rounded or flat bottomed** – rounded not suitable for electric – only suitable for gas burners – traditional woks all rounded.

• **Handles** – long handle/stick and or helper handle – generally heat resistant plastic or wood – long handle facilities tossing action used to sauté ingredients.

Brand Name	Price
Ken Hom non-stick hot wok	€24.99
Casa Professional – 30cm, non-stick, 1.2mm guage carbon steel	€6.95
Judge – non-stick, 30cm	€21.95

Uses/Dishes/Food

• Mostly used for stir-frying but can be used for steaming, deep fat frying, braising, stewing or making soup.

• Chinese cookery

• Sweet and sour dishes.

Main course dishes

• Chinese beef and noodle stir-fry • Chicken satay noodles • Beef coconut curry/rice

• Sweet and sour pork/rice • Chicken stir-fry with noodles.

	Official use only DON OIFIG AMHÁIN	
	1	2

Reasons for popularity

- Quick method, very versatile.
- Low-fat, low cholesterol method.
- Healthy, low GI way of cooking.
- Increasing range of woks and suitable cooking sauces and other ingredients readily available.
- Growing influence of other cultures, e.g. Asian in Ireland.
- Cookery programmes featuring wok cooking.

Key points necessary for the successful use – Chicken Stir-fry – selection criteria

- Cut meat across grain in thin strips and stir-fry in batches over high heat so that the meat will brown quickly.
- Use peanut oil as it won't smoke at high temperatures.
- Wok must be heated to high temperatures before any ingredients are added.
- Oil must be heated to high temperatures before any ingredients are added.
- Meat is stirred in very hot oil then dragged up side of wok to continue cooking and drain off oil.
- Meat can then be removed – vegetables can be cooked – allows cook more control over length of time for which each ingredient is cooked.
- Keep lifting, stirring and moving ingredients while stir-frying. Use wooden spatula – won't damage non-stick interior.

Chosen dish: Chicken stir-fry with noodles

Reasons for choice of dish

- Chicken is a suitable meat to use when using a wook/stir-frying because when cut into thin strips it cooks quickly.
- Chicken stir-fry is a tasty, nourishing dish which is a complete and balanced meal.

Sources of Information | *Foinsí na Faisnéise*

1. Lifelines Carmel Enright and Maureen Flynn
2. Chinese favourites (Pamela Clarke) – Women's Weekly
3. www.easyfood.ie

Practical Application – Preparation and Planning *(6 marks)*
Feidhmiú Praiticiíl – Ulmhúchán agus Pleanáil (6 marc)

Name of dish I *Ainm na Méise*	Chicken stir-fry with noodles
Source of recipe I *Foinse an Oidis*	Lifelines, Carmel Enright and Maureen Flynn
Date of practical I *Dáta an Phraiticiúil*	5/3/07

Ingredients *Comhábhair*	Cost *Costas*	Ingredients *Comhábhair*	Cost *Costas*	Official use only DON OIFIG AMHÁIN 1	2
2 chicken fillets	€5	25g cashew nuts	25c		
1 small carrot	15c	2 tbsp peanut oil	10c		
1 red pepper	20c	1 tbsp soy sauce	10c		
1 clove garlic	10c	1 tsp cornflour	25c		
4 mushrooms	62c	¼ tsp salt, pepper	16c		
½ onion	15c	Water	–		
50g sweetcorn	39c	Noodles	83c		
4 florets broccoli/cauliflower	44c	Fuel	5c		
		(€2.20 per person)			
		Total I *Iomlán*	€8.79		

Key Equipment I *Príomh Fhearas*

Chopping knife, board, wok, 2 wooden spoons, colander, measuring jug, saucepan, tin opener, cutlery, plates

Work Plan I *Plean Oibre*	Official use only DON OIFIG AMHÁIN 1	2
1. Prepare self, collect equipment, weigh ingredients, line bin, set up table.		
2. Wash chicken and cut into strips, wash vegetables, crush garlic, cut carrots, peppers into strips and broccoli into florets. Thinly slice mushrooms and drain sweetcorn.		
3. Heat oil and cook chicken for 10 minutes. Boil noodles for 4 minutes. Add garlic and carrots and cook for 5 mins and add remaining vegetables and nuts, cooking until vegetables are crisp.		
4. Drain noodles. Dissolve cornflour in a little water and add to wok with soy sauce and seasoning. Add noodles to wok, stir-frying for 1 minute.		
5. Serve at once on a heated oval platter.		
6. Do wash up, clean area. Evaluate dish and fill in implementation sheet.		

Implemenation *(28 marks)*
Feidhmiú (28 marc)
(to include procedure followed, key factors considered, safety and hygiene factors)
(an nós inneachtra a leanadh, na príomhthosca a cuireadh san aireamh osca sábhalleacht agus sláinteachas san arreamh)

	Official use only DON OIFIG AMHAIN
	1 / 2

- I set up table, prepared myself, collected equipment and lined bin.
- I washed vegetables, peeled and cut carrots into thin batons, de-seeded and cut peppers into strips, broke broccoli into florets, thinly sliced mushrooms, peeled and diced onion and drained sweetcorn. I cut chicken into strips.
- I heated the wok until it was smoking a little, then added peanut oil and stir-fried the chicken for 6-10 mins, then added carrots for 5-6 mins, added broccoli and peppers for 5 minutes, and added remaining vegetables. Meanwhile, I boiled the kettle and put one serving of noodles into a saucepan and boiled for 4 minutes. I continued to stir-fry until vegetables were crisp. I then dissolved cornflour into a little water and put it and the soy sauce into the stir-fry. I drained the noodles and added them to the wok. I shook the pan to distribute the sauce evenly.
- I served the stir-fry on a heated platter. I evaluated the dish, then did my wash-up and filled in my implementation sheet.

Key factors considered

Make sure the chicken was cut into thin strips and ensure it is thoroughly cooked in a relatively short cooking time.

I used peanut oil which does not smoke at the high temperature required for stir-frying in a wok.

Safety points to be considered

Careful when adding ingredients to the hot oil in the wok so as to prevent any burns, as it might spatter.

Hygiene factors

Washed my hands after handling chicken to avoid cross-contamination with vegetables.

Evaluation *(16 marks)*
FMeasúnúchán *(16 marc)*
(to include ealuation of implementation ans specific requirements of the assignment)
(measúnúchain feidhiniú agus measúnúchán riachtanais shainniúla an tasc san díreamh)

- **Implementation**: The dish was very tasty. It was savoury, mainly due to the soy sauce. The stir-fry had a lot of texture because of some of the vegetables being crunchy and the nuts. The dish was very appetising as it was very colourful, due to all the different vegetables. It was also appetising because it was attractively served on an oval heated platter and garnished with parsley.

- **Modification**: I modified the vegetarian stir fry to include chicken. I thickened the sauce slightly with cornflour and I used noodles instead of rice. These measures ensured that it was a complete, balanced meal suitable for cooking in a wok.

I found the **work plan** really helped me during the preparation and cooking of the stir-fry as it was in the correct order and gave me plenty of time to prepare, cook, serve and evaluate the dish and fill in the implementation sheet.

Skills and processes: I was careful to ensure that all ingredients were cut into evenly sized pieces to ensure even cooking. I kept lifting, stirring and moving ingredients in the wok to ensure that they did not burn.

Safety and hygiene factors: I was very careful when cooking the stir-fry as oil spatters and this could lead to a burn. I used separate boards when preparing the meat and the vegetables so as to avoid cross-contamination.

Advantages

- A wok is a quick method of cooking.
- Not a lot of vitamins and minerals are lost during cooking.
- It doesn't use up a lot of fuel.
- You are able to cook an entire meal in one pan, e.g. chicken stir-fry with noodles.

Disadvantages

- The dishes you are able to cook with a wok take some time to prepare.
- The large surface area means fat can spatter.
- Some woks can be very heavy as they don't feature any helper handle.

Index